Tales of the Hermit ~ Volume II

Yamabushi

and

Homecoming

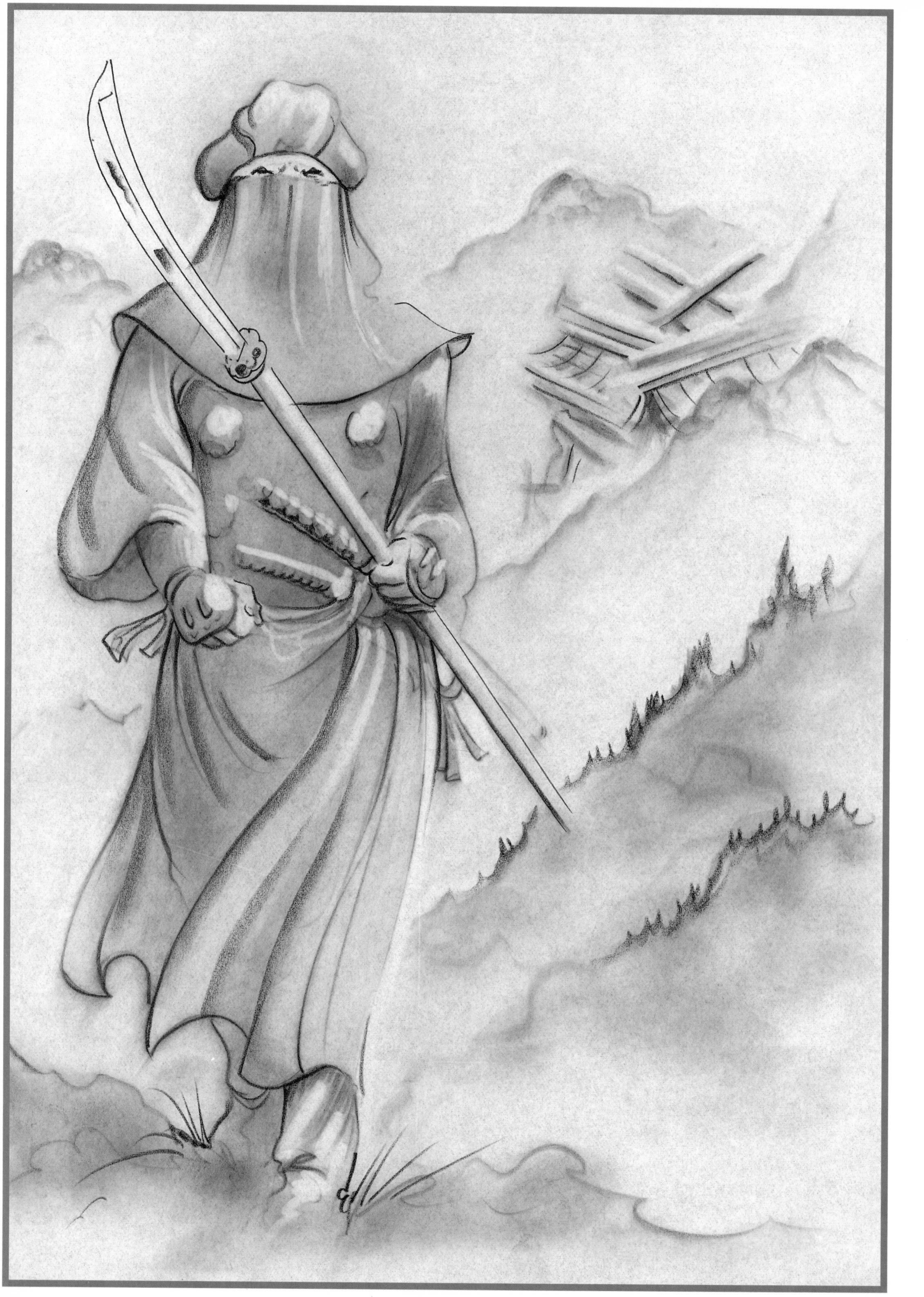

Tales of the Hermit ~ Volume II

Yamabushi

and

Homecoming

Oscar Ratti and Adele Westbrook

Via Media Publishing Company

Dedication
This book is dedicated to
all true peacekeepers and peacemakers,
past, present, and future.

Library of Congress
Cataloging-in-Publication Data

Ratti, O., and Westbrook, A.
      The Tales of the Hermit Volume II:
      Yamabushi and Homecoming/
      Oscar Ratti and Adele Westbrook
ISBN 1-893765-03-2 (alk. paper)

1. Fiction. 2. Martial arts–Social and cultural aspects.
I. Title. II. Ratti, O., and Westbrook, A.

Library of Congress Control Number
2002108975

First published in 2002 by
Via Media Publishing Company
821 West 24th Street • Erie, PA 16502 USA
Tel: 1-800-455-9517 • Fax: 1-877-526-5262
E-mail: info@goviamedia.com
Website: www.goviamedia.com

Copyright © 2002
by Futuro Designs & Publications/
Oscar Ratti and Adele Westbrook.

Printed in the United States of America.

The paper in this book meets the guidelines for permanence
and durability of the Committee on Production Guidelines
for Book Longevity of the Council on Library Resources.

10 9 8 7 6 5 4 3 2 1
06 05 04 03 02

CONTENTS

PROLOGUE

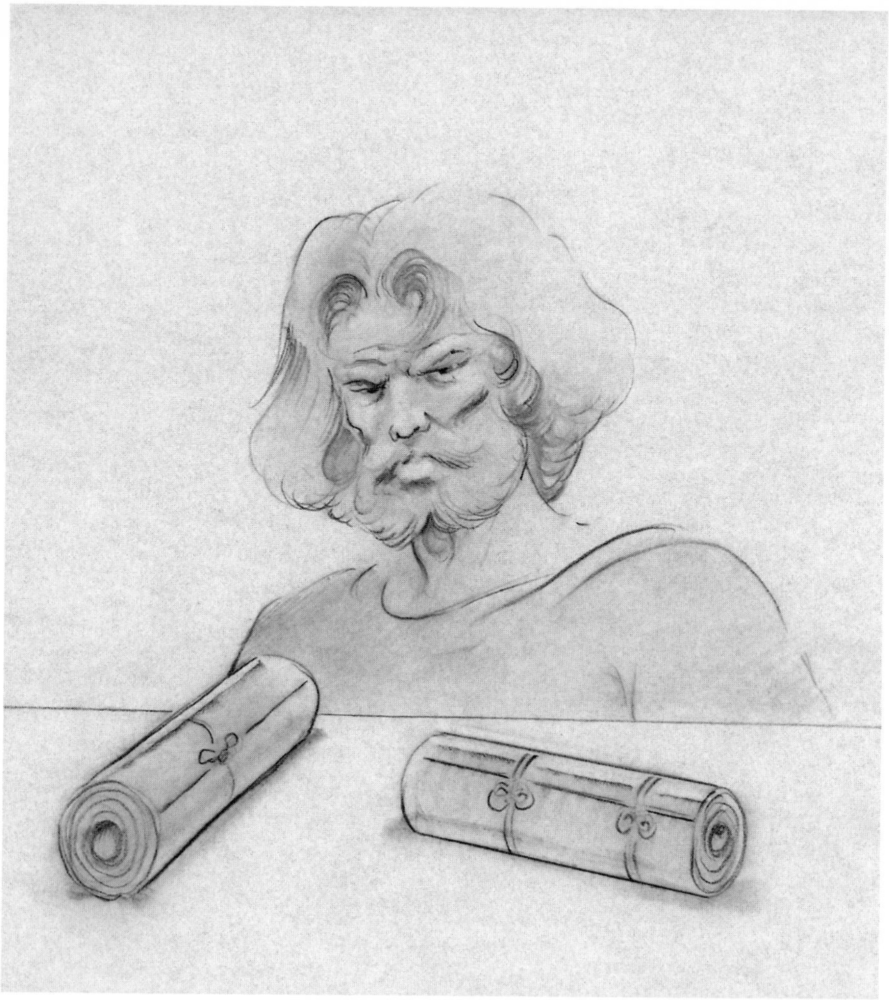

After his long and exhausting flight across the Islands Empire, Père Dominic's arrival at a place of sanctuary on the Summit confronted his hosts, the Residents, with a situation of some urgency. How could they safely accelerate the healing of Père Dominic's mind and body?

They decided that a vital element in his convalescence might be an introduction to those illustrated tales and other forms of literature that had been collected in the Summit Libraries. However, although his physical health improved slowly but steadily, Père Dominic's mental state remained precarious. So many of the core beliefs and convictions—perhaps even hopes—that were central to the early development of his personality and character, had been seriously eroded during the previous, fateful year that he had spent in the Islands Empire. Thus it would be many months before the distraught pilgrim would be able to face the reality of those events that had so deeply affected both him and the parishioners who had been entrusted to his care.

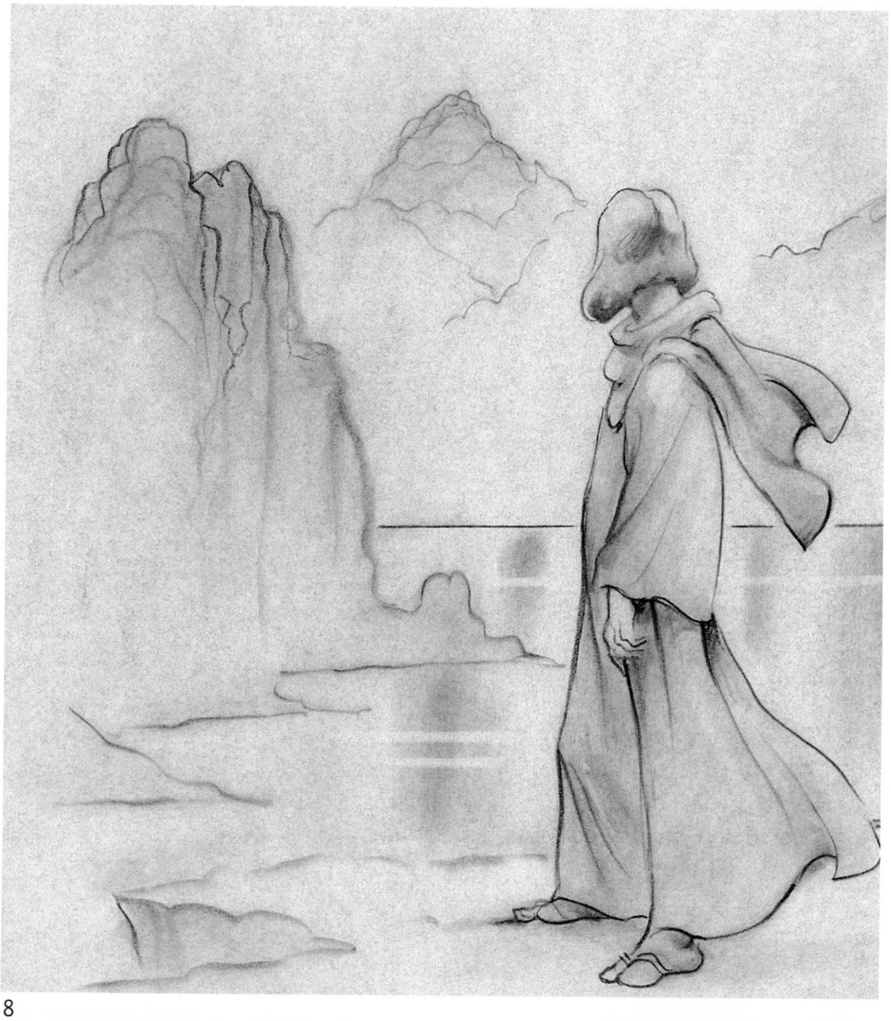

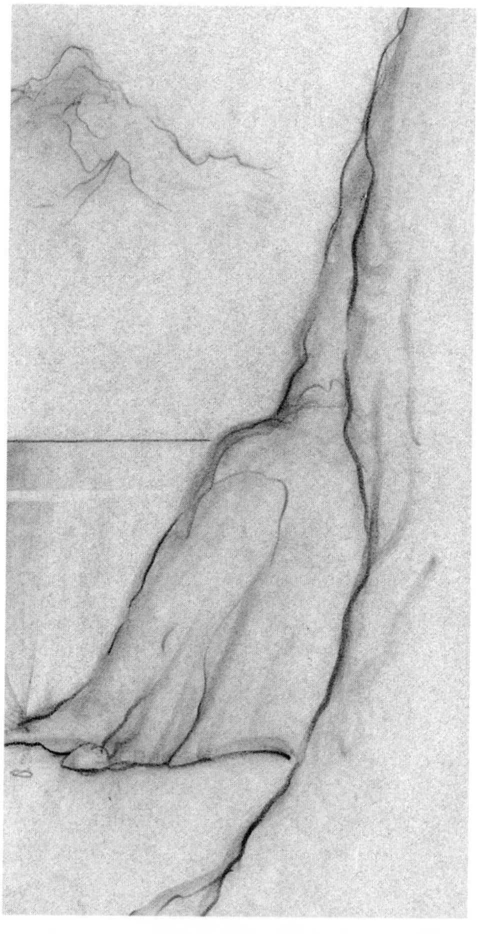

Among the scrolls that made a lasting impression on Père Dominic during the early stages of his recovery, were two illustrated manuscripts entitled, respectively, *Yamabushi* and *Homecoming*. Both were to occupy him for some time as he reflected upon the issues that they embodied, issues which (as he came to realize) had been troubling him since his youth.

He had found them on the Second Level of the Summit's central core—the level directly above the one where he was being sheltered, and the one he had decided to explore as soon as he began to feel his strength returning. The intensive morning and evening bouts of massage to which Residents such as Dandhur and Yi Tai had subjected him with inexorable punctuality every day, combined with the energizing mountain diet supervised by the Abbot, proved to be increasingly effective (at least on the physical level of his recovery), so that he soon felt impelled to move, to act—an improvement in his condition that was welcomed by the Residents. As men and women of action themselves, they never missed an opportunity to encourage his efforts in this dimension. The dictates of Nature, they said, which had endowed human beings with the urge for activity (some Residents wryly suggested "hyperactivity"), would demand nothing less.

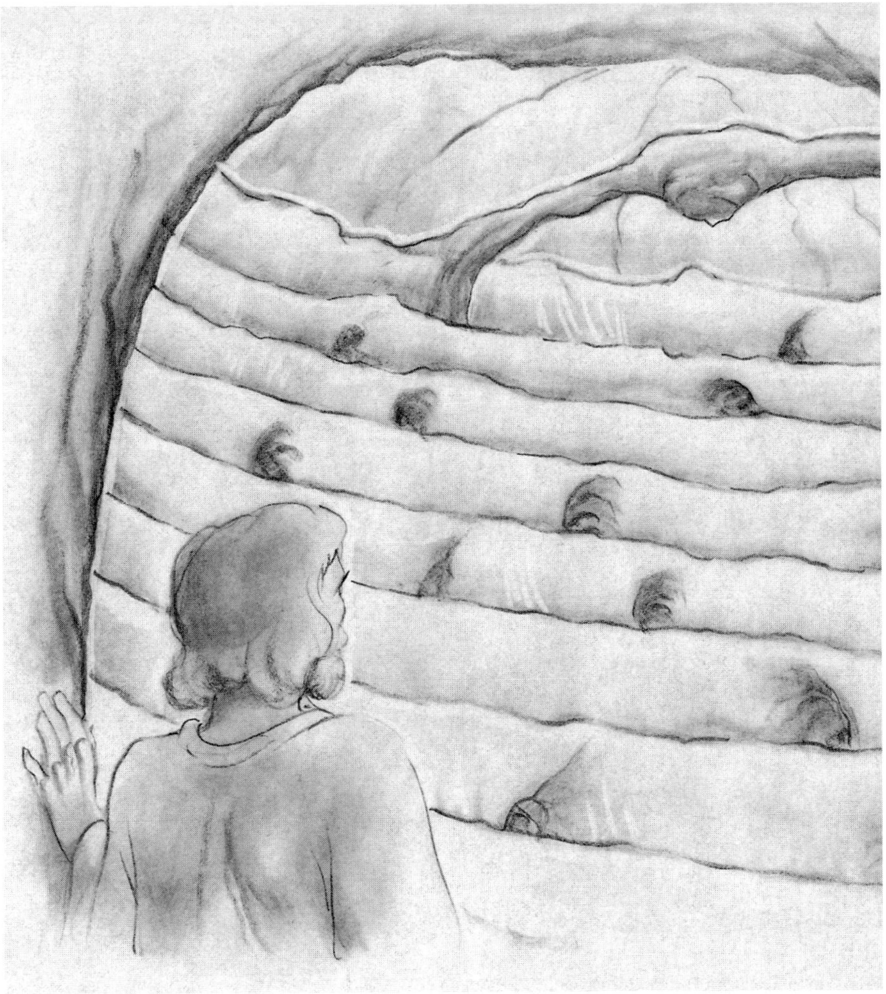

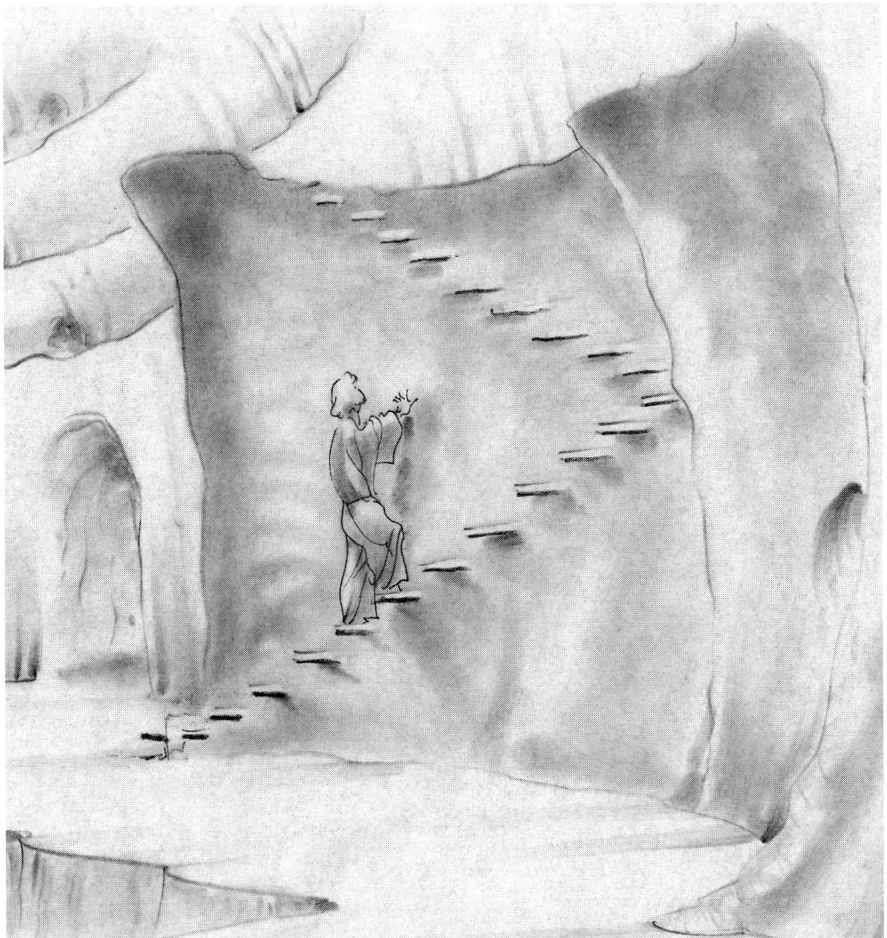

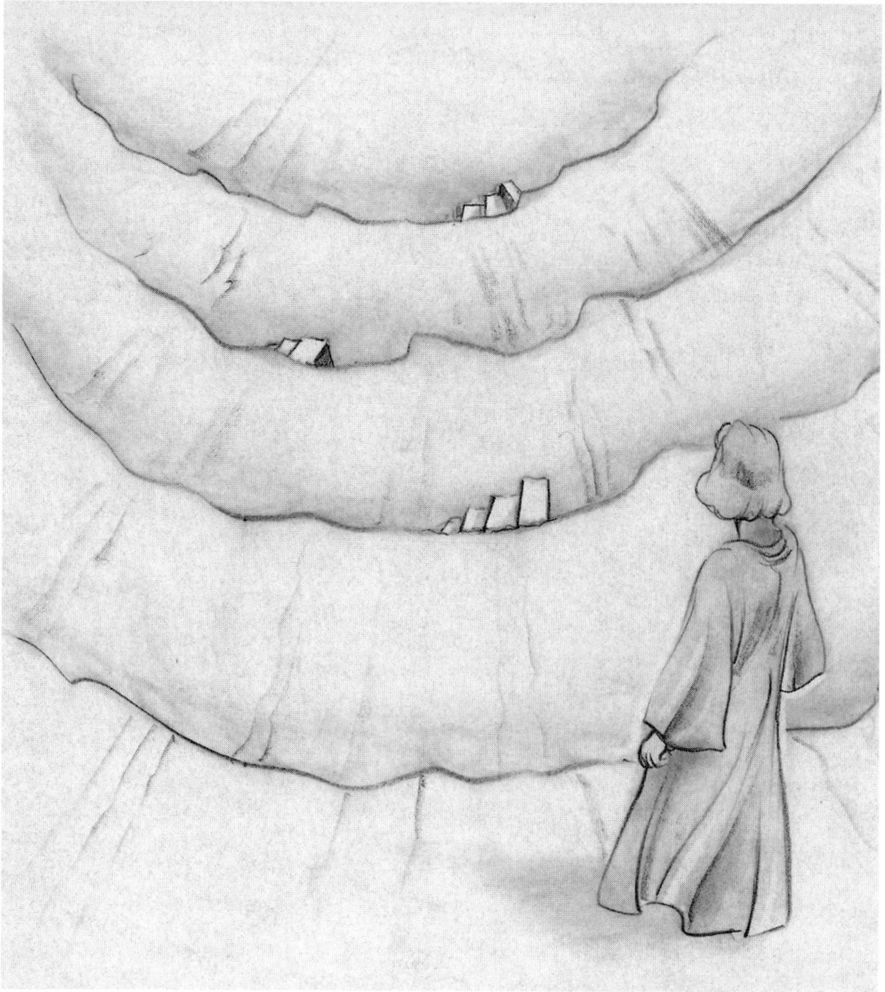

And so it came to pass that, on one particular day, Père Dominic found himself standing unsteadily alone outside the Dormitory, confronting the shadowy stairway that ascended from the First Level to the Second Level. His interest had been aroused by the possibility of gaining a more elevated and comprehensive view of the entire astonishing series of concentric circles that—widening as they rose toward the central and expanded heights—were spanned at the top by a singular rock formation connected by arching bridges to the inner sides of the mountain itself.

He would have ample time to regret somewhat his impulsive decision to attempt a solitary foray in that direction, since he could have benefited in that instance from the companionship of an experienced Resident. It was not so much the threat of unexpected, external danger, as the daunting range of the various caverns, galleries, and caves (both natural and man-made), that branched out in every direction, filled with the richest and most impressive collection of artifacts and representations connected with the human capacity of inflicting violence and even death upon fellow members of their species.

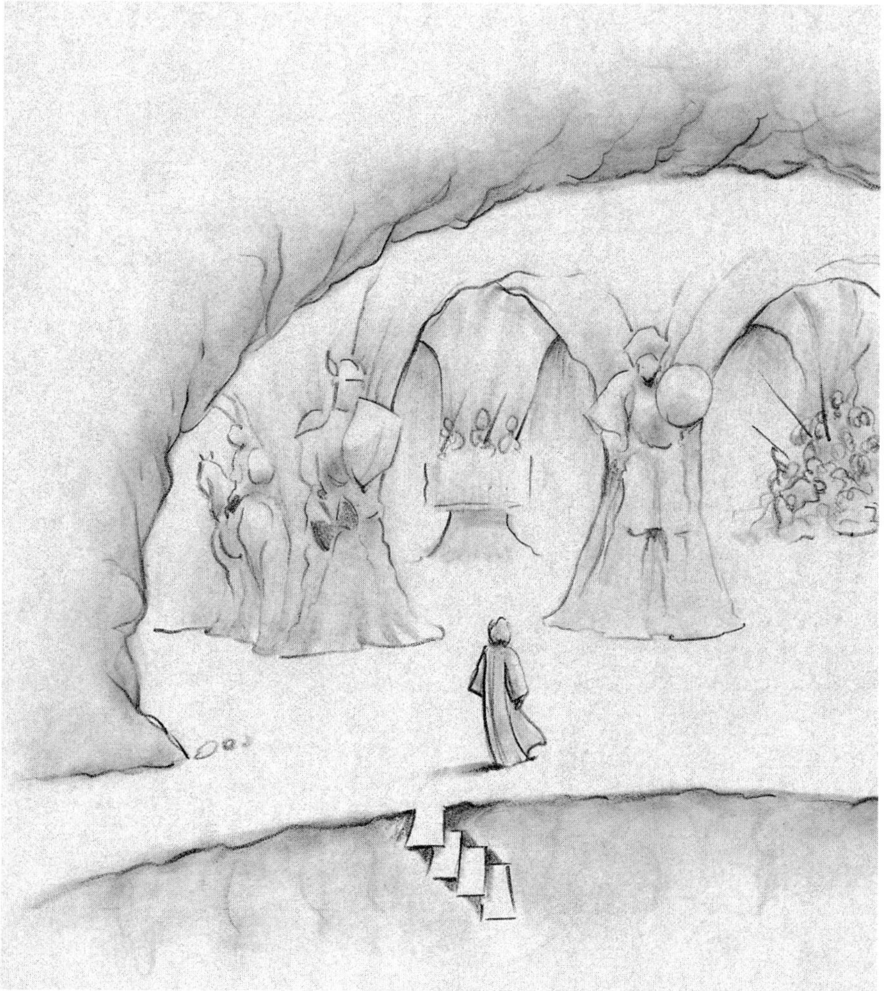

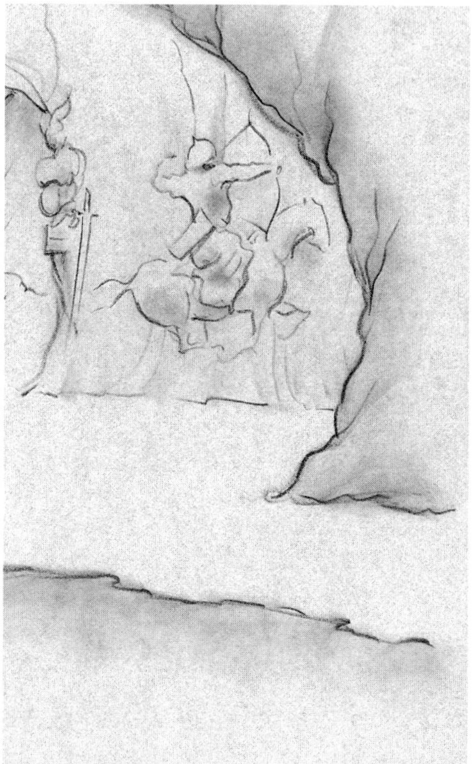

He was to return to this level in the future, when the meaning and value of the collection had been more fully explained to him. But on that day, the impression of a diffused and systematic ferocity proved so overwhelming that Père Dominic found he could only tolerate the briefest glimpses of the extensive ingenuity of the human race in devising weapons and ways of engaging in confrontations clearly destructive in intent and action. The looming sculptures of warriors of every period and, surprisingly, of every land; the bas-reliefs detailing various armed and unarmed forms of conflict; rows upon rows of armor and weapons of previous ages and cultures, all seemed to be alive with a relentless, implacable purpose.

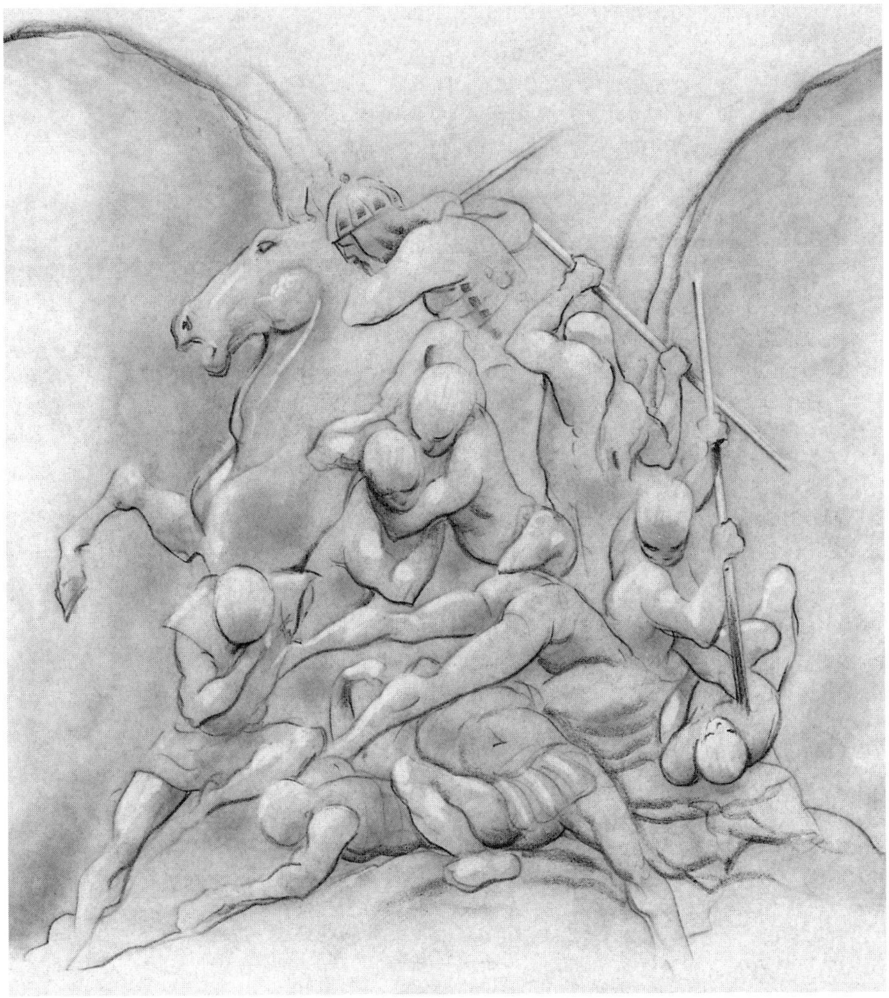

But something else also heightened Père Dominic's pervasive sense of dread at the sights he had glimpsed so fleetingly, and that was the faint echo of combat activities resonating beneath the distant vaults that led to the outside of the Summit, far from its central core. Sharp commands, the clash of metal, and the sounds of colliding bodies, as shadows flickered across the ceilings of distant caves, conveyed a strong impression that this level not only housed the inert symbols of systematic violence, but also contained centers where its ways and means were still being actively pursued and intensely practiced.

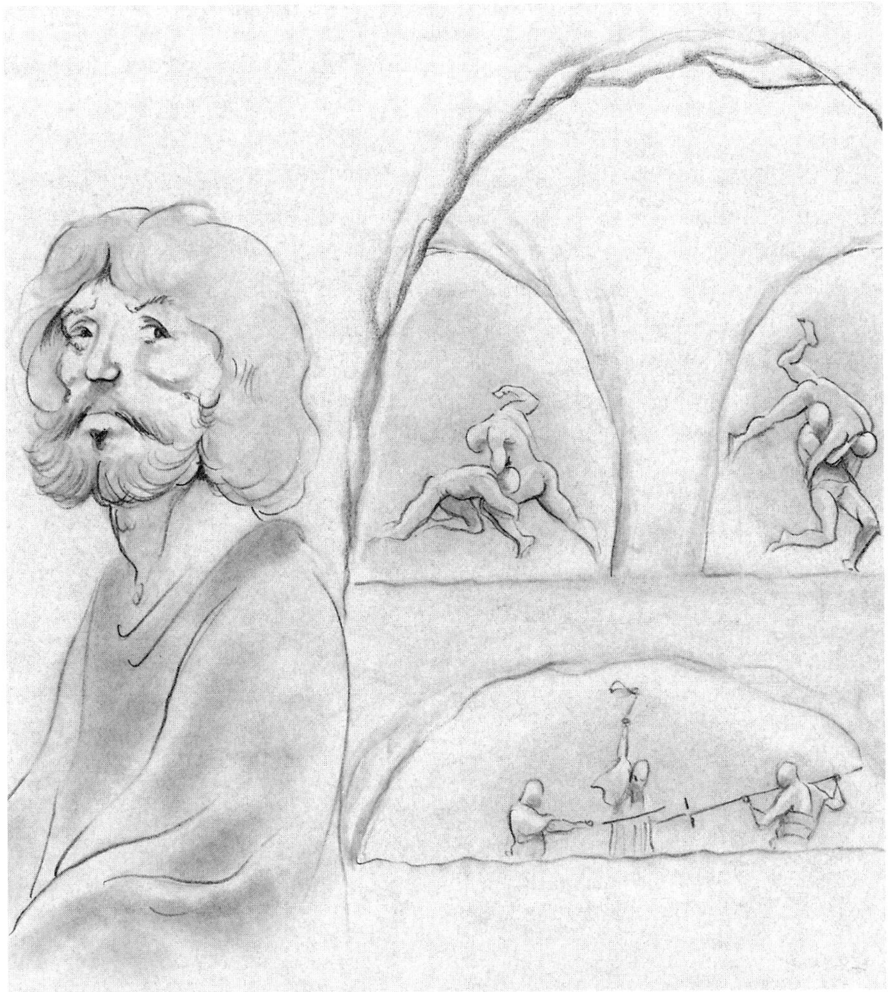

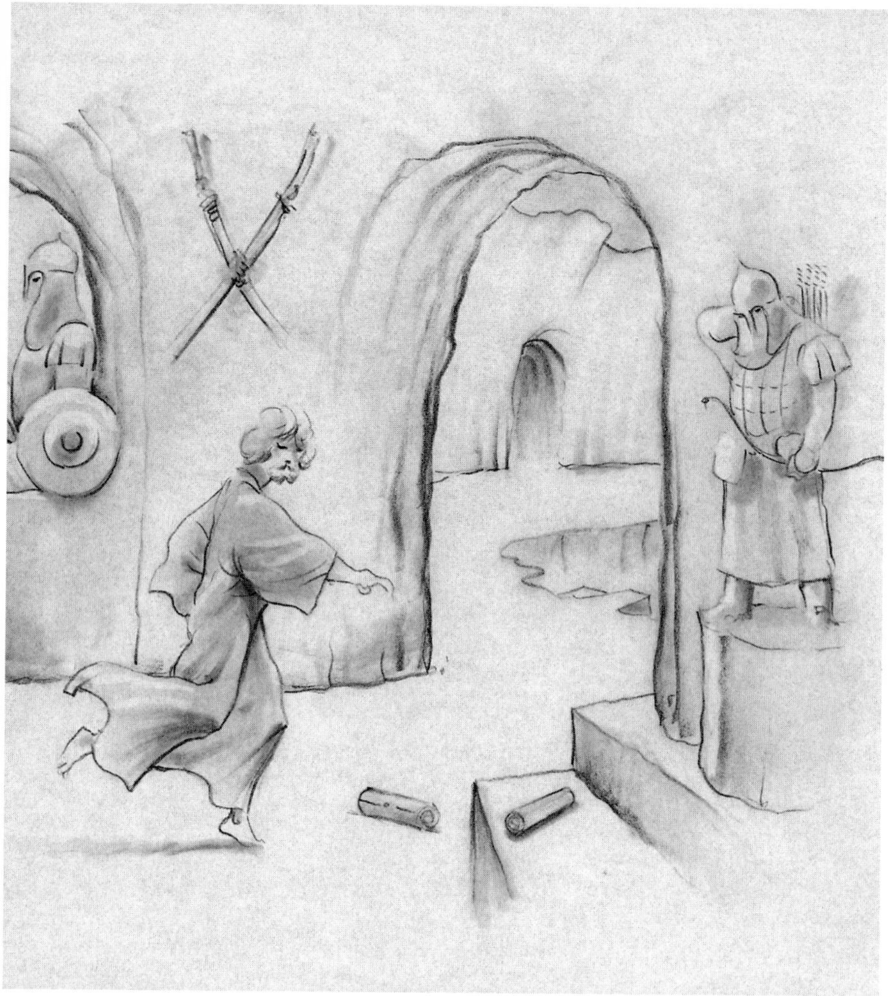

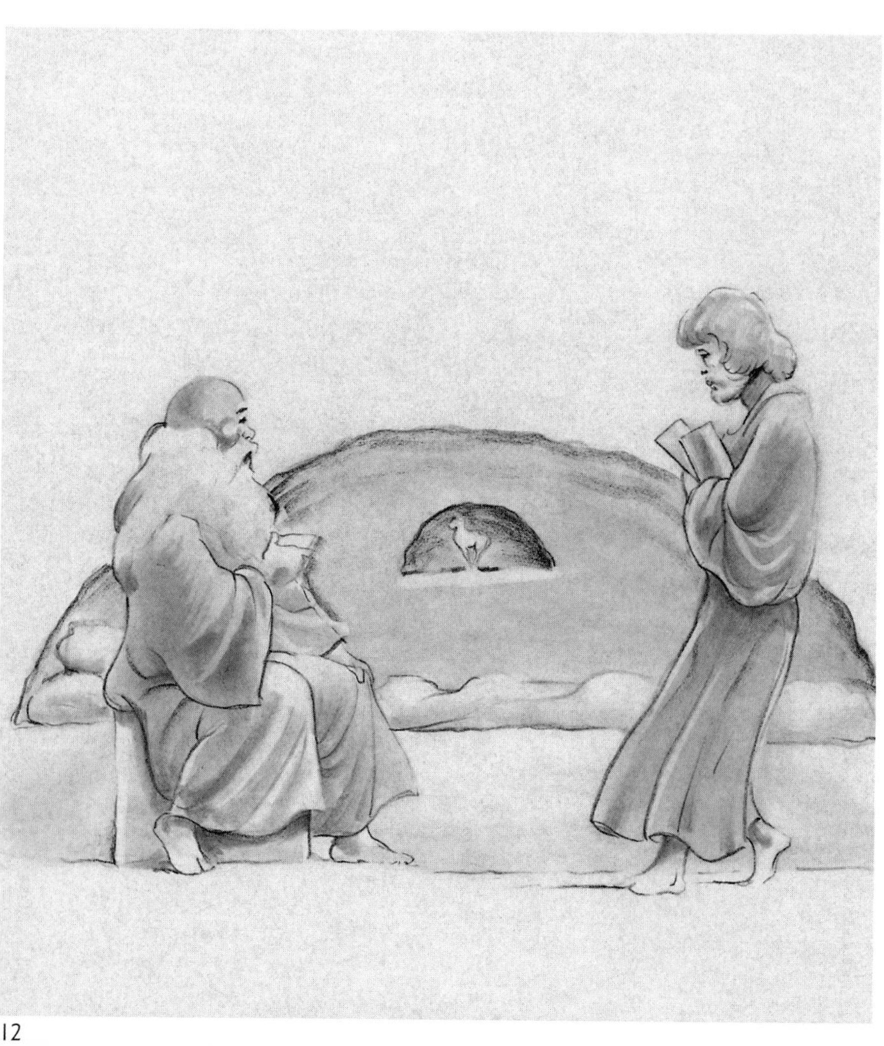

Finally, he could contain himself no longer, and fled back toward the entrance on the broad platform of the Second Level. And, it was while rushing through its main portals that he suddenly saw two scrolls: one half-hidden on a carved seat beneath the sculpture of a mounted warrior, and the other lying on the ground nearby. He had been told that all the records collected on the Summit had been carefully assembled in the Library precincts under the supervision of a particular Resident called Hori. Acting upon instinct, Père Dominic had gathered up both scrolls as he hurried past, partly because he felt that Hori would wish to have them returned to the Summit collection, and partly because he hoped they might contain some clues concerning the disconcerting ambiance of this Second Level.

When he arrived at the Dormitory, Père Dominic encountered the Hermit of the Ninth Level, Yu Xia, who had been waiting there for him, sipping a cup of tea and perusing some of the other scrolls that Hori had left for Père Dominic. The older man recognized instantly that something or someone had seriously disturbed their guest.

"Too much militancy for your taste?" the Hermit suggested, with a gesture toward the Second Level. Père Dominic stopped short, caught by surprise. "How did you know, Yu Xia? I seem to have intruded into precincts that are not only alien to me, but that also embody a powerful and mysterious quality that I find very unsettling."

"Remember that we invited you to do so, my young friend," the Hermit reassured him. "You must be feeling stronger than we thought, since you have begun more extensive explorations than we had expected at this time. But I grant you that the Second Level is a particular site that has disoriented many strong spirits, Celt. It has a definite character that is focused upon an aspect of human existence that is one of the main concerns of the Doctrine which has been evolving here. In time, if you remain so inclined, we can guide your efforts to comprehend its significance and judge for yourself its value. At this juncture, however, I would merely suggest that, just as one principle of existence, Yang, is always balanced by a complementary (some would say opposing) principle, Yin, or just as any ill in Nature has its remedy, so does the Second Level find its integrative balance in the two levels above it: the Third, centered upon the mystical or philosophical aspects of existence, and the Fourth, which encompasses the artistic or aesthetic dimensions. All of this—and more—may become clearer to you, if you remain here with us for awhile, and if you decide to continue those investigations you have already begun . . ."

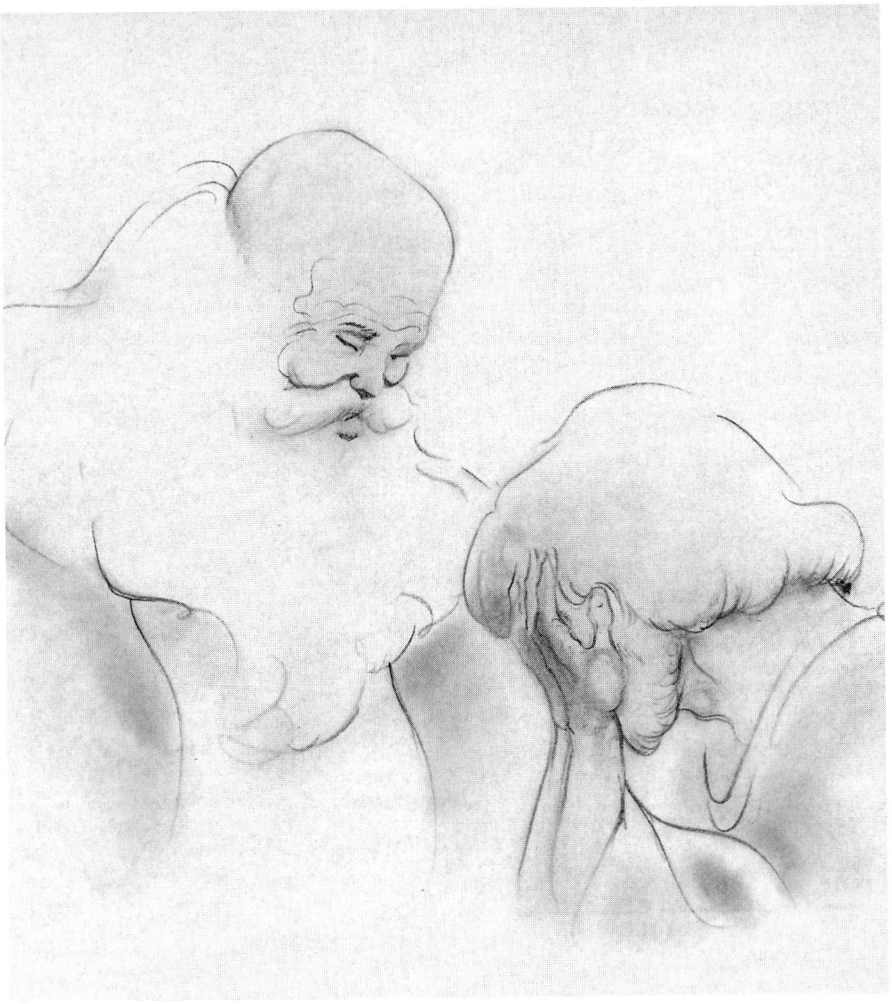

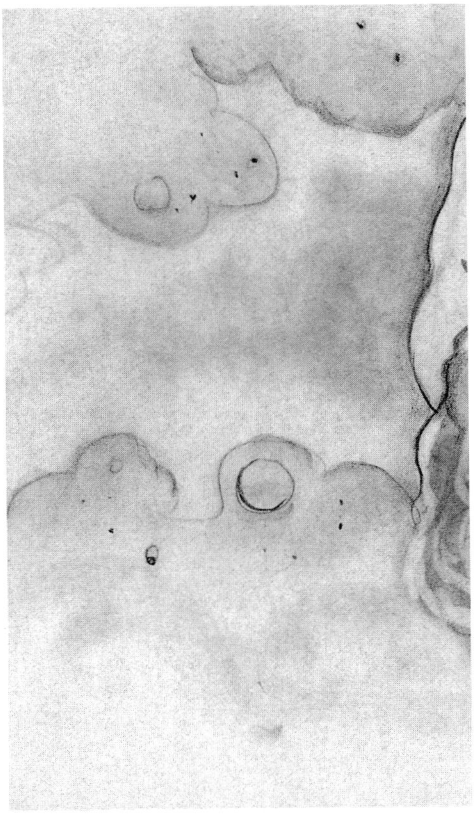

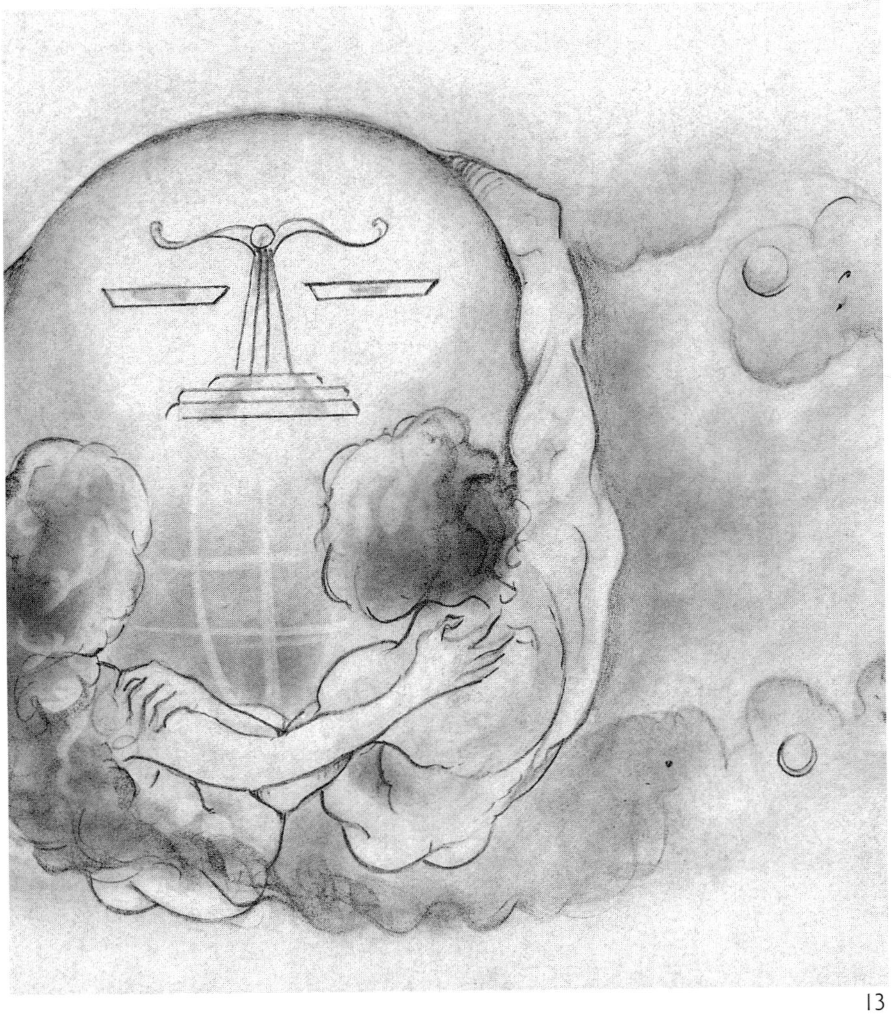

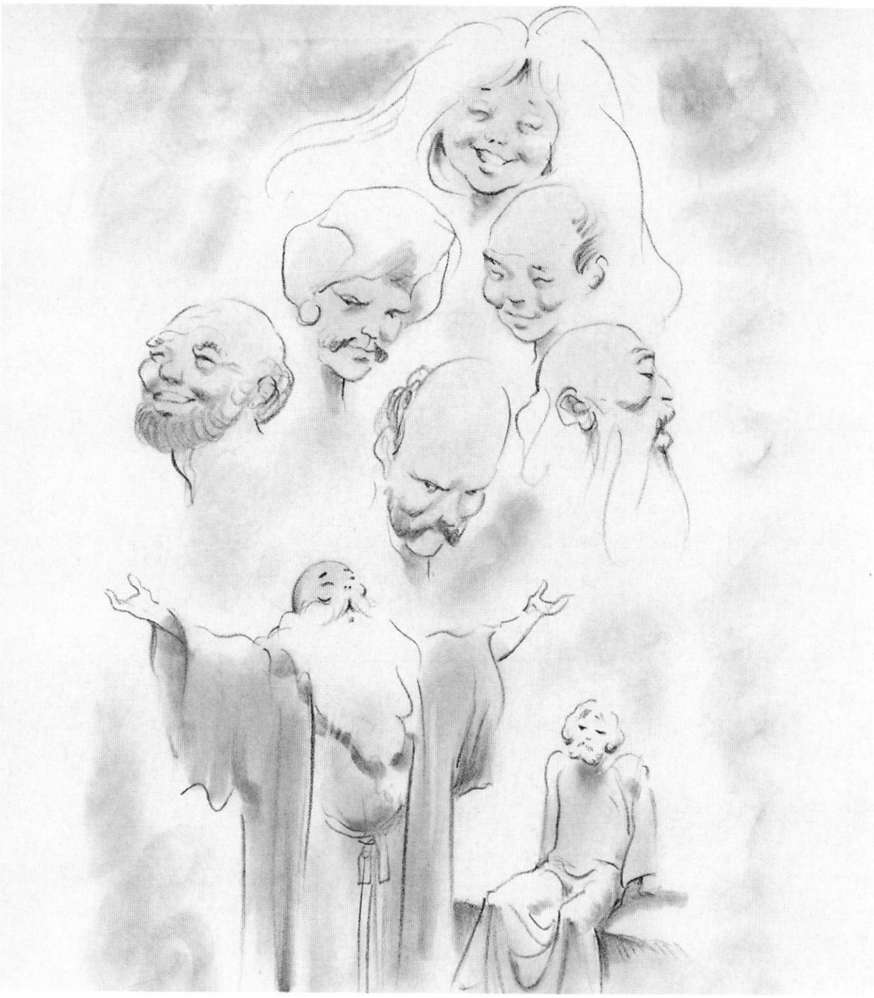

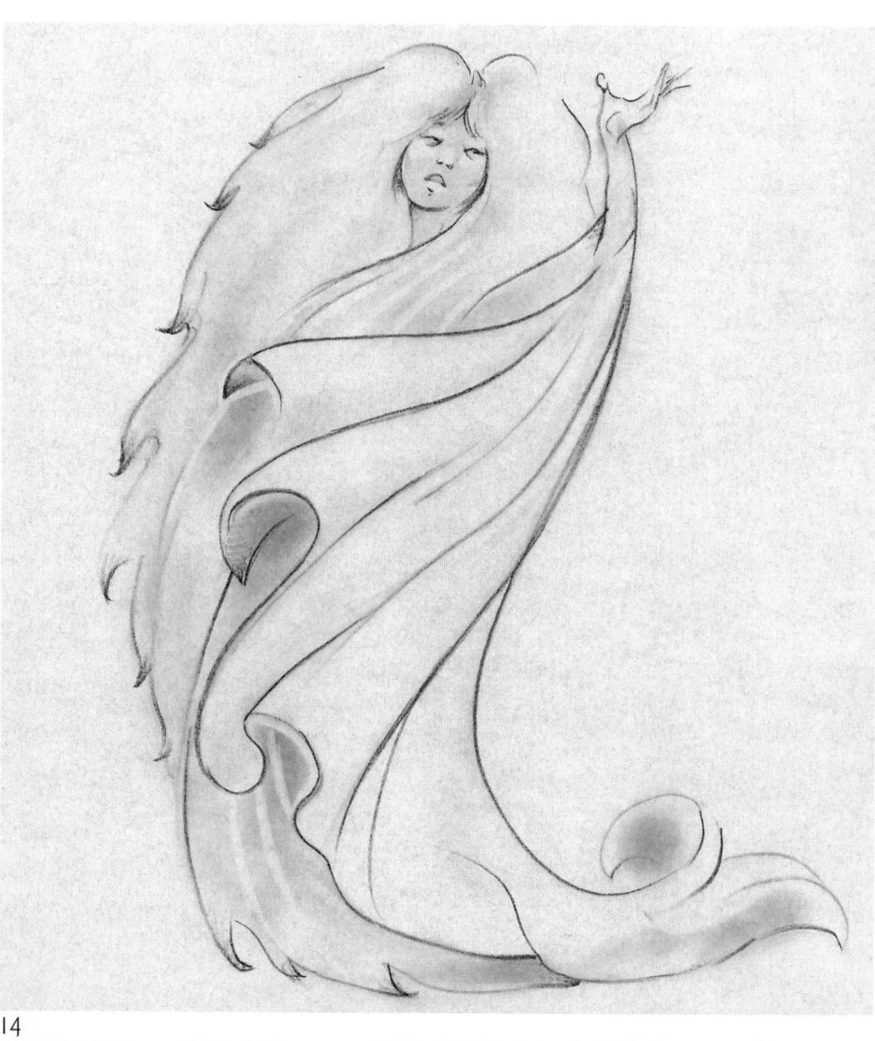

Père Dominic hesitated for a moment, and then responded slowly: "I am certainly interested in the site itself, and in the life of the many Residents who have shown such concern for my welfare. Very interested, in fact. But I fear that I may easily become either overwhelmed by these new experiences on the Summit, or turn into such a nuisance with all my questions that you will regret having extended your hospitality so whole-heartedly to me in the first place. Today, for example, it has become obvious to me that I should proceed more cautiously and, perhaps, that it would be wise to have some guidance in approaching a mountain reality that I still find considerably confusing . . ."

The Hermit's robust laughter resounded under the arches as he patted Père Dominic's shoulder reassuringly. "Certain Residents, in fact, have expressed some doubts about the wisdom of letting you roam about freely and without a guide, within the interior of a mountain that is certainly an unusual site by almost any standards. Ma Hui, on the other hand, is partial to a direct approach, and is in favor of having you plunge into our reality, regardless of how disoriented you may still feel. 'Let him join the company of stalwarts already here! One more, one less—the Ultimate Beginning has a place for him too!' Ma Hui never minces words, Celt. By the way, are those two scrolls in your hands part of the group that came from this case, or did you find them somewhere else?"

Feeling vaguely guilty, Père Dominic told the Hermit where he had discovered the two scrolls he had brought back with him. After examining both scrolls, Yu Xia handed them back, saying: "Some of the Residents borrow specific scrolls for their research, and then forget to return them to the Library. Are you planning to read them, before giving them back to Hori?"

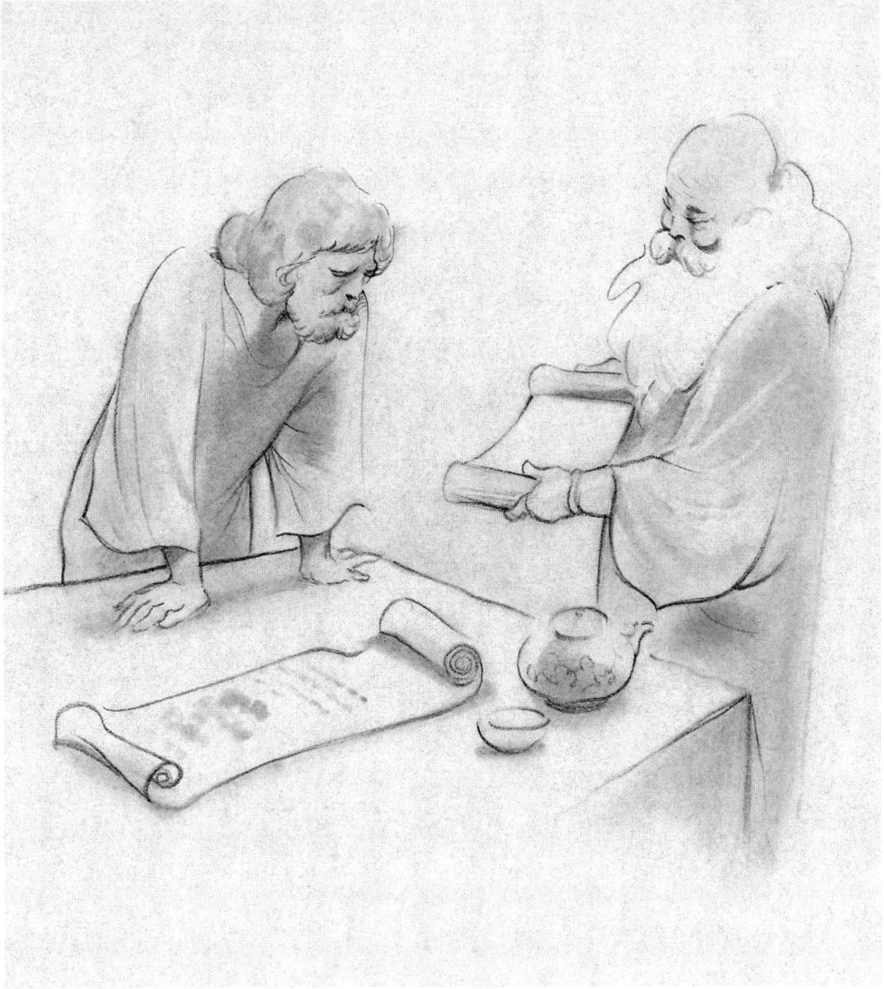

Père Dominic explained that he had wondered if these two scrolls might help to place the sights he had observed on the Second Level in some sort of understandable perspective.

"Well," Yu Xia replied, "they do indeed belong to the martial traditions of the land in the strictest sense, as well as to the larger dimension of systematic violence and its impact upon human affairs and evolution. In the one entitled *Yamabushi*, for instance, you will encounter a world of mystical militancy and the on-going struggle to formulate an ethical response to violence. Do you know what *Yamabushi* means?"

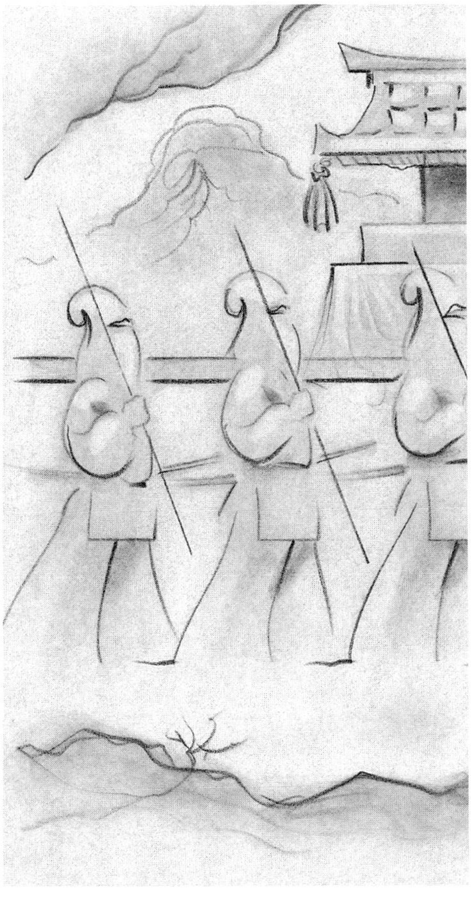

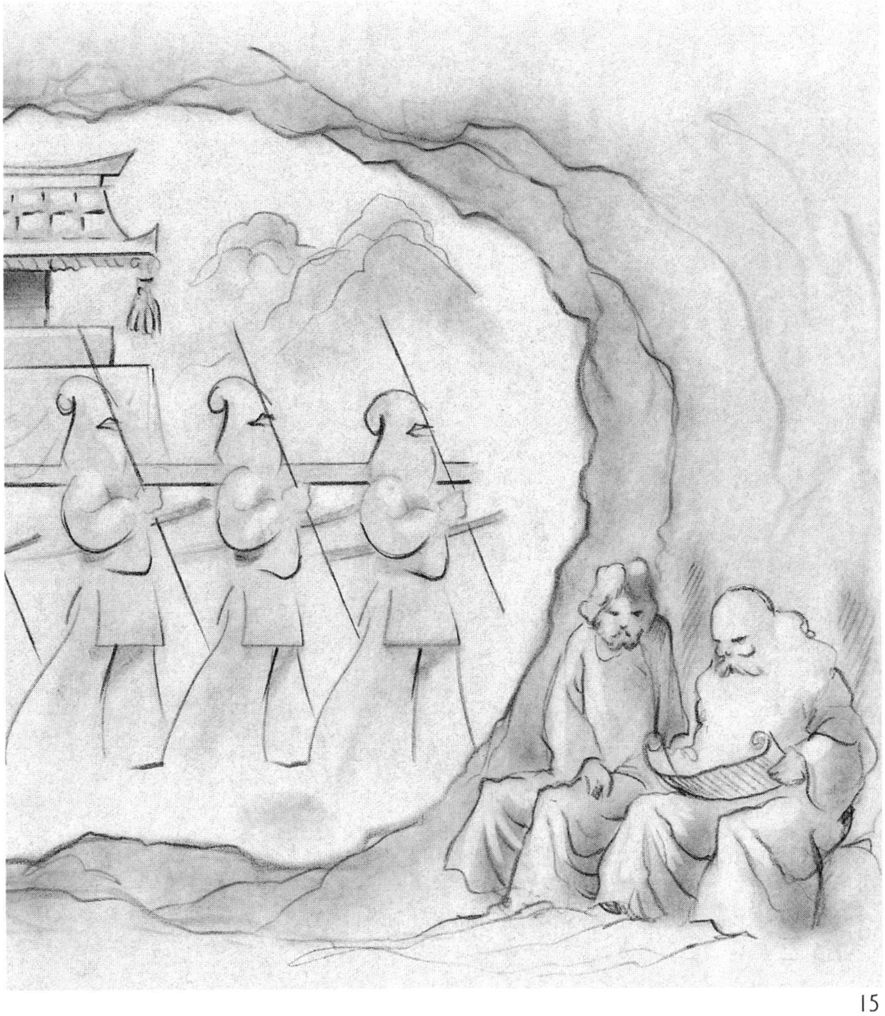

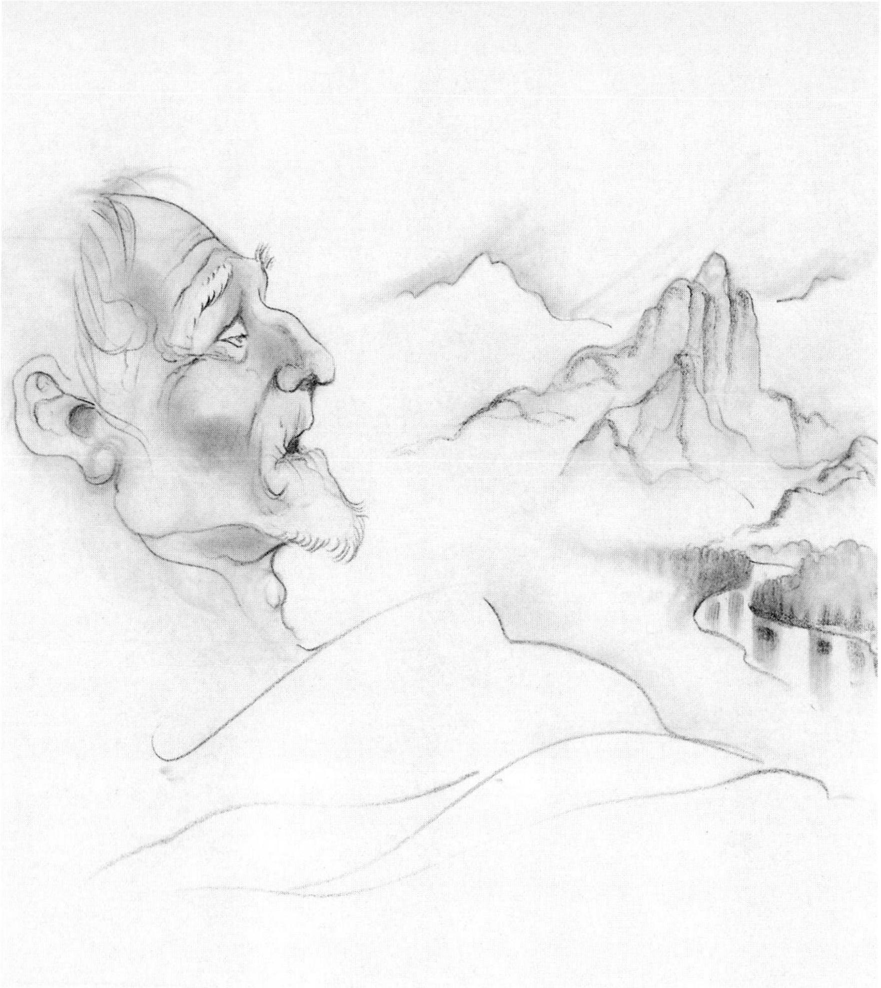

Père Dominic eagerly told Yu Xia about Padre Bartholomew, the ailing prelate who, after decades of missionary work in the Orient, had retired to the Italian town of Siena, but who had kindly agreed to instruct Père Dominic in the ways and customs of the Islands Empire before the younger man began his journey to the East.

Padre Bartholomew had spent many decades among both the meek and the powerful of that nation, dispensing the kind of hope that his faith, as propounded by the Augustinian Order, offered to all those who might benefit from it. And that frail old man had mentioned reflectively that once there had been certain religious sects and cults which, branching out from the ancient creeds of Buddhism and Daoism imported from India and China, had established their own temples and centers of instruction in the remote mountains of the Empire. In time, a number of them had grown extremely powerful both in territory and in revenues, as well as in the number of their adherents, many of whom had become so militant that, eventually, even the samurai class of professional warriors had found themselves confronted more than once on the battlefield by well-armed and organized cohorts of fighting priests and monks.

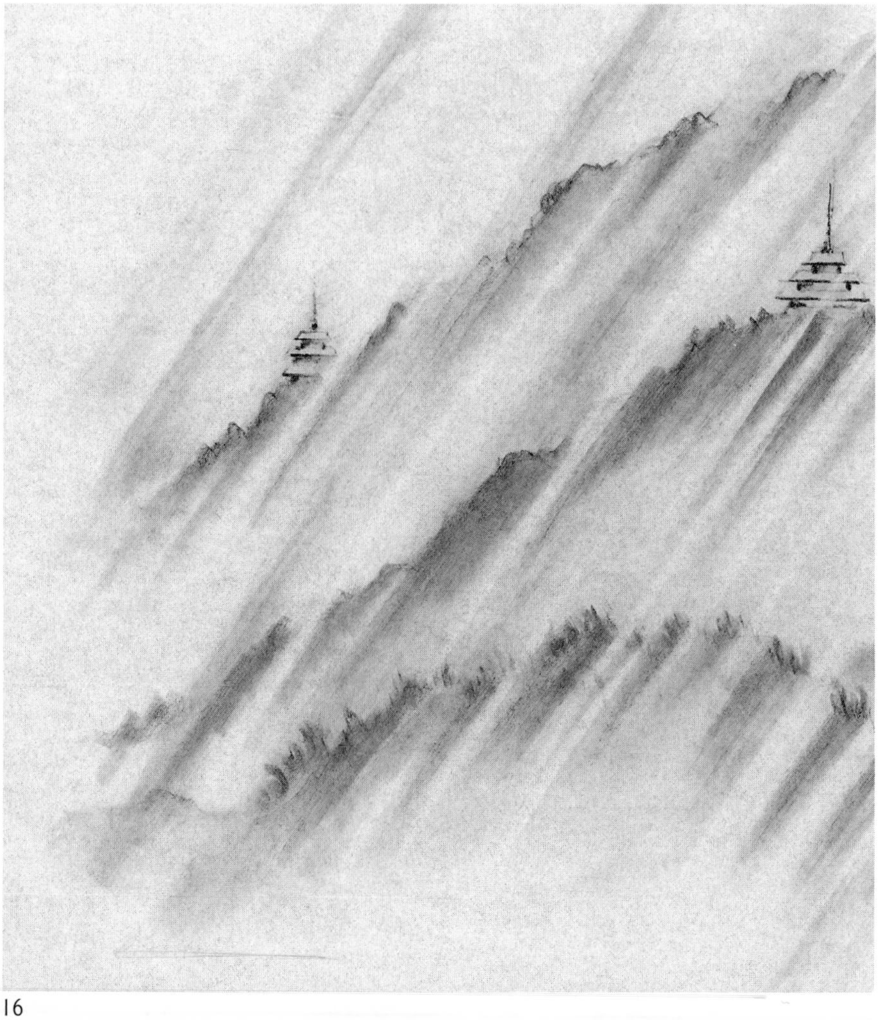

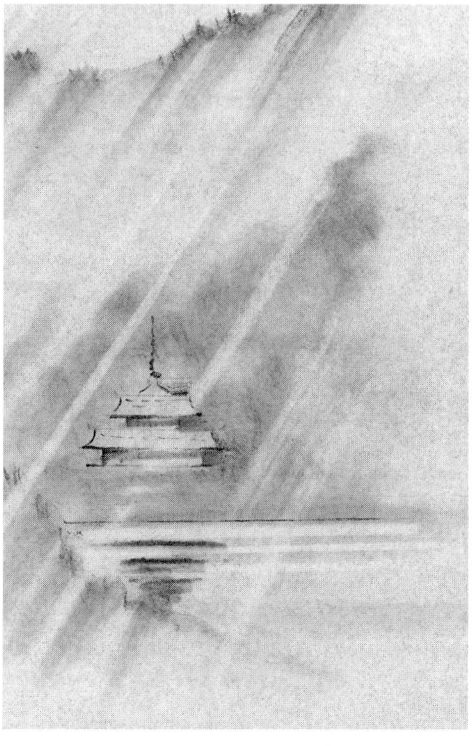

From these mountain sects, Padre Bartholomew told him, had emerged other movements and mountain cults, among which the one known as the "King of the Mountain Way," the famous *shugendo*, and its representatives—the "warriors who slept in the mountains" or *Yamabushi*—reigned supreme for centuries, until the warlords and their retainers inflicted a mortal blow upon them in the course of a series of bloody and merciless confrontations from which these militant mountain mystics never recovered.

"Could these be the same *Yamabushi* to which the first scroll refers, Yu Xia?" Père Dominic asked.

"The very same, Celt," the Hermit responded. "I see that you have sufficient information concerning their background to understand the significance of the tale contained in that scroll, and should you wish to know more, all you have to do is ask Hori, who can locate all the documentation you may wish to consult on those mountain militants. But, be forewarned: If the thought should occur to you that we too may be members of a similar sect because we live in the mountains and espouse an evolving doctrine wherein violence is an issue to be studied, just like all the other issues that inform human life, you should reserve judgement until you get to know us better."

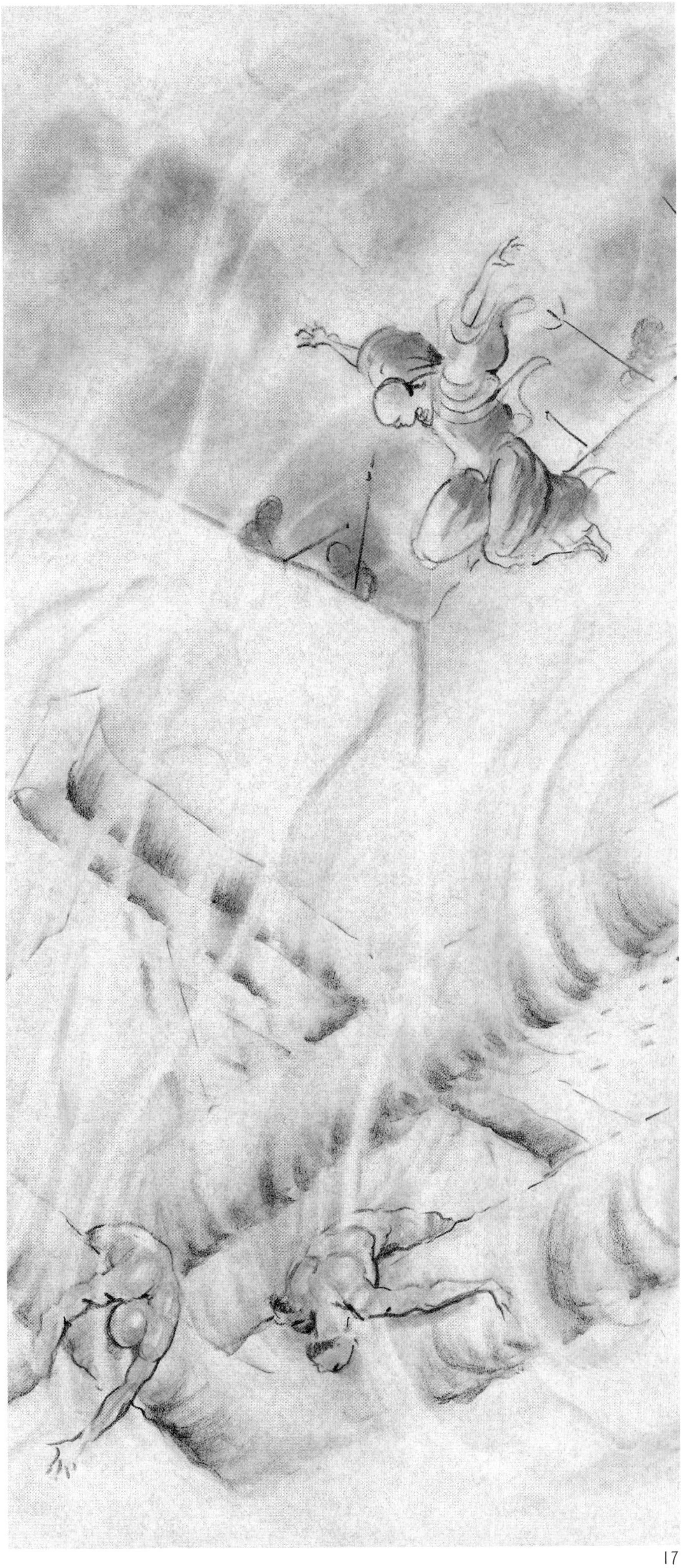

As he rose to his feet, Yu Xia rested his hand lightly on Père Dominic's shoulder. "I hope that you will find your reading to be enlightening and that I will not be reprimanded by other Residents who may feel that you are moving too quickly, and without adequate preparation, into certain inner spheres of the Summit."

With these words, Yu Xia had left Père Dominic alone to enter the world of intermingled light and shadow that was portrayed within the scroll that bore the exotic name of *Yamabushi*.

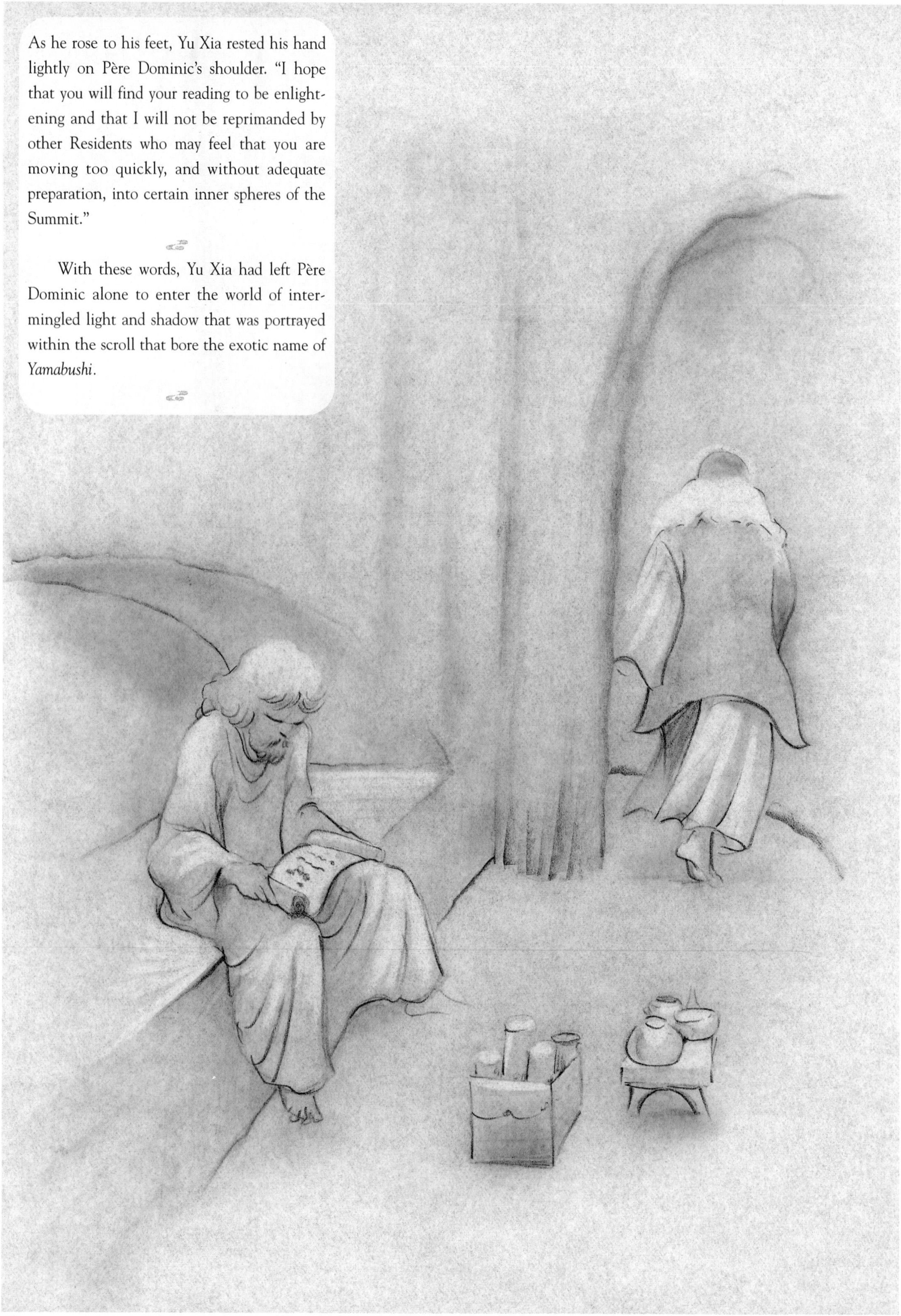

YAMABUSHI

This is a story that begins deep in the Kimbusen Mountains, known for their soaring peaks and shadowed valleys enveloped by dense woods, where waterfalls sing and wild animals thrive, where the untutored eye perceives only beauty, peace, and the integrated rhythms of life.

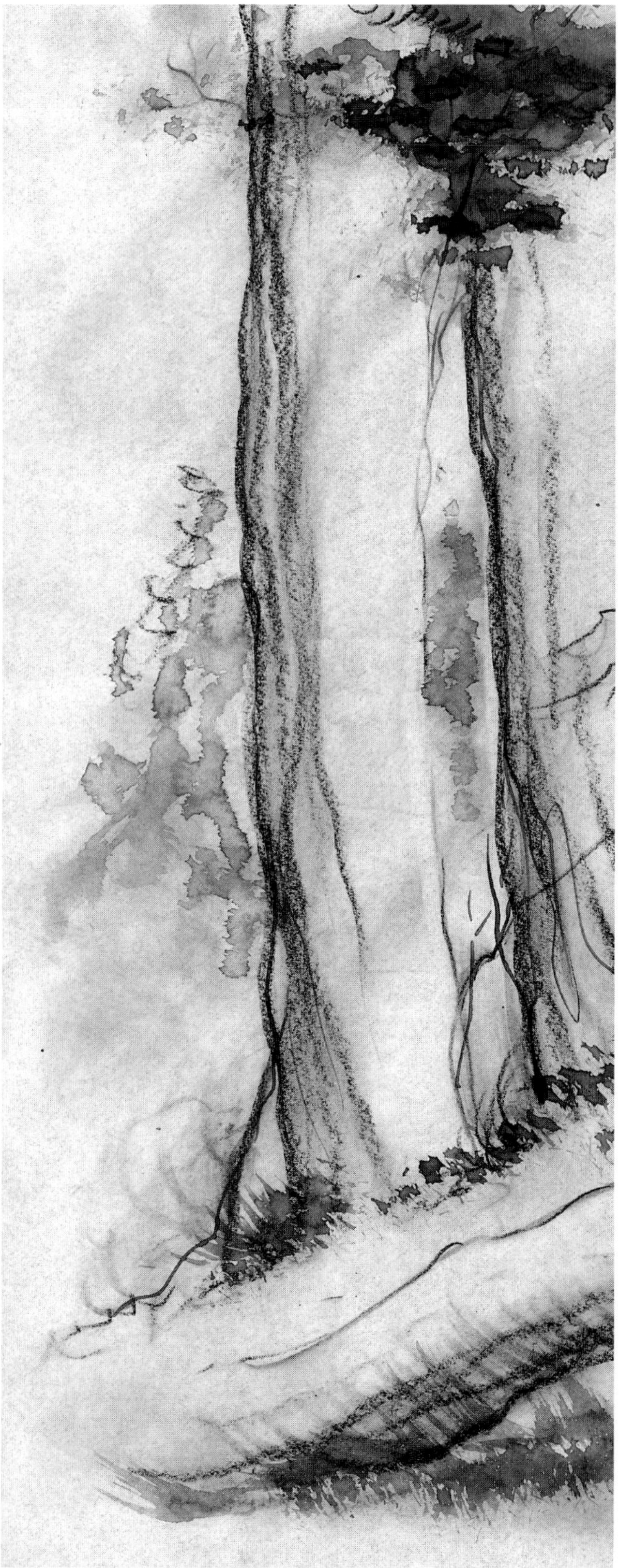

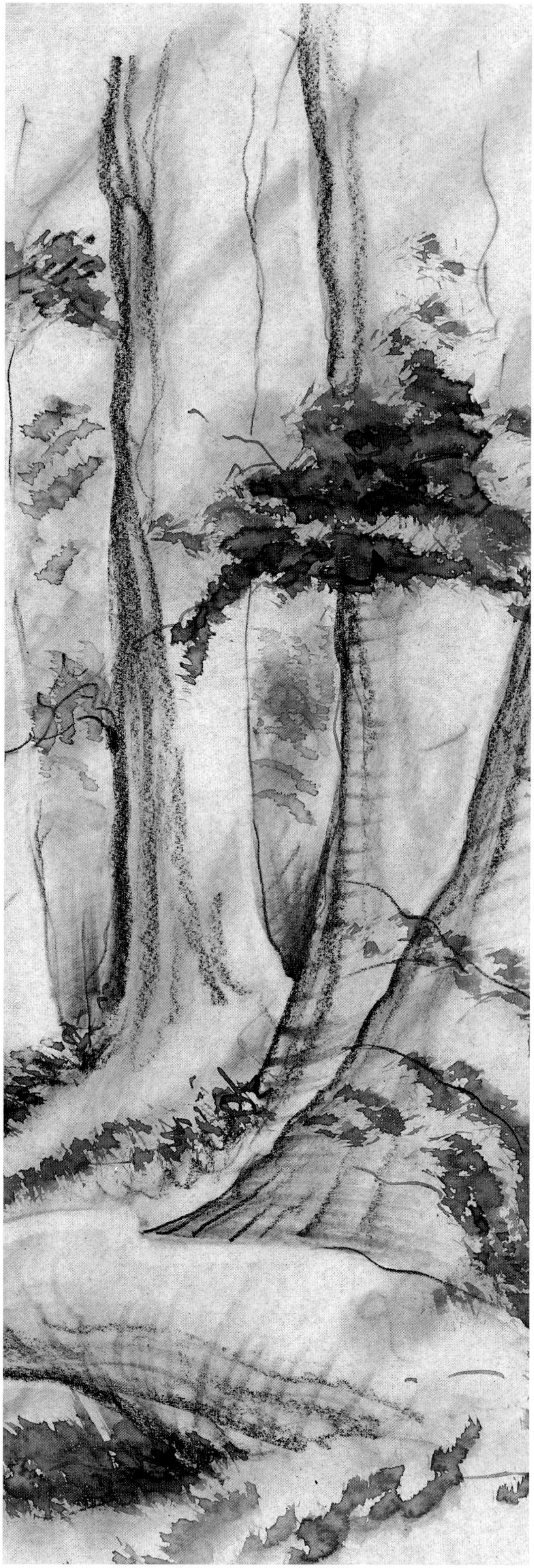

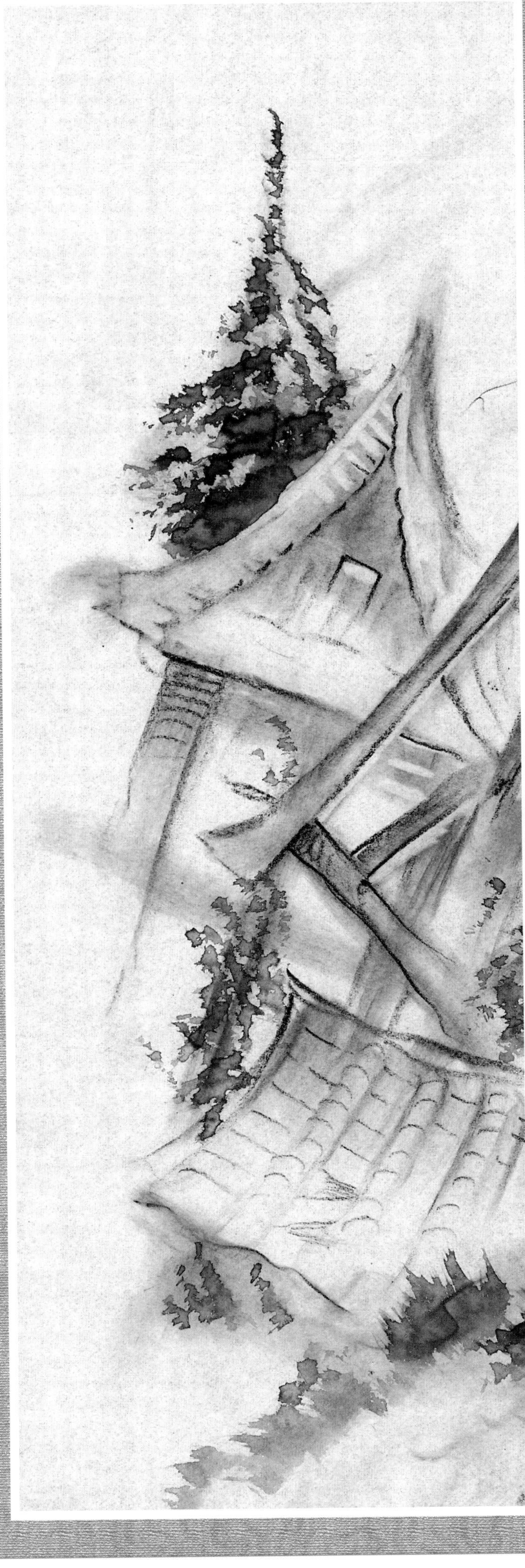

But a returning pilgrim has come upon smoldering ruins where once stood the ancient Kimbusen Temple, whose precincts had resounded with the ringing of bells, the chanting of holy scriptures, and the shouts of young acolytes as they practiced their interpretations of martial skills before the assembled elders.

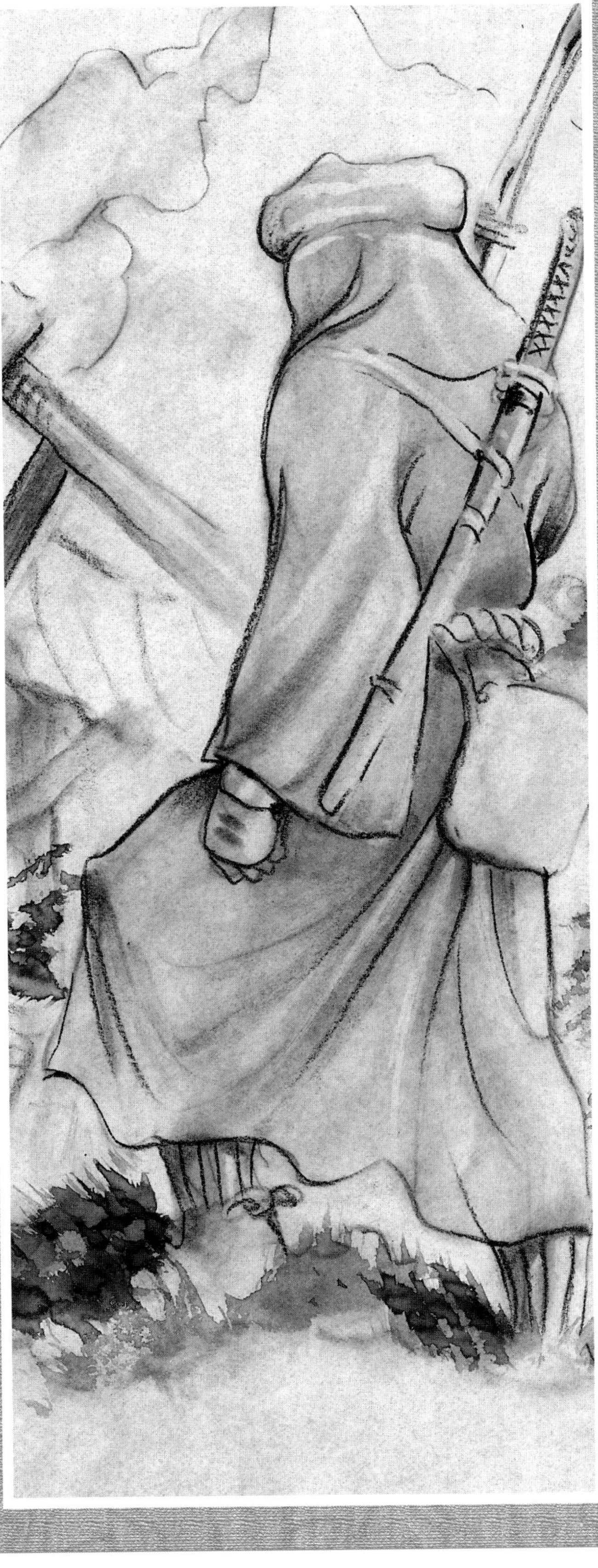

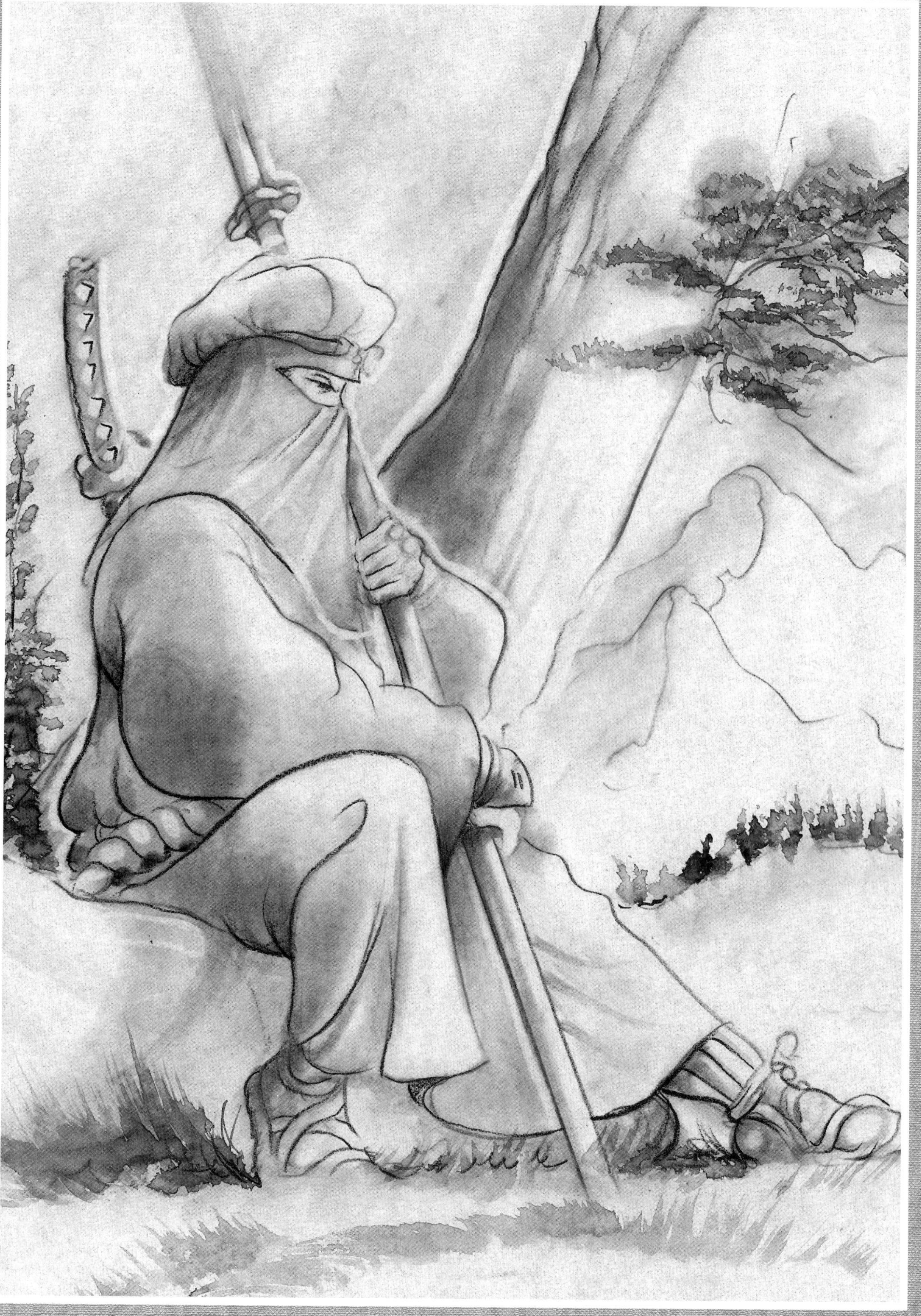

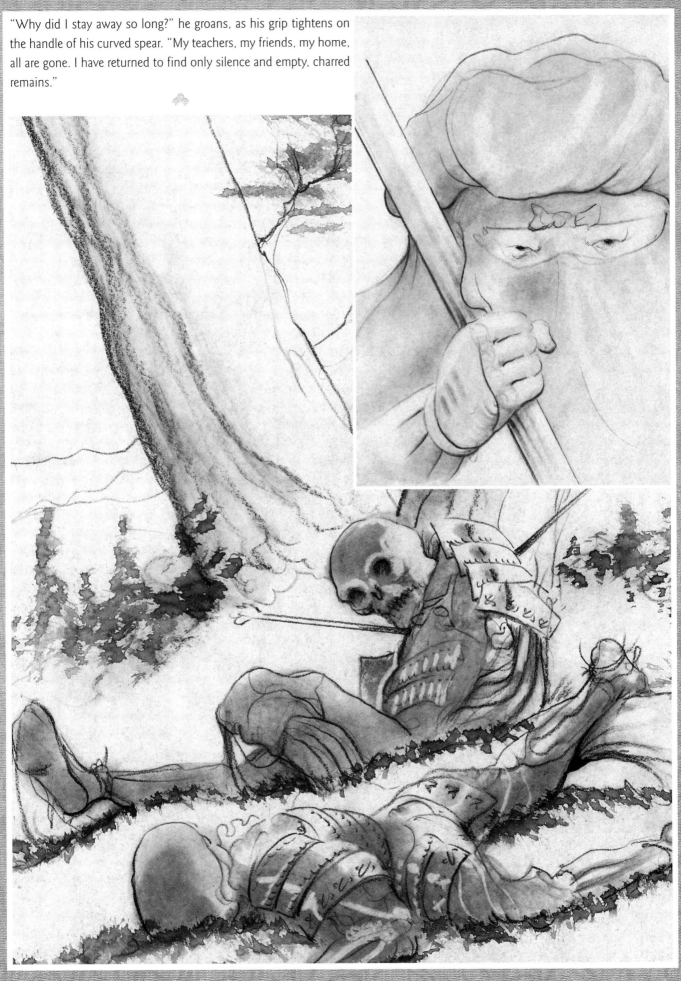

"Why did I stay away so long?" he groans, as his grip tightens on the handle of his curved spear. "My teachers, my friends, my home, all are gone. I have returned to find only silence and empty, charred remains."

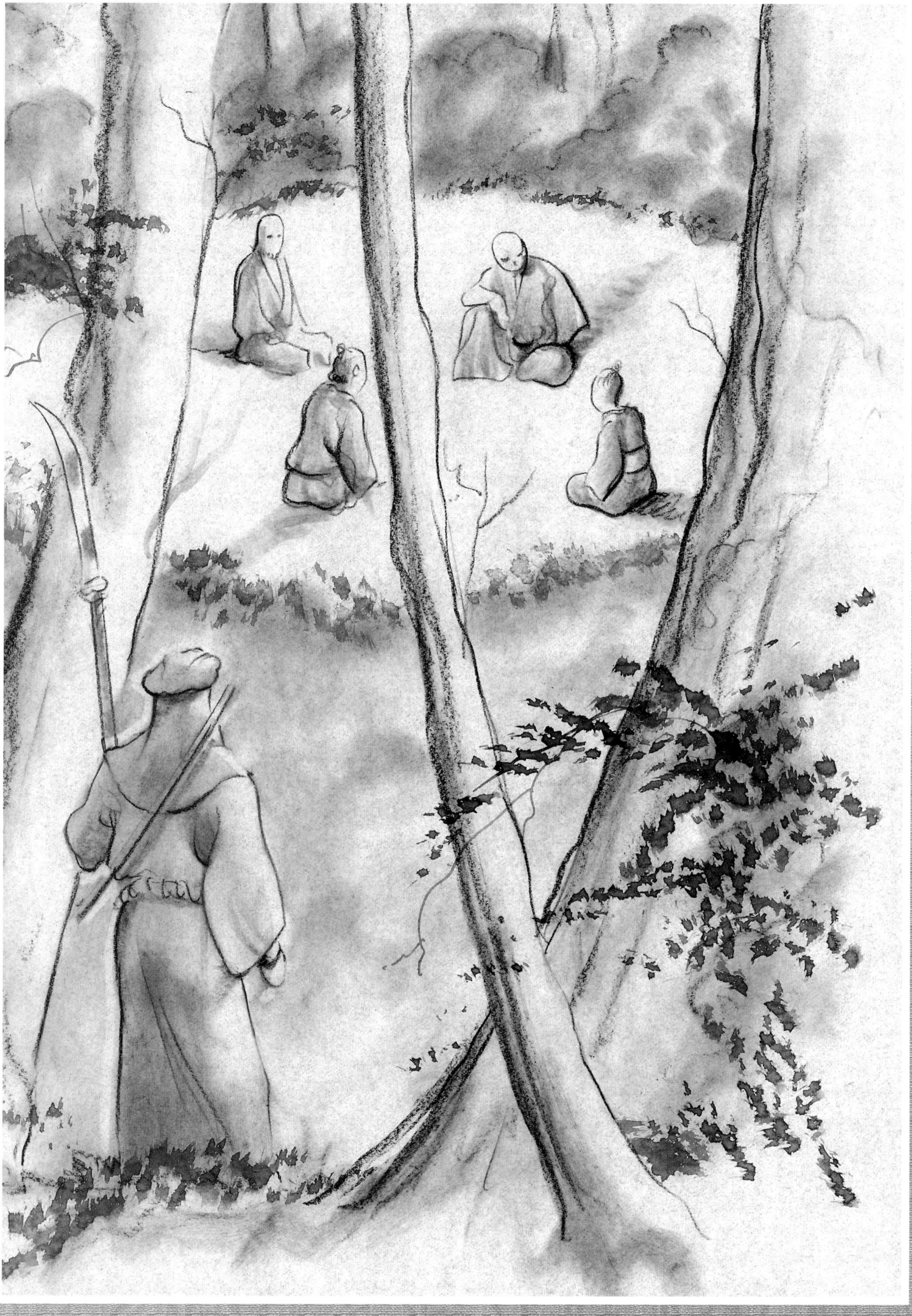

And yet, as he soon discovers, the devastated temple is still sheltering four unarmed travelers who have been making their way through the mountains. Unseen, the pilgrim watches them that night as they huddle around a fire, seeking warmth and comfort for their weary bodies.

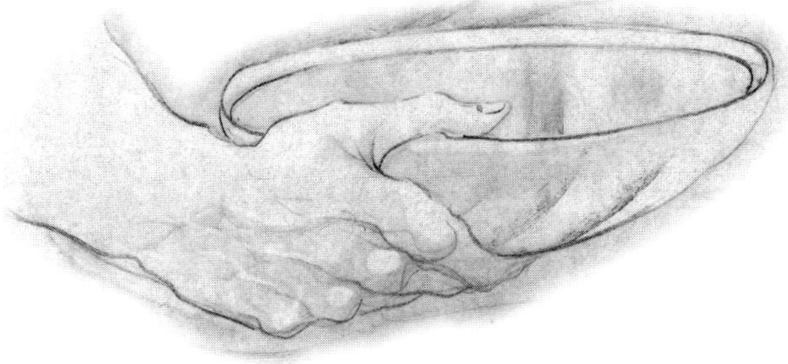

Their leader, Master Naoto, encourages them to rest before they must resume the journey back home, to the courtyards and meditation halls of that school where the venerable Master Kawanari awaits them, offering up his daily prayers for their safe return from these violent lands.

Master Naoto's thoughts turn toward home, as he ponders how best to protect his charges while, at the same time, helping them to perform their duties—to assist those in need, to undertake good works, and to bury the dead in this land ravaged by the furies of war, where the meek find no haven, and the unprotected receive no mercy. Should they continue to journey northward, or return to the Otsugawa Village where, only yesterday, they had all been provided with food and shelter? Dark clouds, billowing ominously at sunset, had signaled possible danger to those hospitable people.

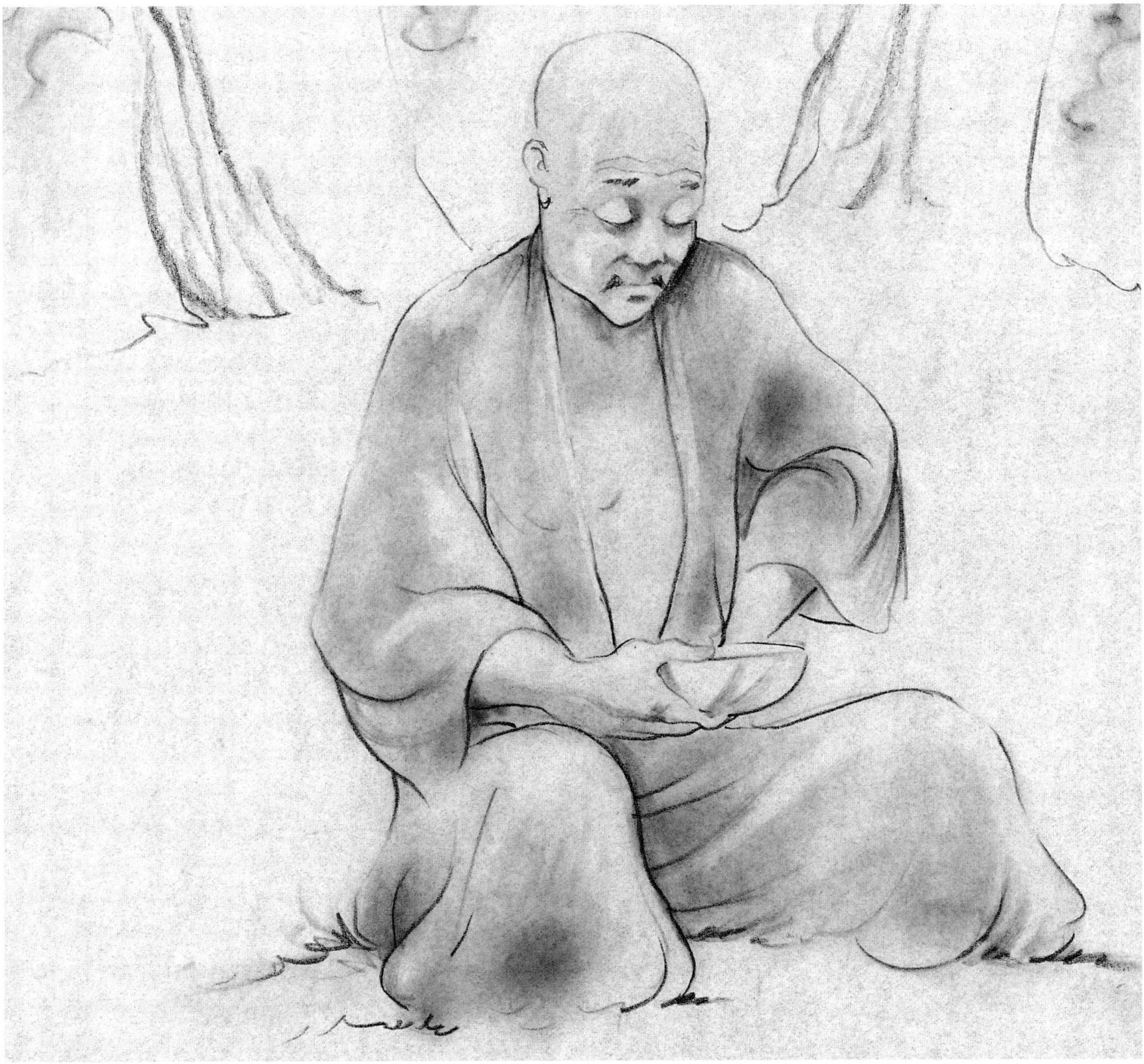

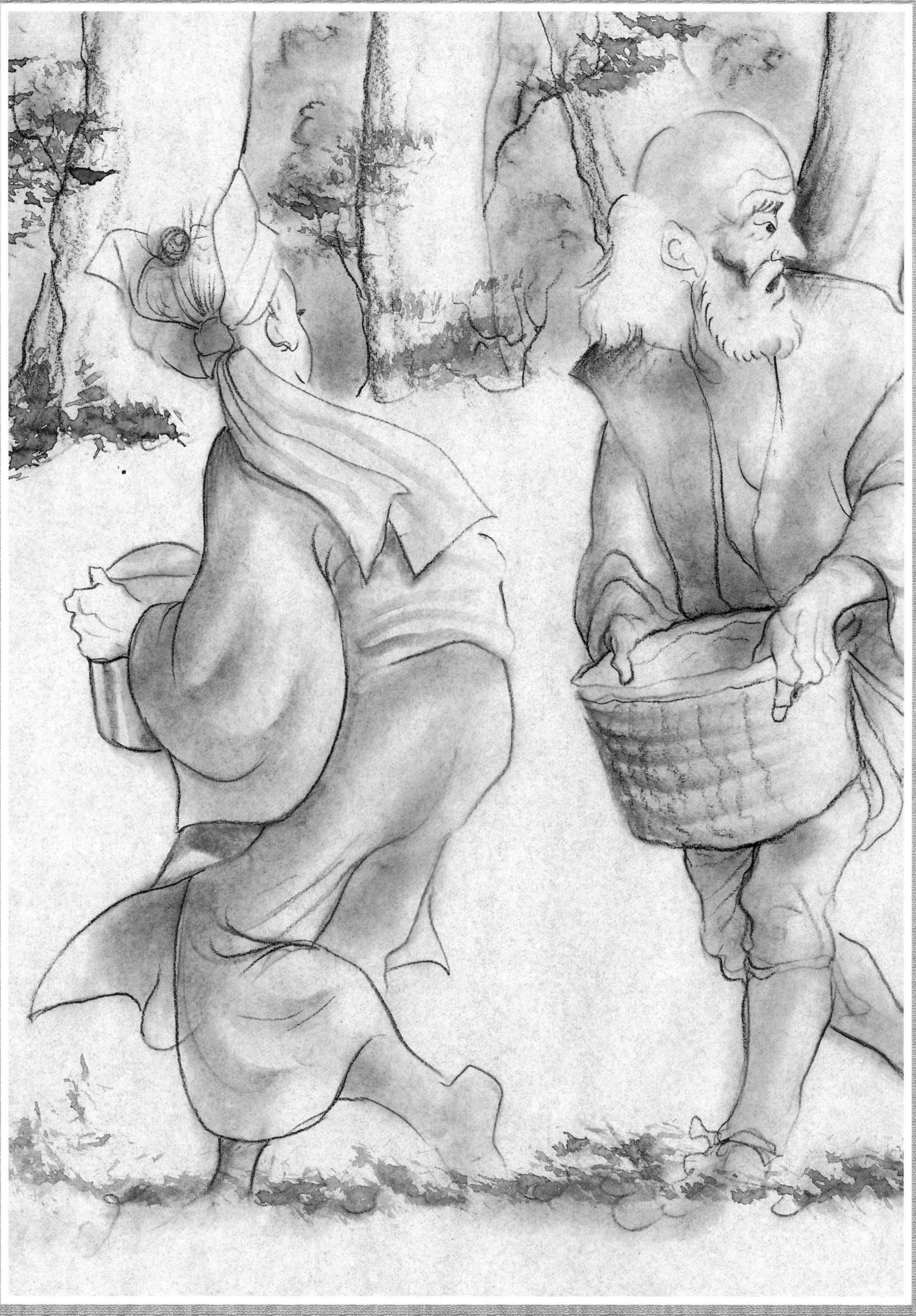

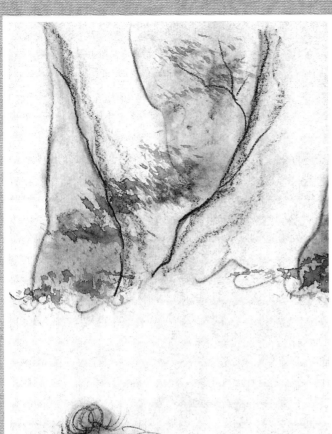

Suddenly, he turns toward the silent shadow in the woods, and courteously invites him to join their group and partake of their bubbling, if meager meal.

"Come, the night is cold and, as you can see, we bear no arms. Step forward in peace, pilgrim, and share our soup, our rice, and our tea—gifts from the Otsugawa people yesterday, despite the scarcity of food in their village."

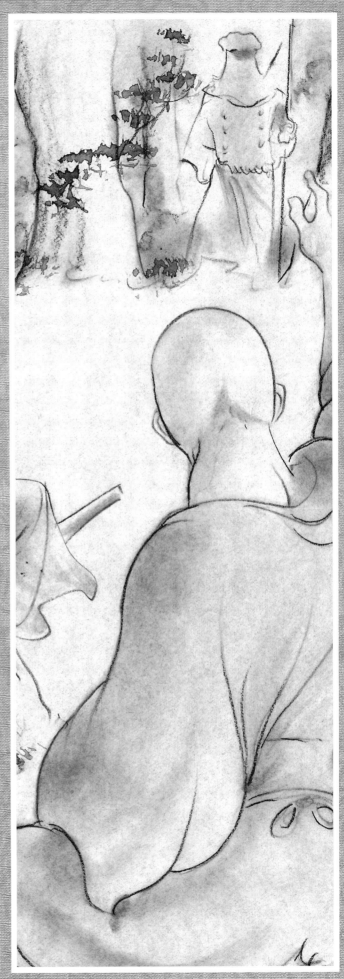

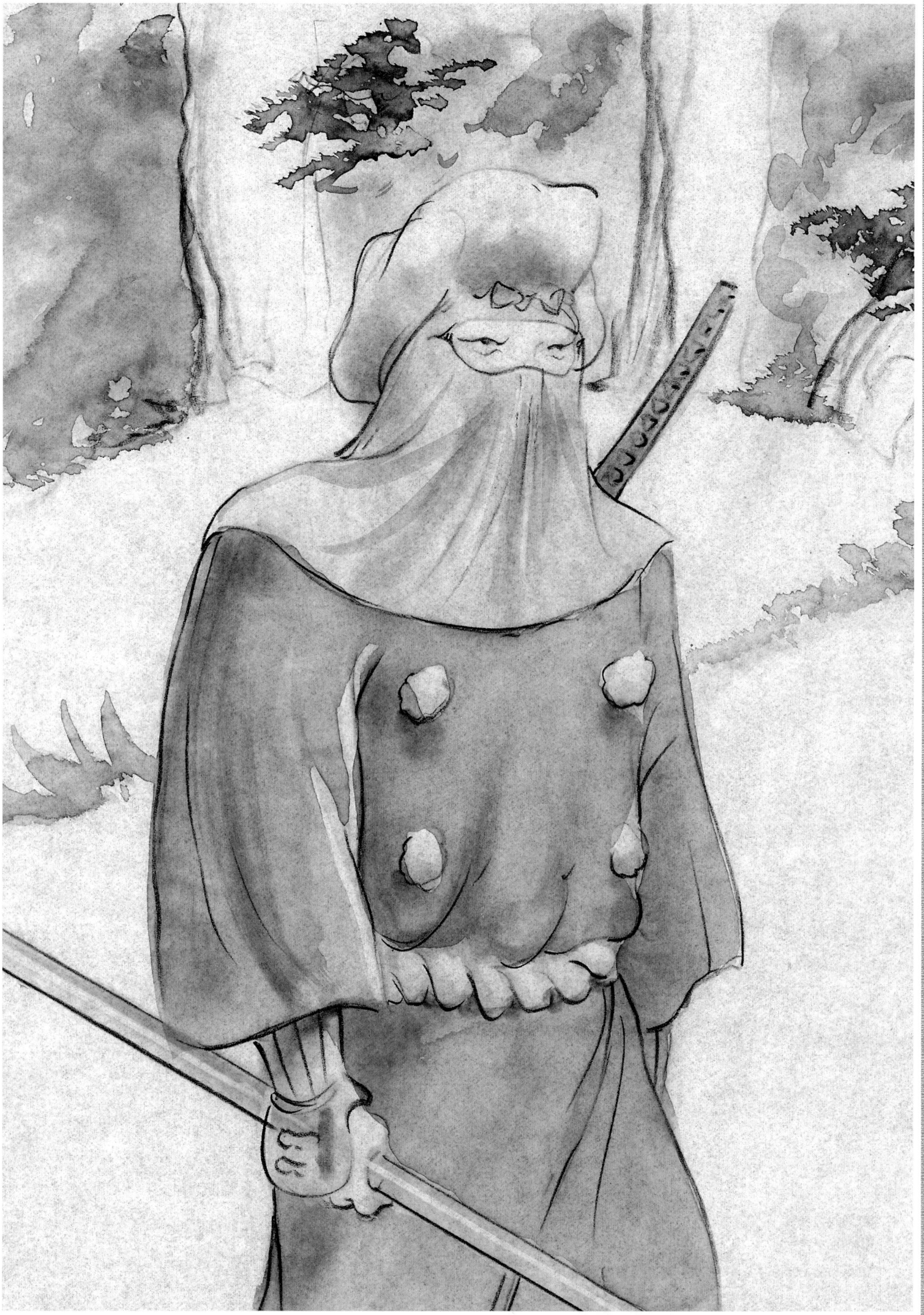

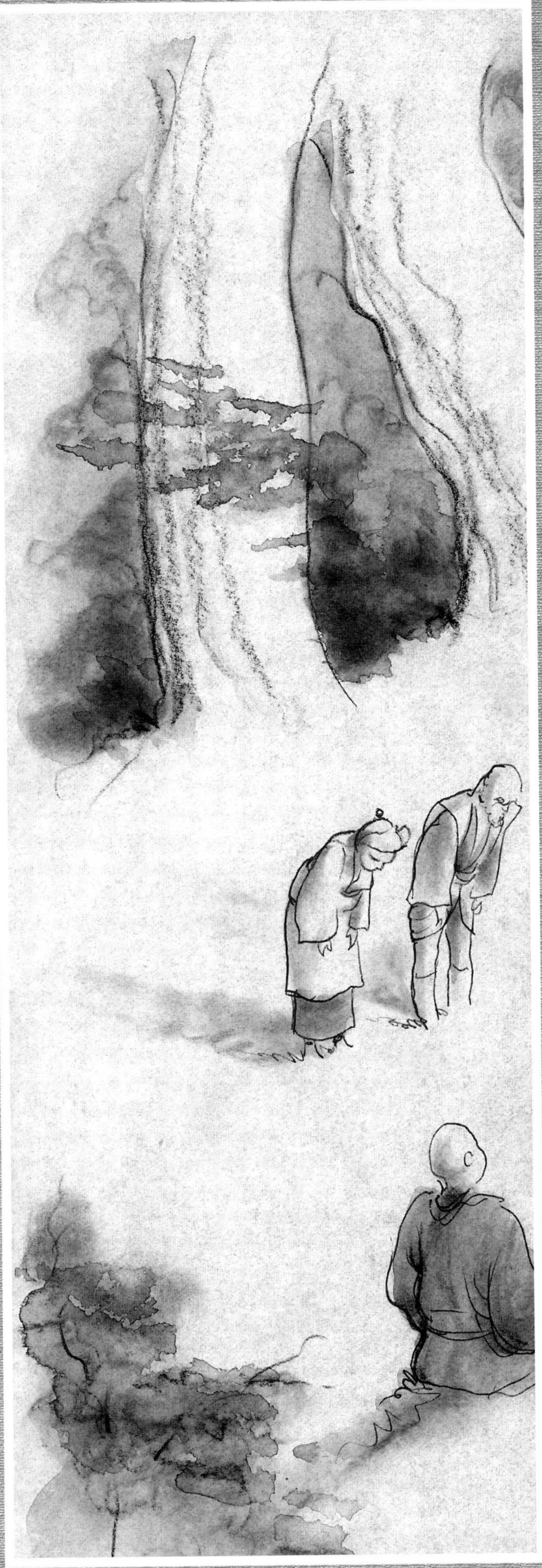

Thus summoned, the Yamabushi steps into the clearing, formidable in appearance, bristling with weapons that catch and reflect the firelight, seething with pain and anger that he does not bother to conceal. "Your senses are indeed keen, traveler," he replies. "Who might you be, seemingly at rest and at peace in these haunted precincts, unarmed, and yet so aware of your surroundings?"

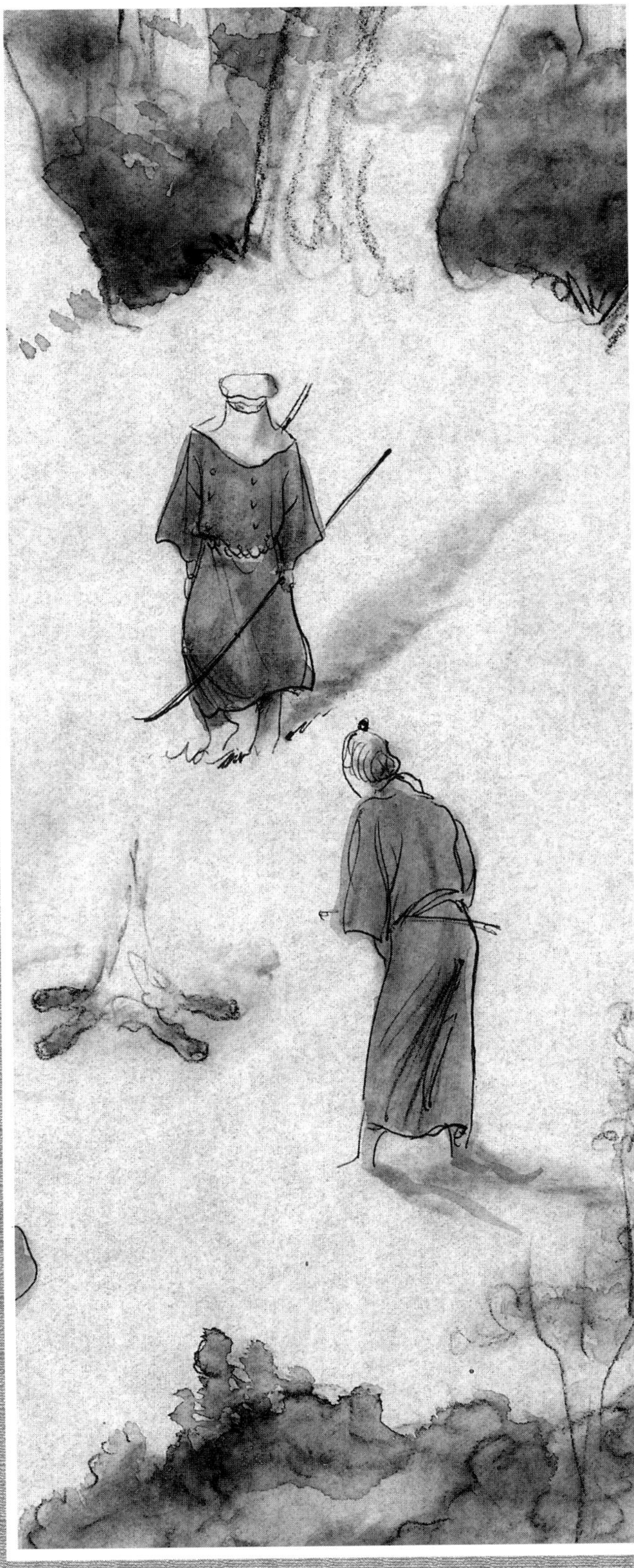

"My name is Naoto, and I am a disciple of Master Kawanari, who—as you may perhaps have heard—teaches the art of conducting streams of violence into the void, where they can harm no one. He sent me south to fetch these three people you see with me, since they also desire to be instructed in Master Kawanari's art."

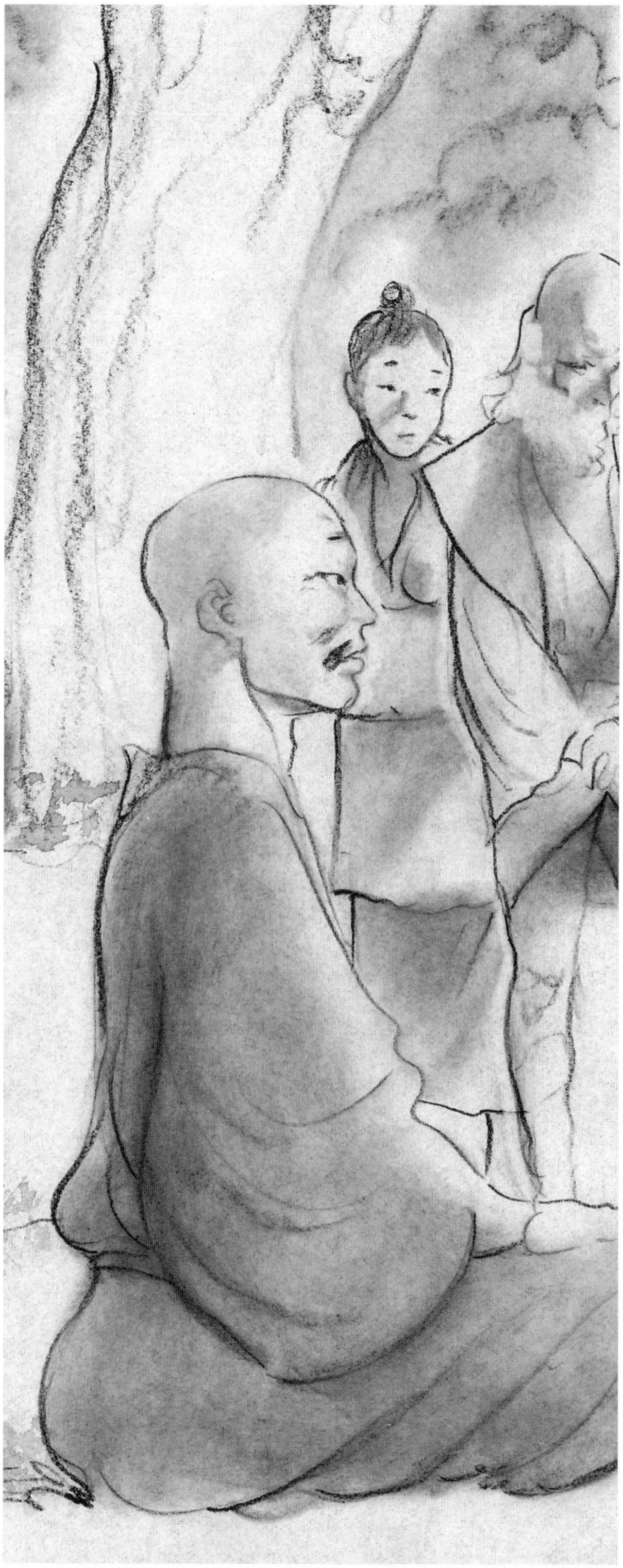

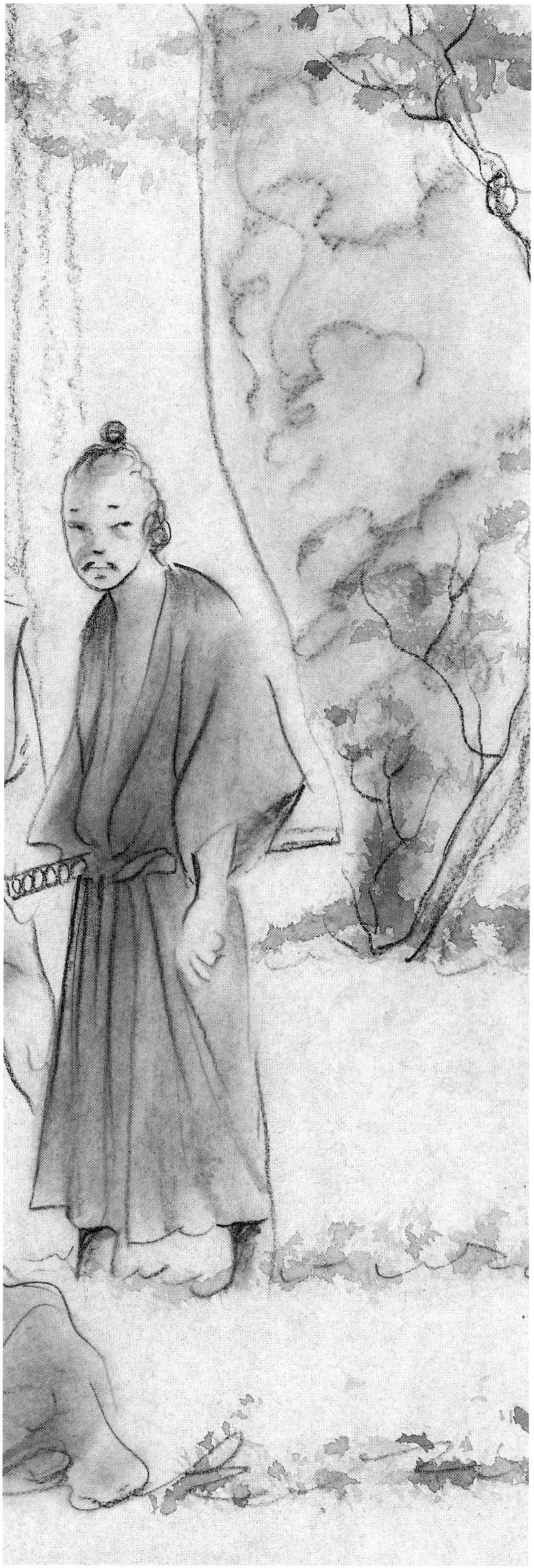

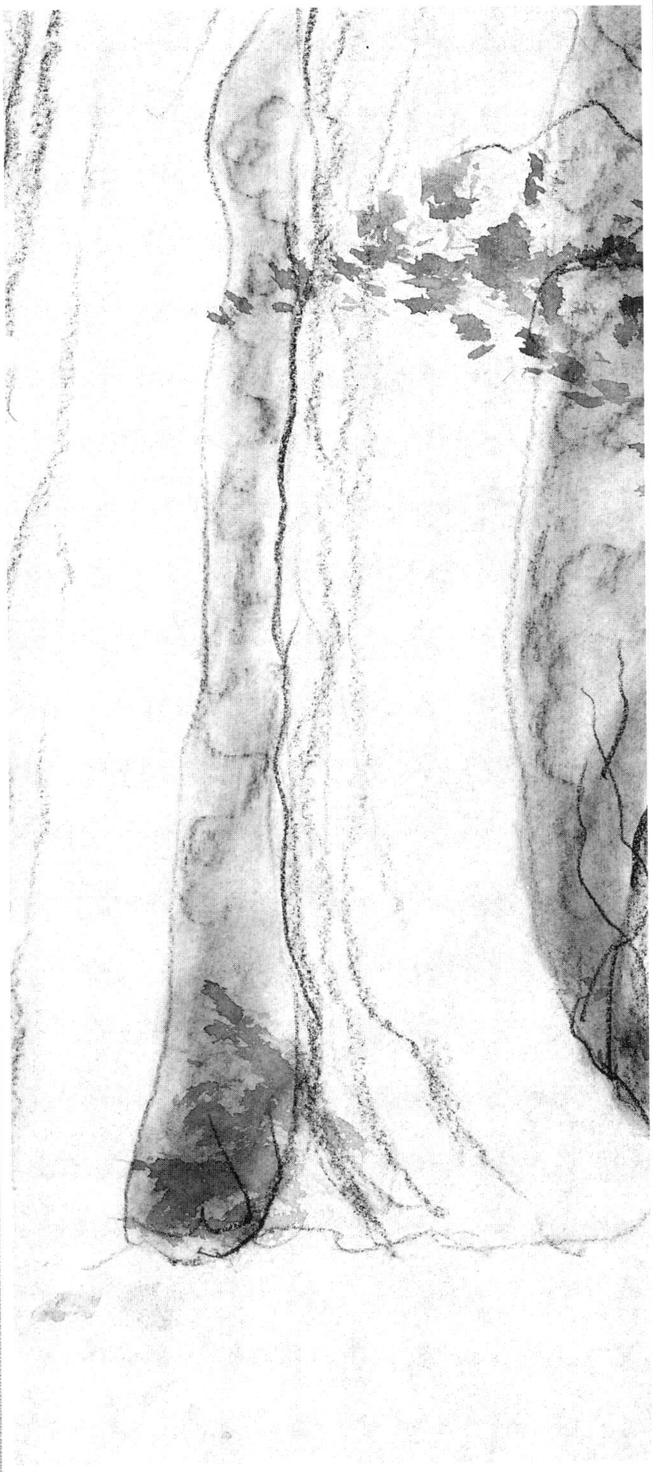

"The young woman on my left is Yamako, whose family was swept up in the latest fighting in the Koro District, and whose members have all been reported missing. She will be sheltered at our school until it is safe for her to search for them. This young man, obviously still reluctant to relinquish his short sword, is Ishi, a young warrior from the Bungo Province, who wishes to seek paths other than those of the martial arts. And my other companion is Kudara, who can bend matter such as clay into shapes useful to men and women, a skilled artisan, and a man of peace."

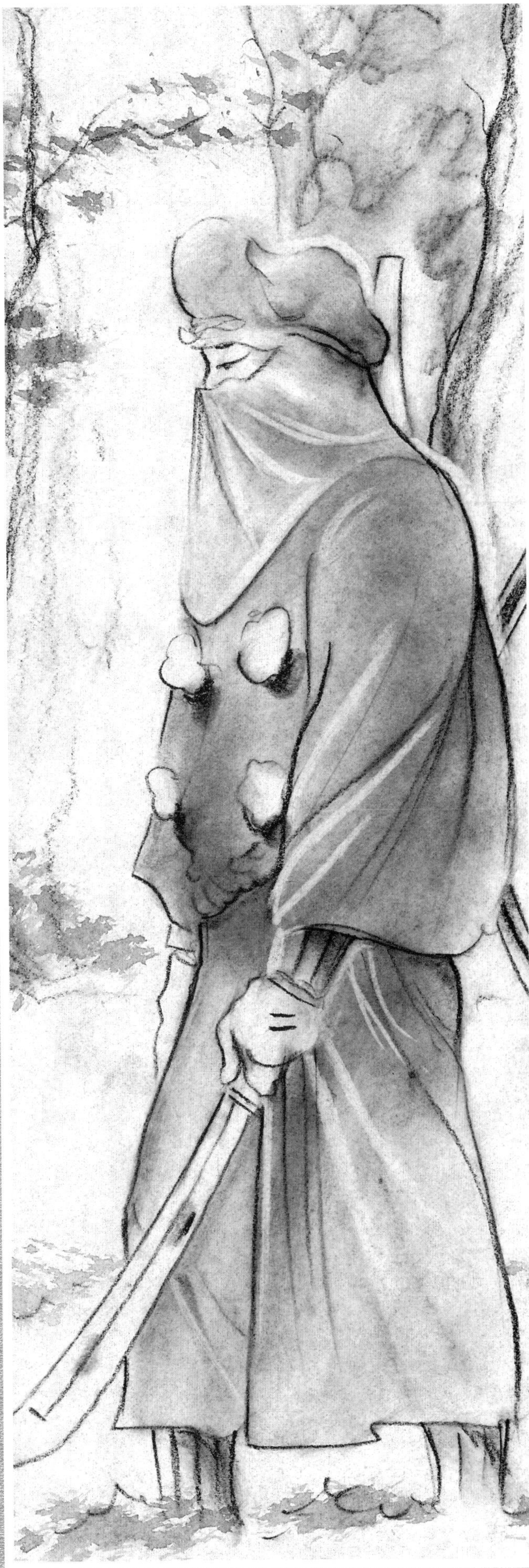

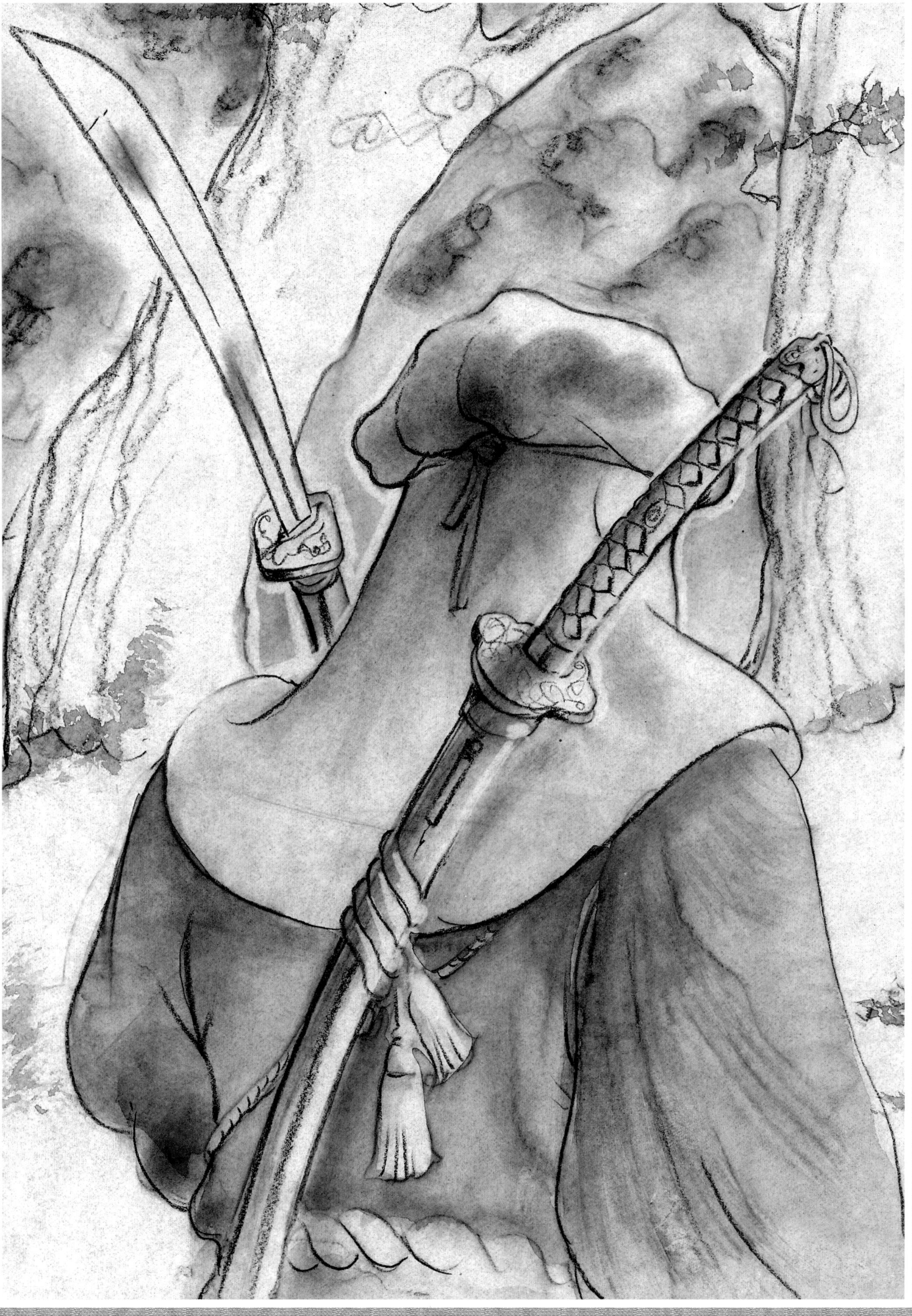

"But what of you, who walk alone in these woods you seem to know so well, holding your spear in a grip of iron and gazing about you with eyes like burning coals? Was this perhaps your home, this temple that now lies around us in charred ruins, bereft of is inhabitants whose bodies a merciful hand (perhaps yours) has buried? If this should be so, please believe that we share your grief. May Gauthama Buddha ease your pain, and may his teachings comfort you in this dark moment of your life, and of our mutual history."

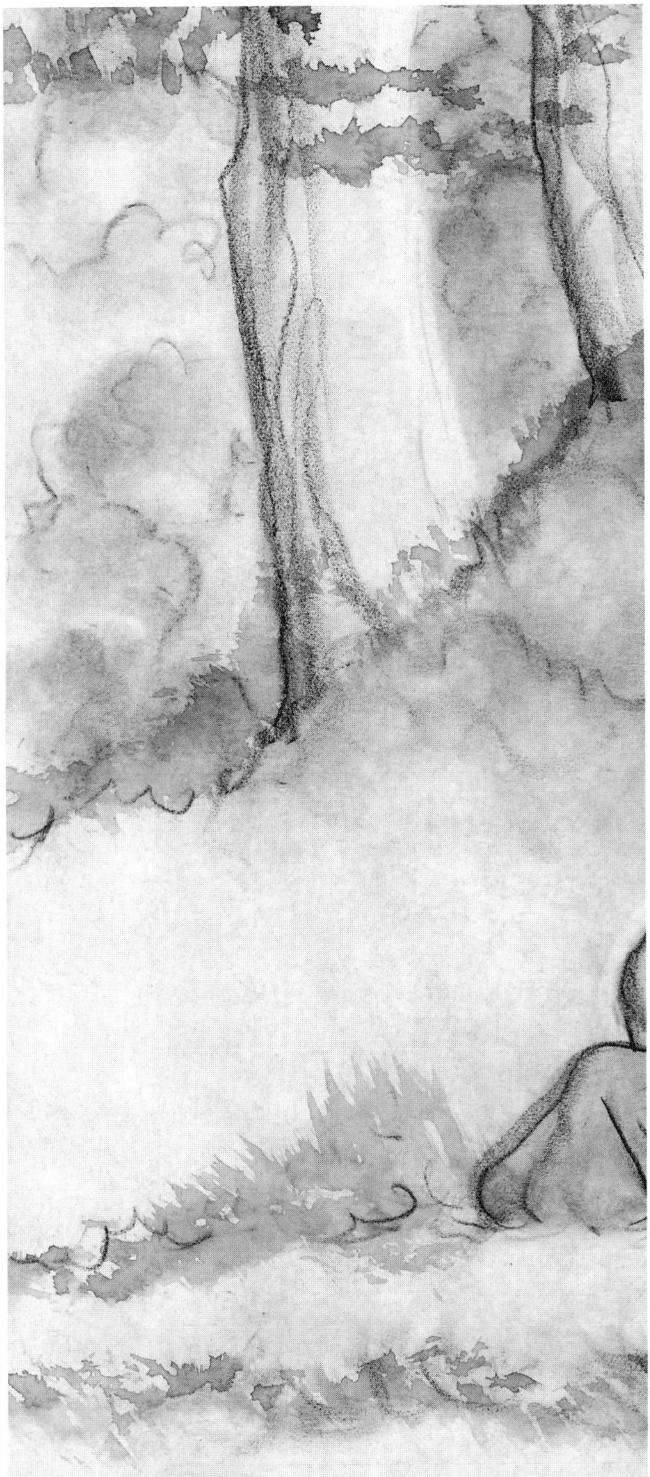

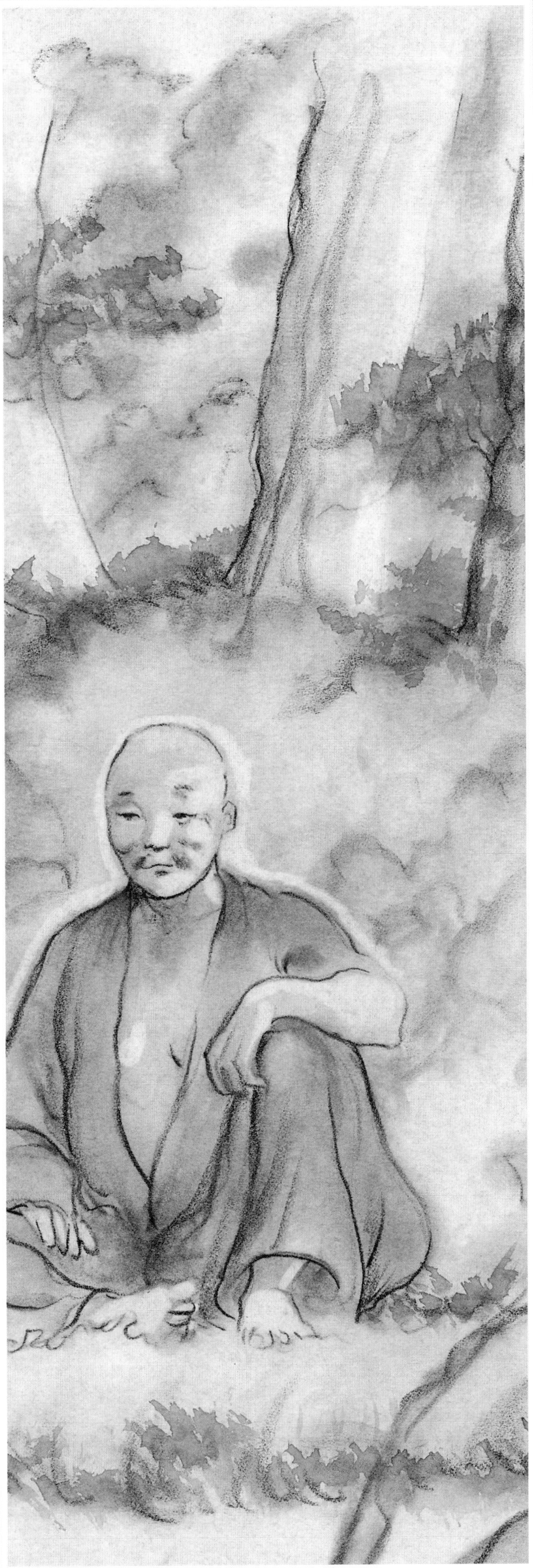

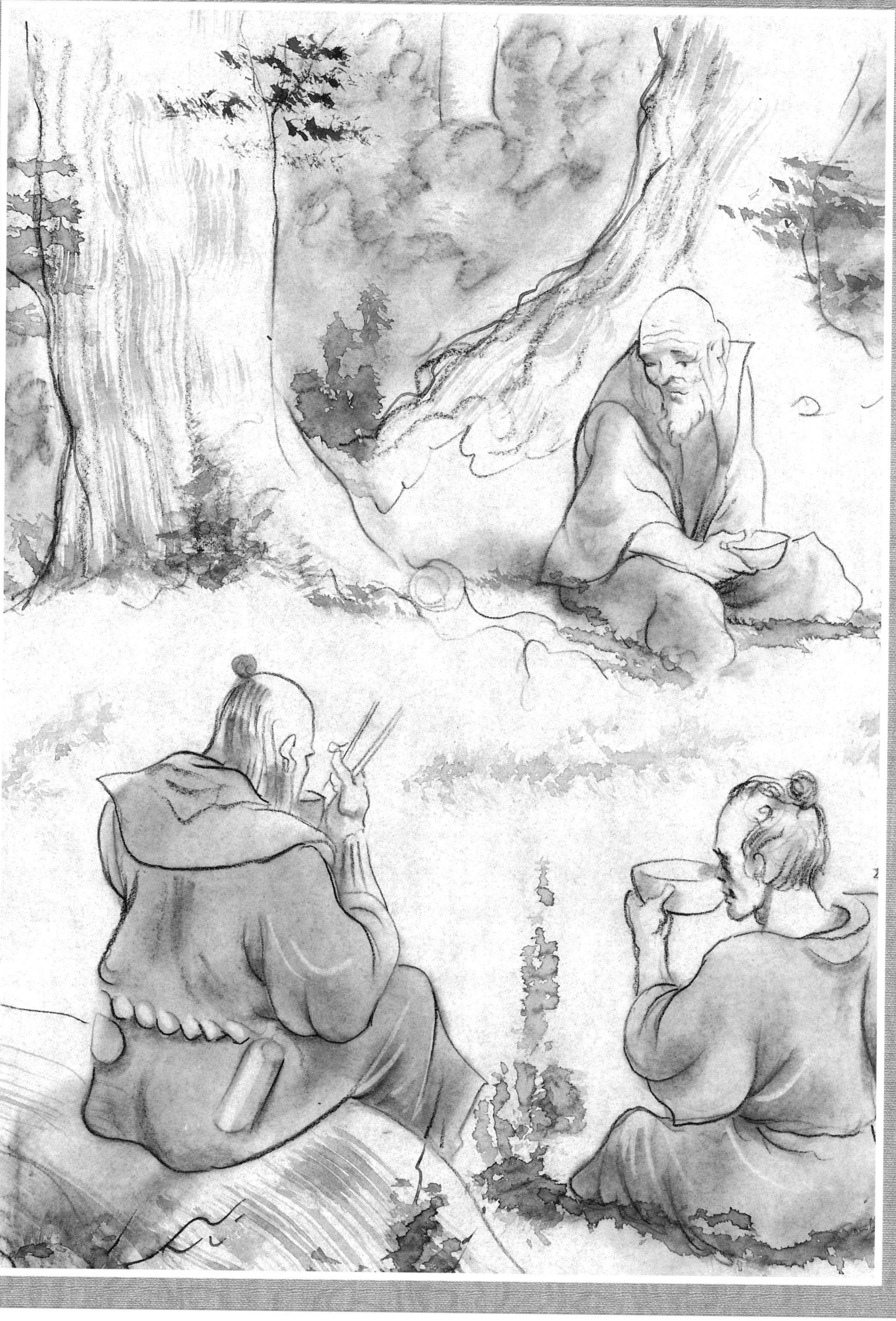

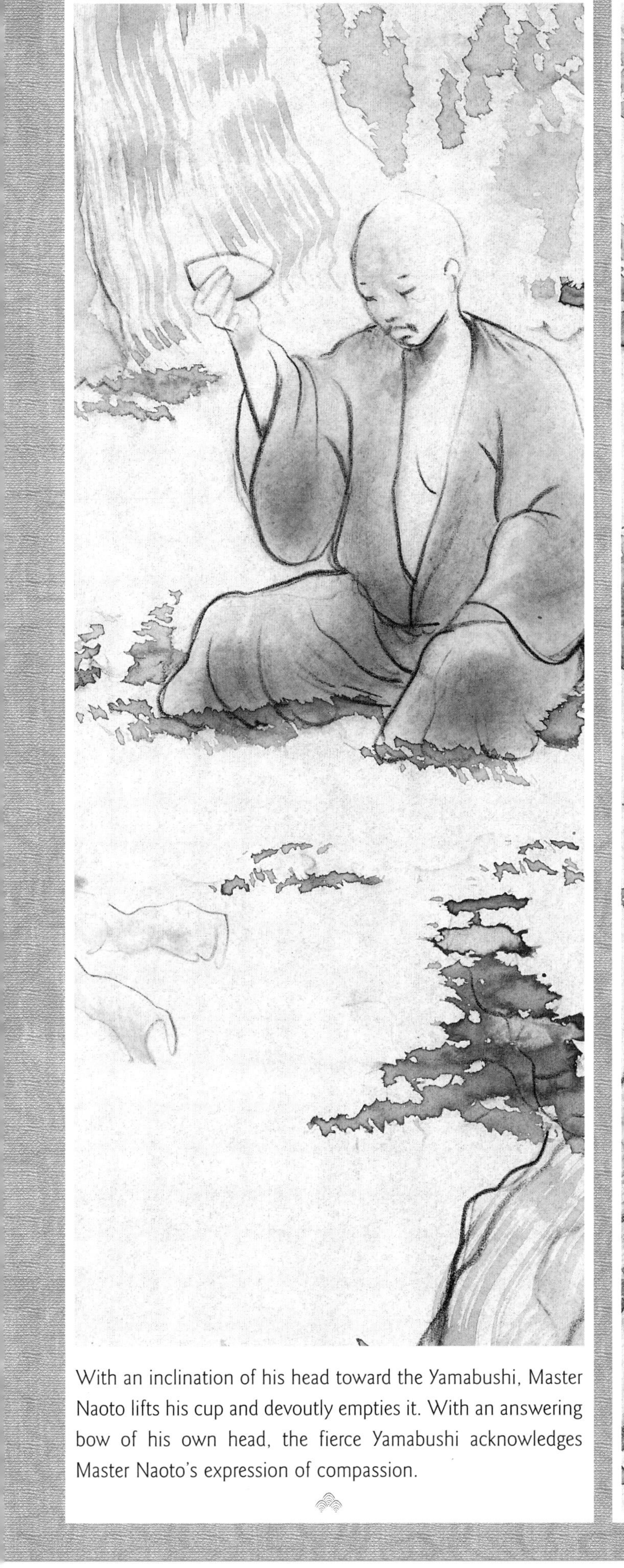

With an inclination of his head toward the Yamabushi, Master Naoto lifts his cup and devoutly empties it. With an answering bow of his own head, the fierce Yamabushi acknowledges Master Naoto's expression of compassion.

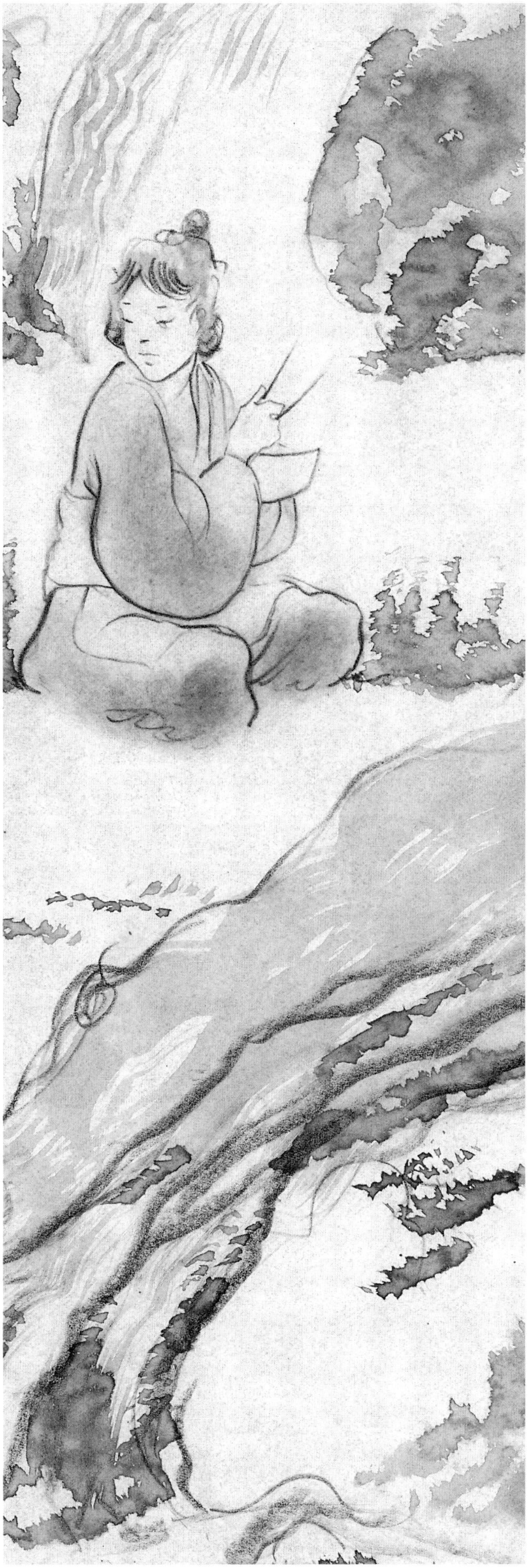

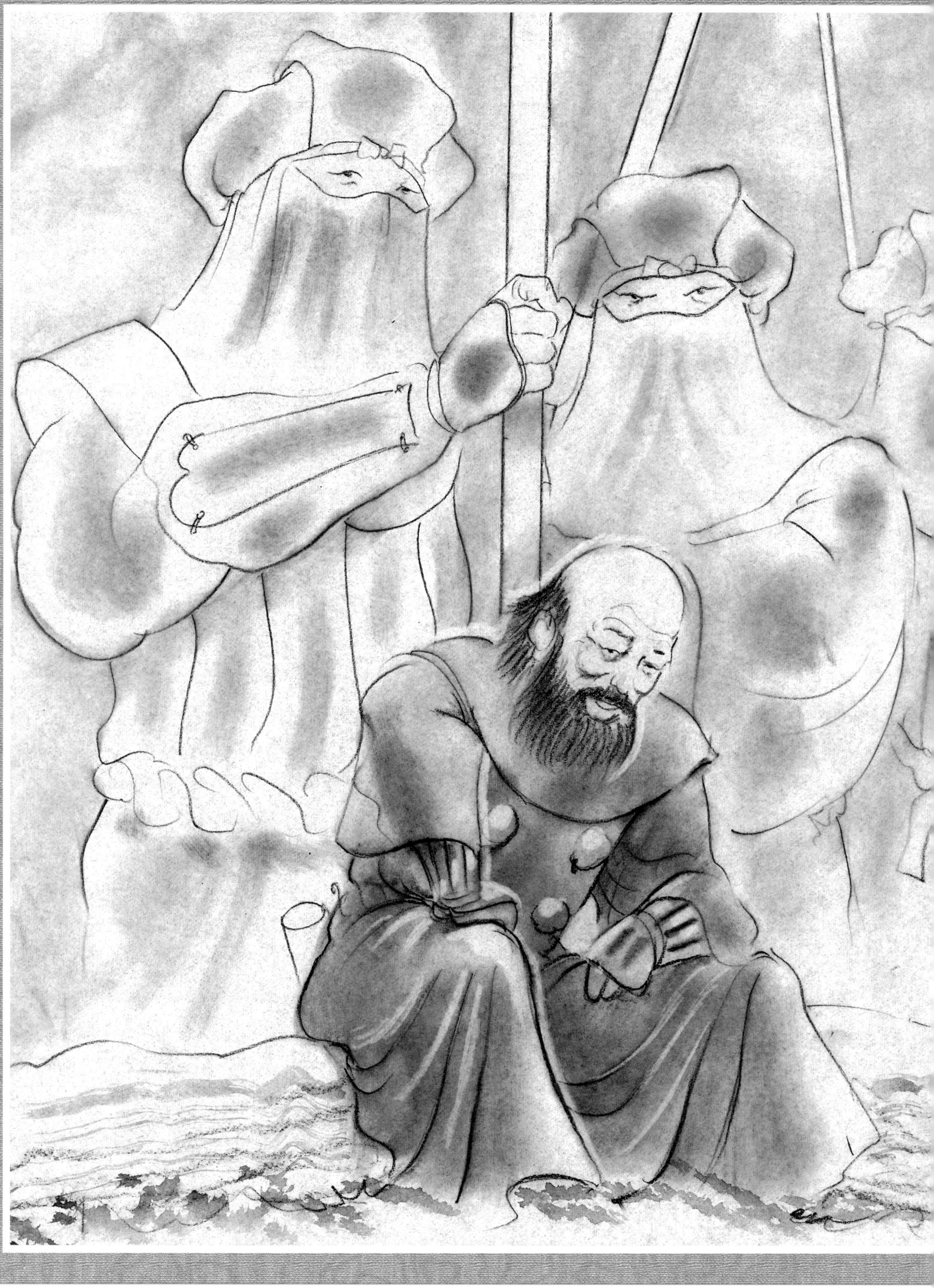

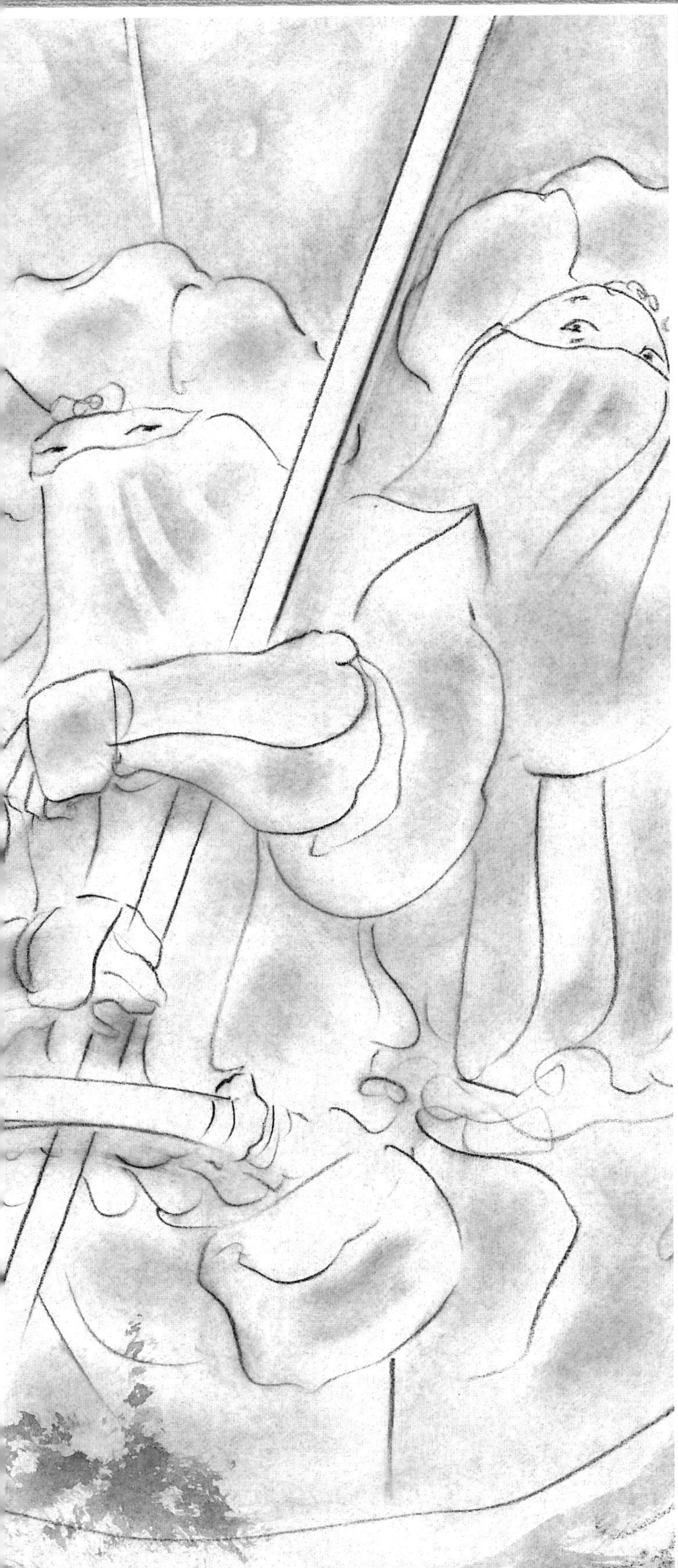

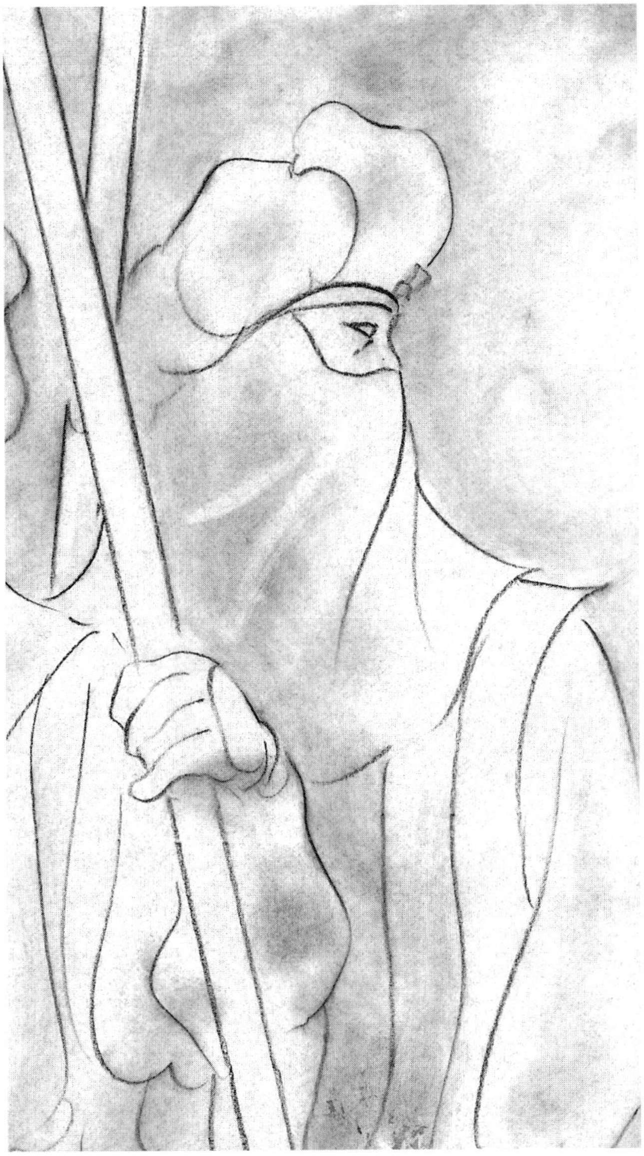

"Once again, you astonish me, sir. This was indeed the temple where I came to maturity; the burial mounds you see cover my teachers, my friends, my comrades-in-arms, all slain while I was away, studying at the Shingu Temple where I was sent three years ago to learn the secret spearfighting arts taught there by Master Kiyohara. My name is Haru. When rumors began to reach us of the troubles in these sacred mountains, I rushed back—to discover this! Instead of testing my skills shoulder to shoulder with teachers and friends against a common foe; instead of performing heroic deeds before the eyes of my mentors, as we barred the way to the temple, driving the cursed warriors back, step by step, blow by blow; instead I returned to find all the inhabitants of the temple slain, their bodies mutilated, and the temple precincts desecrated by the professional killers of the plains. Thus it is that I wander amidst these ruins, now that I have paid my respects to the dead, unwilling to remain where my past has been blotted out, and yet unable to leave."

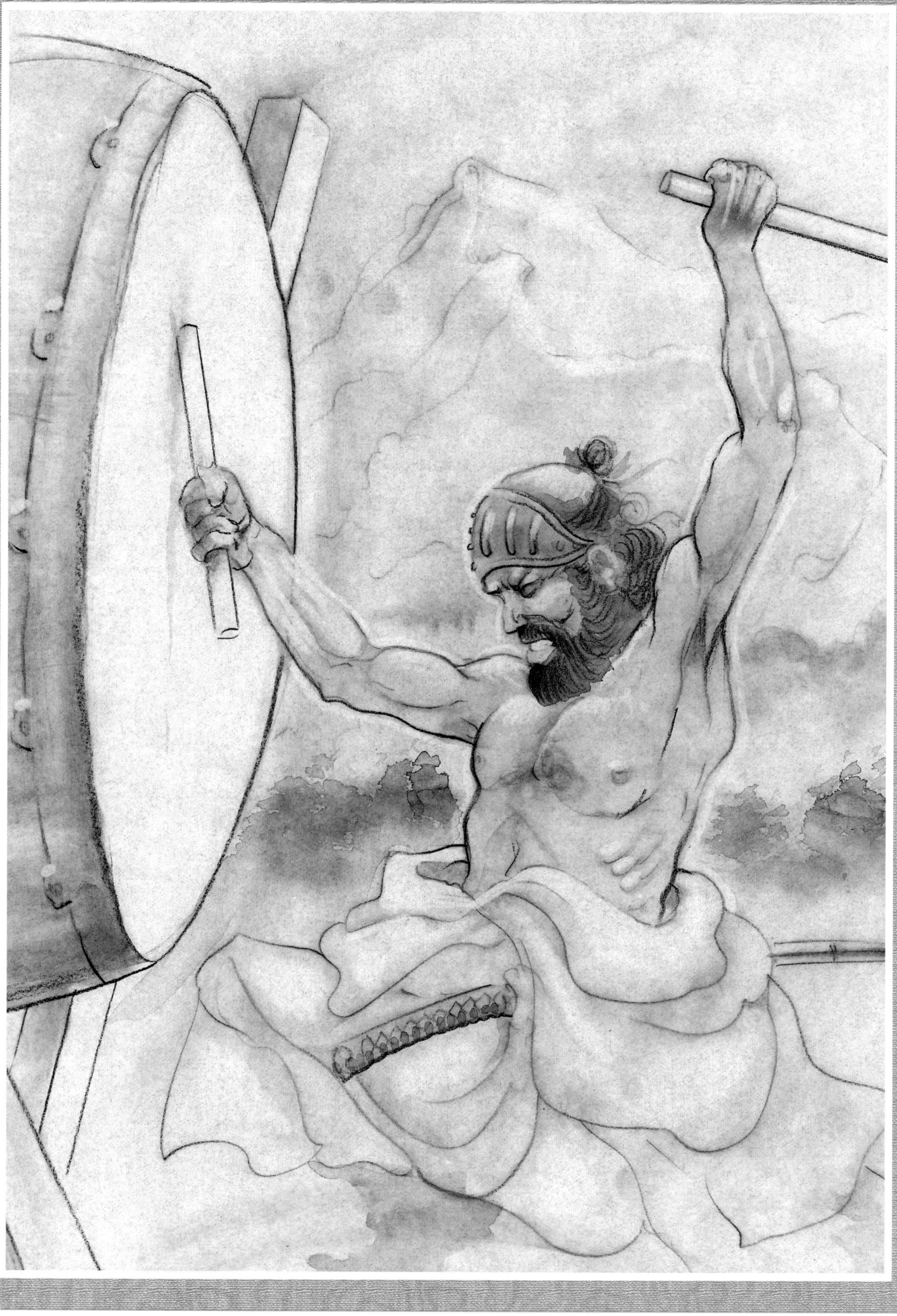

"I can only resurrect memories of other times, when the mountain winds carried the sounds of our war drums far and wide, and the ringing of our temple bells called us to sacred battles on the plains below, where the Court and our venerable Emperor were being slowly but inexorably suffocated by the growing masses of warriors whose power was not sanctified . . ."

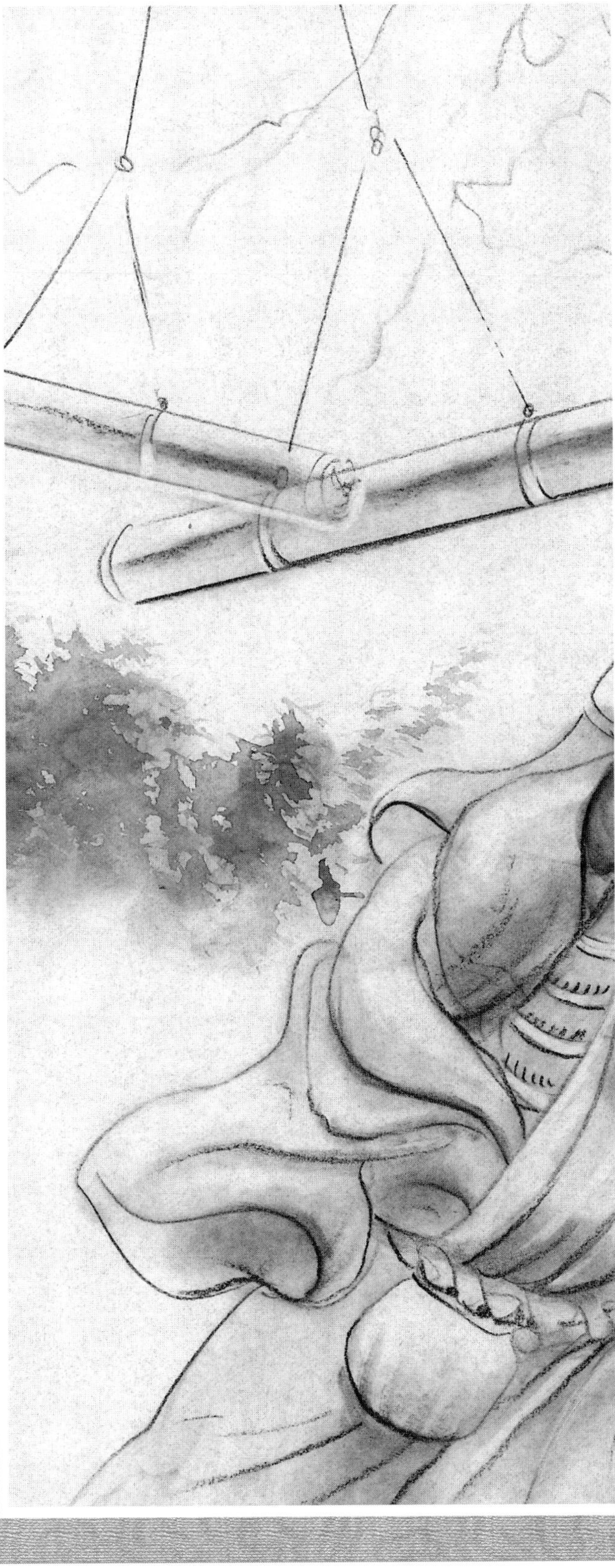

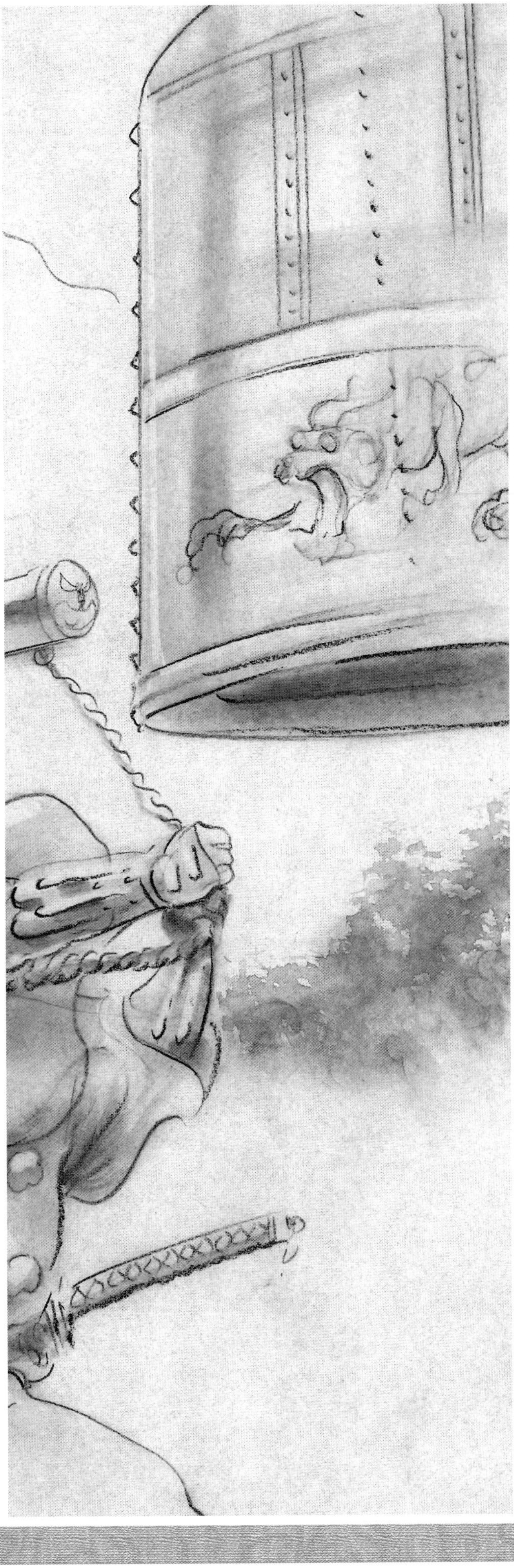

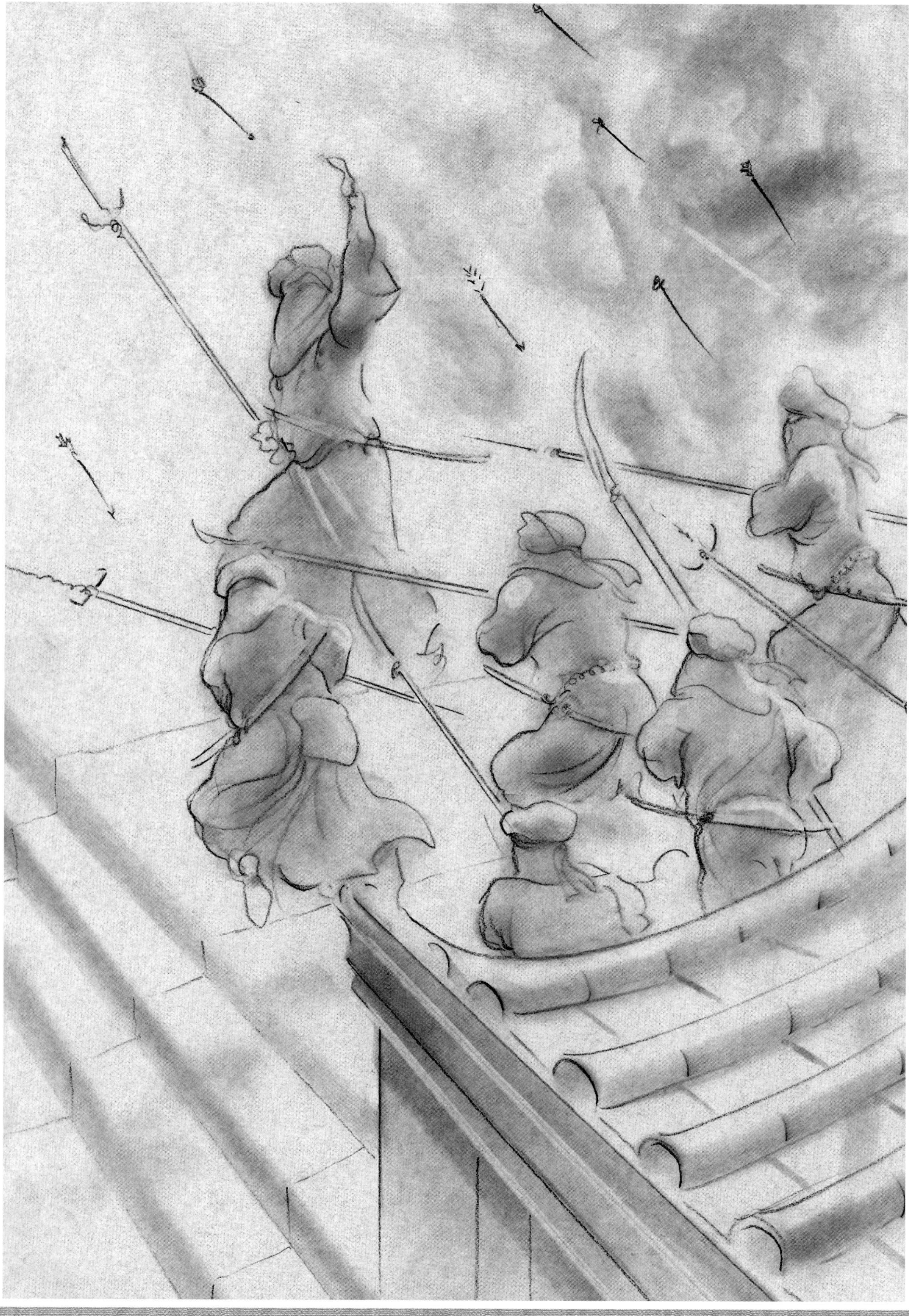

". . . until those same warriors eventually brought their sinful wars up these blessed slopes and left no one alive in the charred remains of those temples and monasteries you can see all around us, where even the forest seems stunned by the aftermath of their blasphemous attack. . . ."

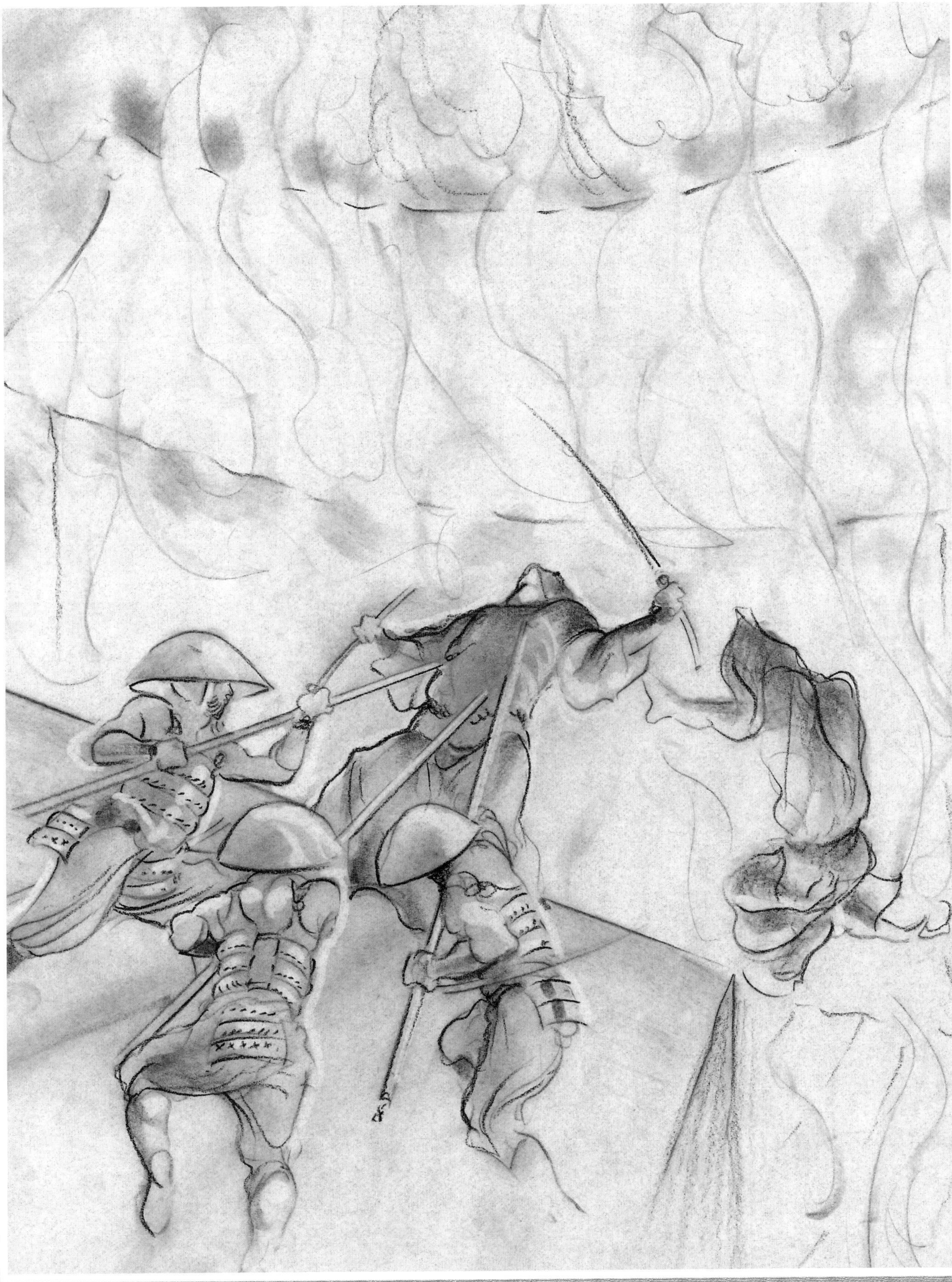

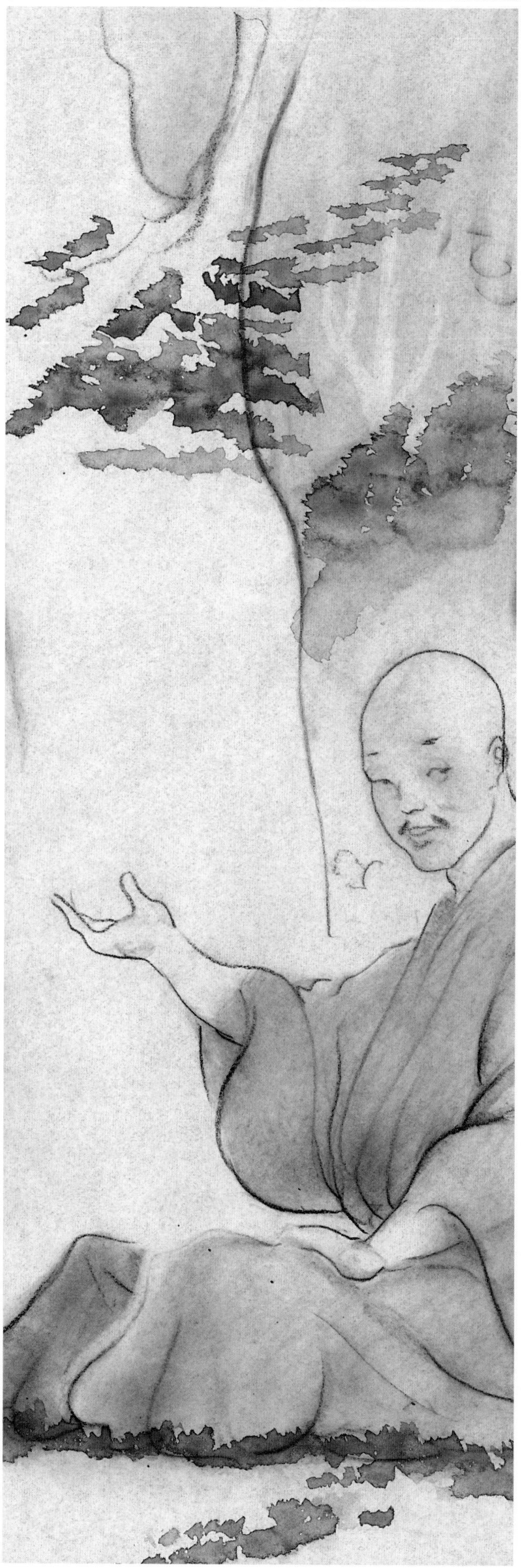

They all sit in silence for several minutes, as the *Yamabushi's* voice trails off, while the fire crackles and the shadows dance beneath the low, dark branches.

"You are still young, Haru," says Master Naoto. "You could rebuild this temple and, it would be our hope, find some peace in this world. However, if you wish, you may choose to join us for a time. I am sure that my teacher will be able to convey more about that center where life finds both its main source and its fullest scope, where pain can be absorbed and balanced in the vast harmony of creation. At one time or another, we have all been wounded, my friend. Come with us. You would be very welcome."

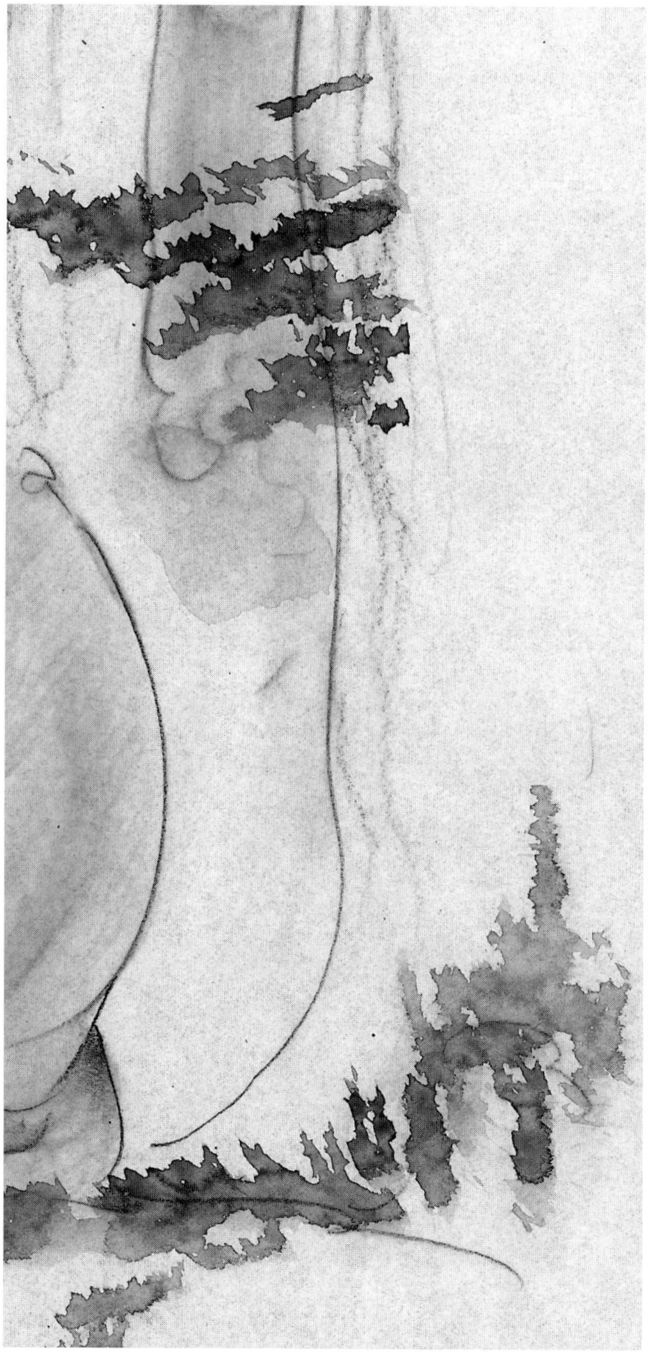

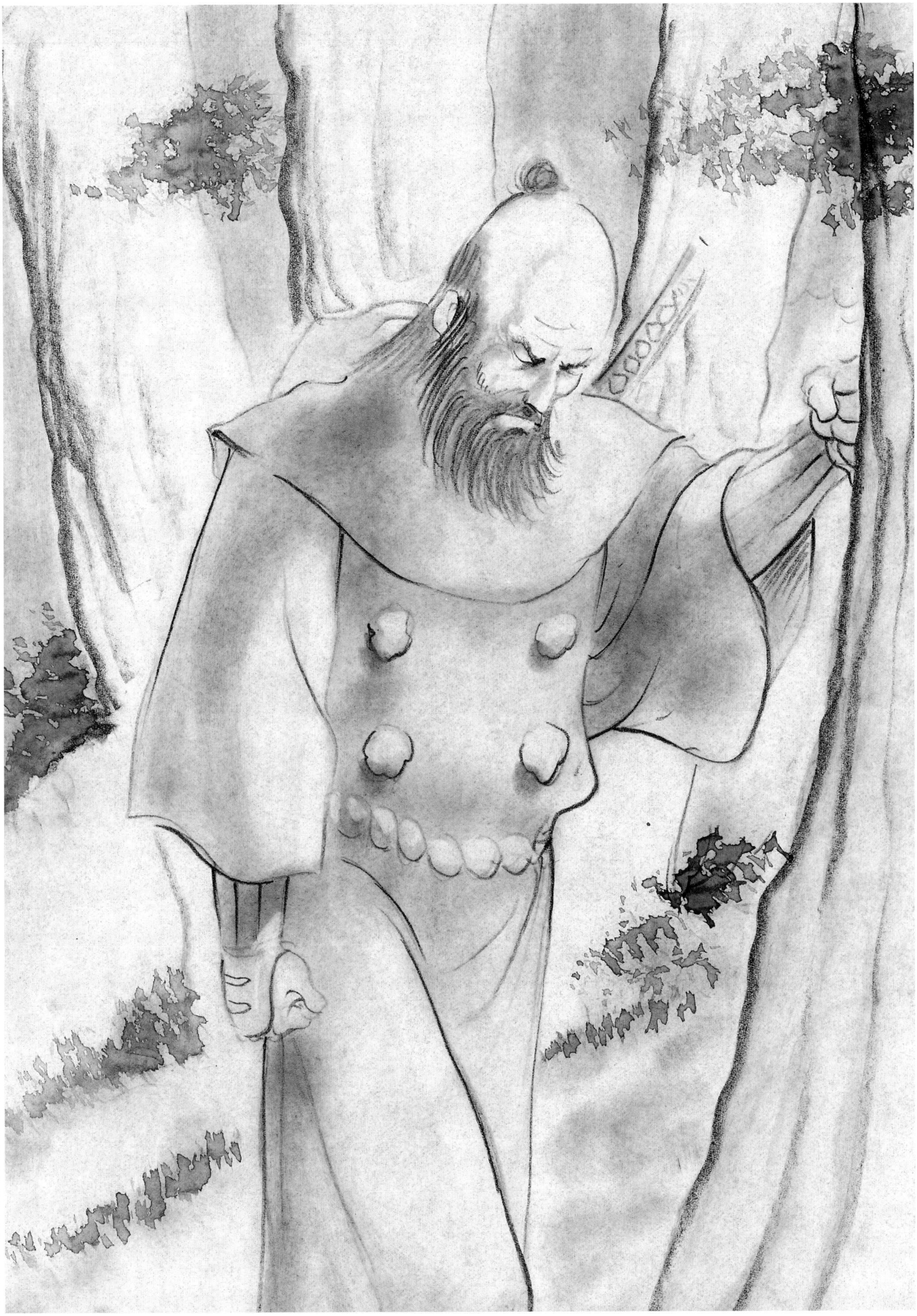

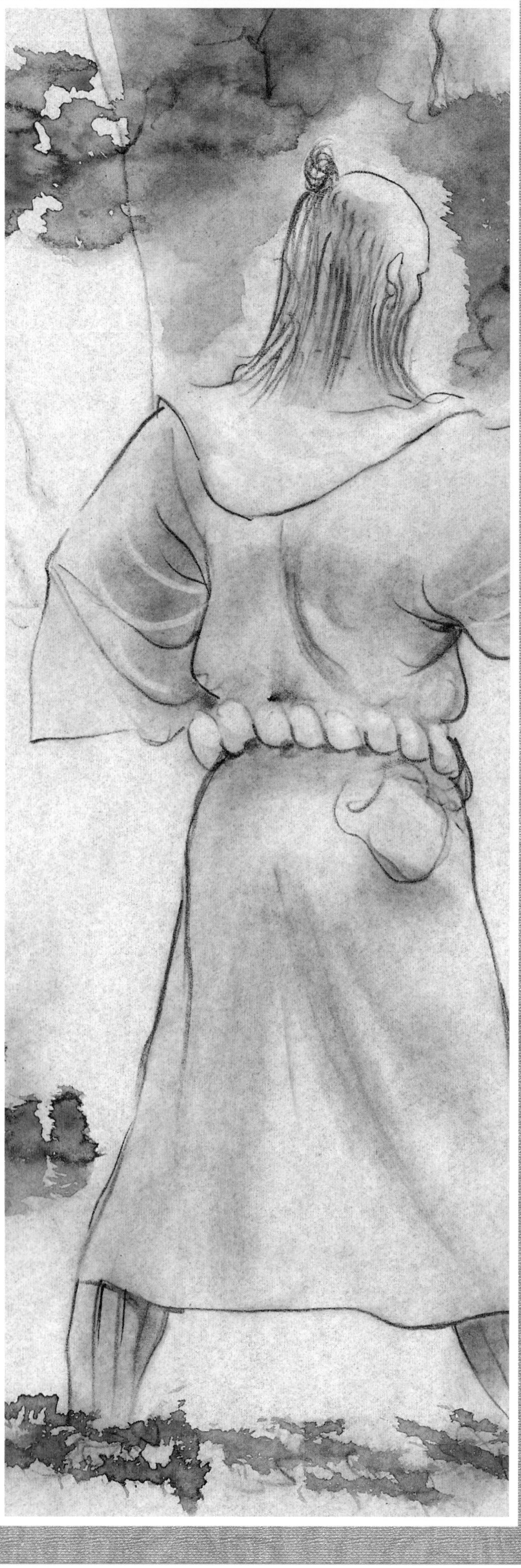

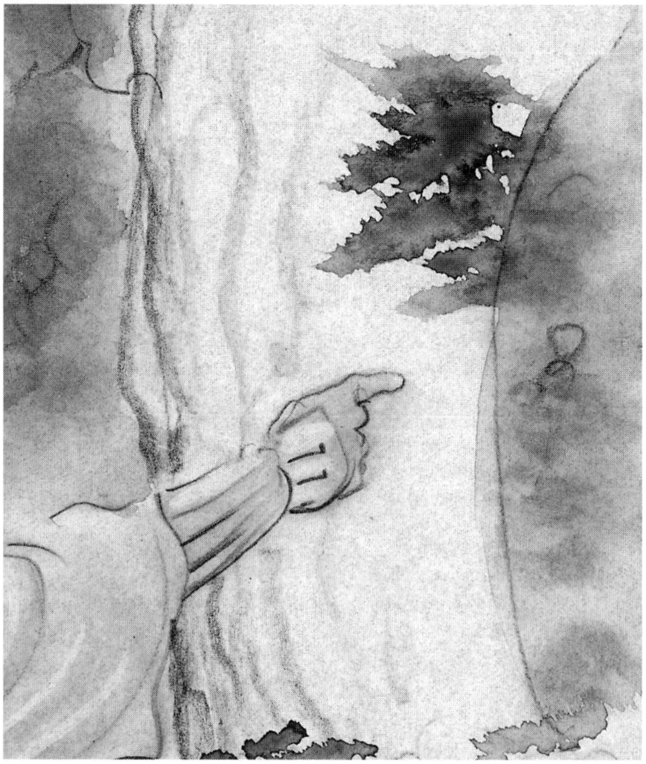

The Yamabushi is intrigued by the invitation but, after a moment's reflection, shakes his head regretfully. "I thank you most sincerely, Master Naoto. Perhaps some day I may join you, but at this point your teacher's doctrine of refusing to return a blow, of sparing a deadly foe, is a concept that I find difficult—if not impossible—to accept. Although our sect also began by following the gentle instruction of the Buddha, we have developed our own forceful search for the Way; we still seek to remove—with the use of our weapons if necessary—every obstacle in His Path."

"We believe, Master Naoto, that the Divine Will can be implemented by force of arms and the righteous application of martial skills, as well as by chanting and preaching. And, in times such as these, such a forceful way has begun to seem the only way to us. The meek appear doomed to perish—like those villagers who provided you with food and shelter. I, too, saw those black clouds, and from my vantage point I could see that they rose from the very village you have left behind."

Master Naoto's heart is heavy. "We must return then," he murmurs. Without a word, his companions begin to collect their belongings. "Why?" asks the Yamabushi. "Everyone in the village is dead by this time and scavenging bands may even now be roaming the site in the wake of the army, looting whatever the warriors have left behind. What can you possibly do for the dead, and what could you do, unarmed as you are, against any such predators?"

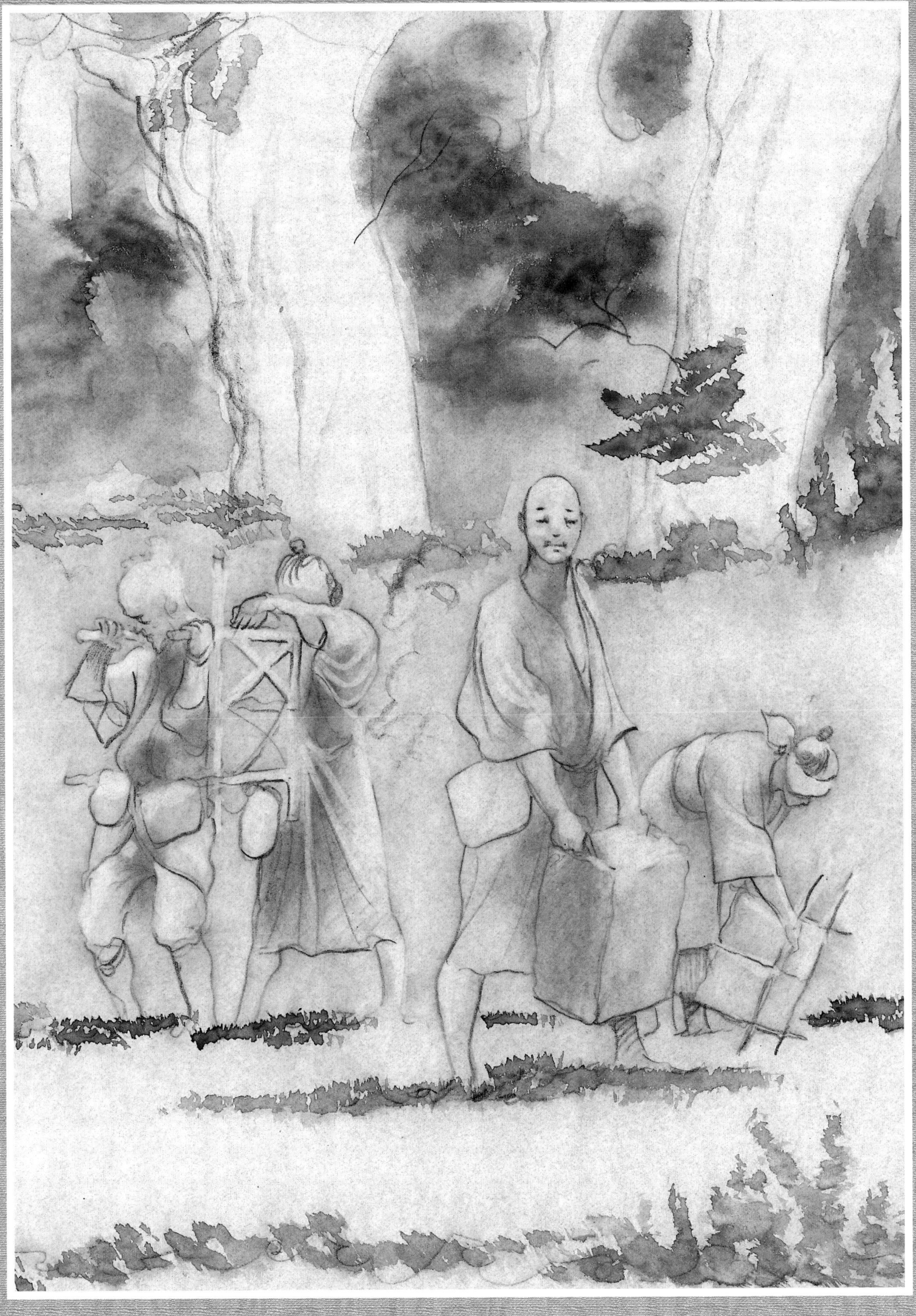

"Bury the former and try to avoid the latter, my friend. Wish us the Buddha's protection, as we wish you a fruitful reconstruction of your past." With these words, Master Naoto lifts his pack onto his shoulders and passes noiselessly beyond the light of the fire and into the enveloping woods. Bowing, one by one, the others follow their leader, leaving the Yamabushi staring after them, shaking his head as they disappear into the shadows.

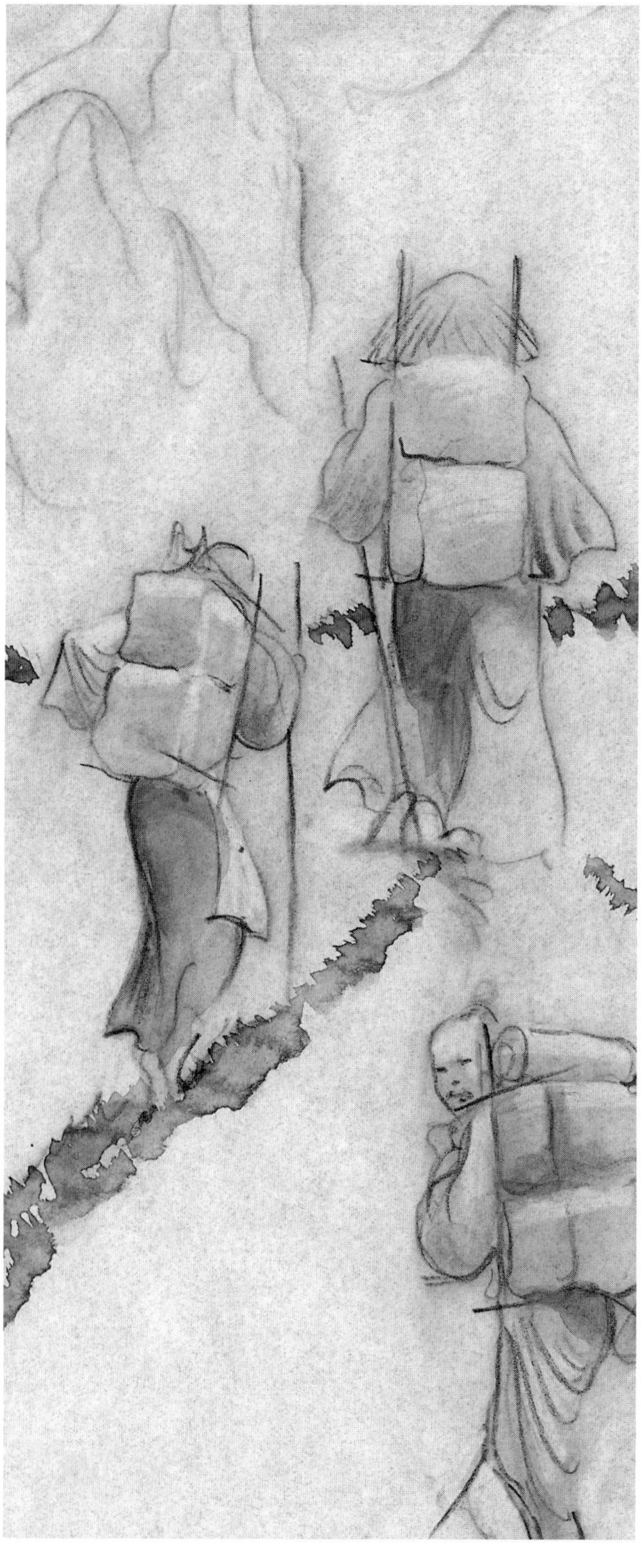

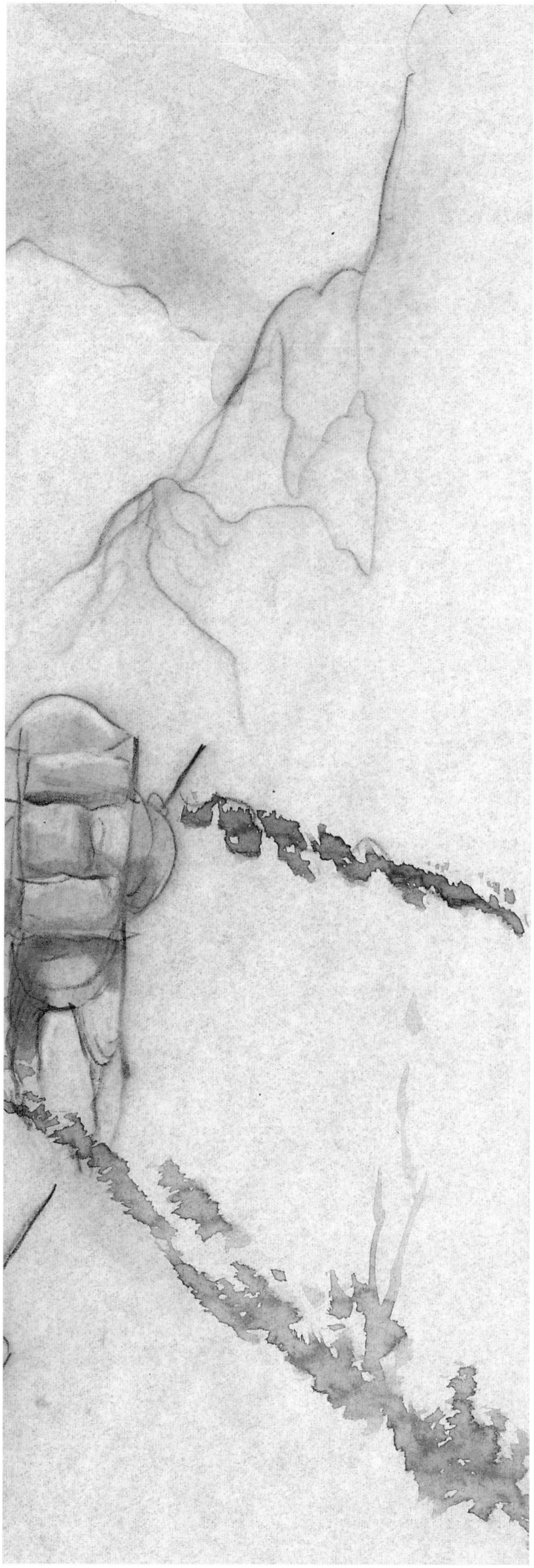

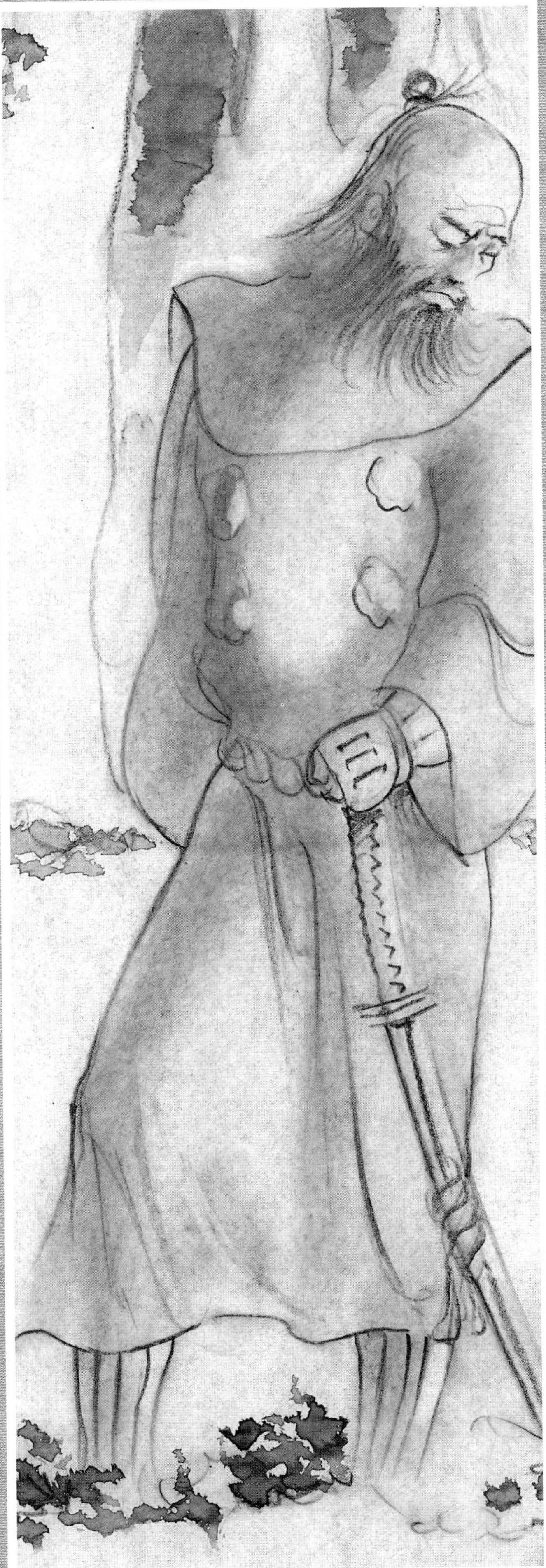

Then, turning his gaze to the dancing flames of the fire, he sees in their reflection the grimacing, helmeted faces of his foes, and the writhing shapes of his people as they are consumed and reduced to ashes.

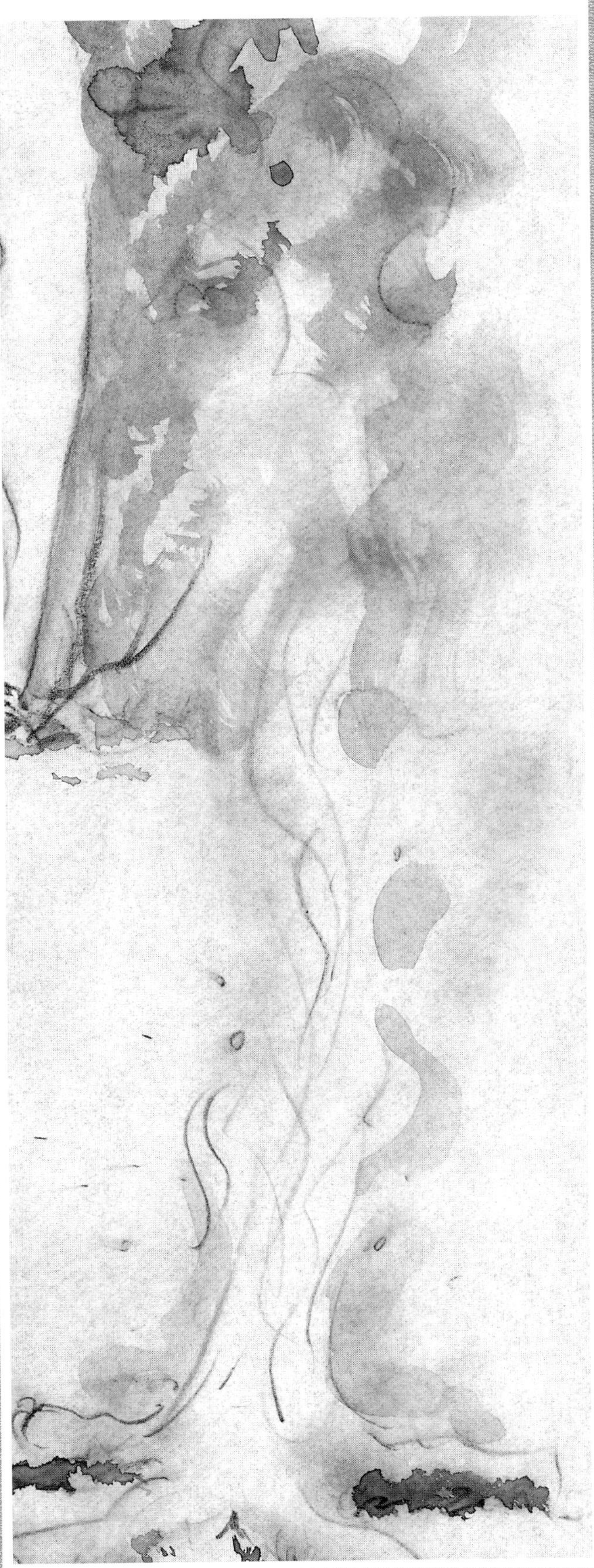

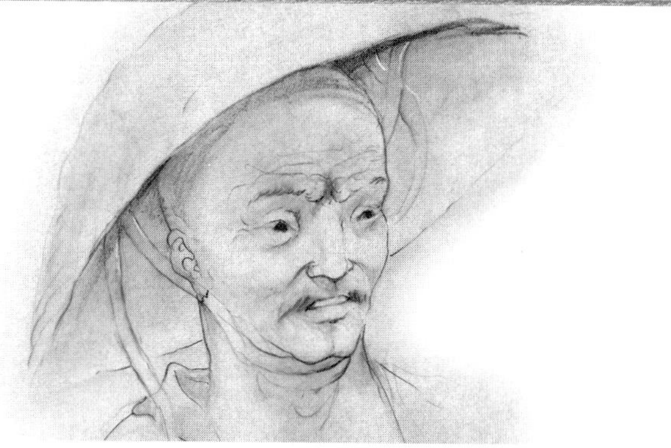

Throughout the night, Master Naoto and his companions travel, following the stars and using as guideposts the dark outlines of the surrounding mountains. They proceed in silence, stepping carefully, each following the indistinct shadow of their leader that forges ahead until, finally, they reach cultivated land: those fields where people have toiled for generations to reap Nature's bounty.

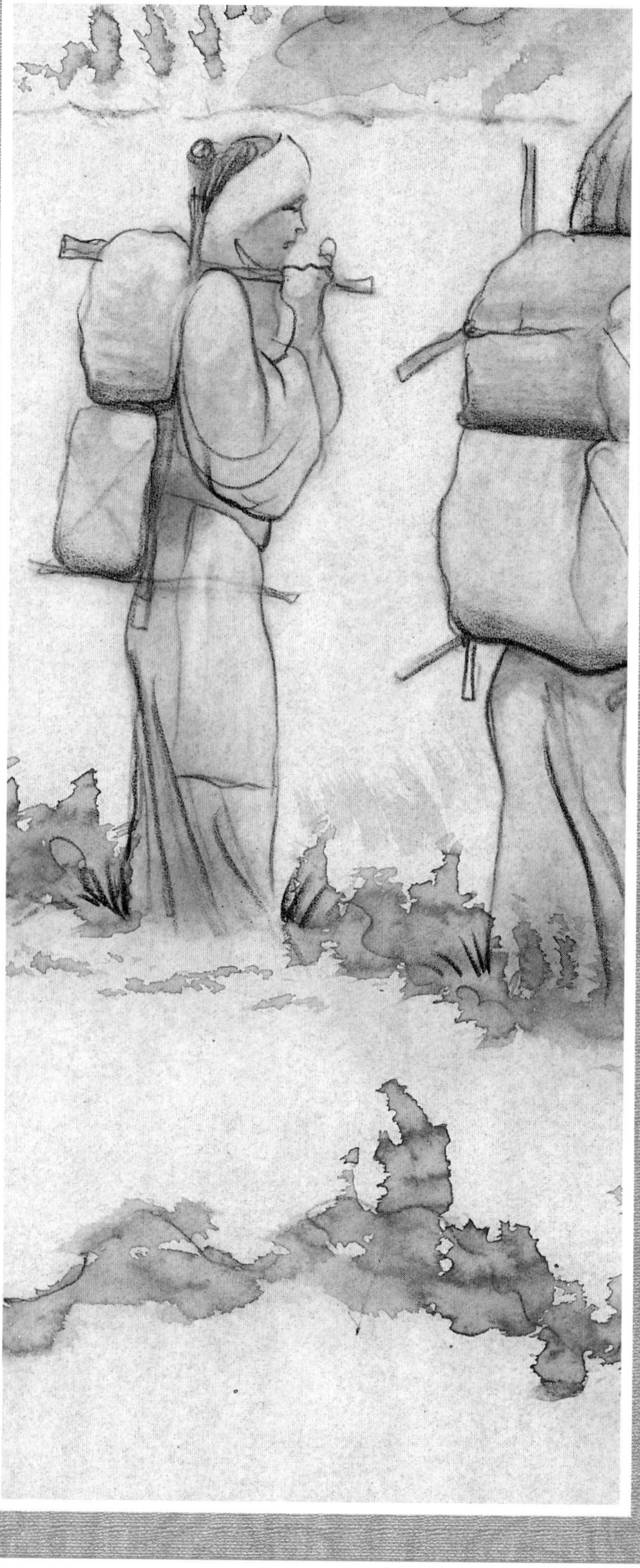

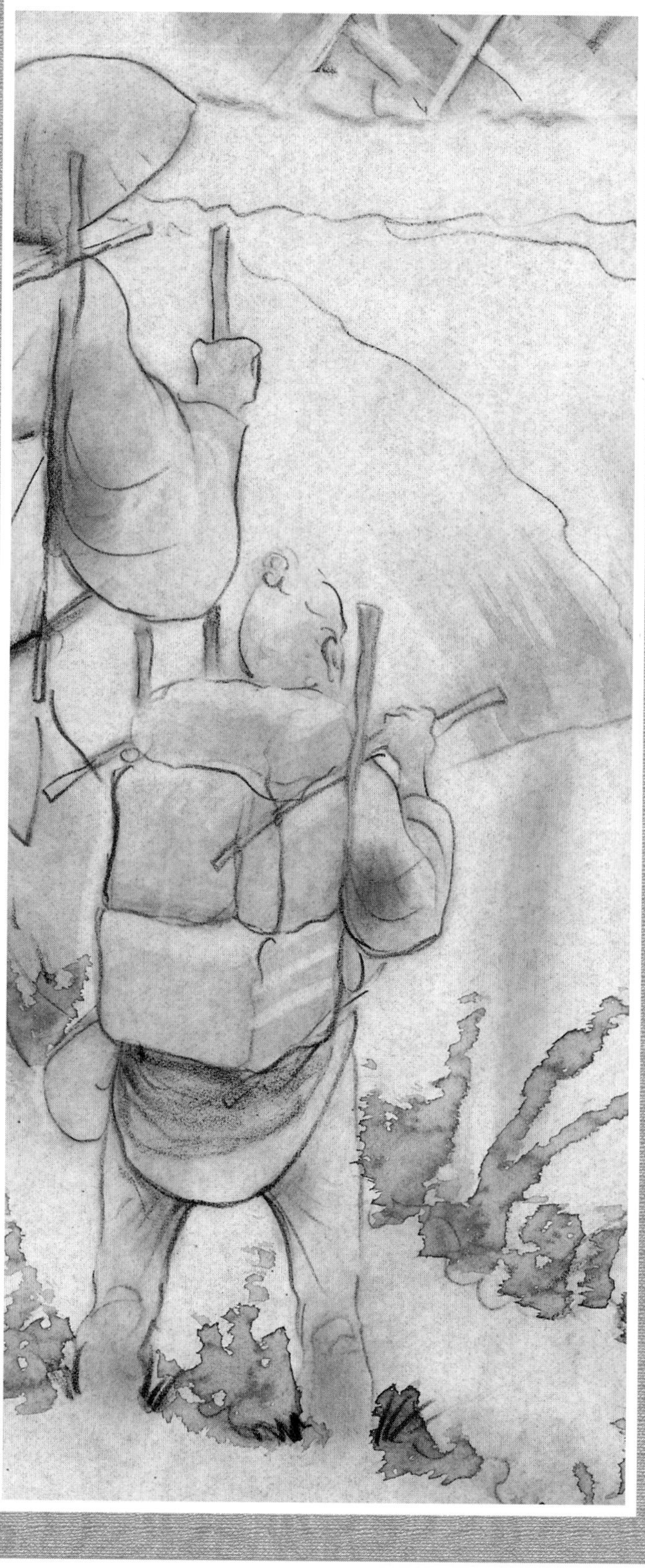

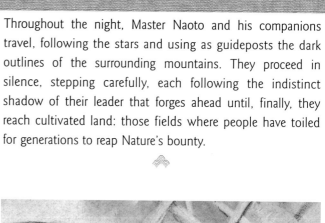

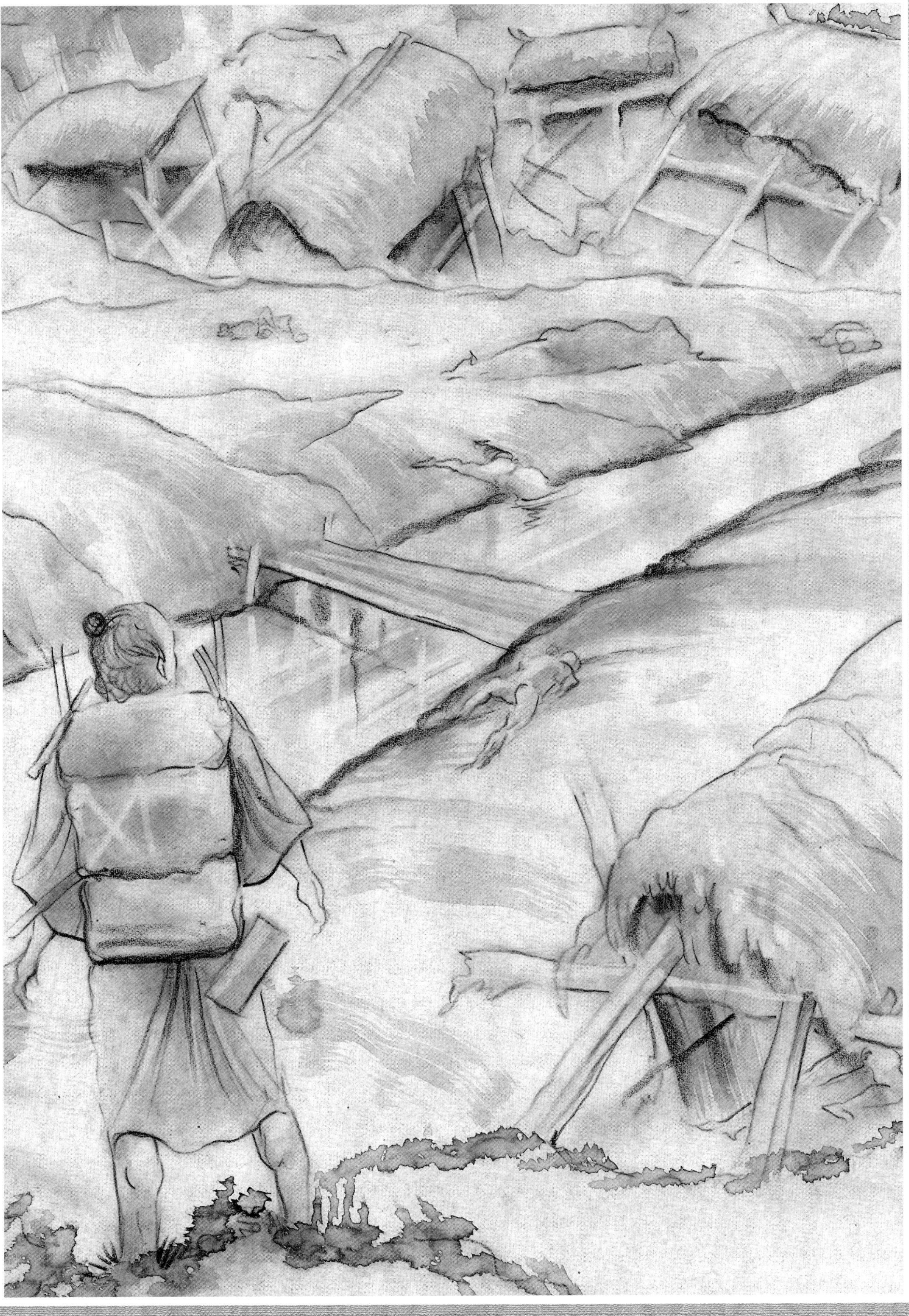

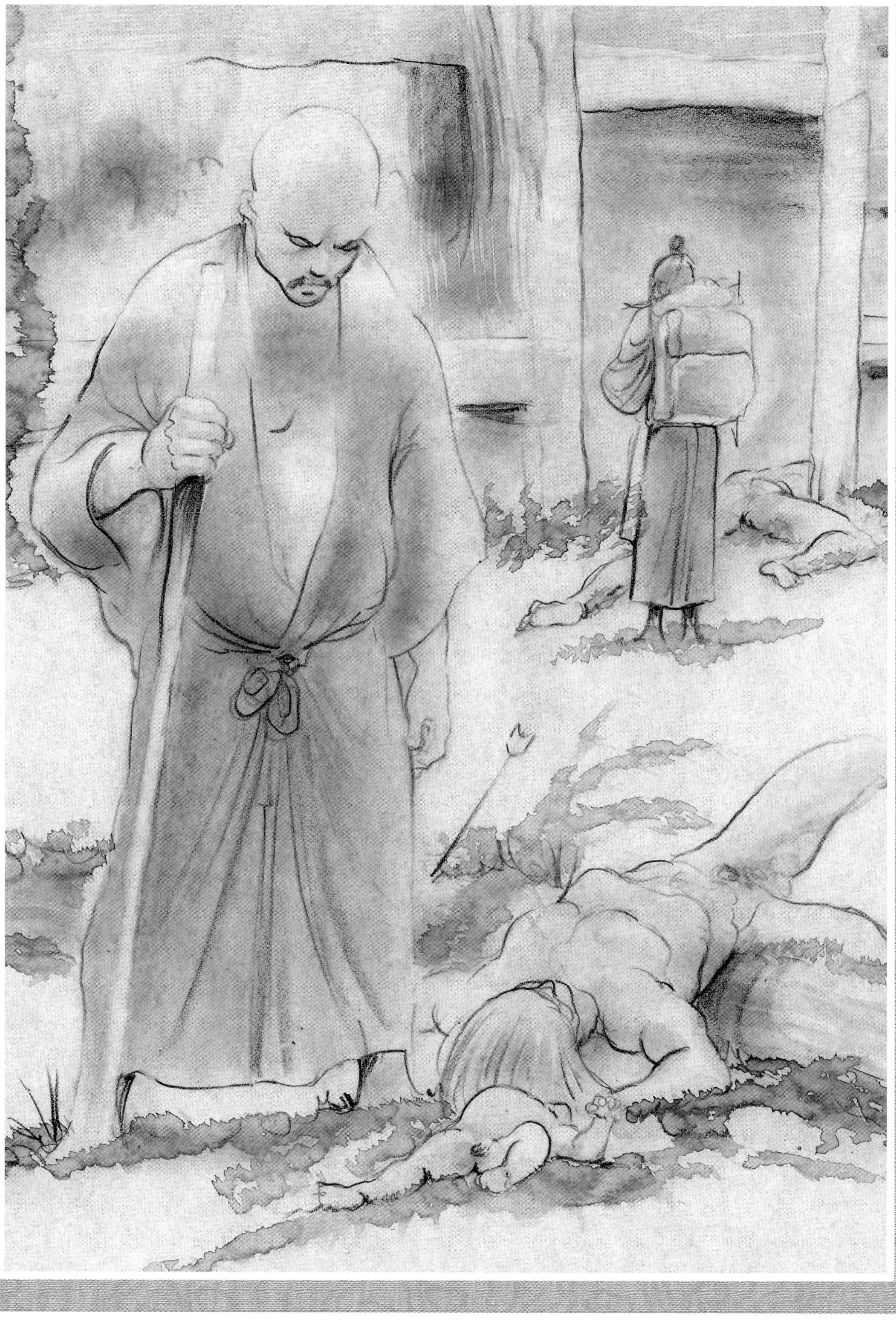

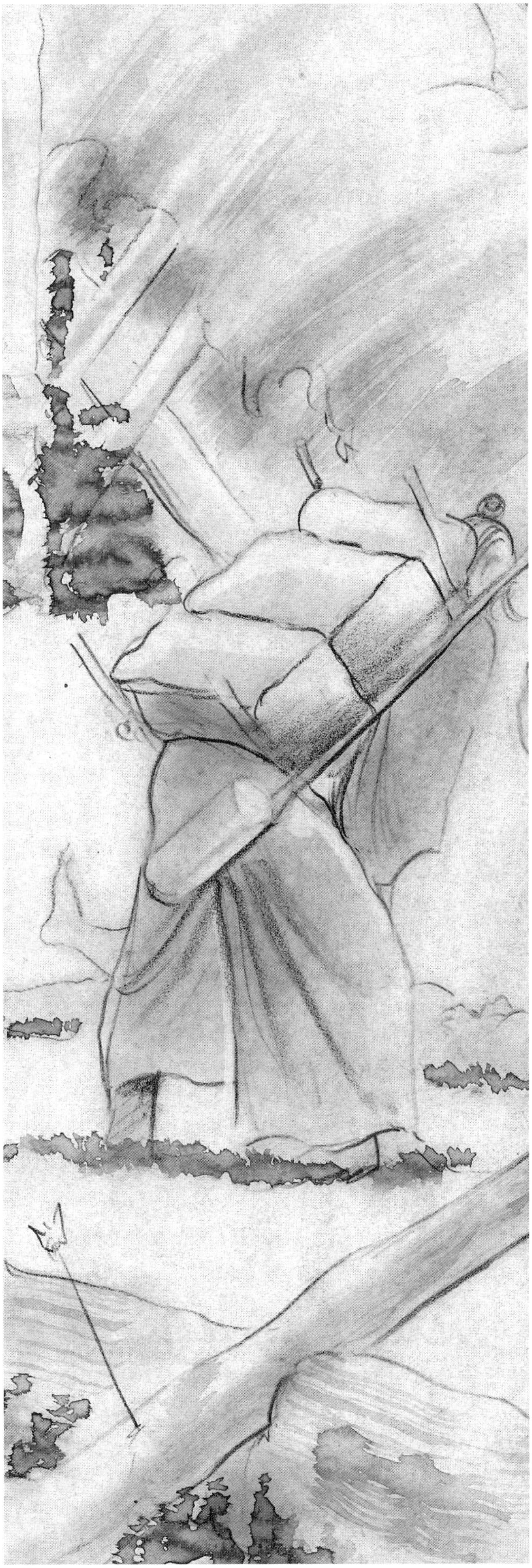

It is here, where men and women have struggled to establish a productive order, that they come upon the first signs of man-made disorder—in the lifeless bodies strewn about like pitiful, discarded dolls, in the still smoldering ruins of the fields themselves where the warriors' weapons have lain everything waste.

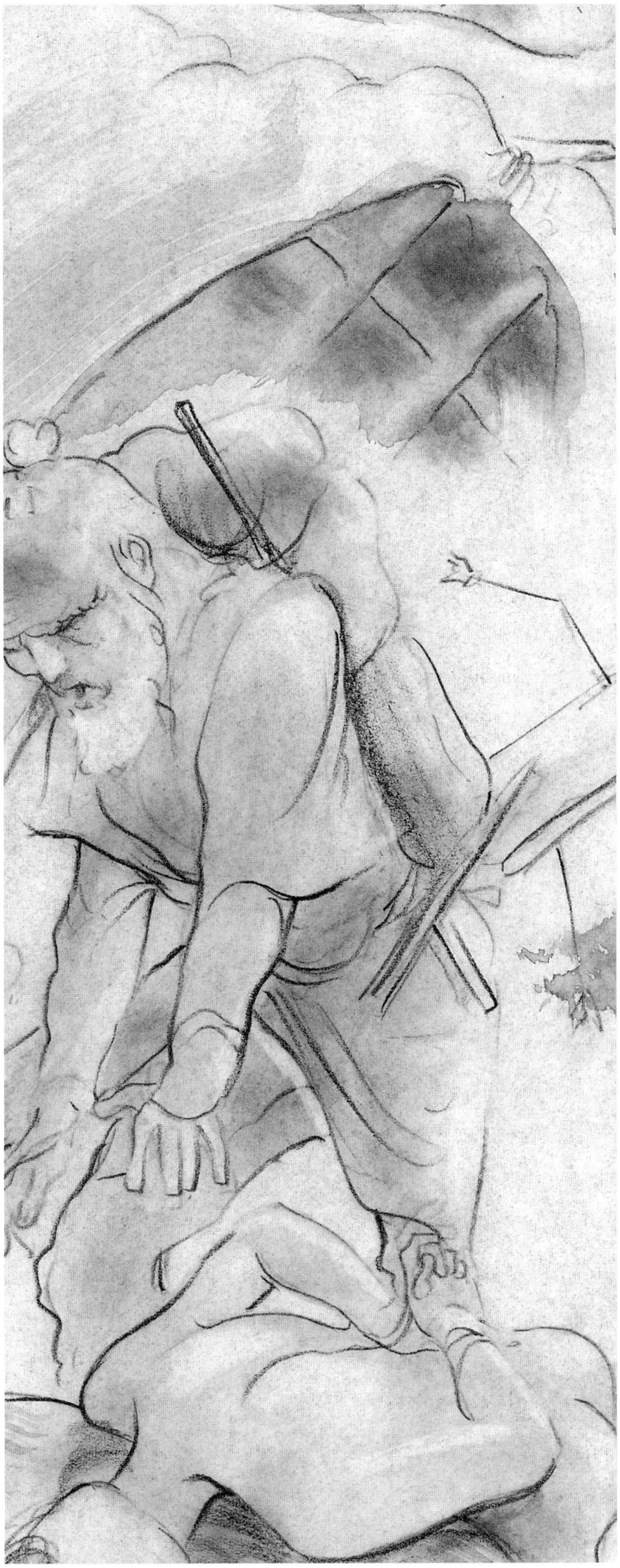

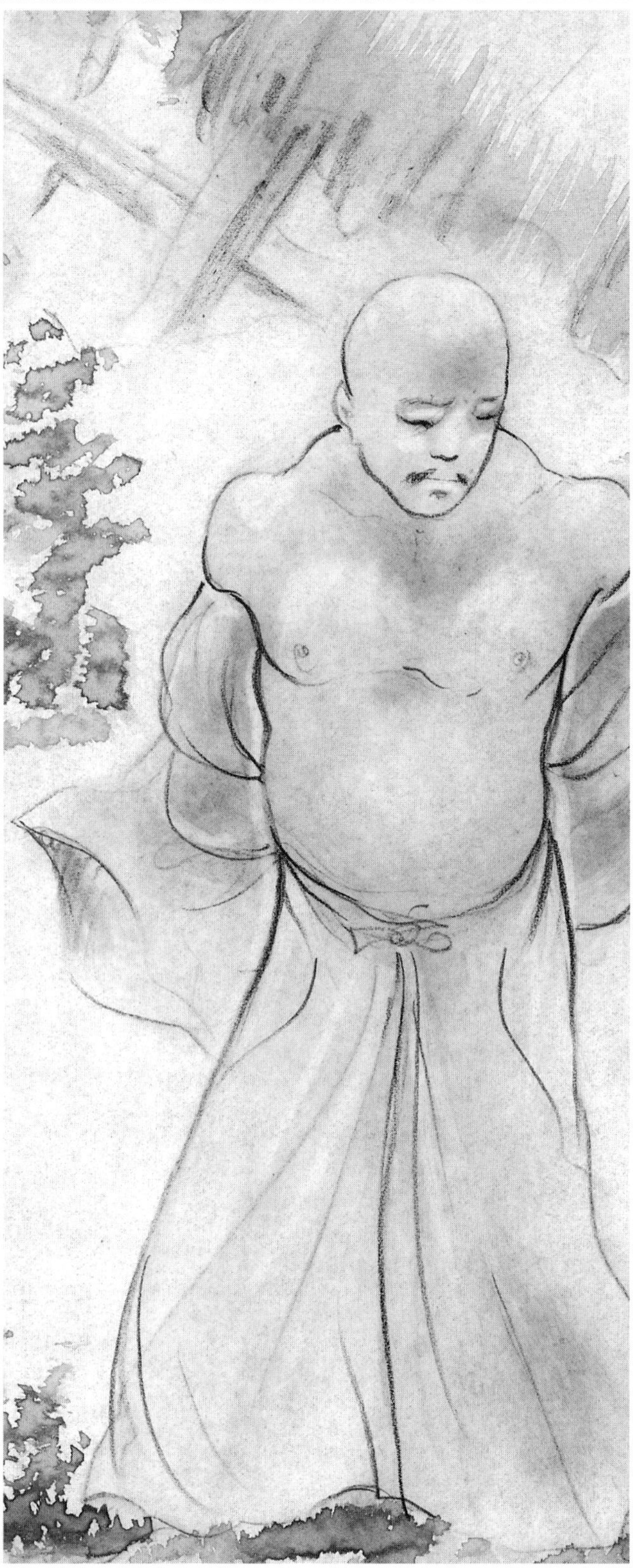

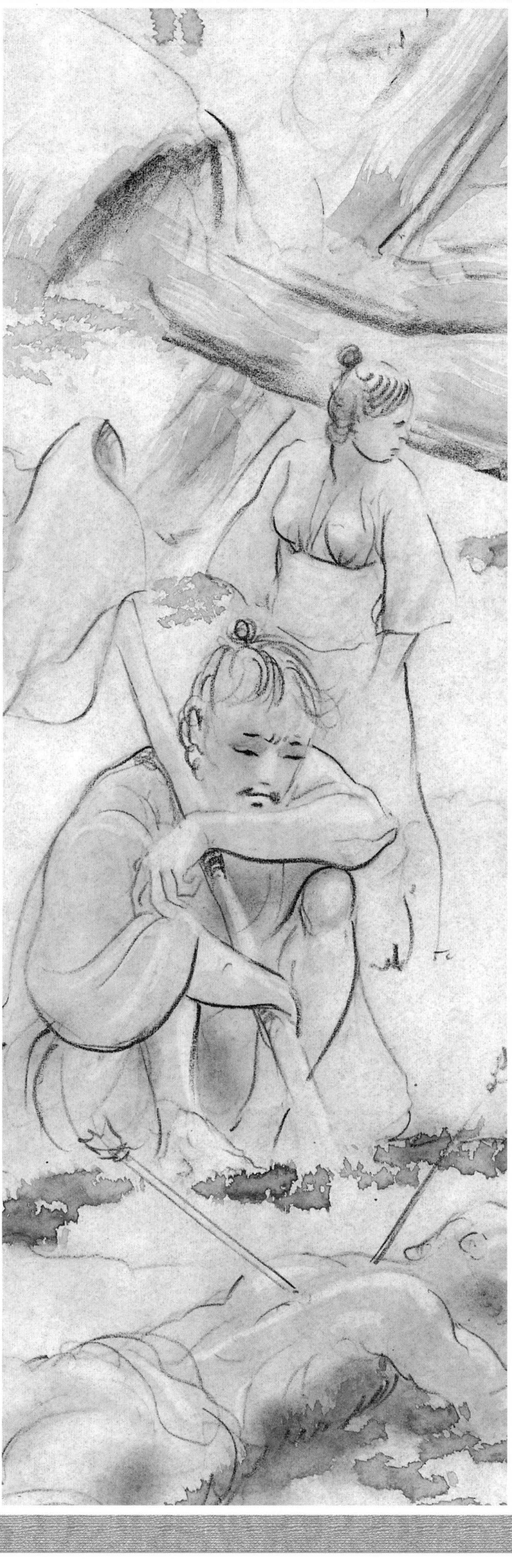

As pain and anger war in his breast, Master Naoto and his companions set about their grim task of returning the bodies to that earth which, only a few hours earlier, had borne, nurtured, and sustained these villagers. They work silently, gathering the inert forms together beneath the cliff, where they will prepare the final resting place for those who can no longer seek any for themselves.

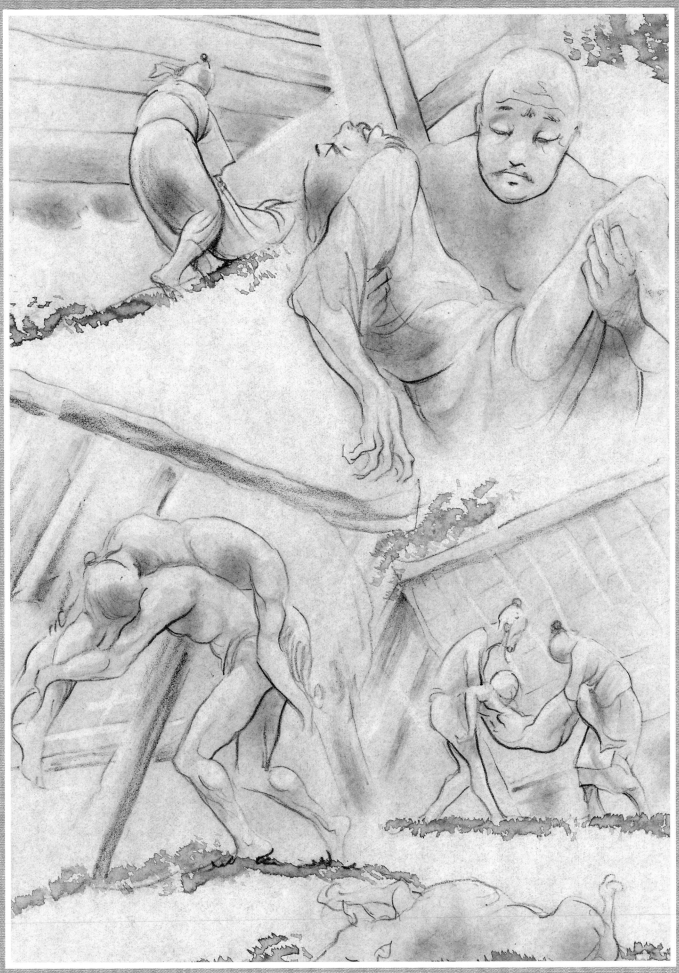

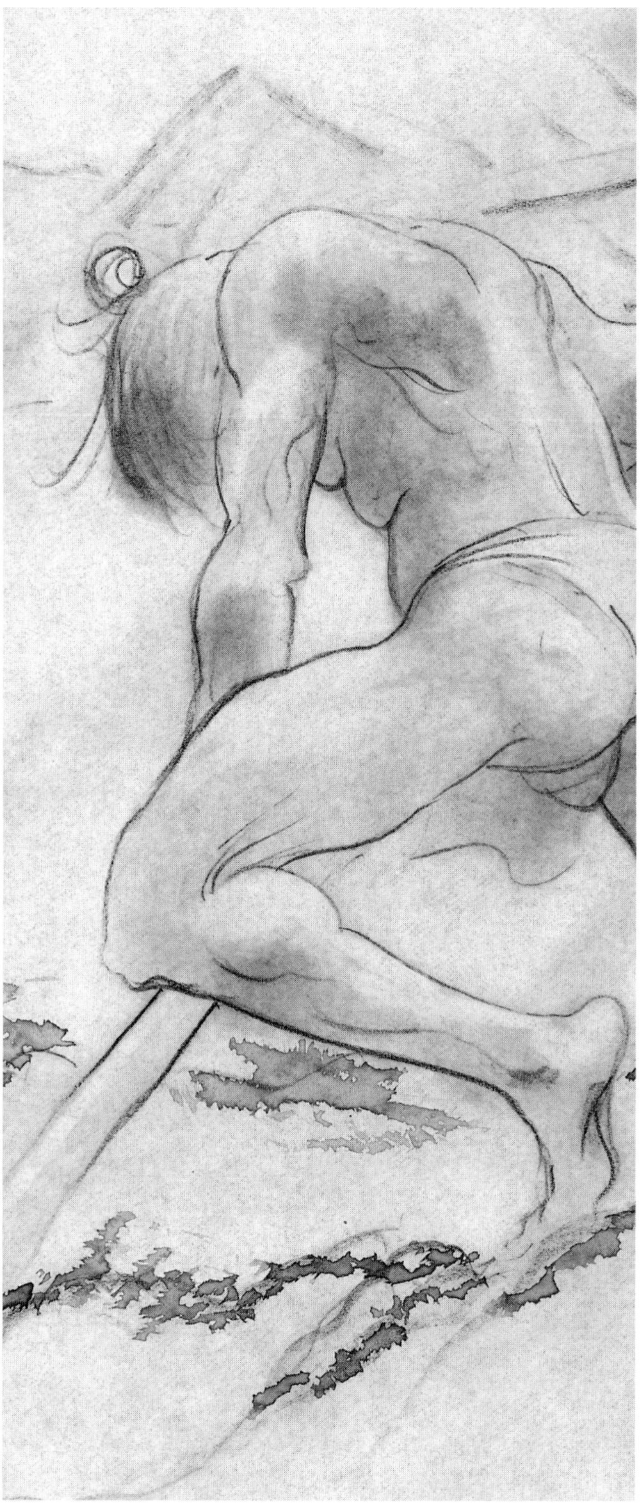

They toil without respite as the sun, unable to gaze directly at what man has wrought, passes behind the clouds and so across the sky. They continue their work of mercy with increasing speed, in the hope of completing their task before nightfall. Heavy are those inert bodies and unyielding is the earth that Ishi must remove. Halting for a moment to catch his breath, he rests his hands on the cold stones, and it is then that he hears the clanking of weapons, of wooden shafts rattling against plates of armor.

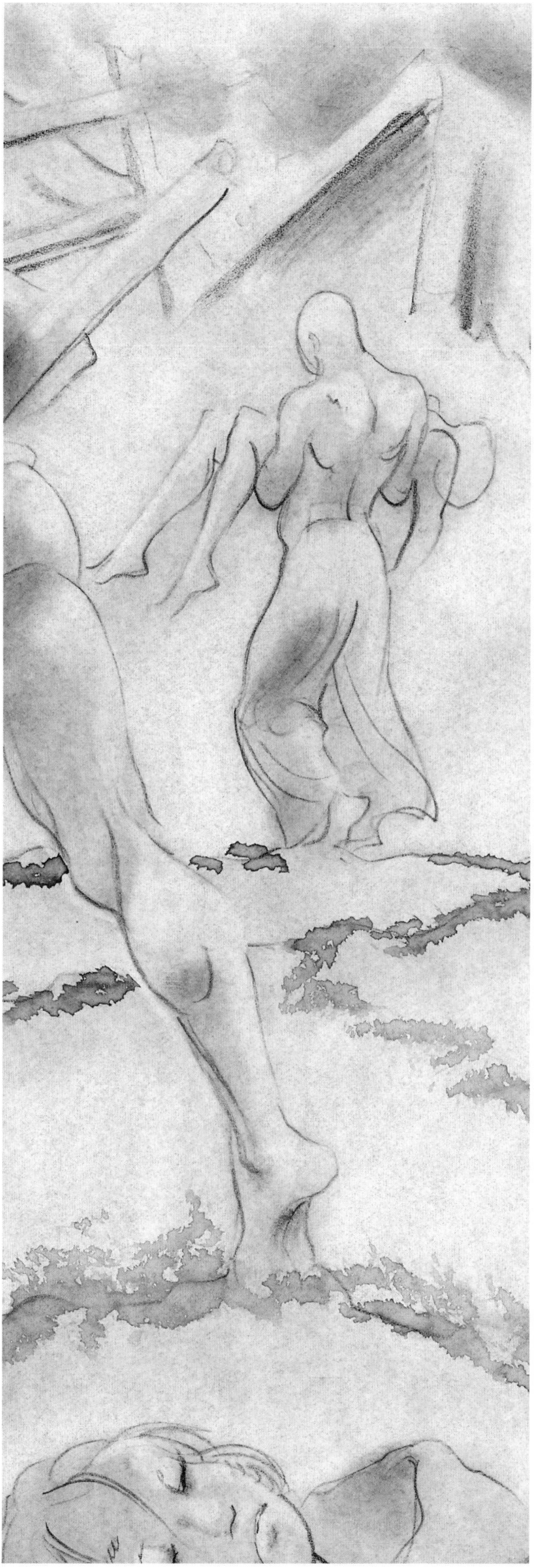

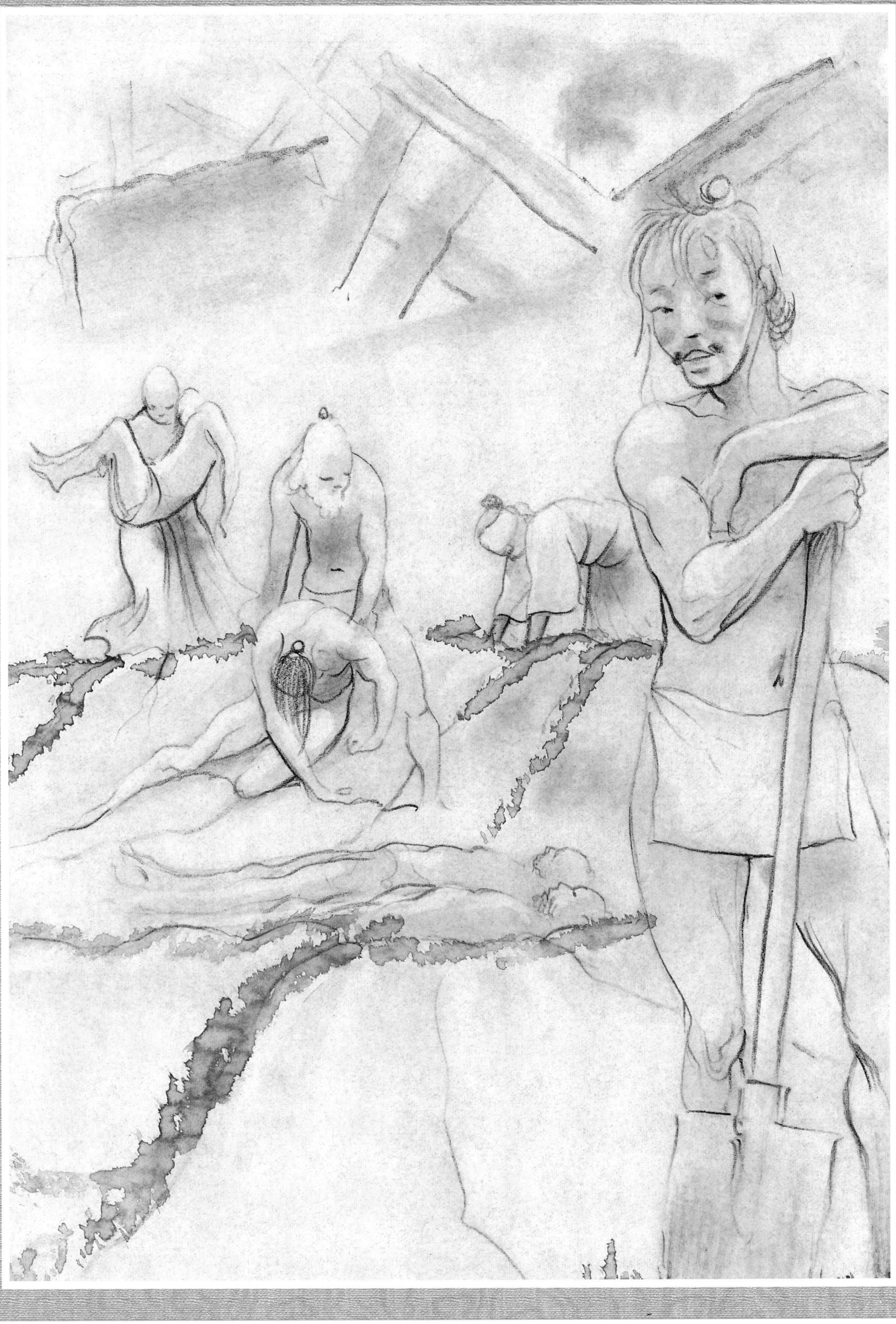

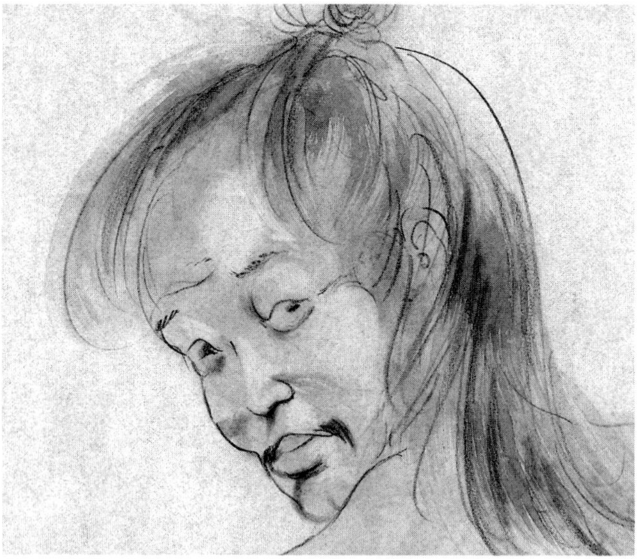

Looking up, he catches sight of a line of shadows approaching from the West. Still enveloped in the dissipating haze, the shadows grow more formidable as they approach, and suddenly Ishi and his companions are surrounded. These armed men are an odd assortment, some of whom betray their peasant origins.

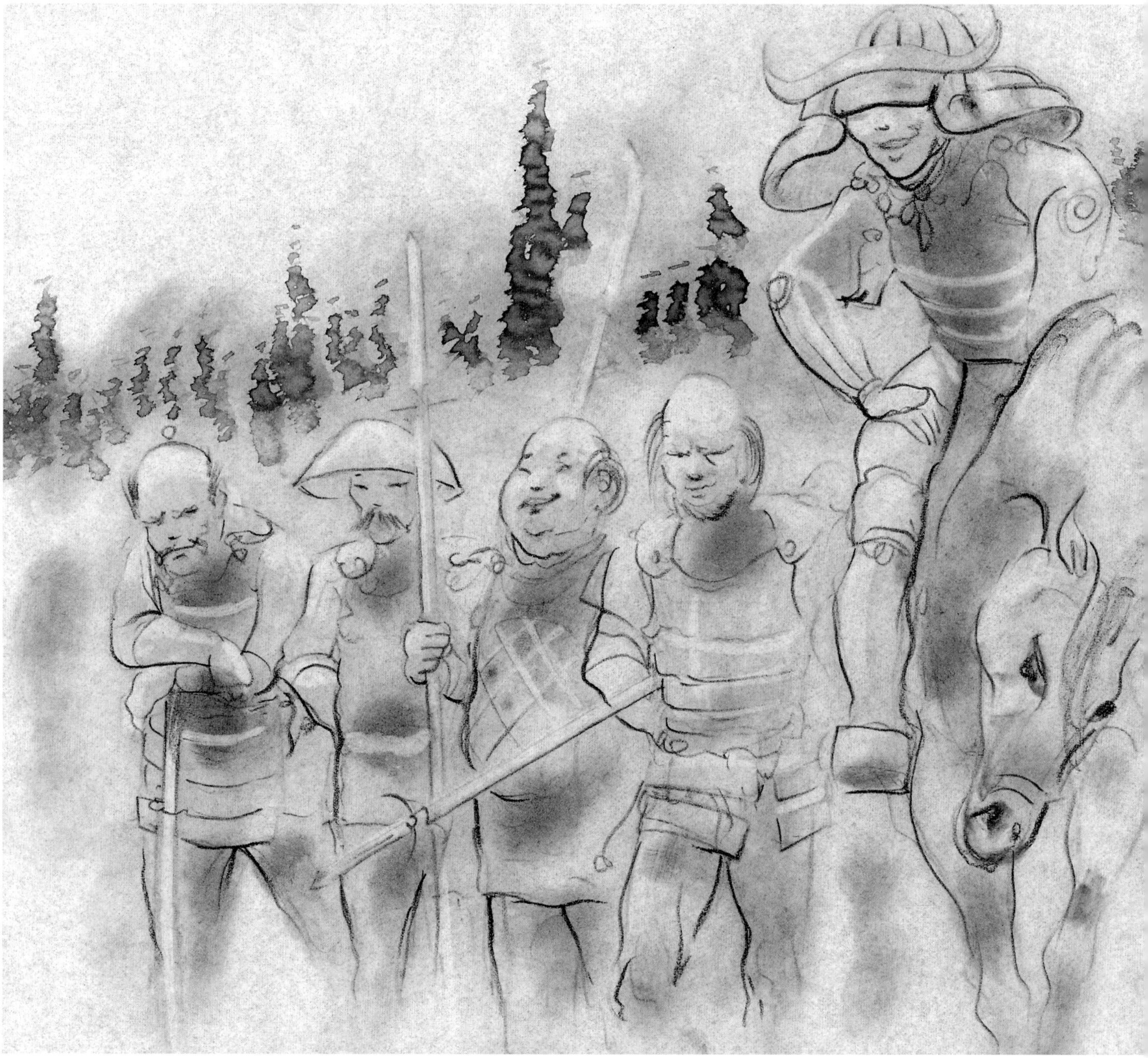

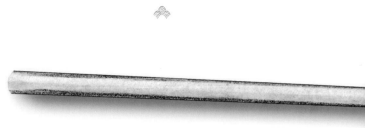

Adorned with mismatched pieces of armor, evidently scavenged from the bodies of dead warriors left behind on various battlefields, they display a distinct lack of discipline in maintaining any sort of formation, providing clear evidence of their lack of samurai affiliation. Their leader, however, the only horseman among them, shows signs of having had some military training.

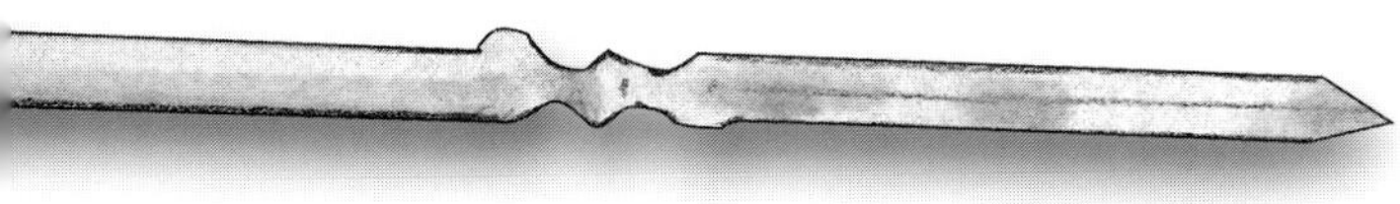

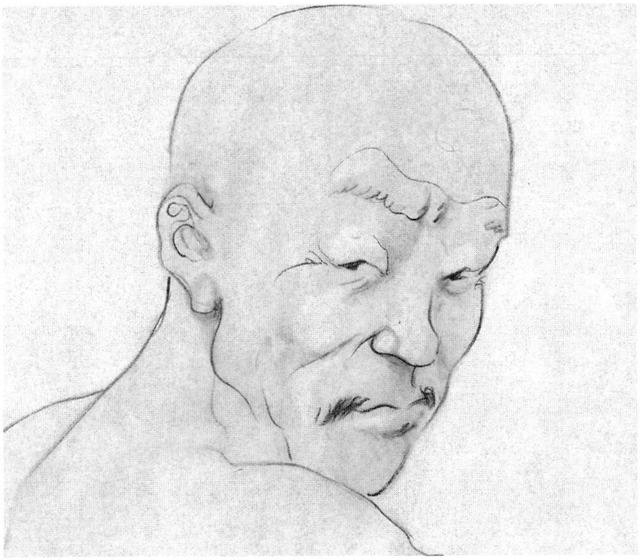

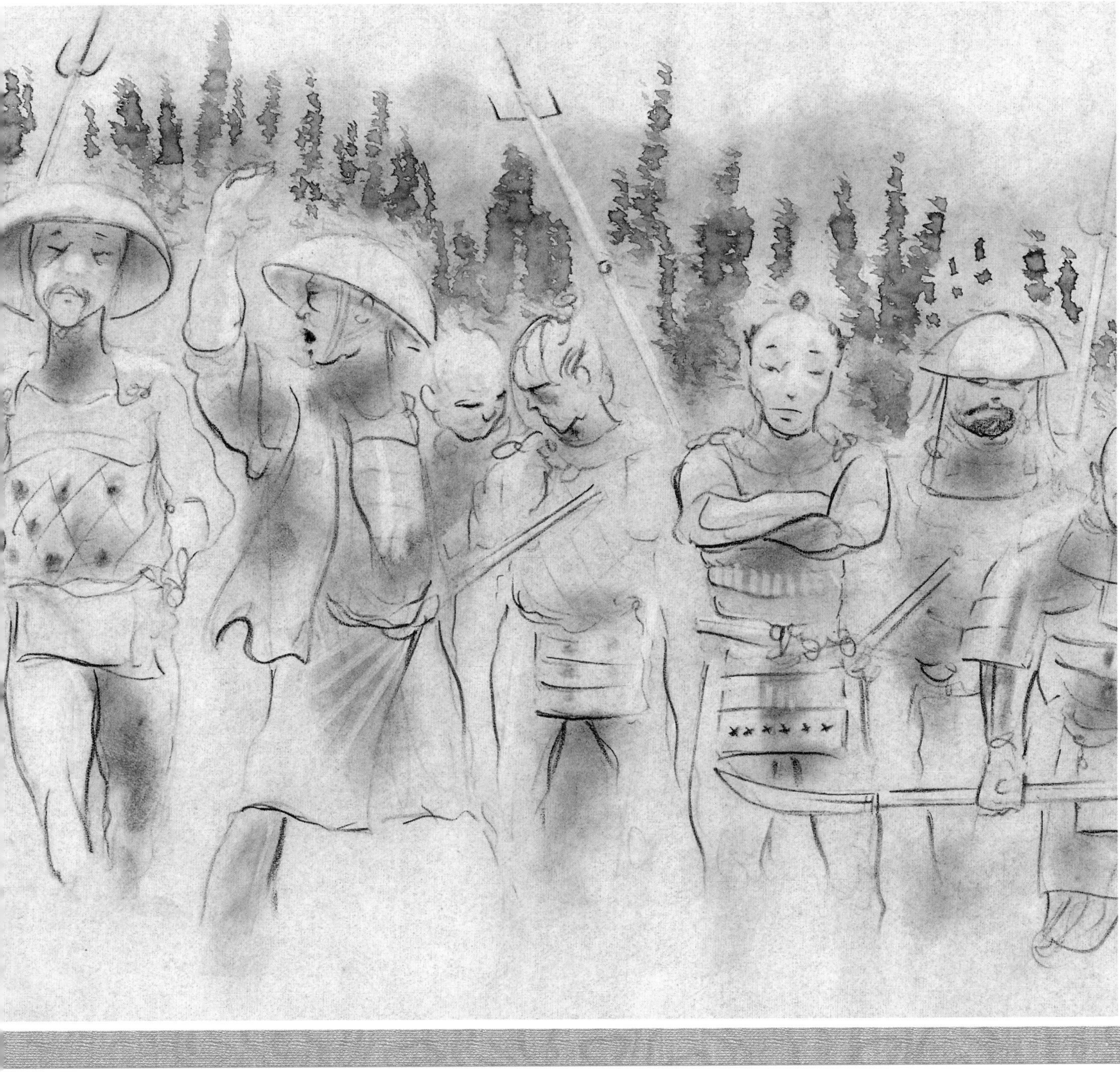

Ishi retreats instinctively before the silent, sullen stares of these armed men and whispers a hoarse warning to his companions: "They have returned! Master Naoto, what are we to do?"

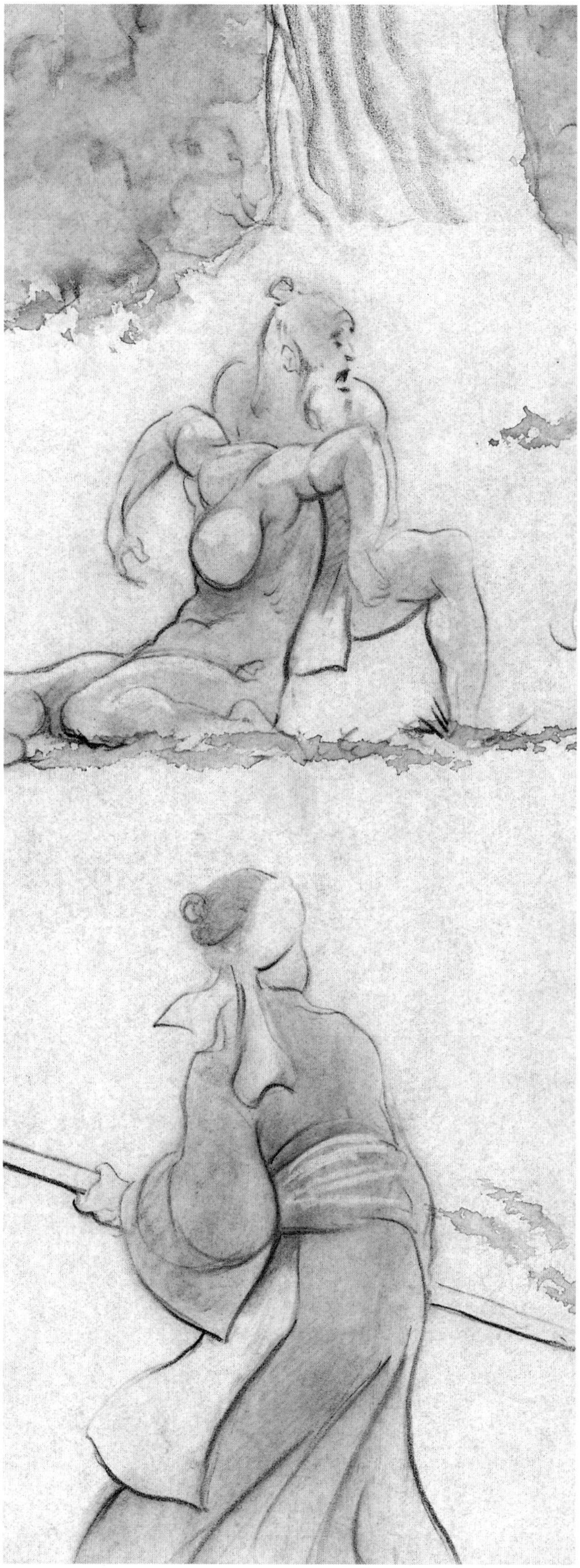

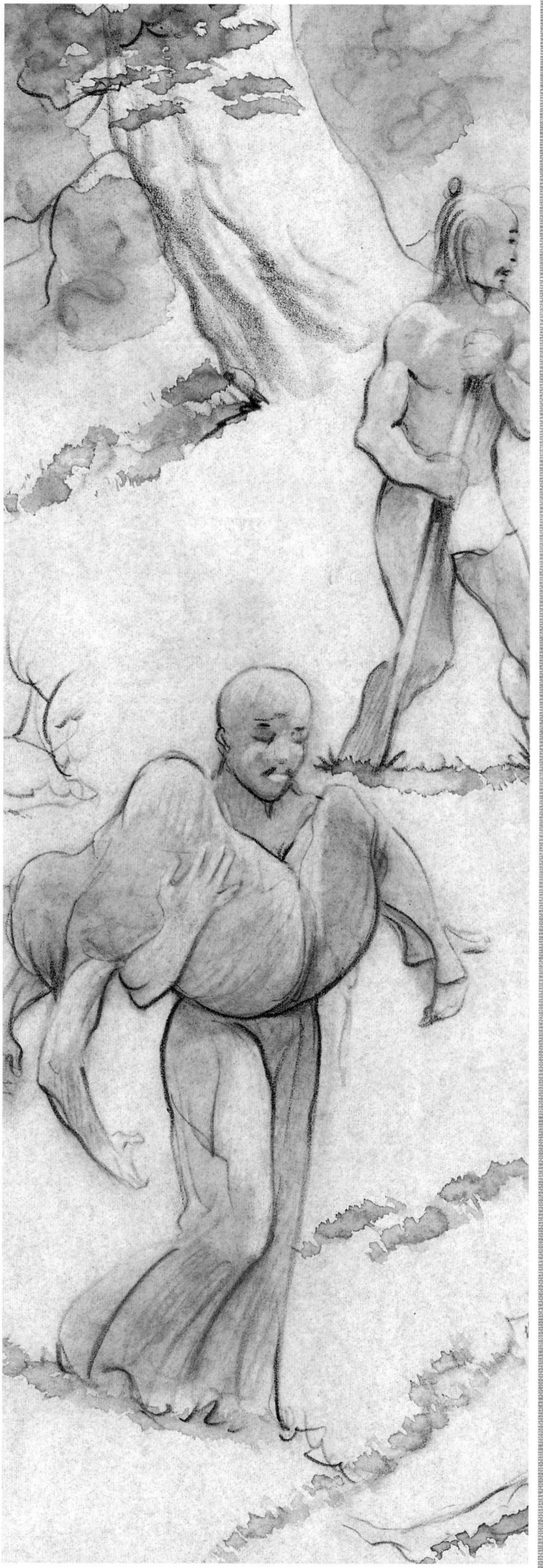

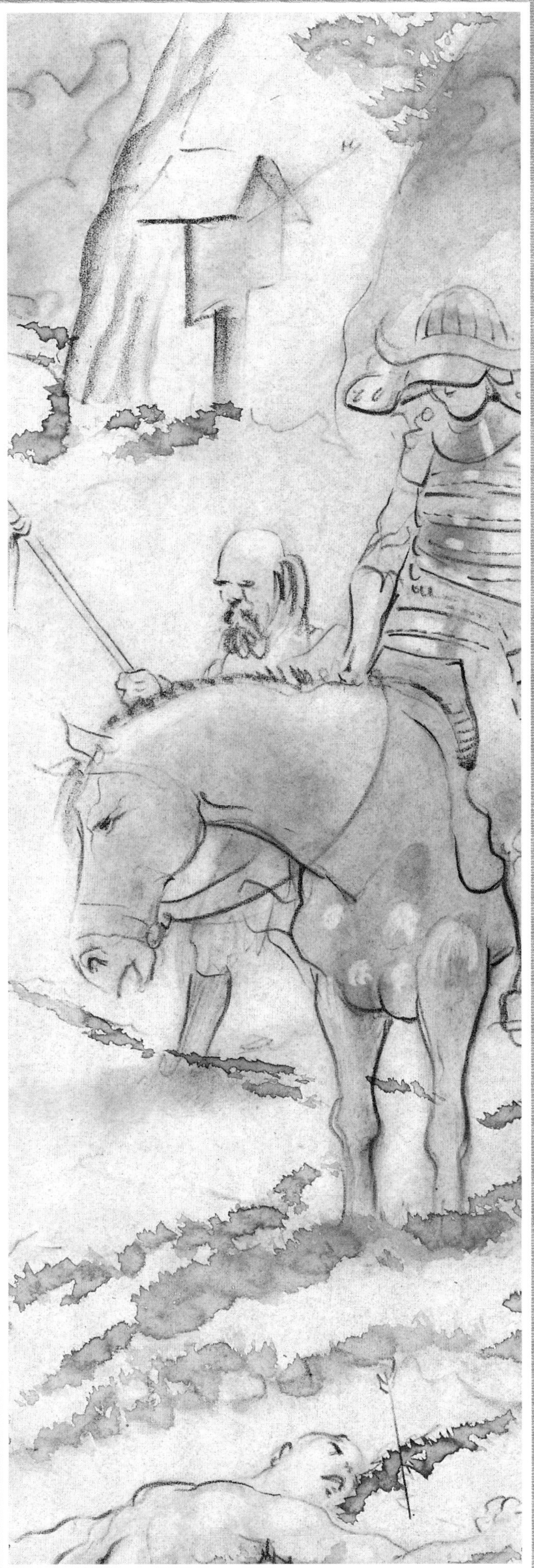

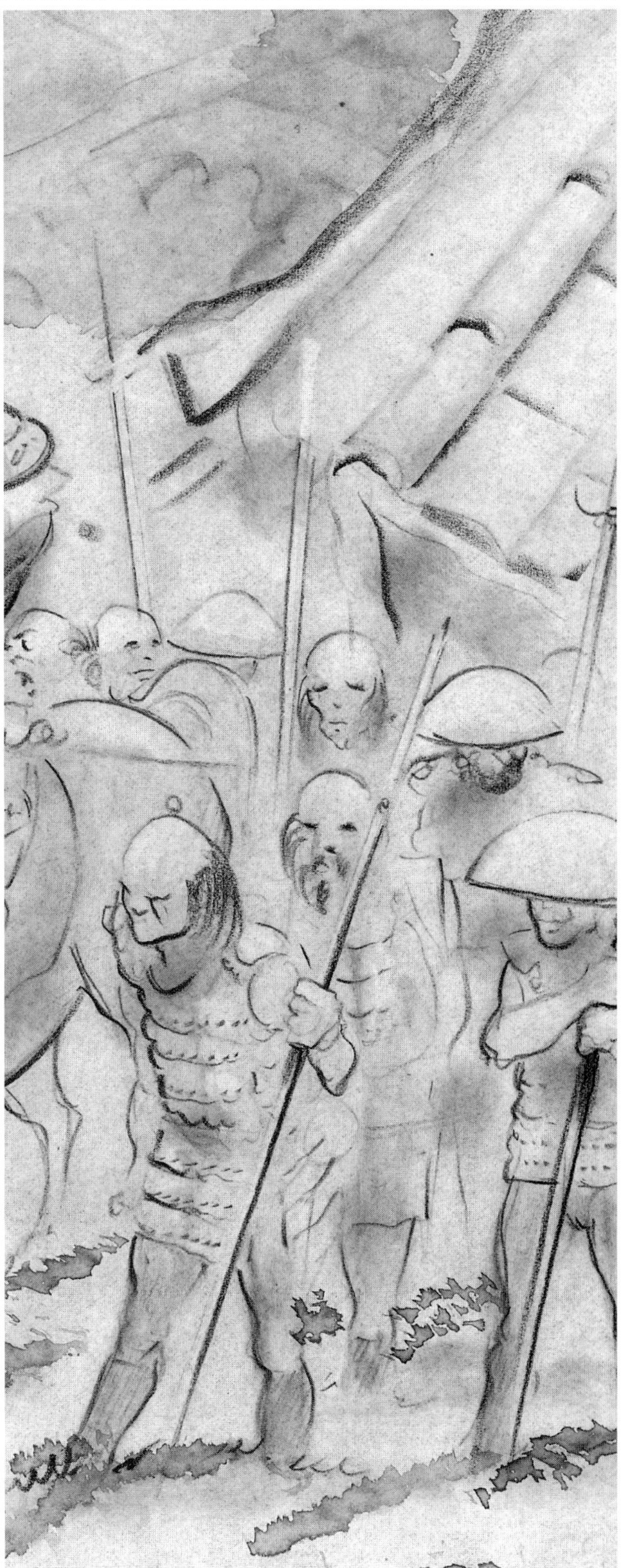

But Naoto, after gazing at the motley assembly for a moment, returns to work, his soothing voice filling the silence: "Be calm Ishi, and continue with your task. You too, Kudara." He nods encouragingly to the young man who is clutching the shaft of his spade, as if fearful that death may be close at hand.

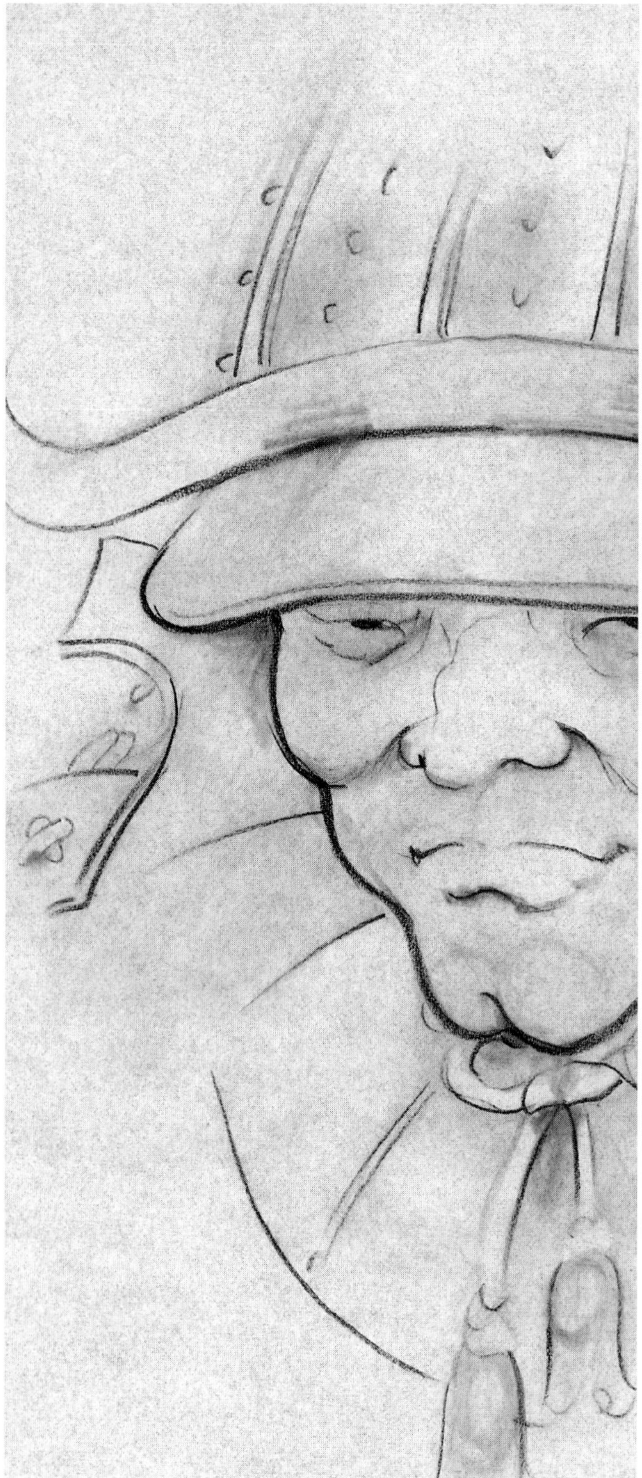

With many awkward, nervous glances in the direction of the undulating line of armed men, Master Naoto's companions join him once again as he continues to assemble the bodies of the dead near the cliff. The man on horseback stares menacingly at Naoto's broad back for some time, as he shifts back and forth in his saddle. "What do we have here, Kimbei?" he finally asks of the man standing on his right. "Didn't you assure me that you had cleared this place yesterday?"

Kimbei tries to muster a grin, but his face is red. "I certainly had, Kisaichi. These must be four new arrivals—priests associated with some crazy sect that doesn't approve of our efforts. This is obvious, since they are trying to conceal them beneath the earth." His leader leans down and growls: "Then finish the job. And start with that tall one over there who is trying to ignore us. Yes, by all means, start with him."

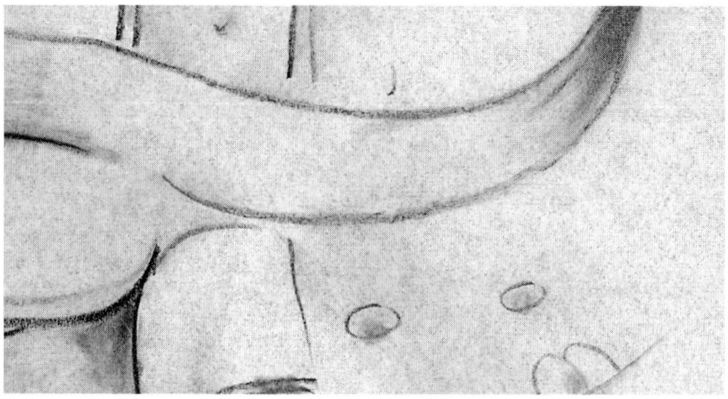

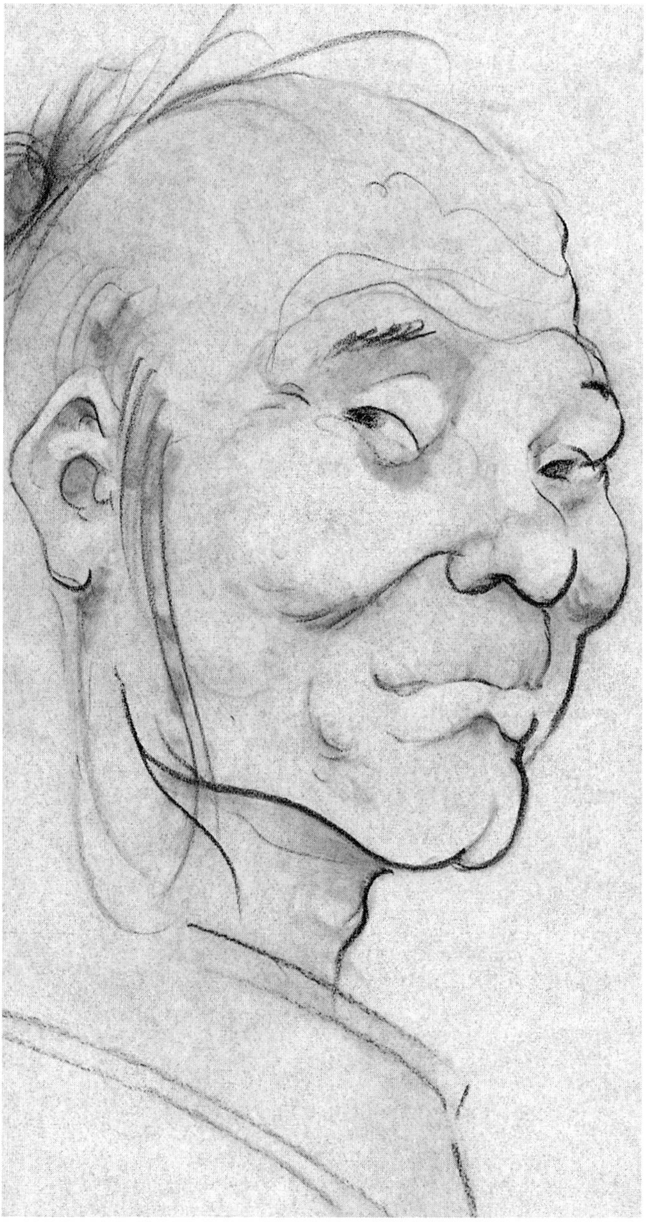

Thus encouraged, the would-be soldier named Kimbei steps boldly forward, buoyed up by a wave of shouts and cries that erupt from his companions, who are eager to be entertained (at no risk to themselves). Kimbei's sword gleams in the misty air as he strides toward Naoto.

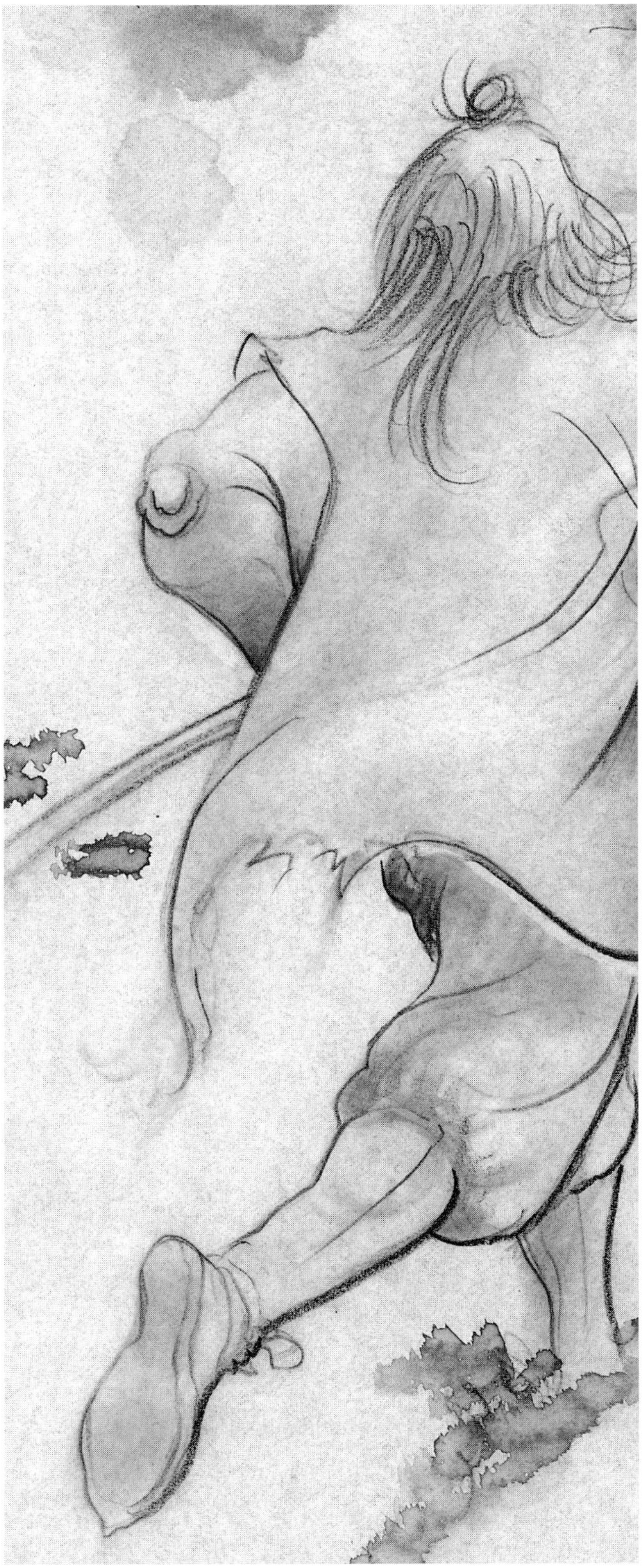

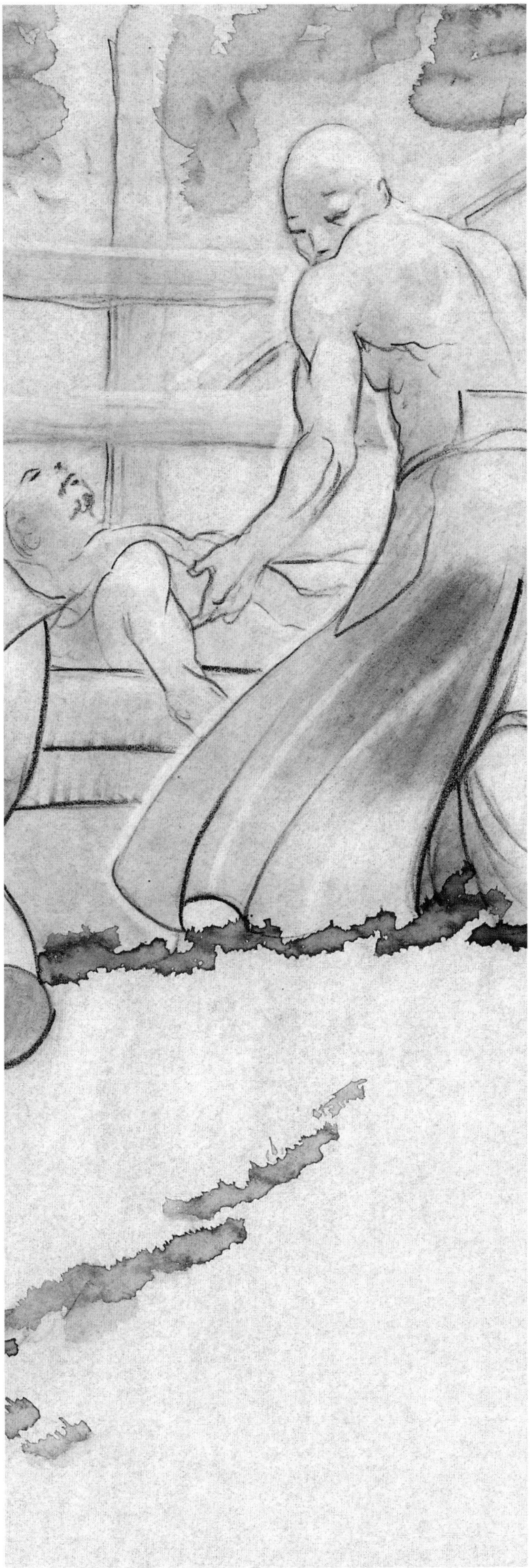

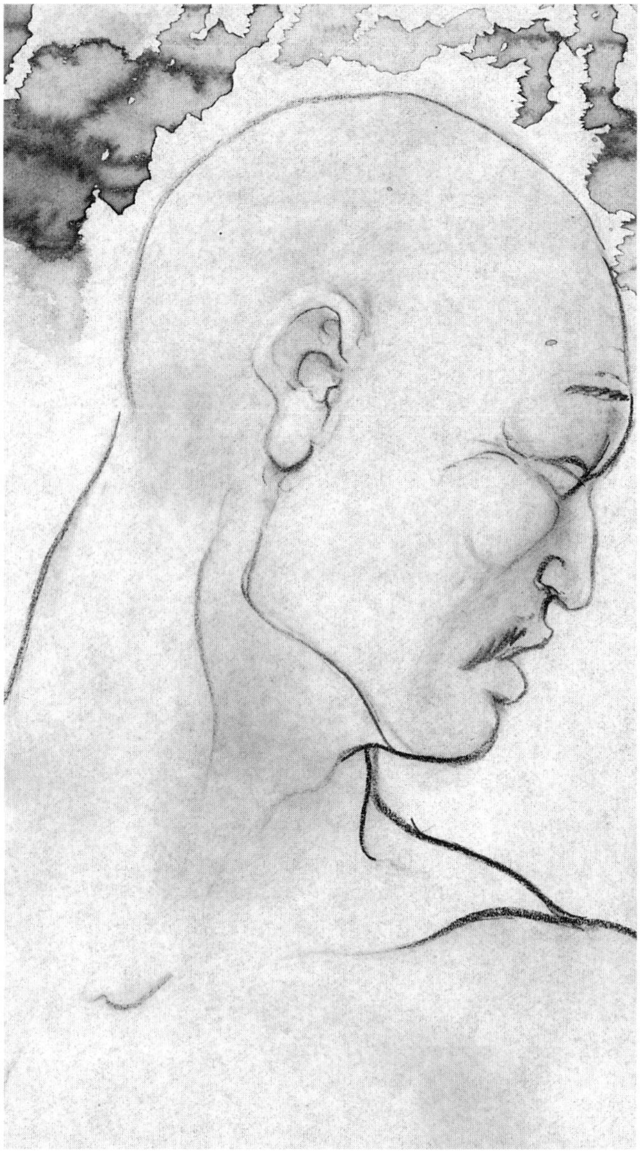

Something about the tall, imposing figure, still turned away from him, seems disconcerting, however, because he feels called upon to deliver a final warning: "You dog of a mad priest! Don't you know the penalty for acting in a disrespectful manner toward your betters? Toward a warrior? Turn around and die like a man, or I'll cut you down like the cur that you and your sort always are!"

At this, Master Naoto does indeed turn to face the blustering, would-be warrior, as the words die away on Kimbei's lips. When Naoto speaks, his voice is low, but Kimbei retreats before it. "Go away. You and your companions have caused enough harm here. Leave us in peace to finish our task."

Silence greets his words, as the rag-tag group of men shuffle uneasily and drop their gaze, while Naoto looks at each one serenely. But their leader is someone of a different mettle and is not inclined to overlook any slights.

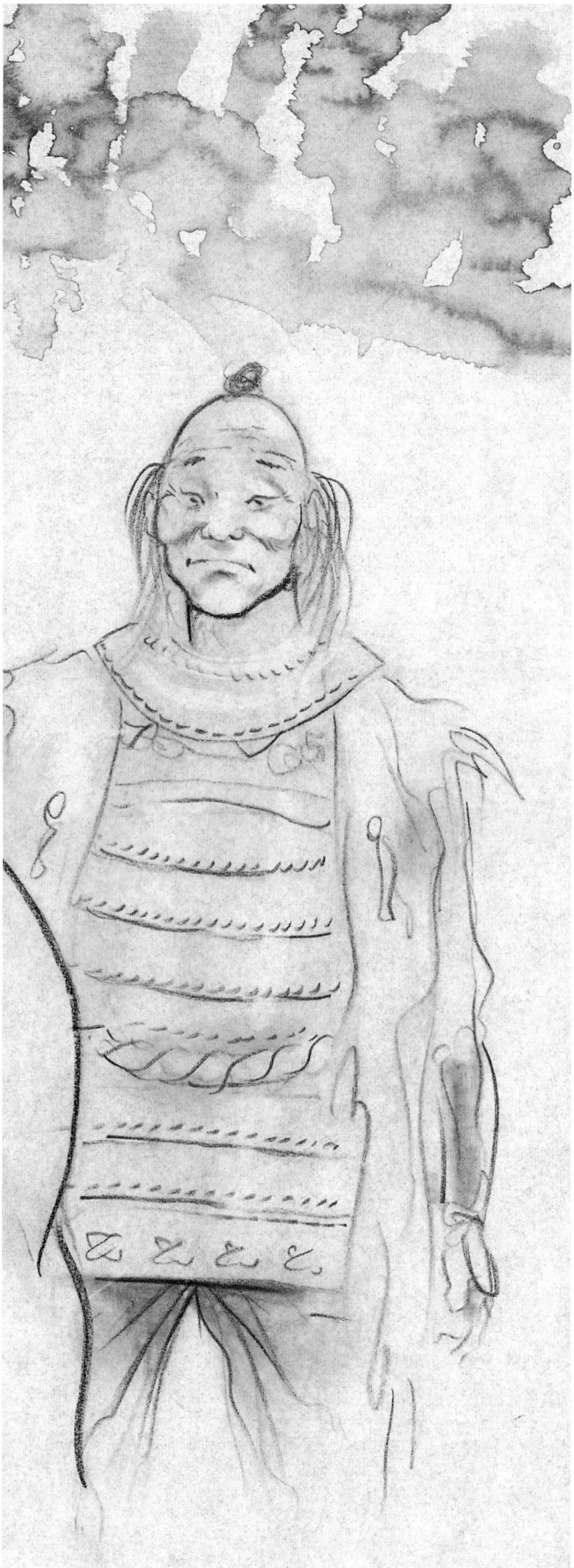

"What's the matter, Kimbei?" he calls out. "Do you wish to join his ranks? If he has converted you, we will pass around a collection helmet for your parting gift. But if he hasn't, do what you have been ordered to do, and let's move on!"

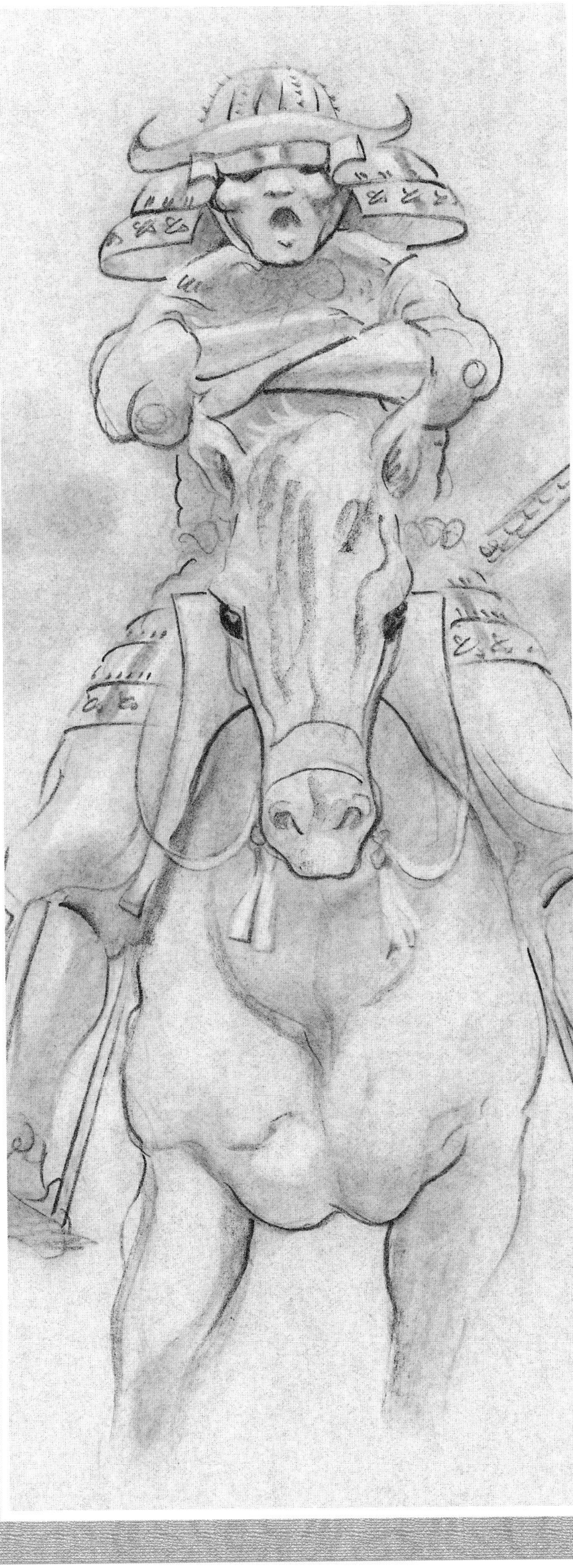

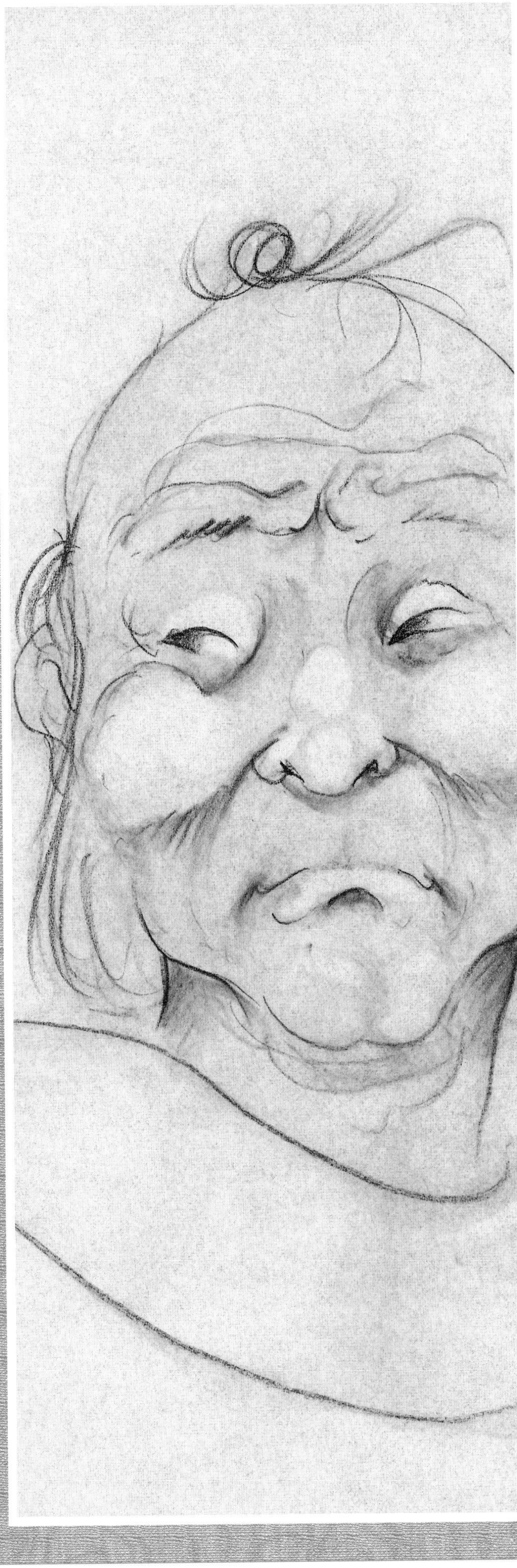

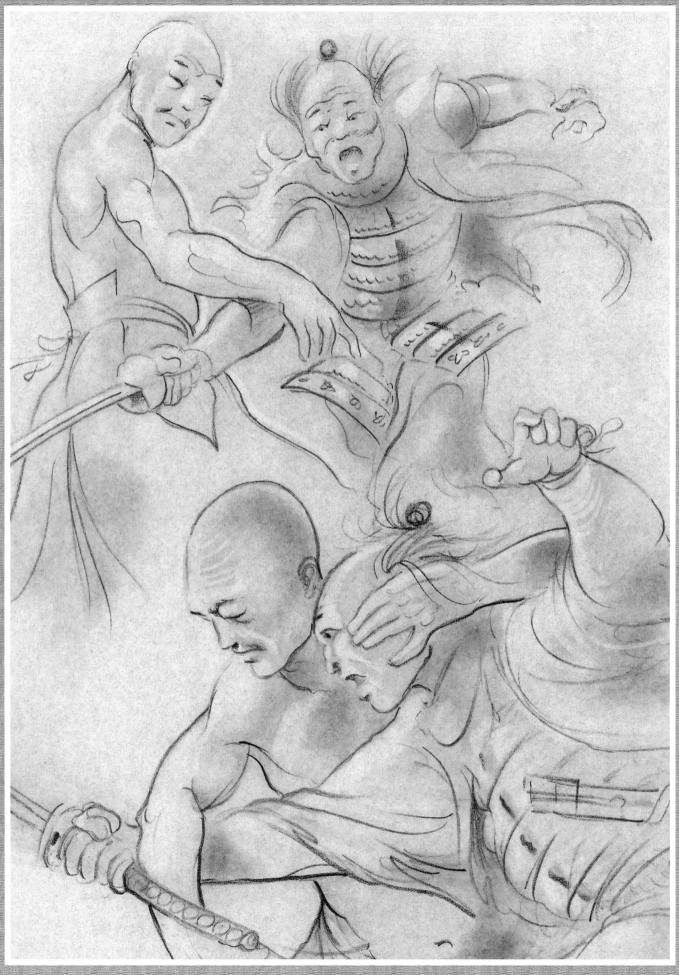

Goaded now by the mocking tone in his leader's voice, Kimbei hurls himself forward with a shout of rage, aiming a diagonal cut at the left shoulder of the unarmed man. But the long blade whirls by unopposed toward the ground as Naoto seems to

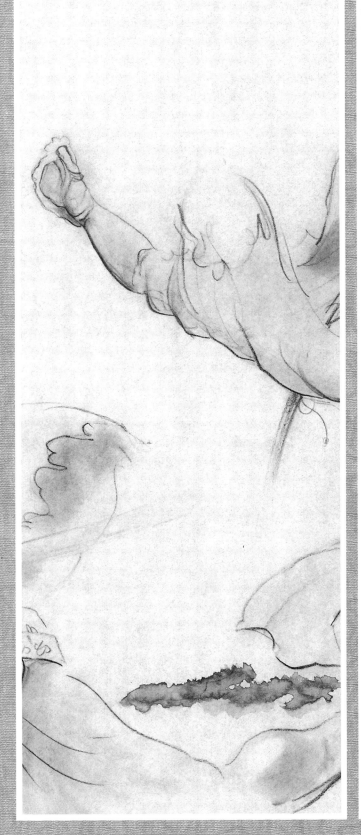

vanish from its path, reappearing almost instantly at Kimbei's side. From this position, his powerful arms spin the amazed man into a soaring flight that brings him crashing back to the earth almost beneath the hooves of the leader's horse.

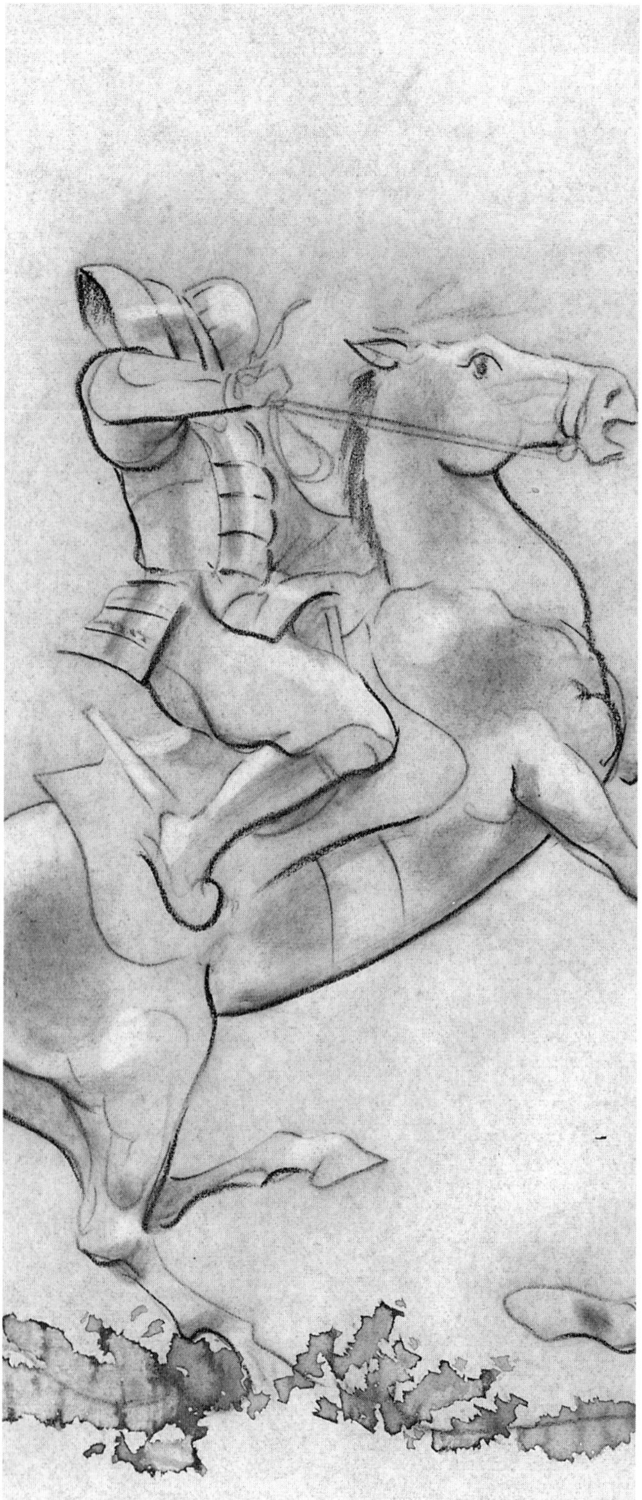

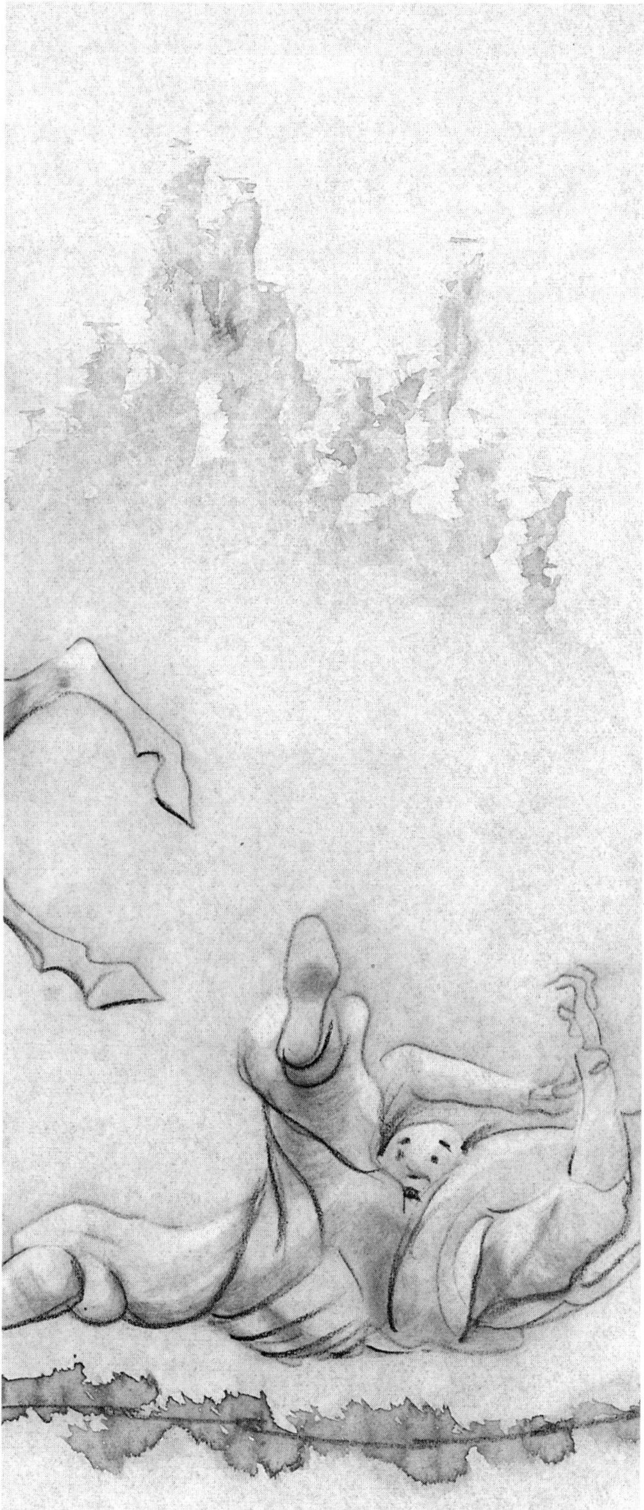

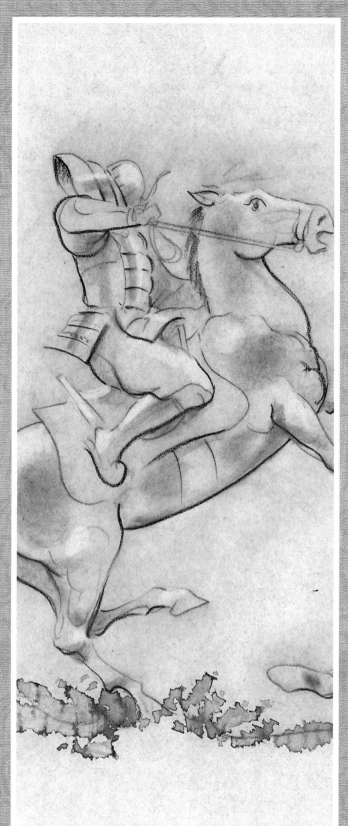

In the ensuing confusion, as the surprised and now alarmed marauders jostle one another without any semblance of order, Master Naoto looks with distaste at the sword he has removed from Kimbei's hand and then whips it down against a nearby stone, snapping the silvery blade in two. Shaking his head, he tosses the handle away and sighs as his eyes follow its flight, remembering other times, so many other times. . . .

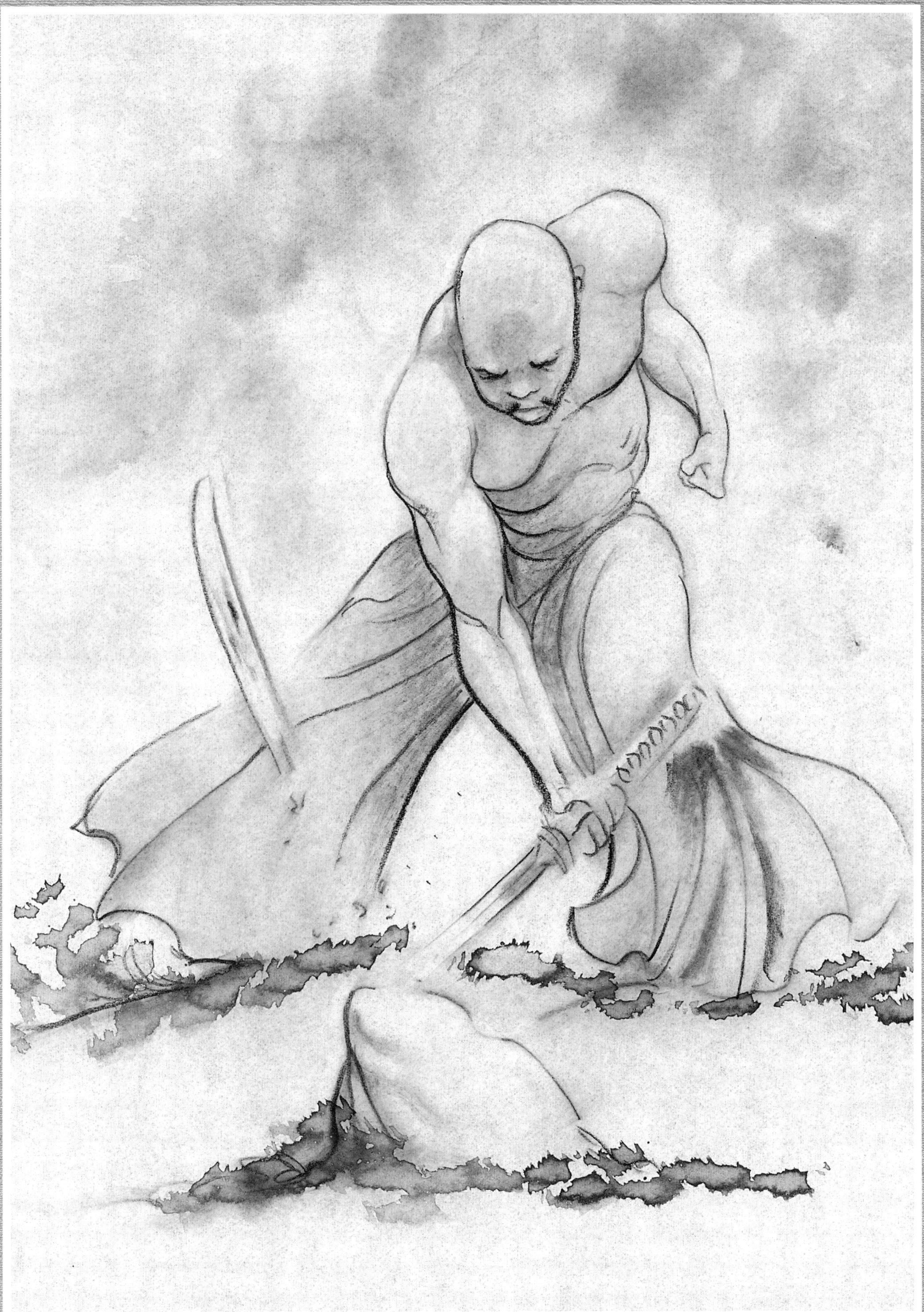

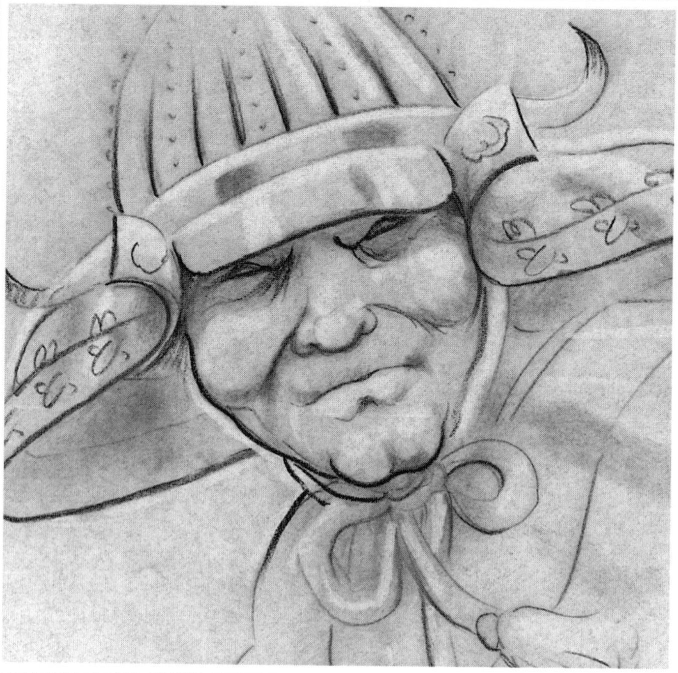

During the entire encounter, Kisaichi had kept his gaze fixed upon Naoto. Even now, as he signals to a pair of spearmen, he continues to stare at him. "Enough! Motobeisan, Mogojiro, I want to see his head on the tip of a spear. Whoever succeeds will be given Kimbei's spoils as well!"

Kimbei, bruised and dazed, is dragging himself to the rear, as the two spearmen hurl themselves at Naoto. But to their astonishment, he meets them halfway, where he spins between them, deflecting the thrusts of the spears and grasping them in his huge hands. Caught up and drawn into the priest's whirling displacement, both men cling desperately to their weapons, which are now dragging them with an irresistible surge in one direction that culminates in a snapping whiplash in the opposite one, as their bodies soar up and then down again into the whirling dust.

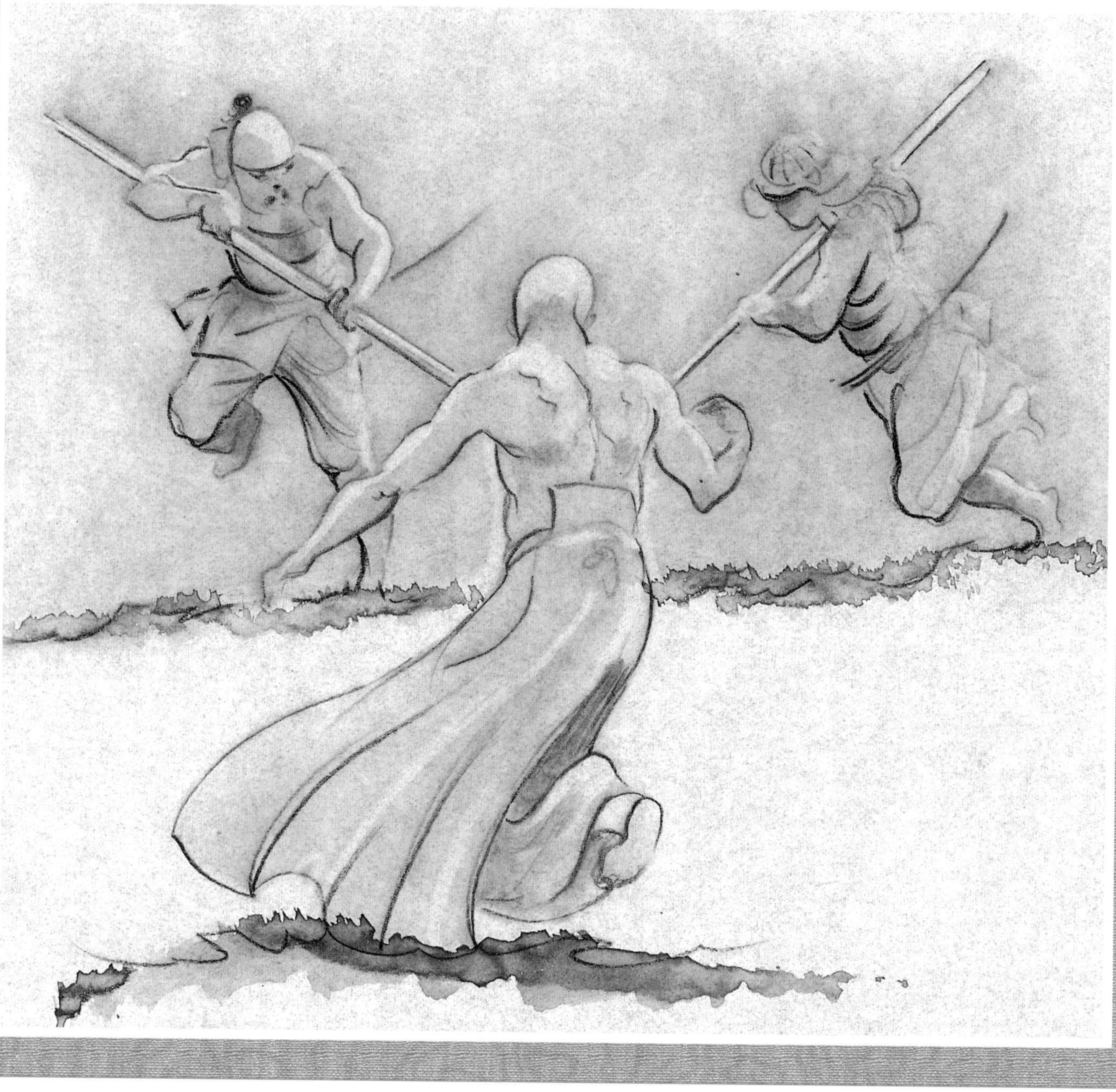

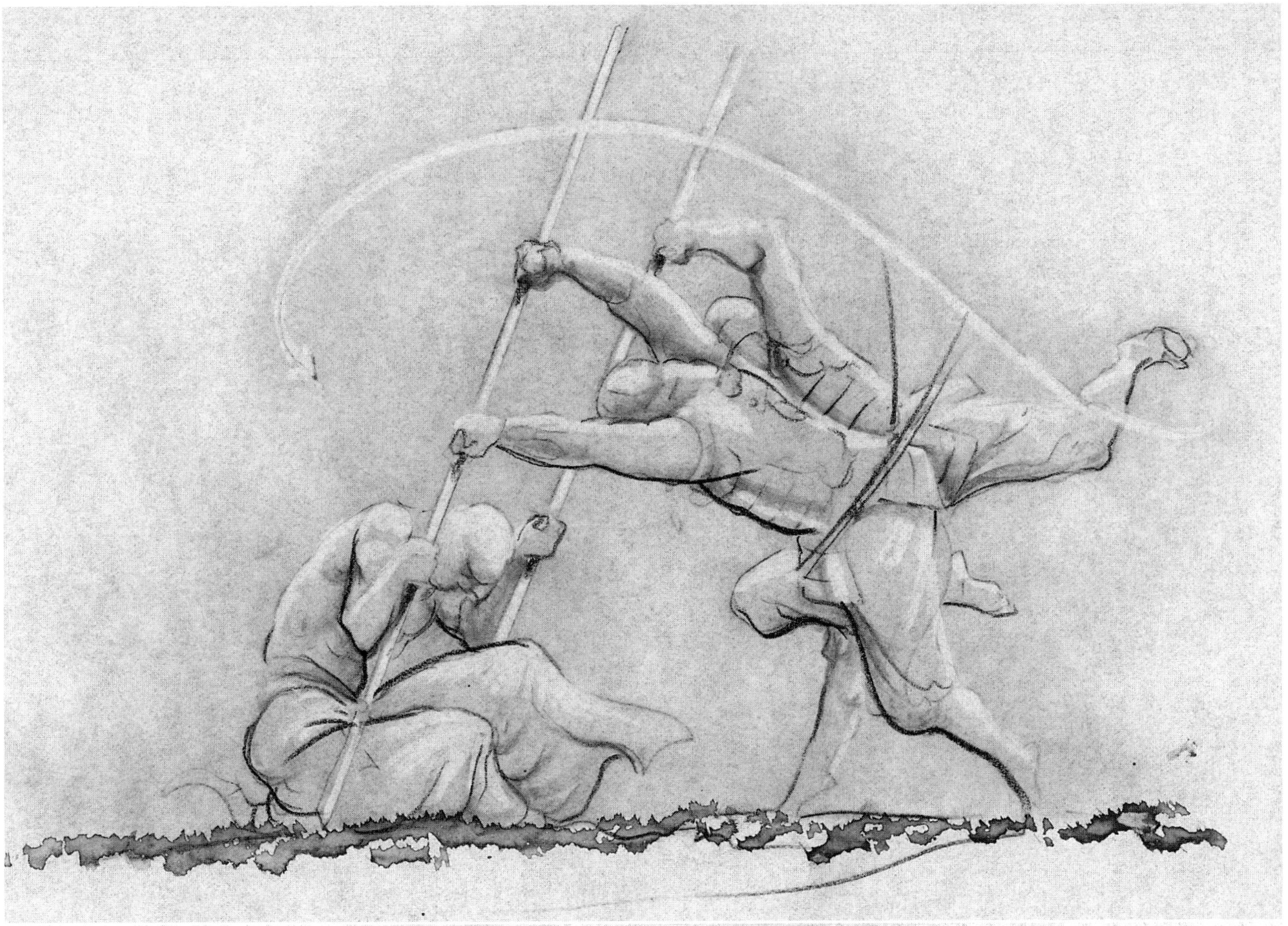

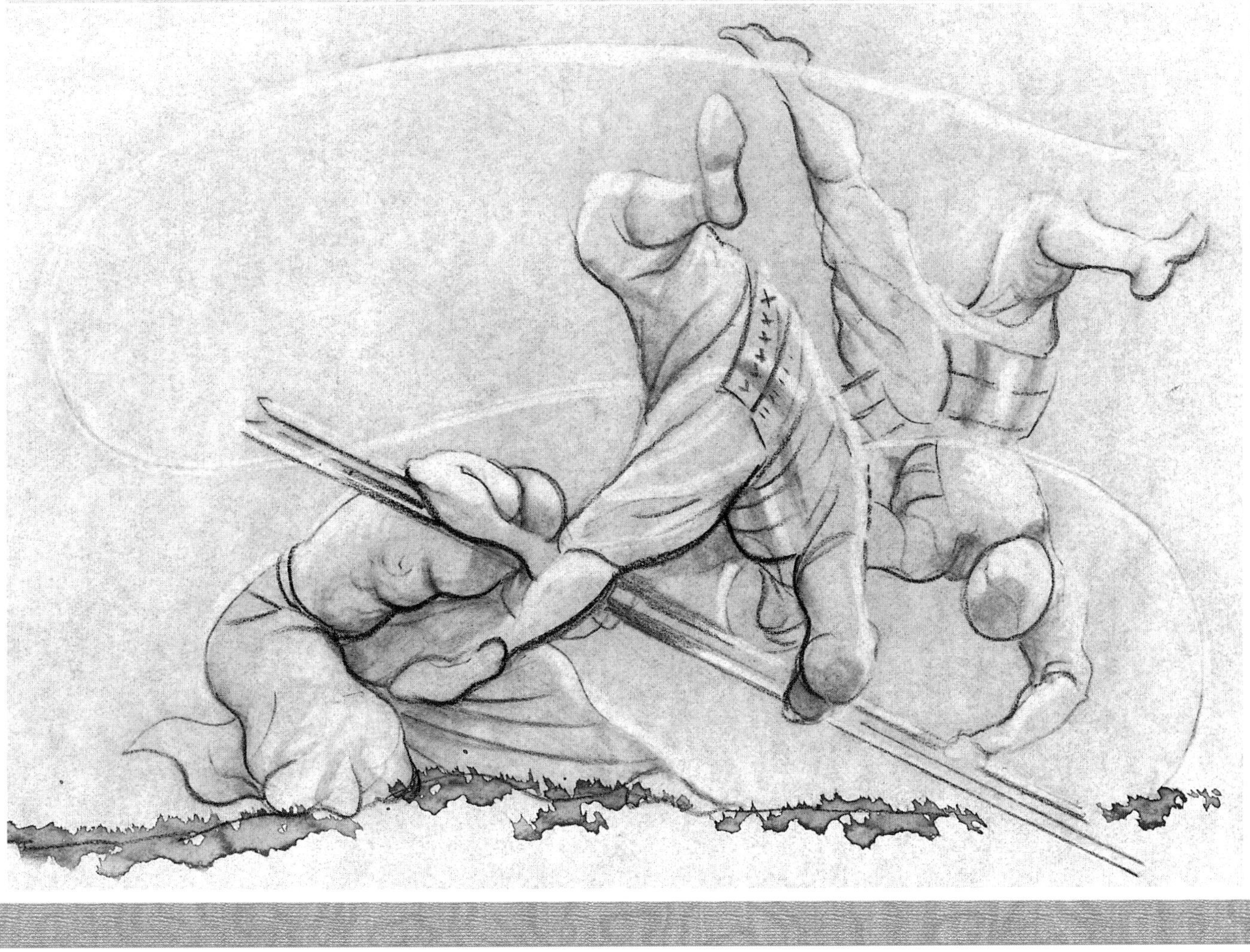

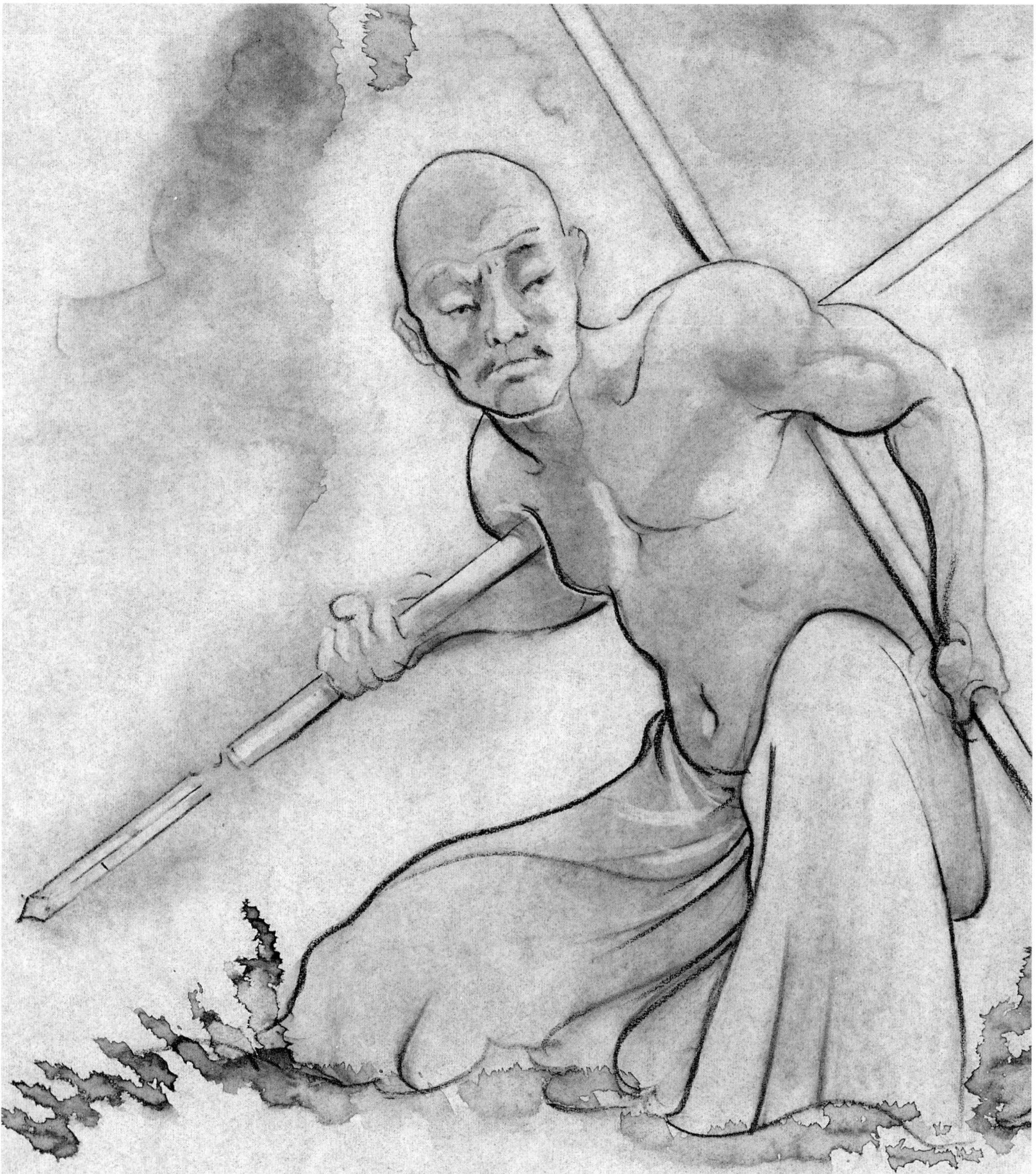

Master Naoto now has full possession of their weapons, as he returns the leader's stare. His voice is still soft, but the marauders can detect the undercurrent of rage: "What will it take to make you understand? We must complete our task, in the name of Amidha, the Buddha. Leave this place—now! Take your weapons and go. May Amidha pity you. Go!"

But Kisaichi shakes his head. He motions to Karoku, who moves suddenly to seize the dumbfounded Ishi from behind, choking him and forcing him to his knees. The unfortunate young man had approached too close to the center of the confrontation, torn between his fear and the desire to help his teacher.

Kisaichi grins. "Hold it right there, priest. I obviously made a mistake starting with you. One of your followers should have been first. Now, why not be sensible and drop those spears? You have insulted us and I am bound to punish any such insults whether to me or to my men. Beneath that priestly garb you seem to be a man familiar with the Way of the Sword and I am sure you can understand my position."

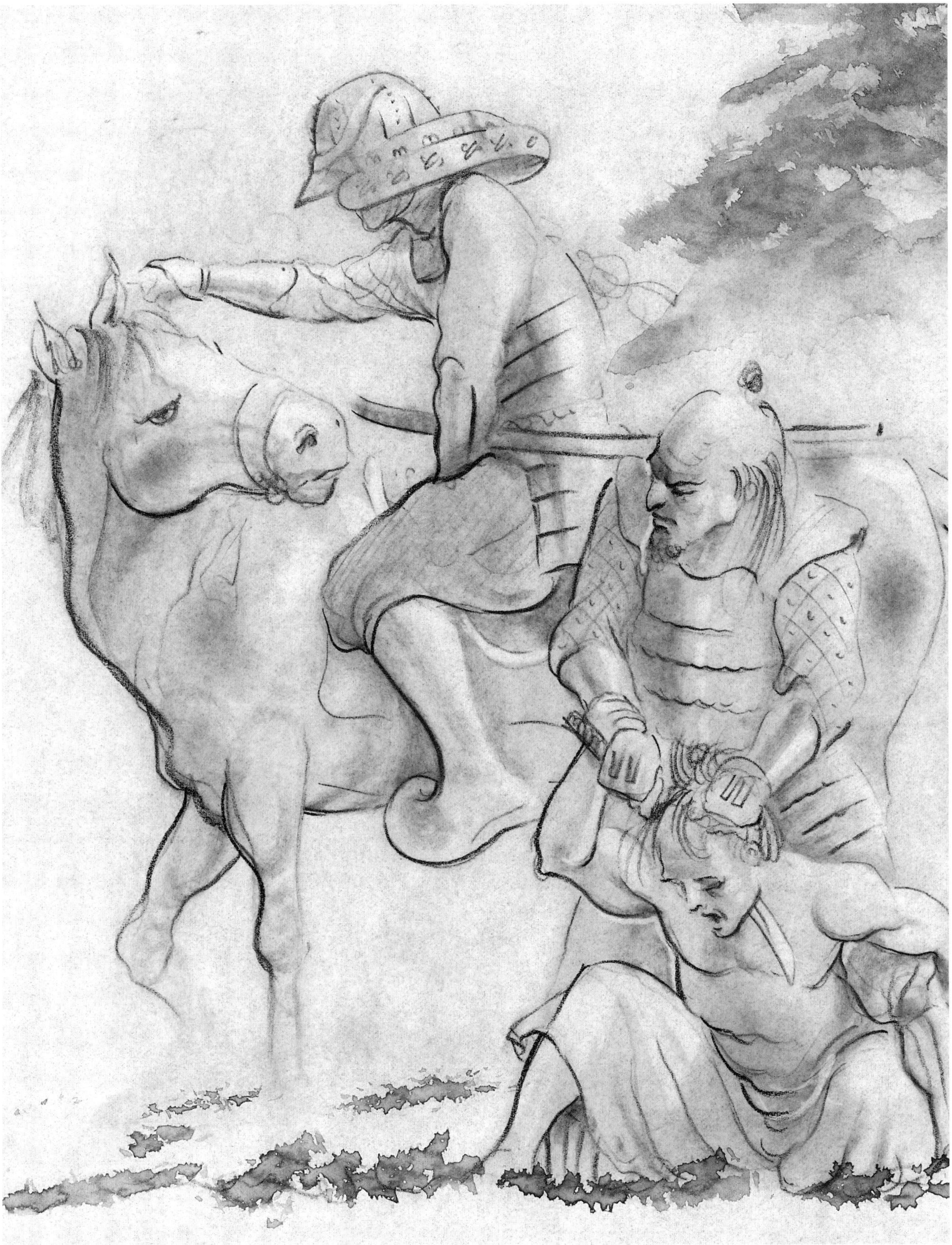

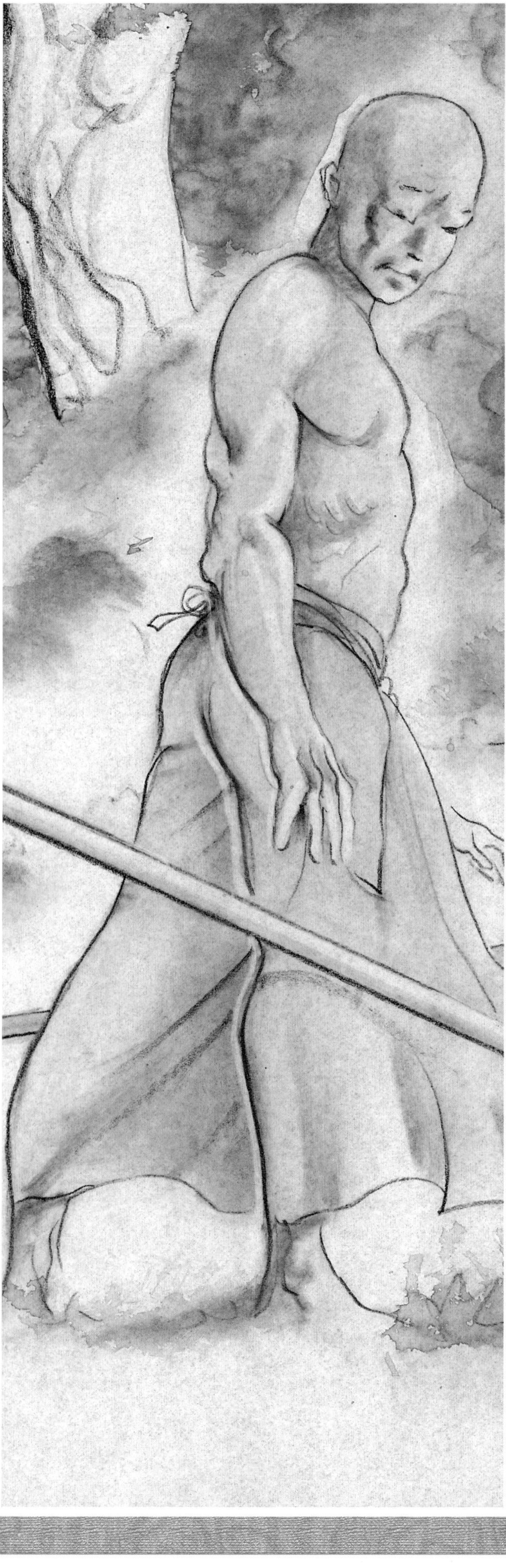

Naoto's shoulders drop. There may always be a vulnerable chink in anyone's armor—or strategy. He allows the spears to fall from his hands as he tries another tactic: "This is unworthy of you, whether or not you are a warrior. I am the one you want, not unarmed youngsters. Let him and the other two go and I promise to provide you with sufficient entertainment, if that should be your pleasure."

But Kisaichi has other plans and is enjoying his moment of triumph to the fullest: "My pleasure is to watch your expression as we begin with him, priest. Then we will move on to the others. Go ahead, Karoku—let's have the first head to roll this morning."

Naoto's body tenses as he watches Ishi's head tremble beneath Karoku's grip, while the marauder's short dagger arches upward. Naoto's thoughts are anguished. He may retrieve one of those spears and hurl it at the butcher, but Ishi will already be dead. "Master Kawanari, what would you do?" "Ah Naoto, Naoto, always begin at the beginning. Your charges, remember? You should have seen to it that they were all safely behind you and kept yourself between them and those brutes. You still have two to protect. Poor Ishi . . ."

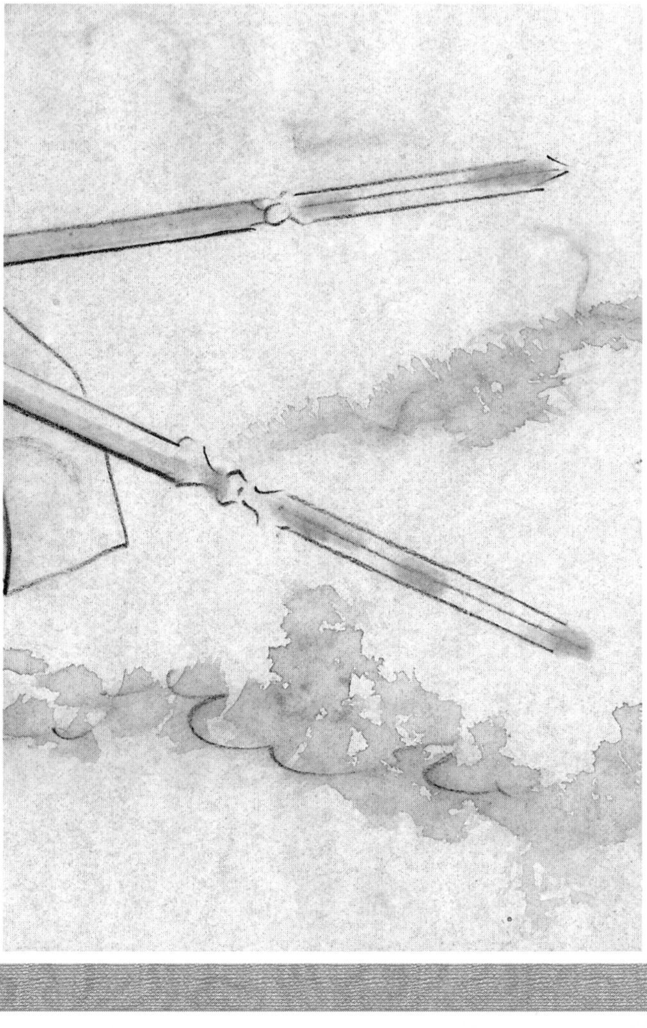

Suddenly, Karoku's dagger halts in mid-air and his body stiffens, as his eyes widen for a brief instant, then shrink into a frozen, lifeless stare. Ishi falls to the ground, gasping for air. Alarmed, the renegades withdraw noisily as Karoku pitches forward, revealing the shadow of a spearman who calmly withdraws the curved blade of his spear from the renegade's back. Naoto recognizes Haru, the Yamabushi, and his heart contracts within his breast. Now there will be more death amid the ruins of the Otsugawa Village. . . .

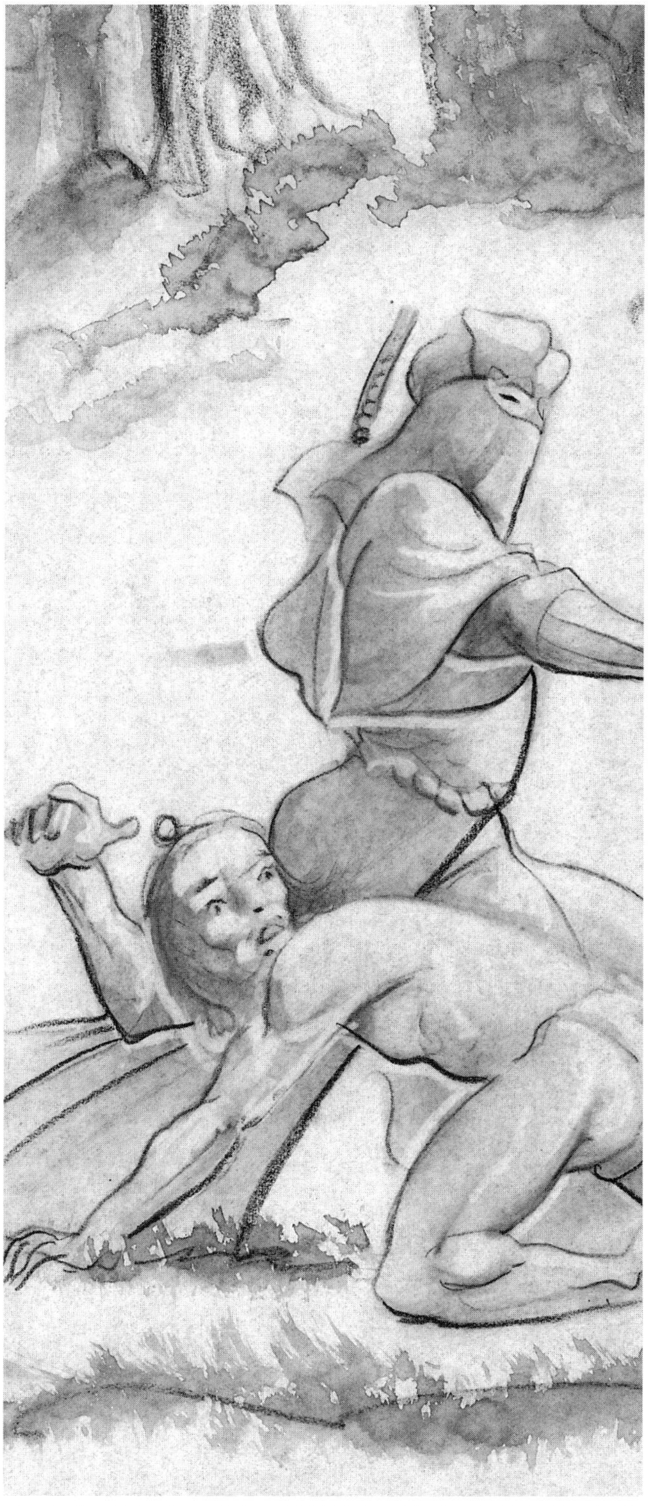

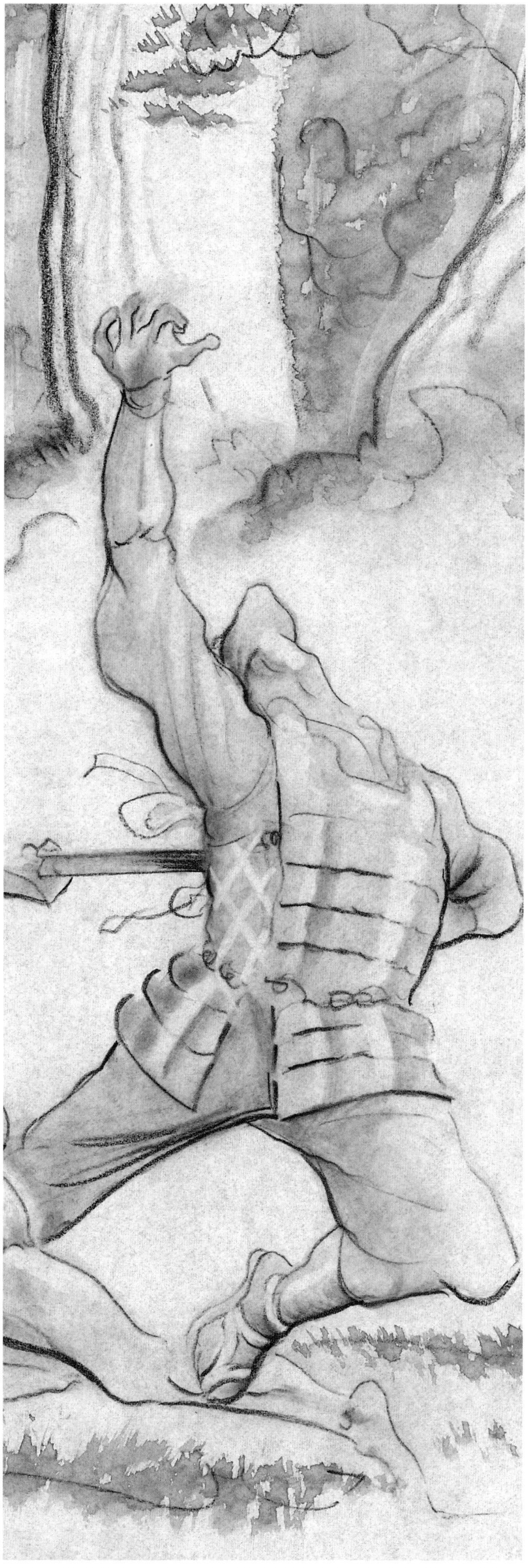

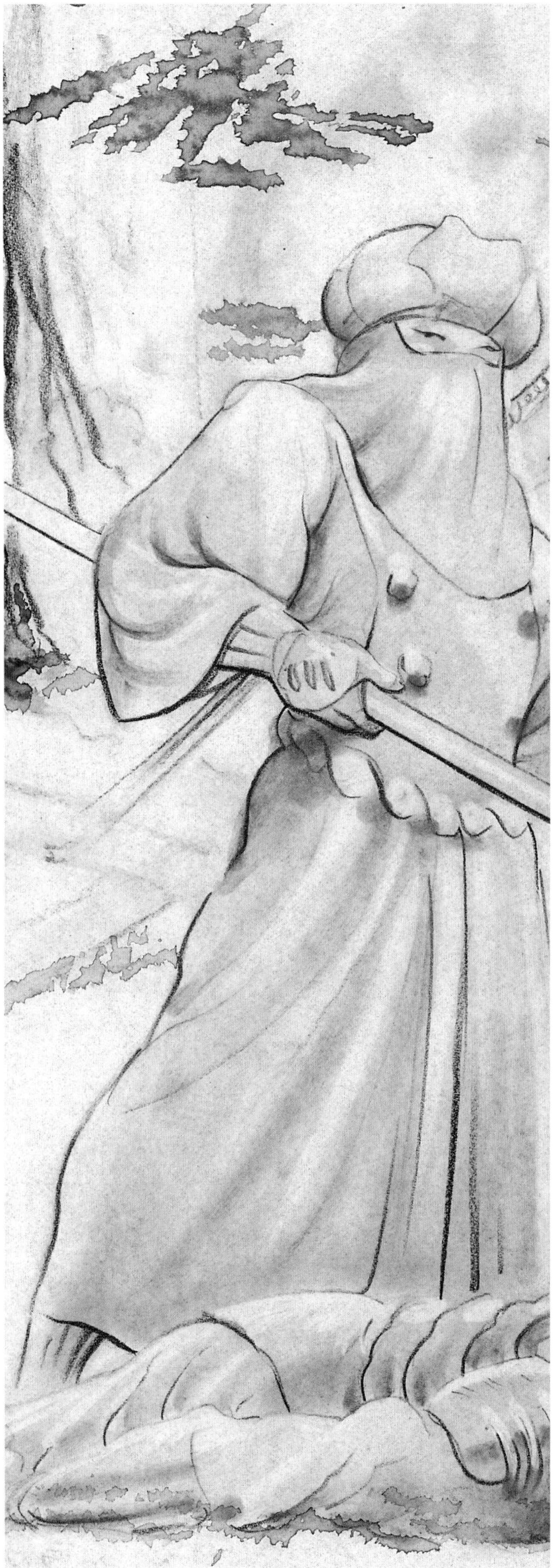

As the Yamabushi steps over Karoku's lifeless body, he laughs and addresses Naoto. "Well, what did I tell you? You insist upon sparing the lives of such scum, and they turn around and savage you. But my method works differently. My way pacifies them—completely—as you can see for yourself. Now, are there any true warriors among you?"

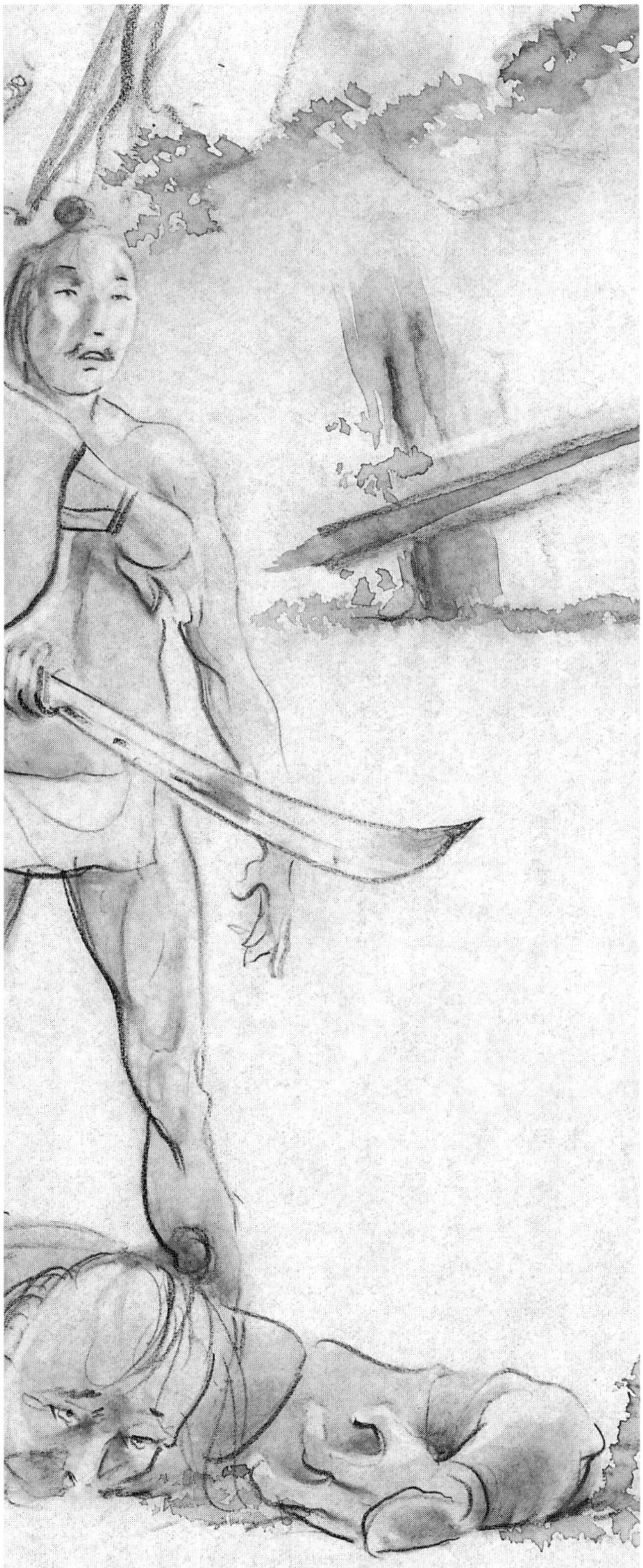

The *Yamabushi* whirls his spear before the widening circle of the rag-tag assembly, all of whom are beginning to find this morning too full of surprises for their liking. Where might Kisaichi—who was usually so well aware of their limitations when confronted by professional warriors—be leading them today?

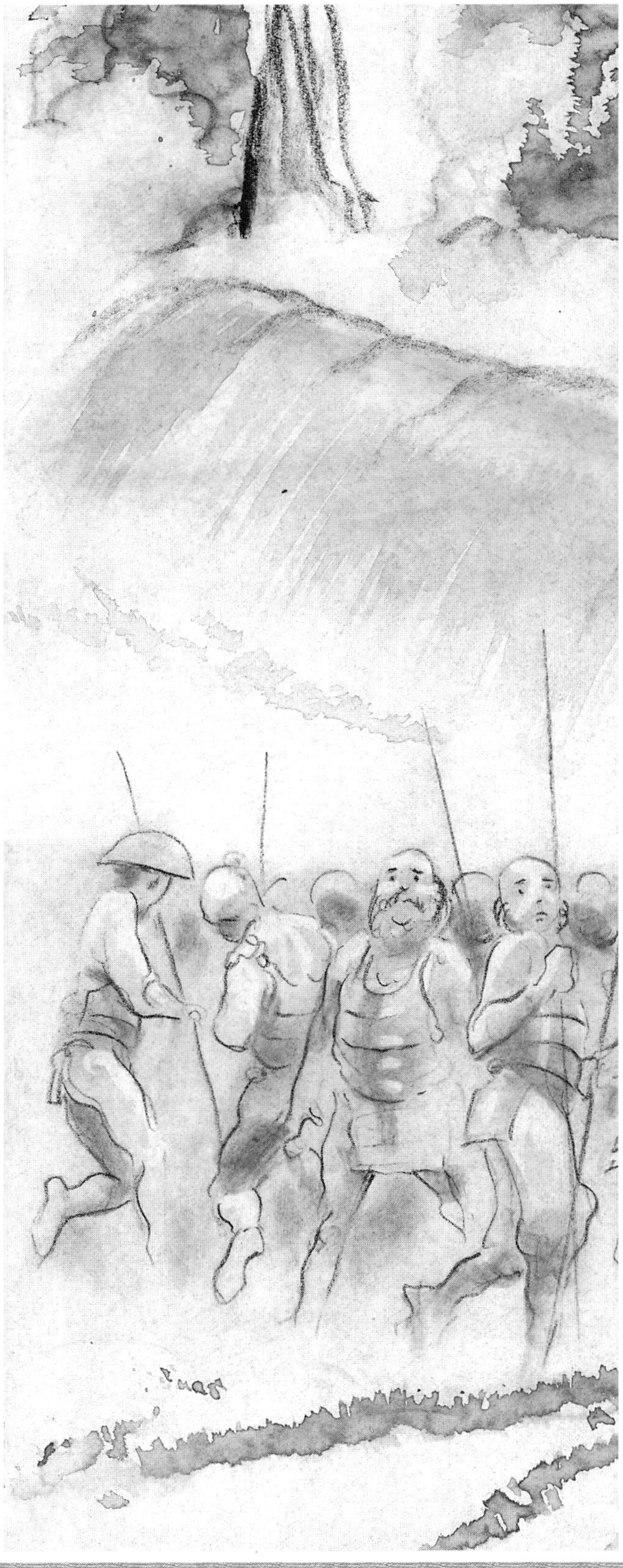

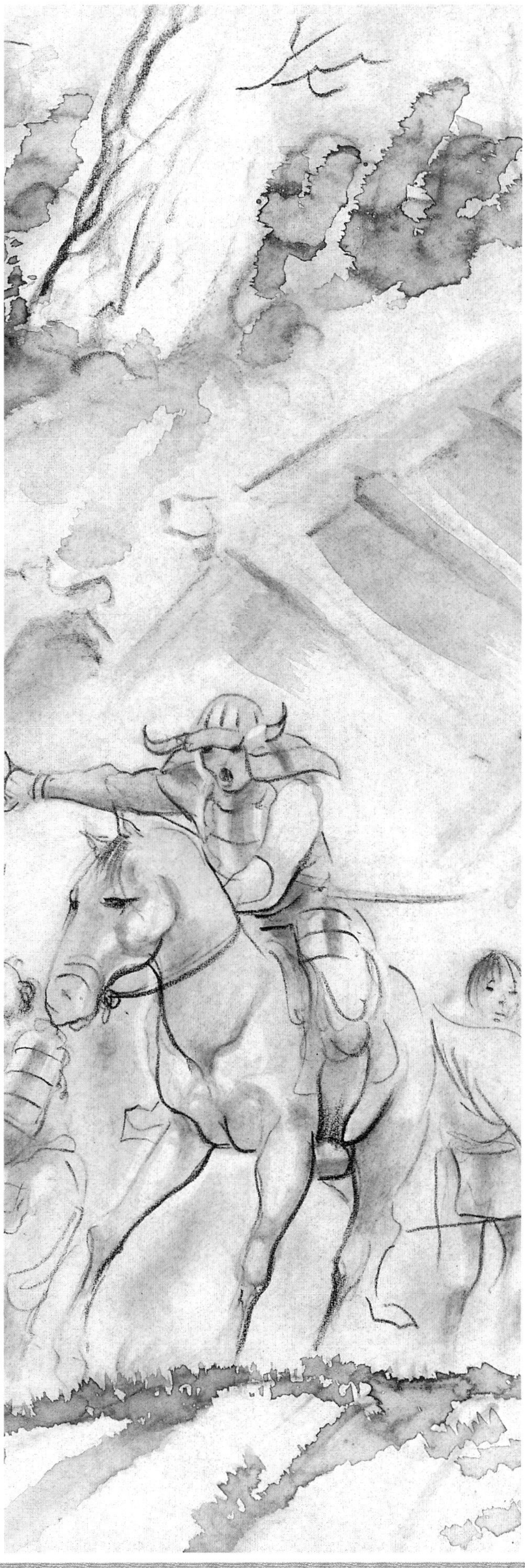

But Kisaichi recovers quickly. "Another one! Straight from the pits of hell! This place certainly must be some sort of shrine. It is frequented by all kinds of religious gnats—some harmless and some that would bite a samurai, if they could. Tosuke, Irobei: no one has ever been able to touch you. Dispatch this one and the spoils of those idiots who have fallen ignominiously in the dust this morning will be yours. Come on, show us some real combat!" He leans back in his saddle, holding his spear securely.

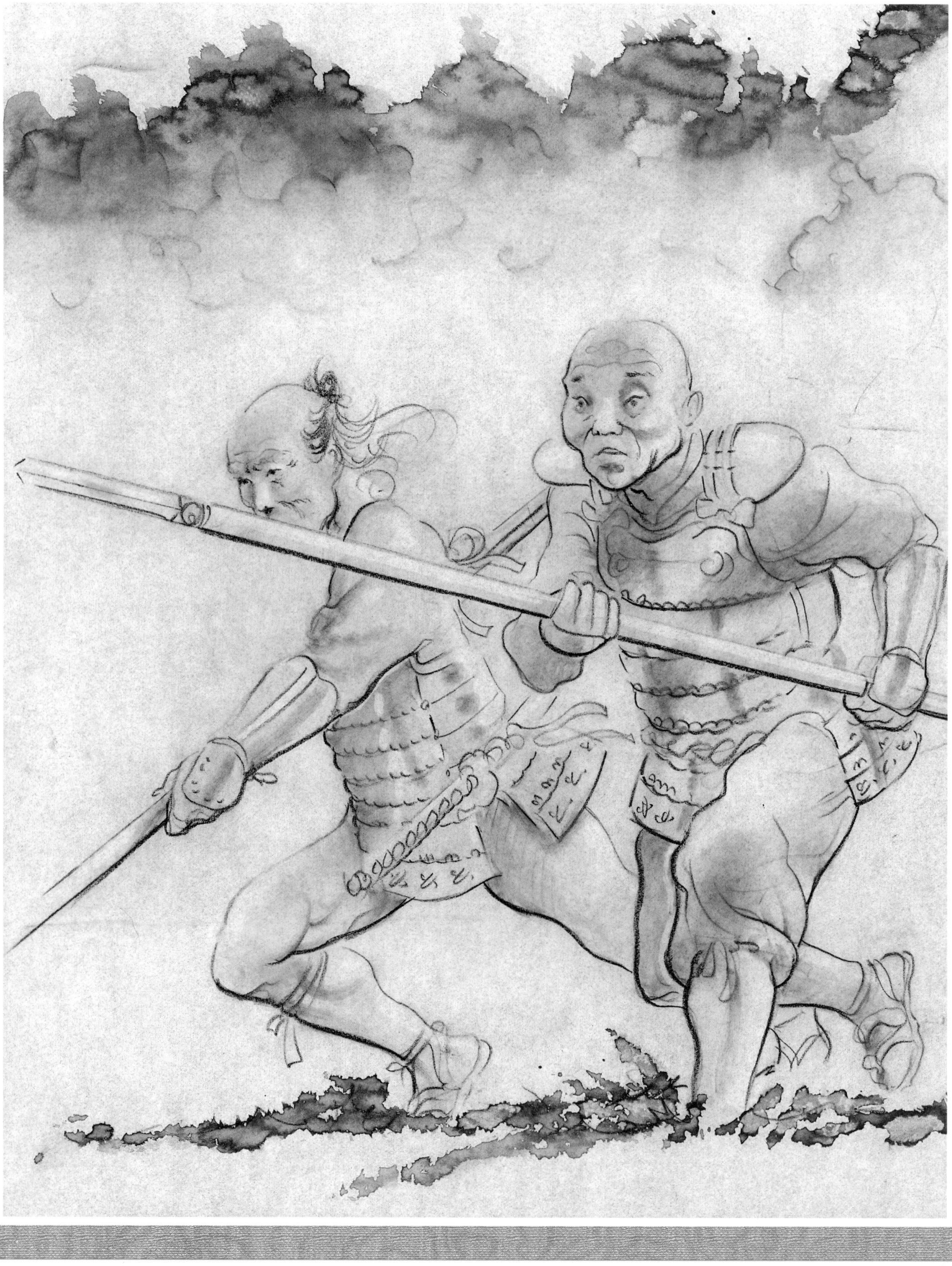

Both Tosuke and Irobei have seen action in battle before, although the conditions then had been less challenging. Here, facing a masked mountain priest, they find themselves decidedly uneasy. Still, as Kisaichi had pointed out, he was only one man, even if a member of a redoubtable mountain order. . . .

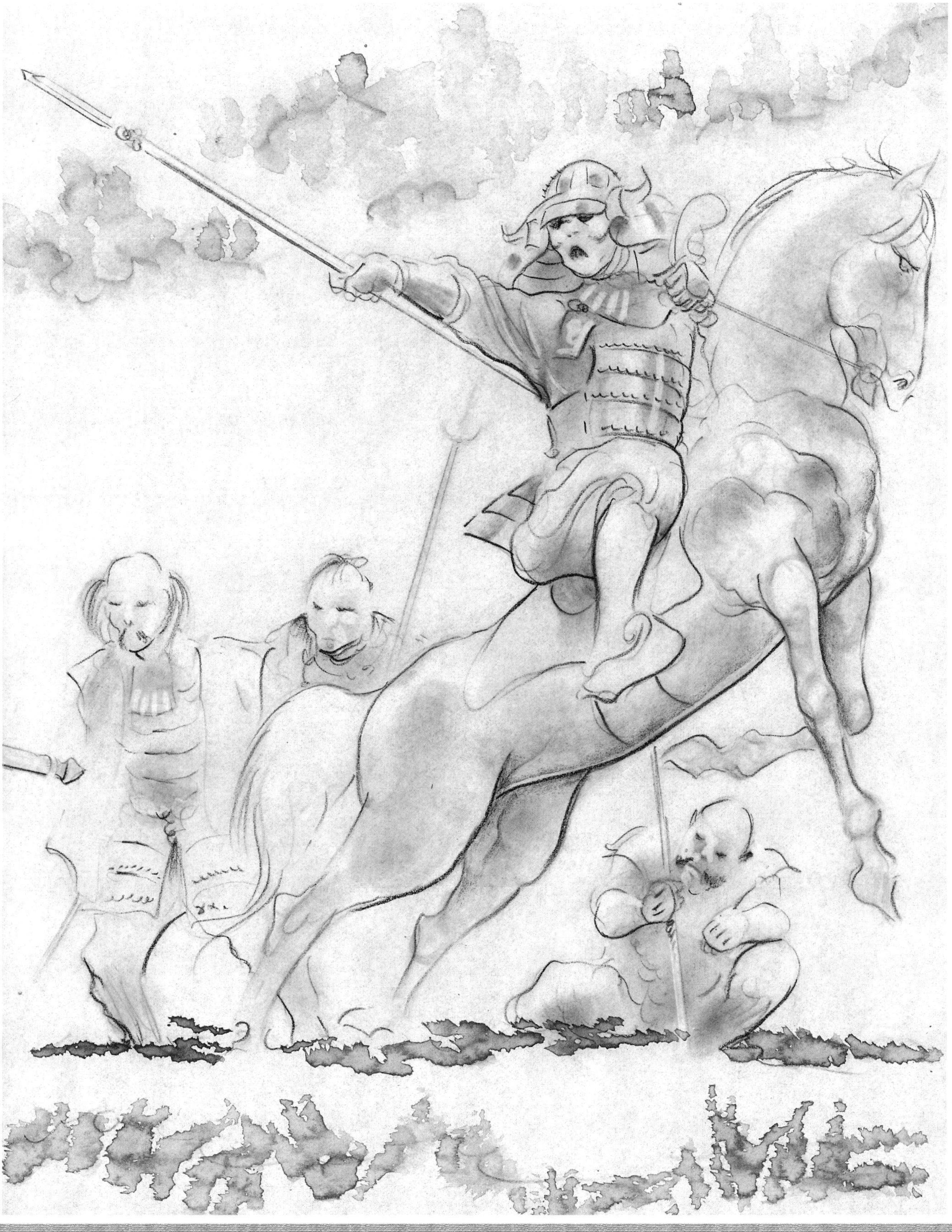

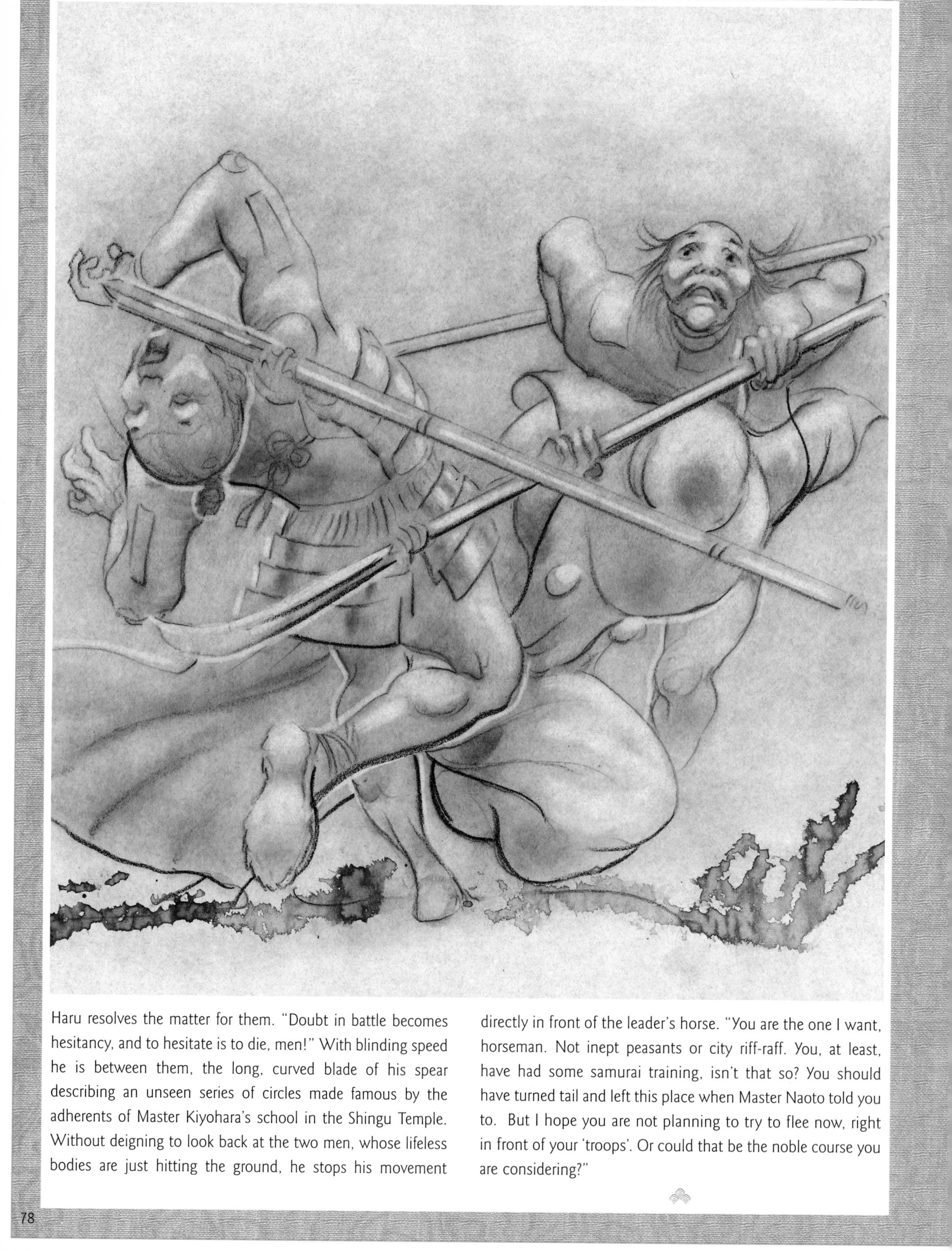

Haru resolves the matter for them. "Doubt in battle becomes hesitancy, and to hesitate is to die, men!" With blinding speed he is between them, the long, curved blade of his spear describing an unseen series of circles made famous by the adherents of Master Kiyohara's school in the Shingu Temple. Without deigning to look back at the two men, whose lifeless bodies are just hitting the ground, he stops his movement directly in front of the leader's horse. "You are the one I want, horseman. Not inept peasants or city riff-raff. *You*, at least, have had some samurai training, isn't that so? *You* should have turned tail and left this place when Master Naoto told you to. But I hope you are not planning to try to flee now, right in front of your 'troops'. Or could that be the noble course you are considering?"

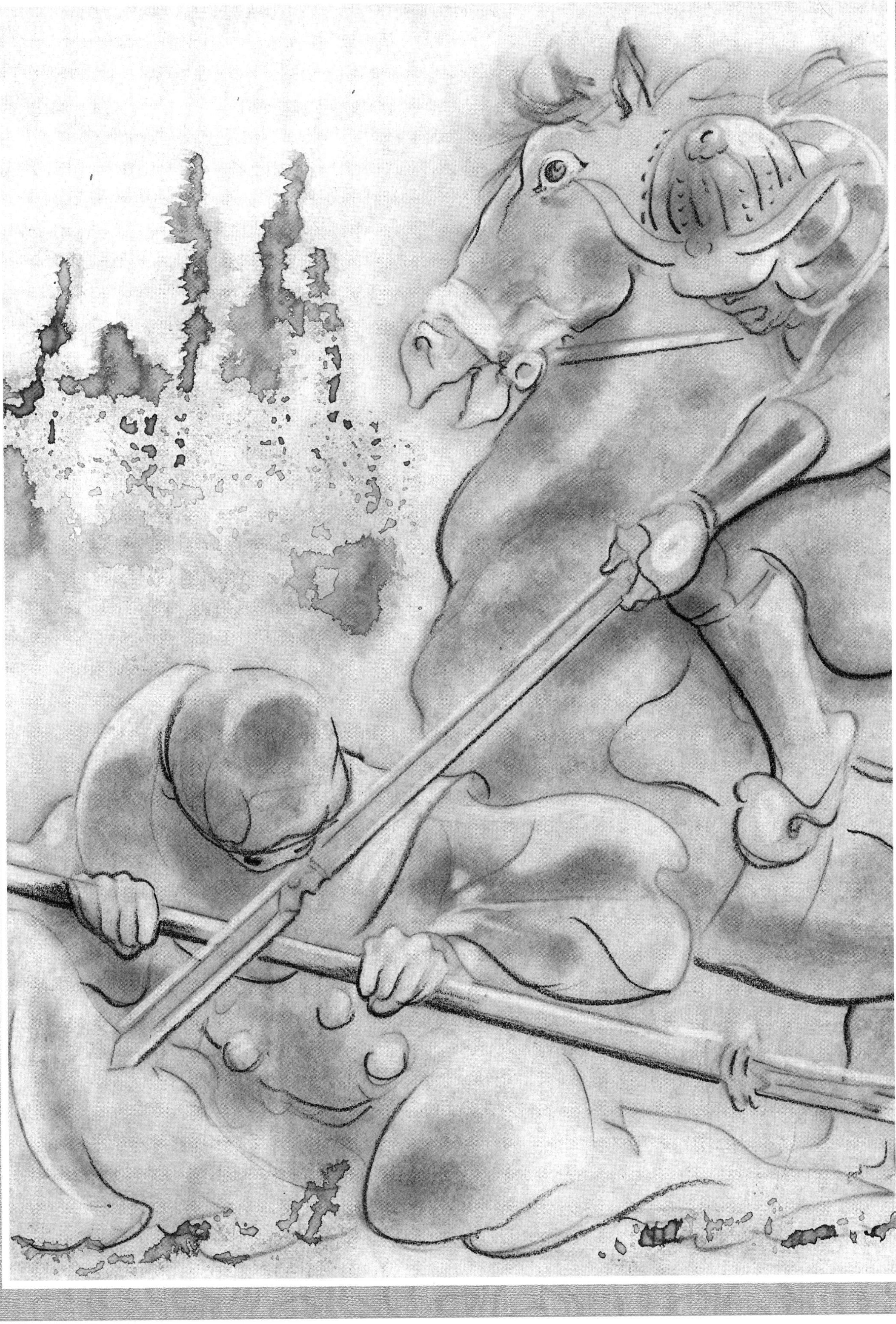

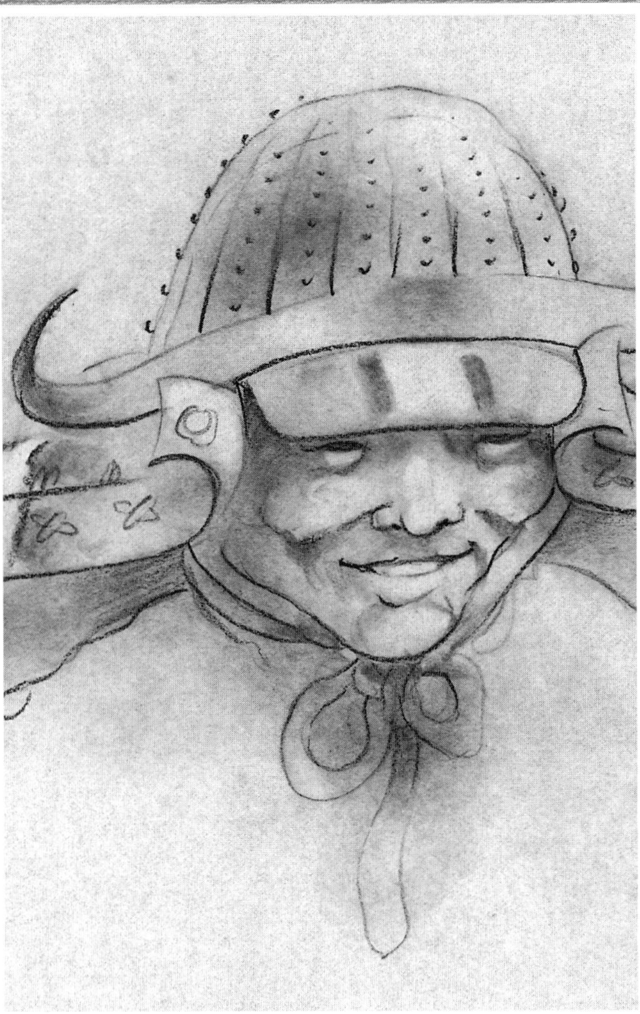

Naoto is about to intervene, hoping to interrupt a chain of events he abhors, but Kisaichi has made up his mind—a seemingly inevitable decision because his tone in response is almost jaunty. "No, priest, I wouldn't consider leaving. And you are quite right. I am not like these misfits you see all around me. Admittedly, they are not much, but still, I have shaped them into a semblance of a fighting force. I was a samurai once, and a good one, too. Although I may now be unaffiliated, a *ronin,* I still hate all priests, especially those who skulk around in the mountains. I shall take great pleasure in dealing with you myself."

Even as he speaks, his mount whirls, trained to respond to the pressure of his rider's knees, and the horseman's spear is suddenly aimed at Haru's throat. But the accompanying thrust is parried by the curved blade that Haru handles so dexterously, and the Yamabushi slips right under the horse's legs, entangling them and uprooting the unfortunate beast with the thick handle of his spear. Neighing loudly, the animal thunders to the ground, hurling his rider into a somersault from which the warrior emerges unscathed and ready for combat, except for his helmet, loosely secured all morning, which has rolled away.

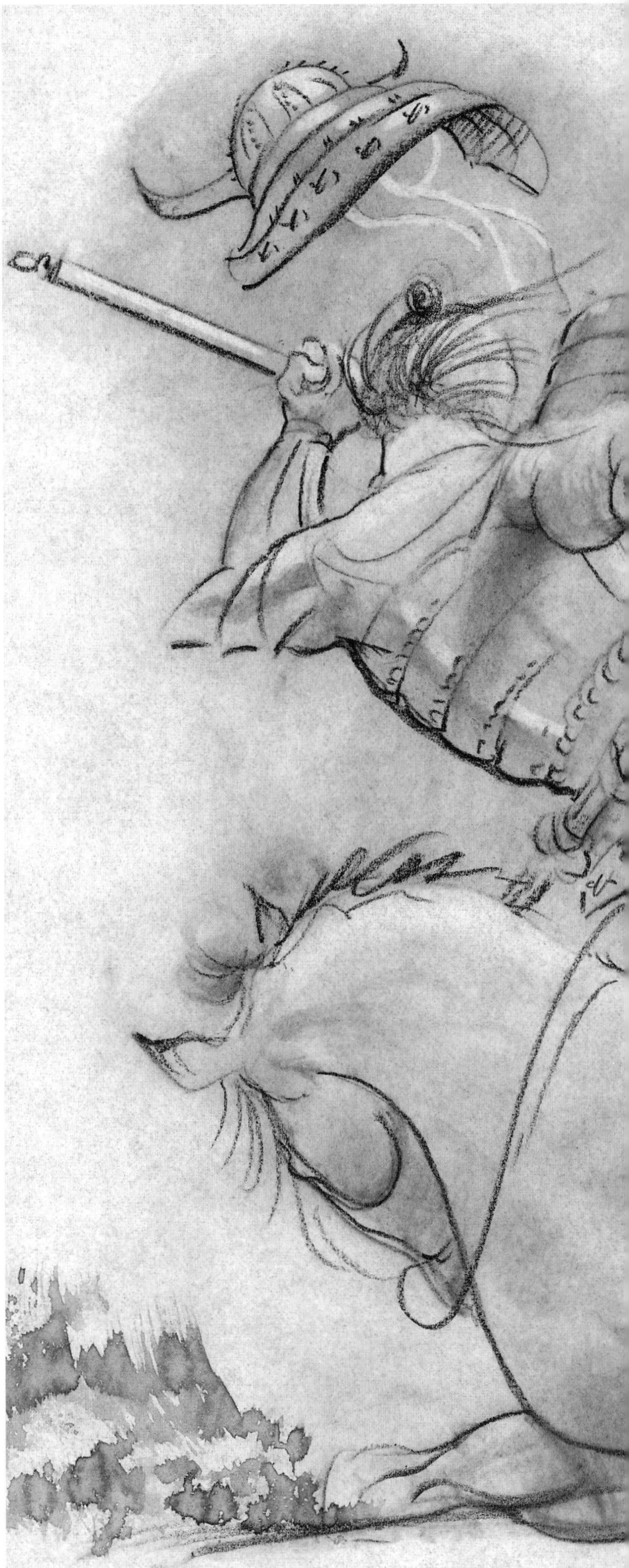

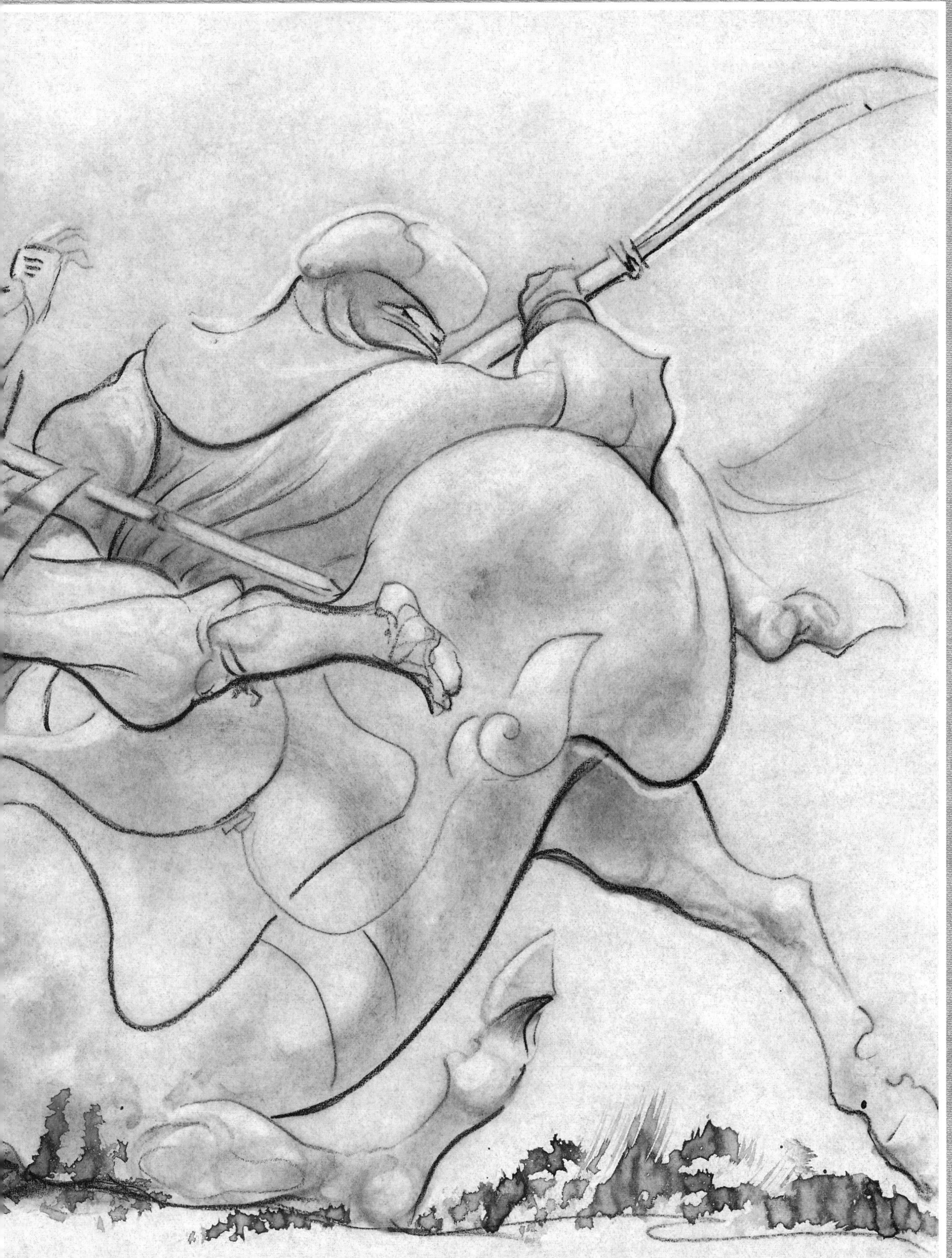

Kisaichi salutes the *Yamabushi*. "Well done, priest. It has been a long time since I have had an opportunity to cross spears with anyone accustomed to wielding anything deadlier than a pitchfork. Still, you are doomed, priest. I will kill you not so much for shaming me before the band of rowdies I happen to be leading at the moment, but because you have lessened me in my own eyes. But if you give me a good fight, I shall dispatch you in a way befitting an honorable man-of-arms."

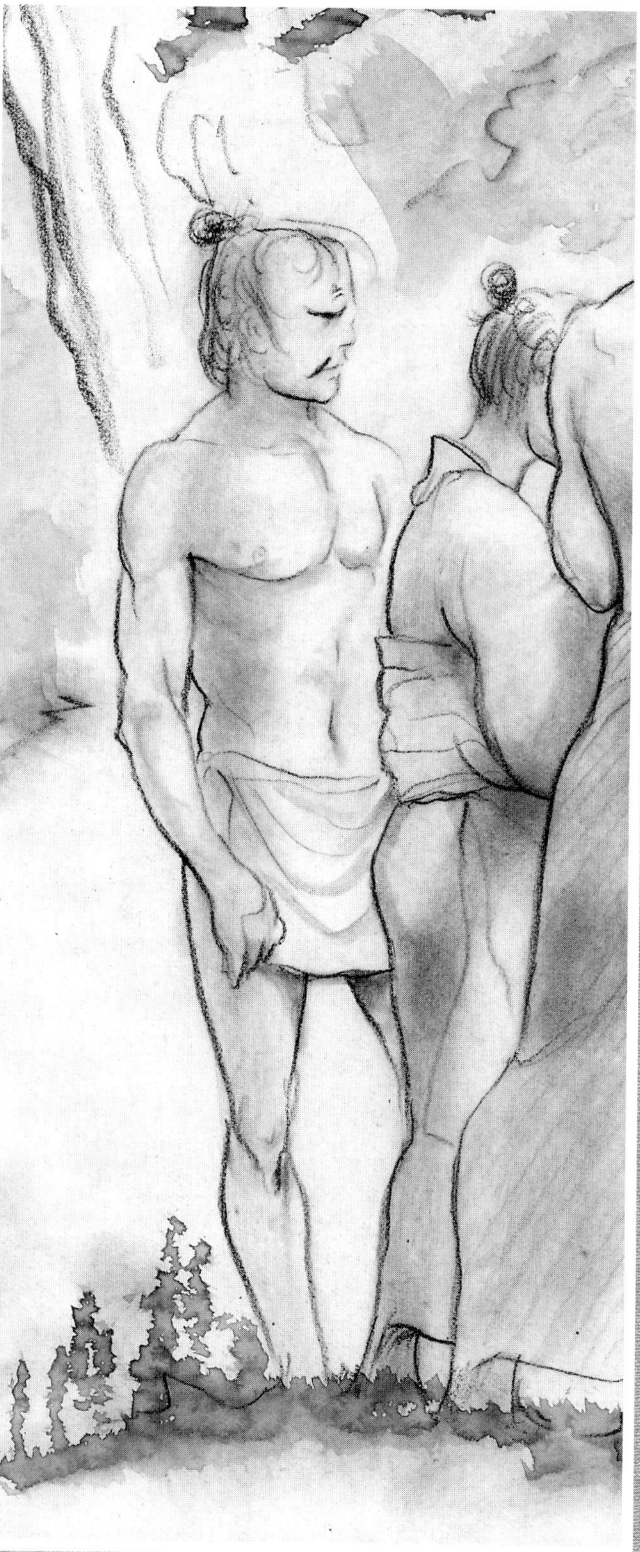

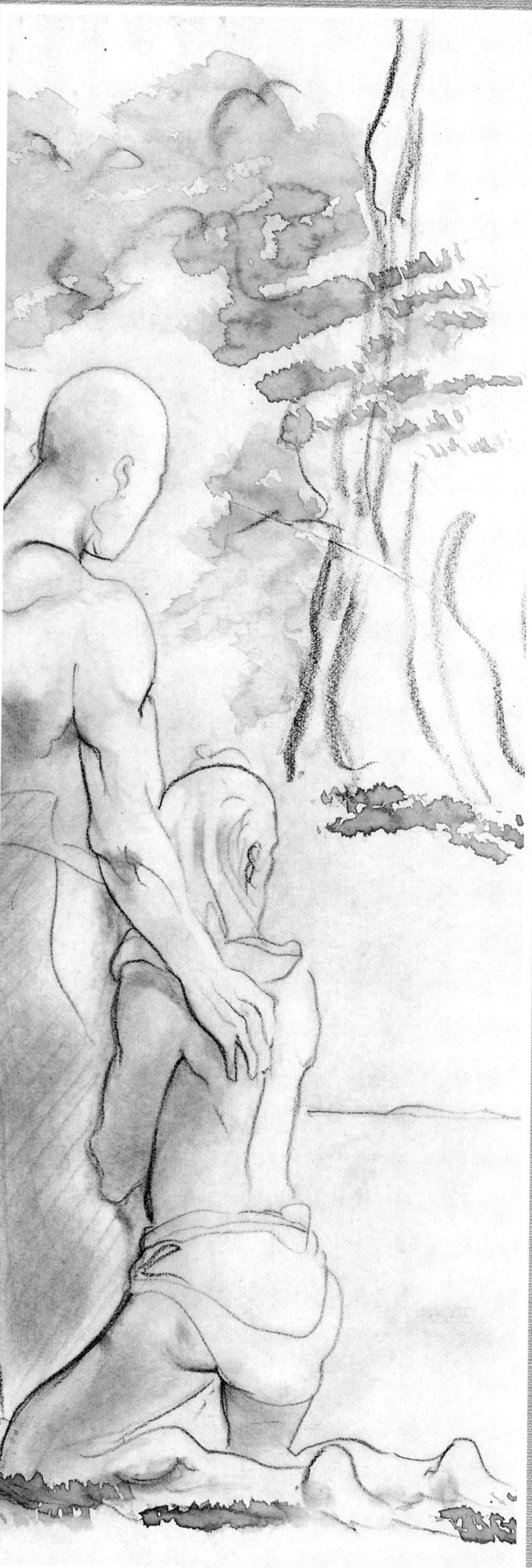

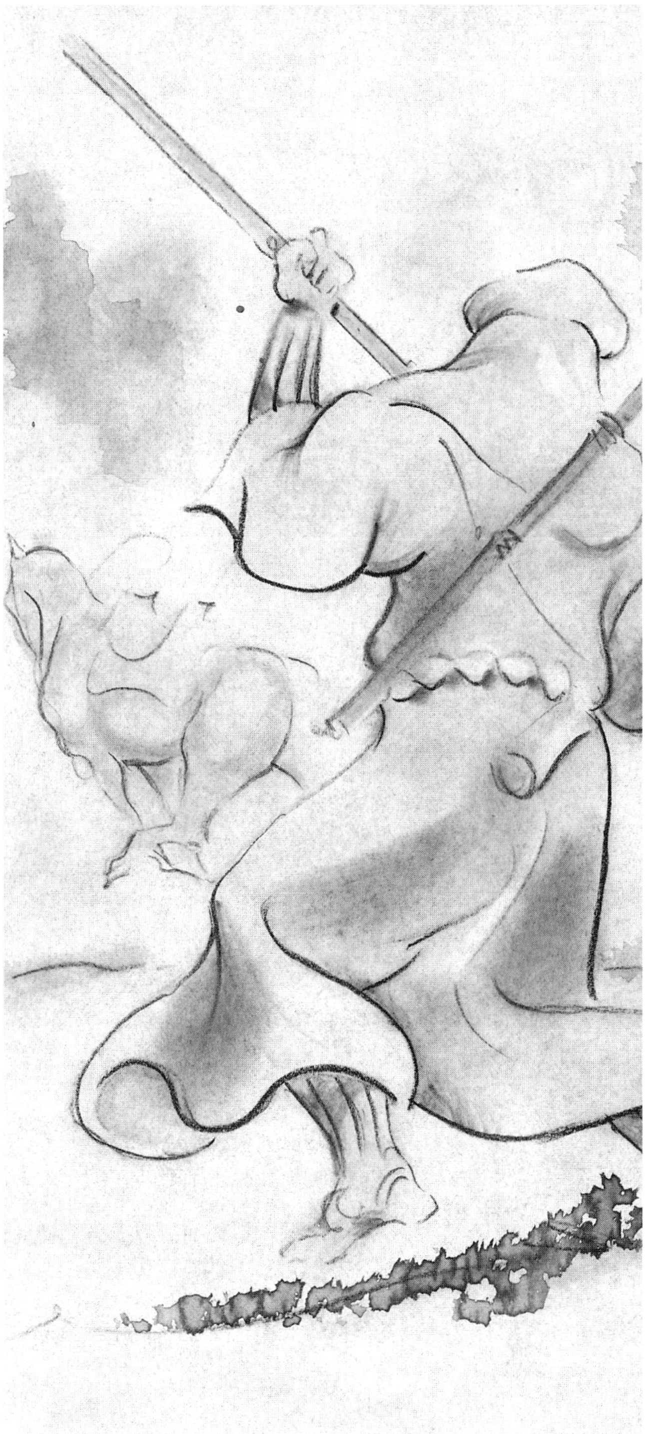

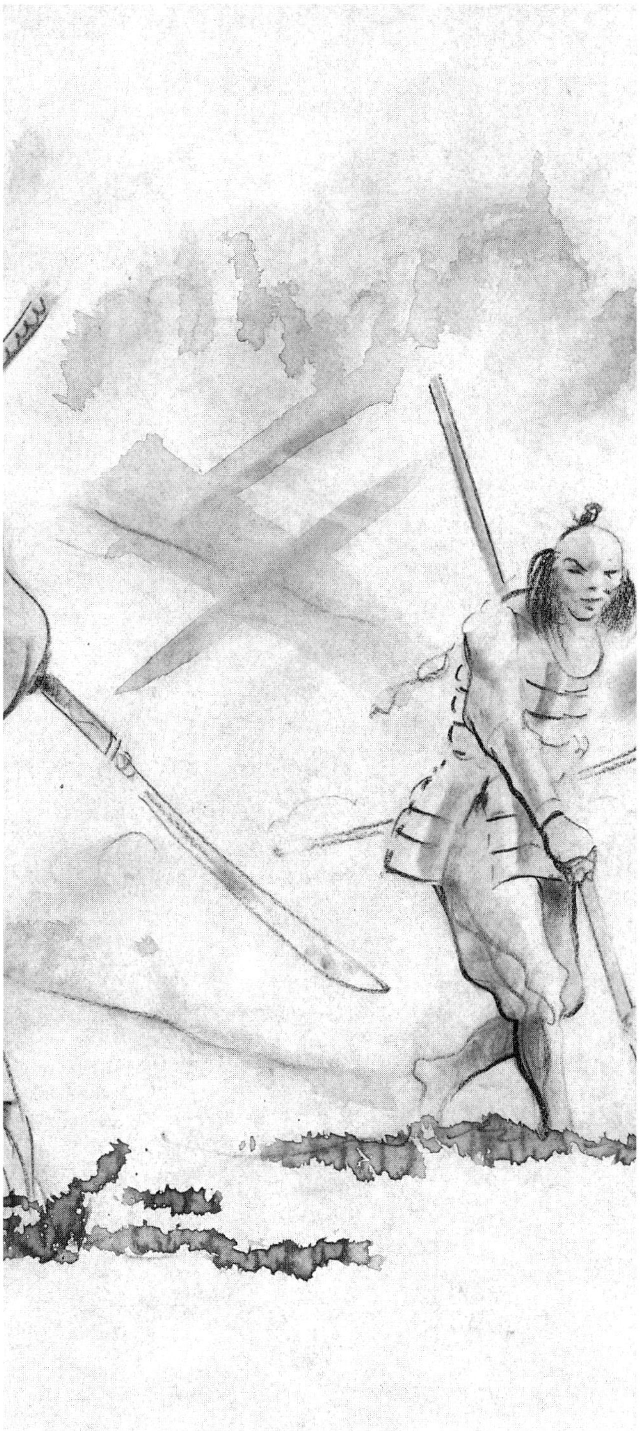

Thus the two men prepare to engage in what they both know will be a mortal bout. Naoto, who has witnessed such encounters before, judges that they are well matched. The Yamabushi is younger and fresh from the training halls, but his all-encompassing hatred for any samurai and his yet untested skill in a battle such as this, may cause an opening, a *suki,* in his strategy. On the other hand, the renegade leader has obviously had both training and battlefield experience. Moreover, his mind, as he has already shown, is devious and full of stratagems. His longstanding hatred for the mountain priests, however, and a certain coarsening of the warrior's fine edge, stemming from the time he has spent among the rabble, may just give the advantage to the Yamabushi.

In any case, Naoto realizes that he must turn his attention to his companions—they are his first responsibility. He motions to Ishi to join Yamako and Kudara near the river's edge.

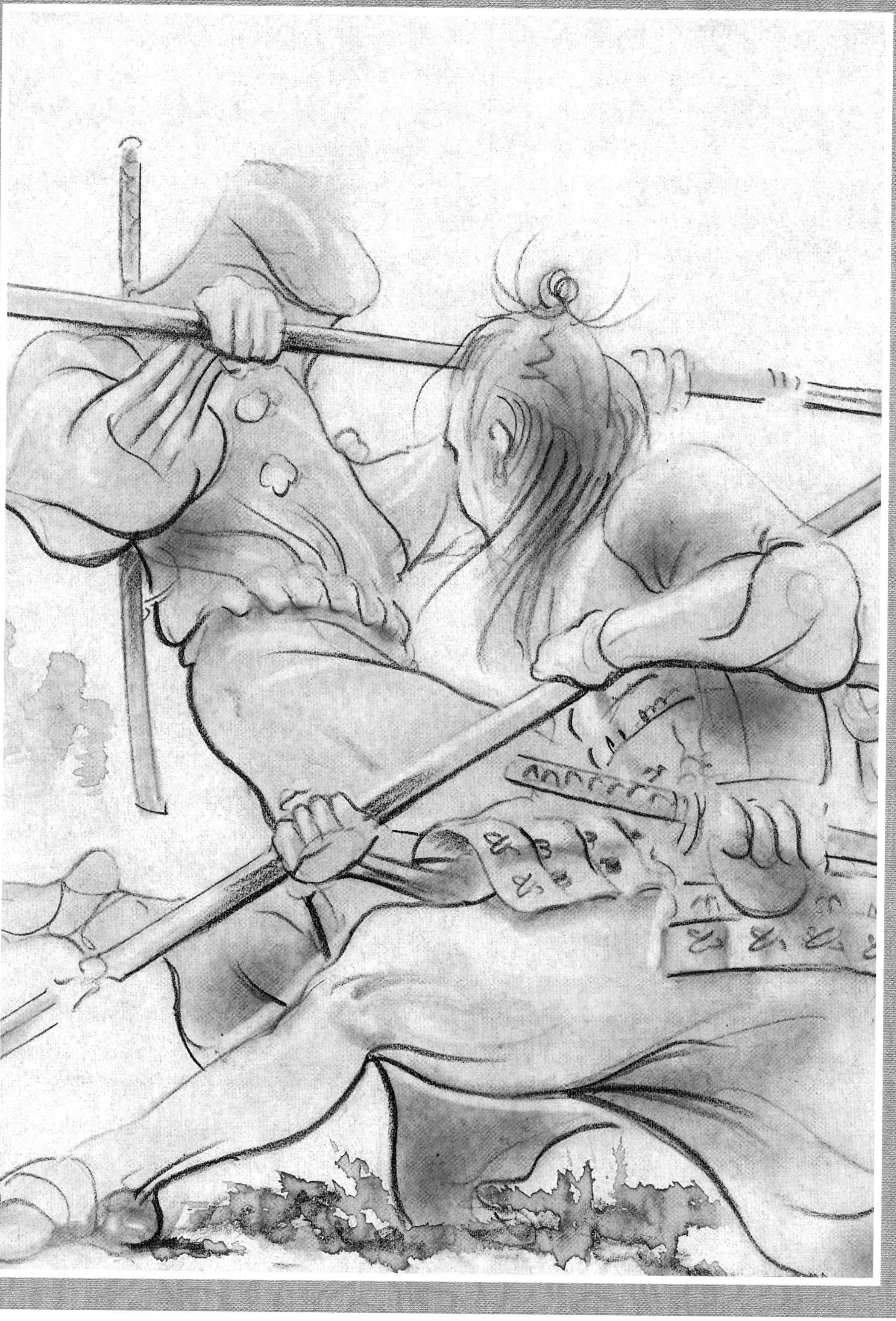

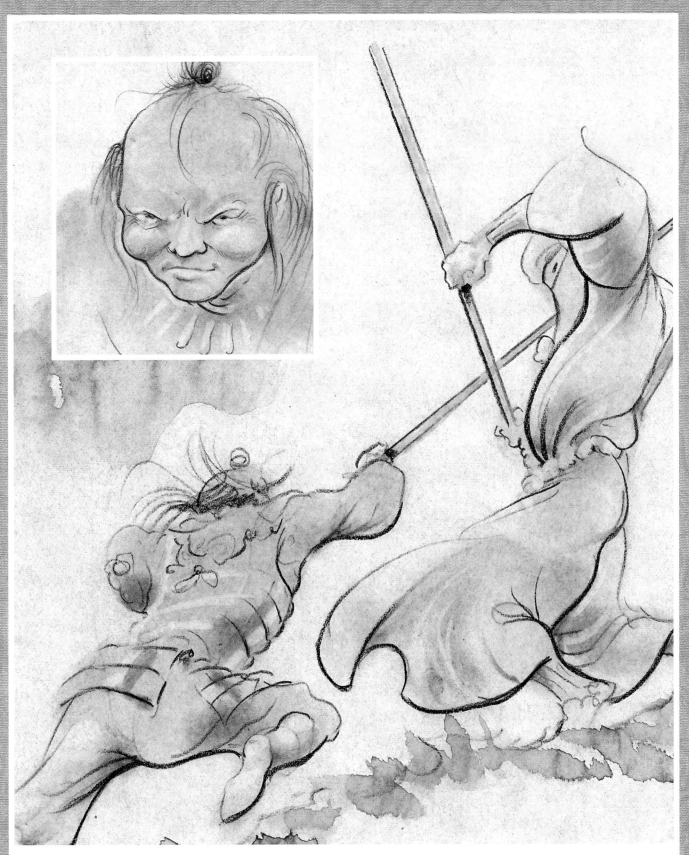

Twice now, the straight blade of Kisaichi's spear has penetrated Haru's guard, and once its butt, as well. The Yamabushi continues to deflect the thrusts but that gleaming point follows him, pressing, probing, and forcing him to retreat across the uneven terrain, where sure-footed movement is difficult. "A price must be paid," the young monk mutters to himself, realizing now the full extent of the difficulties facing his religious order of mountain fighters. Warriors are always dangerous and one should never underestimate any of them. A price must always be paid. . . .

And so he sinks forward, as if about to fall, stretching out his neck, which now makes an attractive target. In a blurring movement, Kisaichi's spear flicks in, but it clangs against the Yamabushi's neck-protector. Before Kisaichi can twist away or retreat, the young monk is beneath his guard and the curved spear clears the ground with a sweep that makes a deep cut in the warrior's tendon.

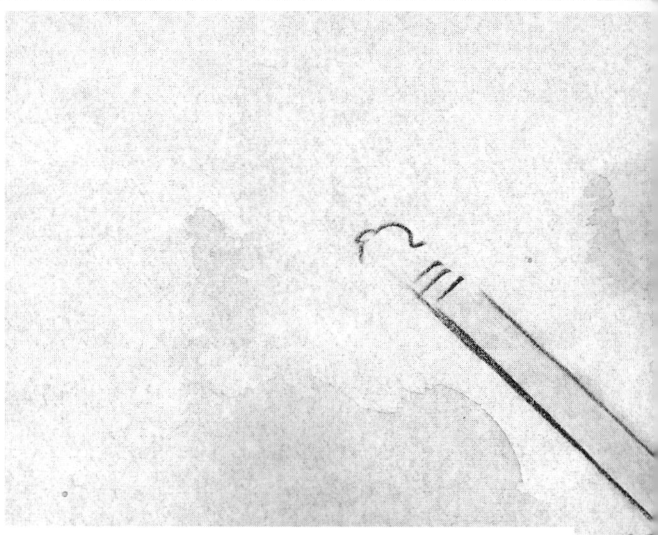

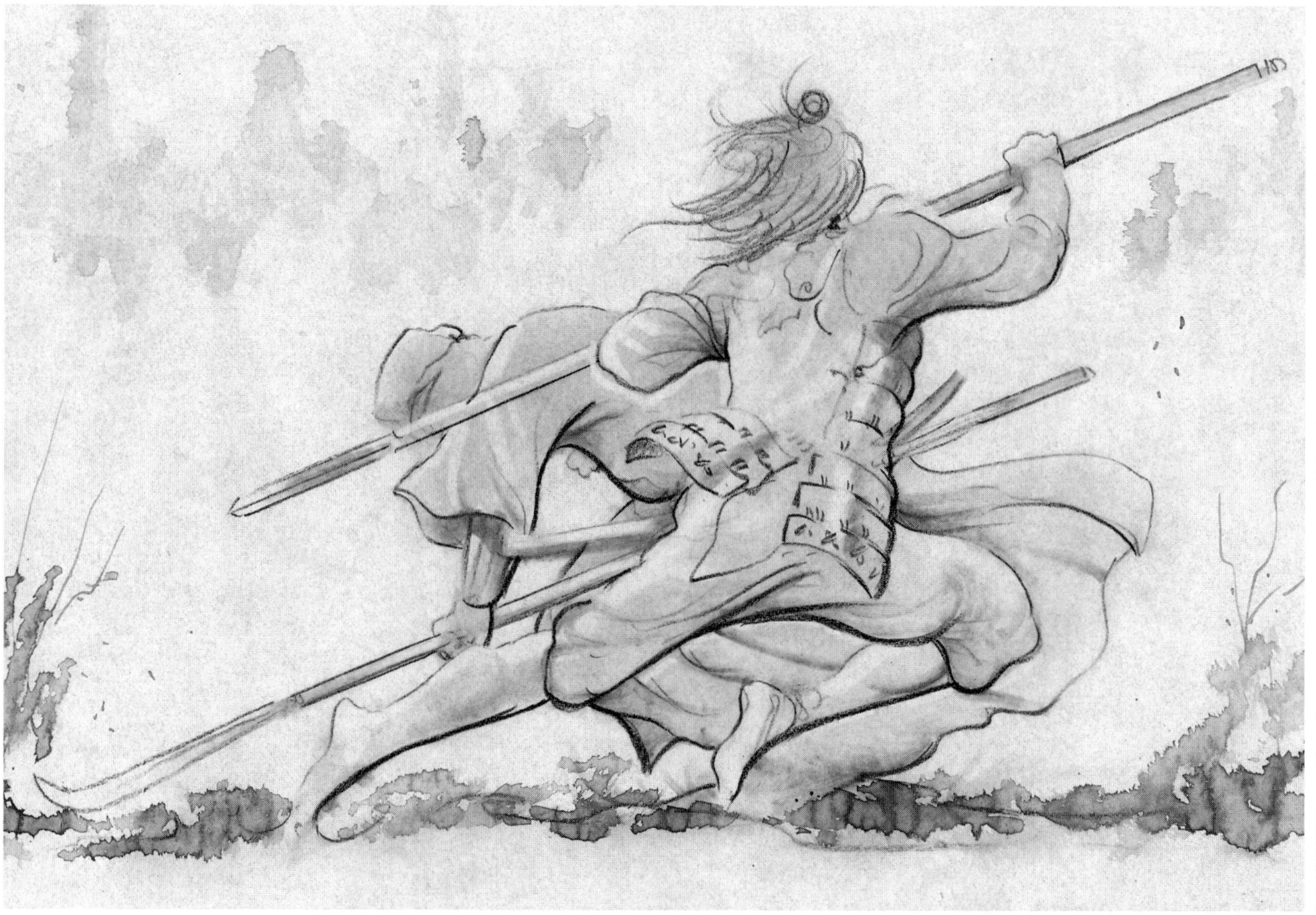

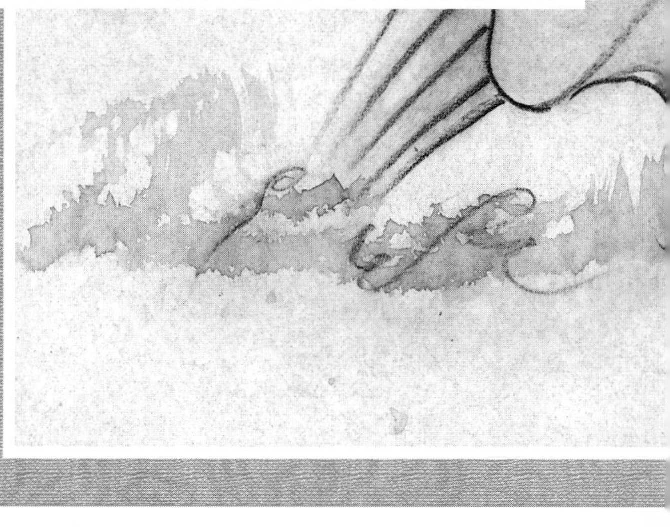

As Kisaichi falls on his back, the curved blade returns to his throat. In a last, savage attempt, the fallen warrior slashes viciously with the sword that he has extracted from its scabbard almost instinctively, but his universe is suddenly engulfed in blackness.

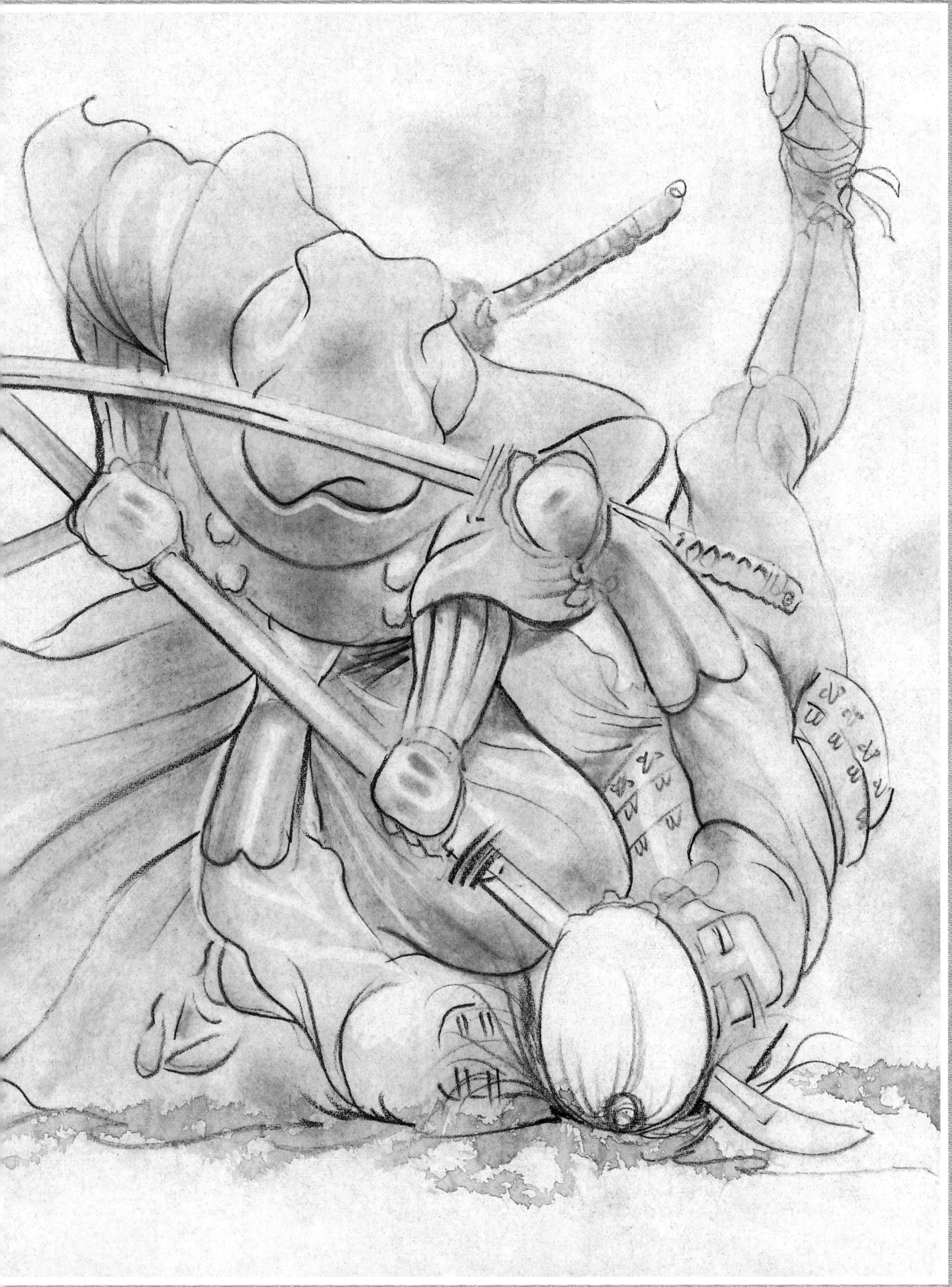

For a few moments, the bleeding Yamabushi stares at his decapitated foe, oblivious to everything else. When at last he emerges from his dazed concentration, his eyes still reflect the shadow of such an encounter's madness. Before that terrifying gaze, the group of renegades scatters, withdrawing with increasing speed and leaving the four bodies of their former companions as mute, lifeless proof of their presence in the pillaged village today.

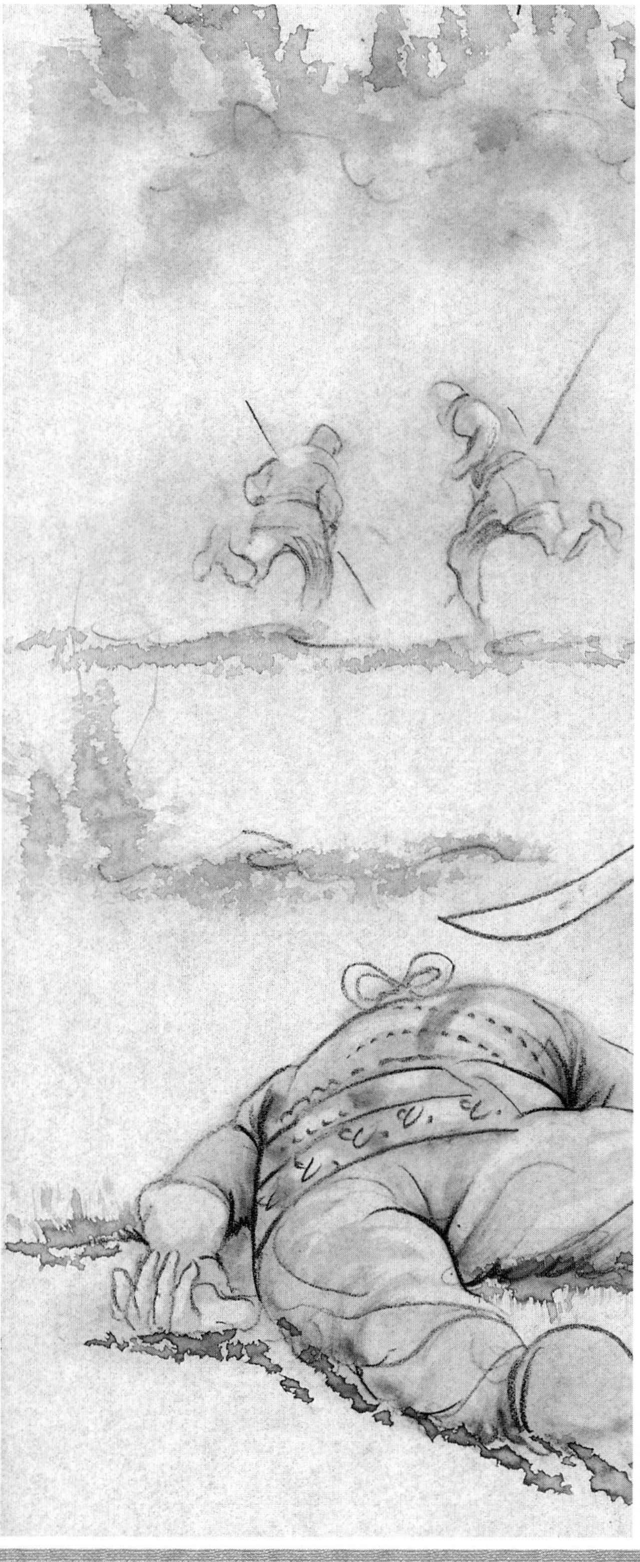

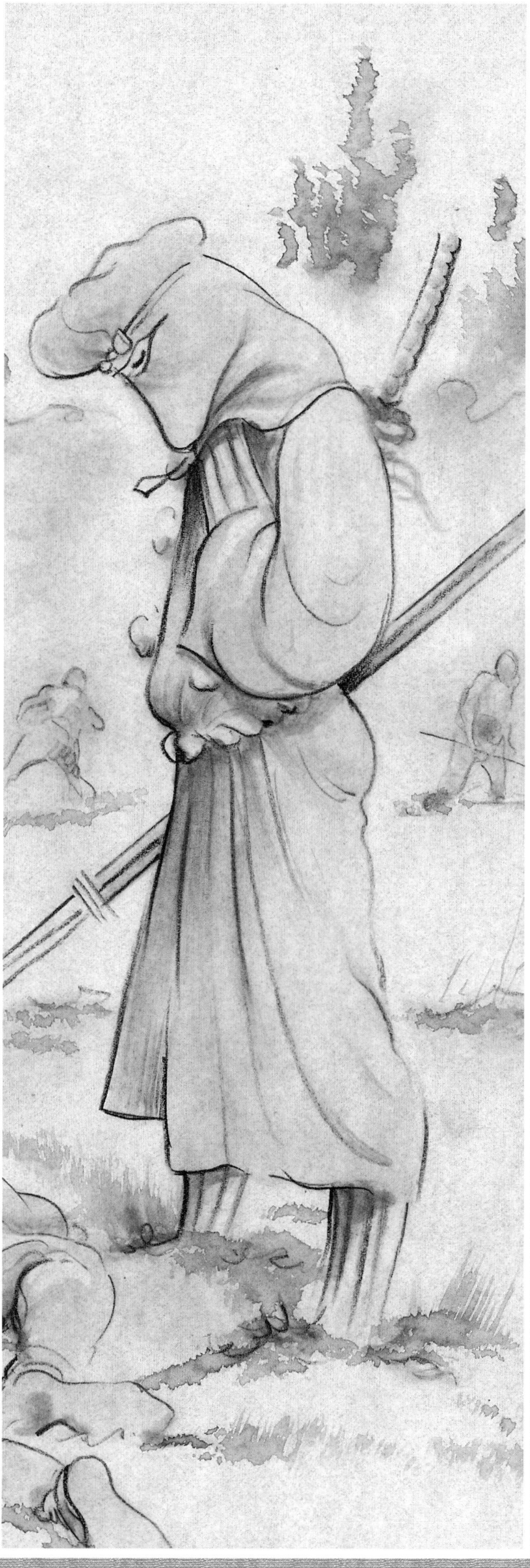

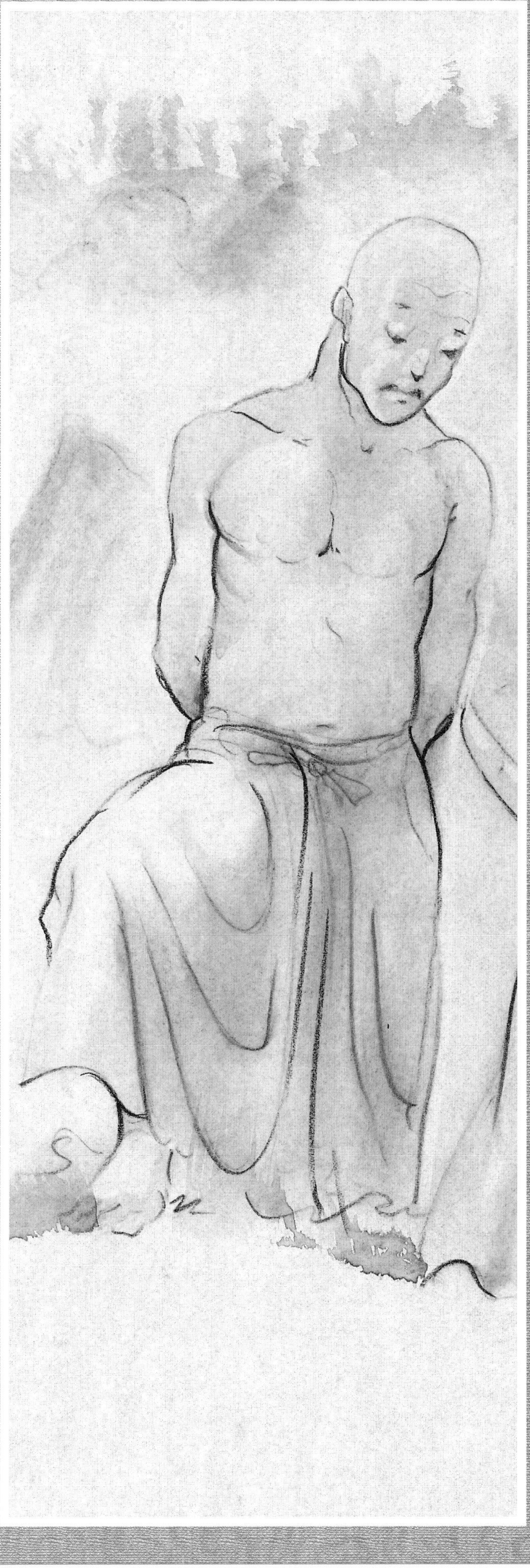

Naoto approaches the silent Yamabushi and says gently: "It is over, Haru. I thank you for saving Ishi's life." He can see that Haru needs time to re-assert control over himself, and so he asks: "Do you need our help?"

The Yamabushi slowly lowers his spear, shaking his head as if to clear it. "It is nothing, Master Naoto. Fortunately, I always wear a neck-protector. But he wasn't bad, that one. And what about you? I watched you with those two would-be spearmen. Incredible! Master Kiyohara would be honored to teach you—that is, if you still need to learn anything more in the way of techniques. We could really decimate the accursed samurai then! Don t you agree?"

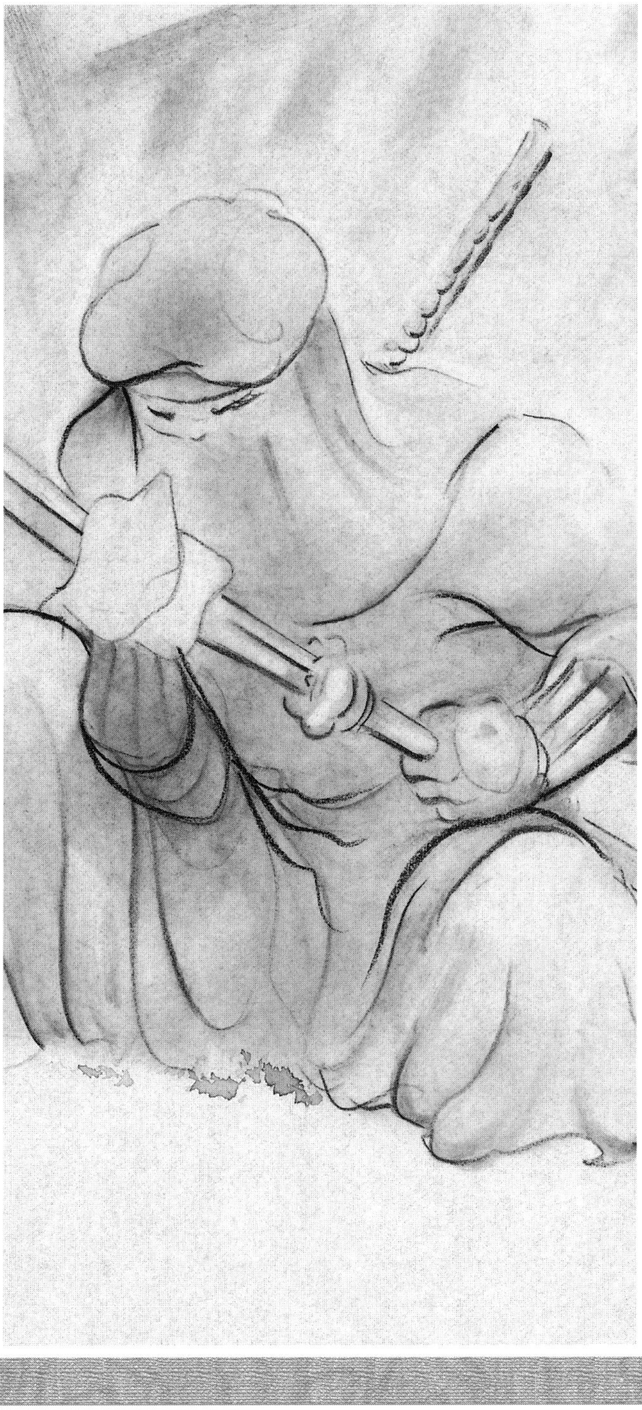

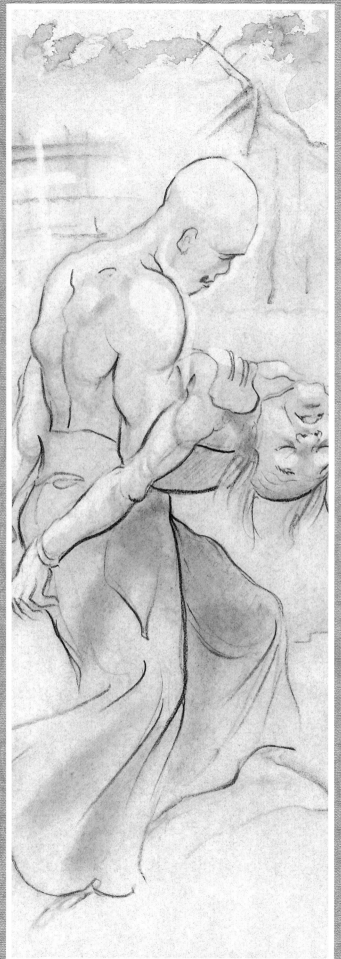

But Naoto has already resumed his work, followed by his three companions. "No, Haru. You know that I cannot agree. Look around you—four more bodies to add to all the others. There has to be a better way."

❀

He sees the Yamabushi frown and draw himself up to his full height, but before he can speak, Naoto continues, "We are grateful to you—but also sad that the price has had to be so high."

❀

The Yamabushi bows and then shrugs: "Perhaps, Master Naoto, until there are more battalions of peacemakers such as yourself, and fewer of those destructive forces we have just encountered, there will continue to be a need for a certain number of Yamabushi like me."

❀

The four pilgrims continue their labors as the Yamabushi watches their efforts. Finally, he addresses Naoto: "I cannot witness violence, aggression, and death without reacting, Master. It is in man's nature to resist the ways of inflicting pain, of causing destruction."

"Indeed it is, Haru," is Naoto's response. "The question then becomes one of means—how is one to resist? If you will join us and spend some time in our school, I am sure some possible answers will suggest themselves to you. But it takes time. Sometimes a very long period is required, and much patience." The Yamabushi shakes his head. "Time is exactly what I don't have right now, Master Naoto." The older man bows and answers: "I hope—we all hope—that you will find it some day soon, Haru."

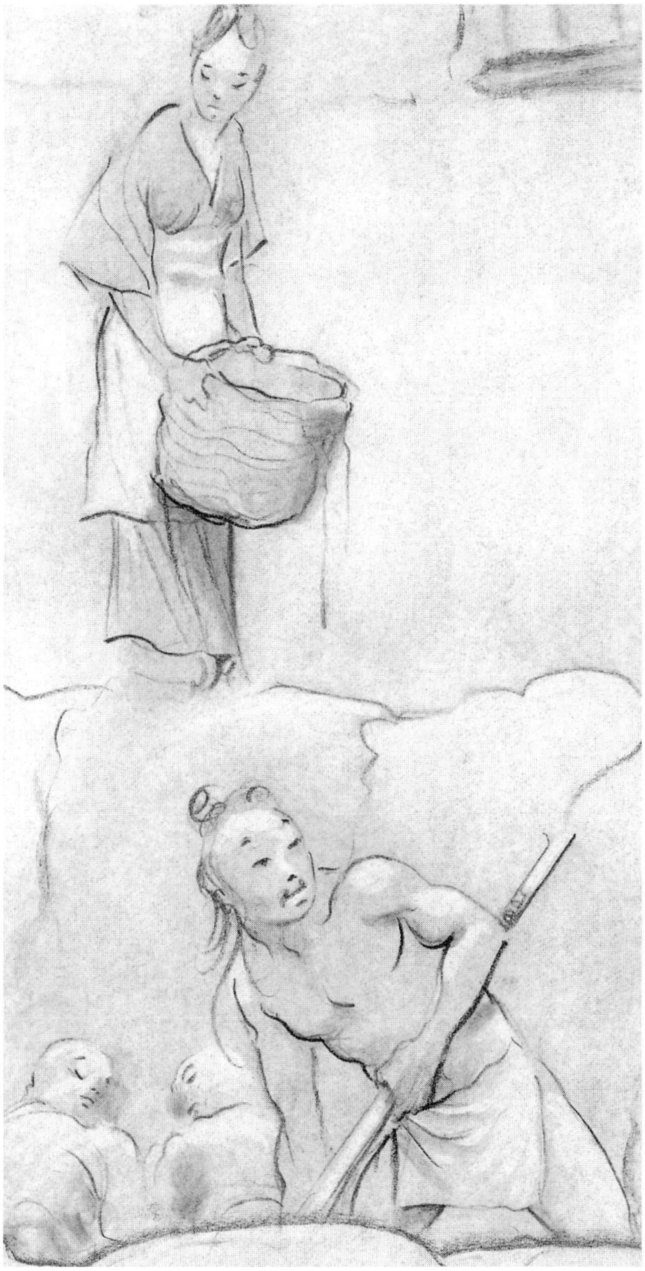

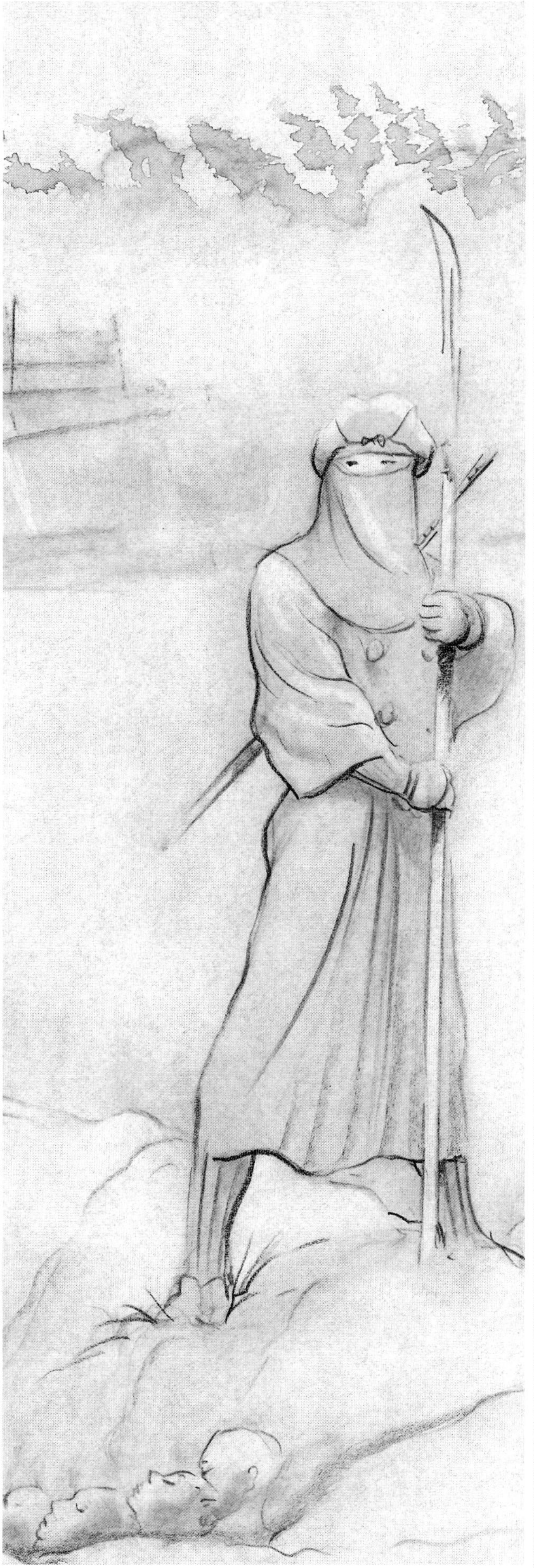

The Yamabushi stands silent as the burial mound is completed and adorned with ritualistic symbols and flowers. As the four companions gather to offer a last prayer on behalf of those who have died, the Yamabushi bows again in their direction and takes his leave. His mind is still suffused with too much anger, and his hands still clutch the spear too tightly for prayerful thoughts to intrude. Before he can address the merciful Amidha again, he must seek the healing silence of the mountains, so that he can face the shrine once more and perform properly the rites of purification.

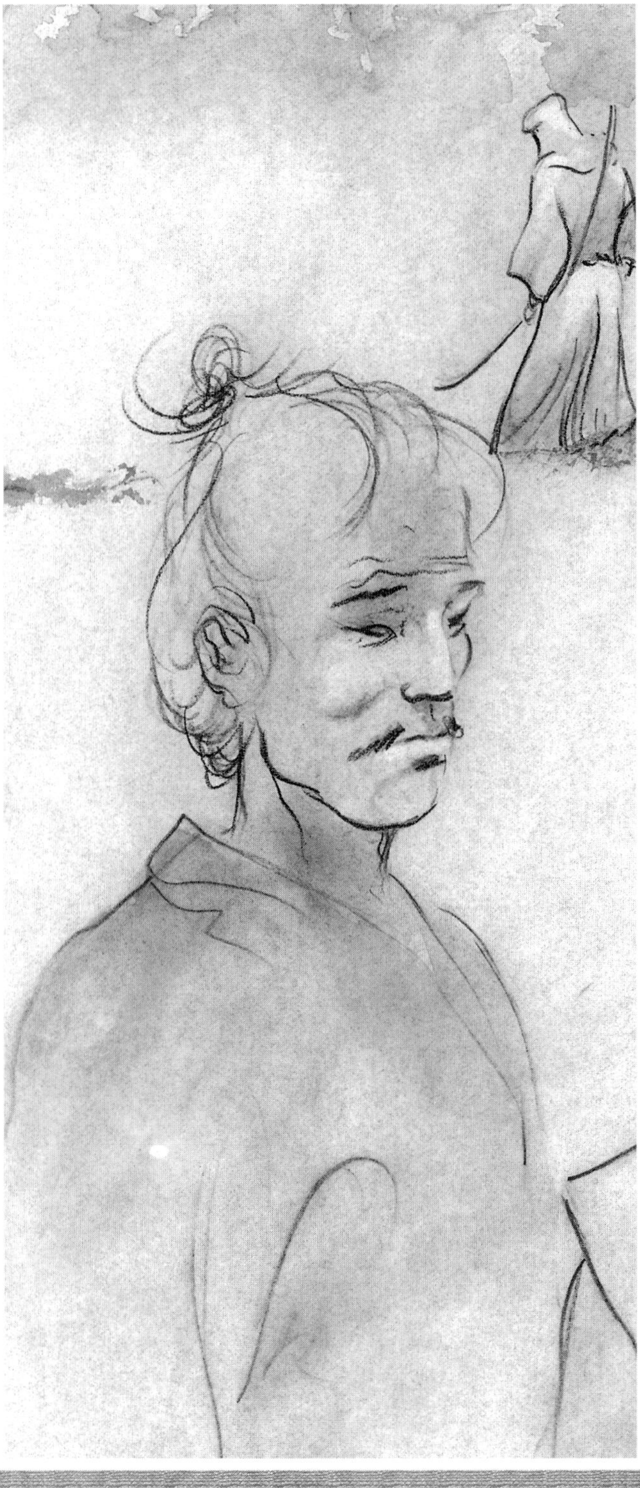

Naoto's gaze follows the departing figure until the Yamabushi can no longer be seen, disappearing into the morning mist. With a sigh, the priest turns away. The road to their Yadon Temple still lies before them, and he, too, needs the silence the woods can provide if he is to re-examine the recent events and try to make some sense of the madness they have encountered. He looks at his three companions and wonders if they are asking themselves the same questions with which he is grappling, or if they have accepted the world as it seems to be today, bleak and without peace or security.

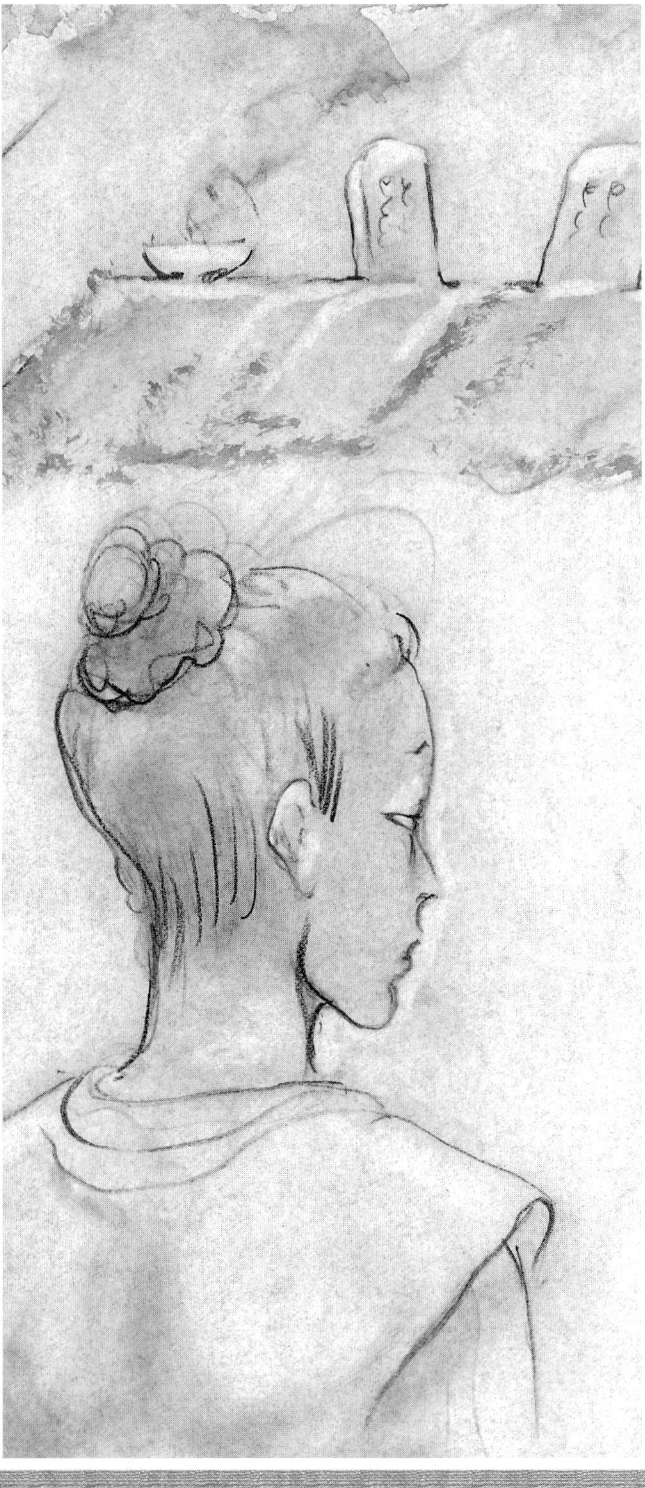

No, he tells himself, lifting his eyes toward heaven. No. Kudara is an artist who continues to create useful and beautiful things with his own hands. The other two are young people who have already felt the chilling shadow of death skim across their bodies and yet, here they still are, trying to make amends for the vile deeds of others. There is no reason for despair. Great evil there may be, but equally great hope rises strongly to contend against it. *Yes*, great hope still beckons. . . .

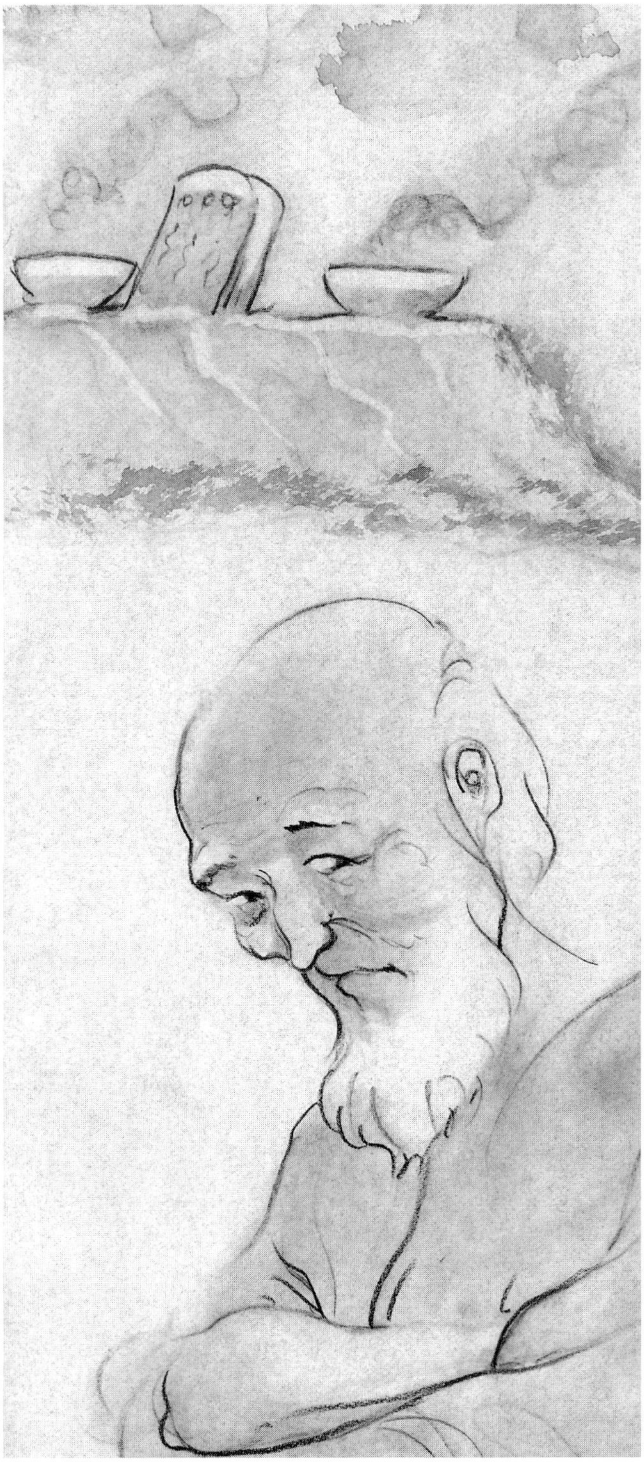

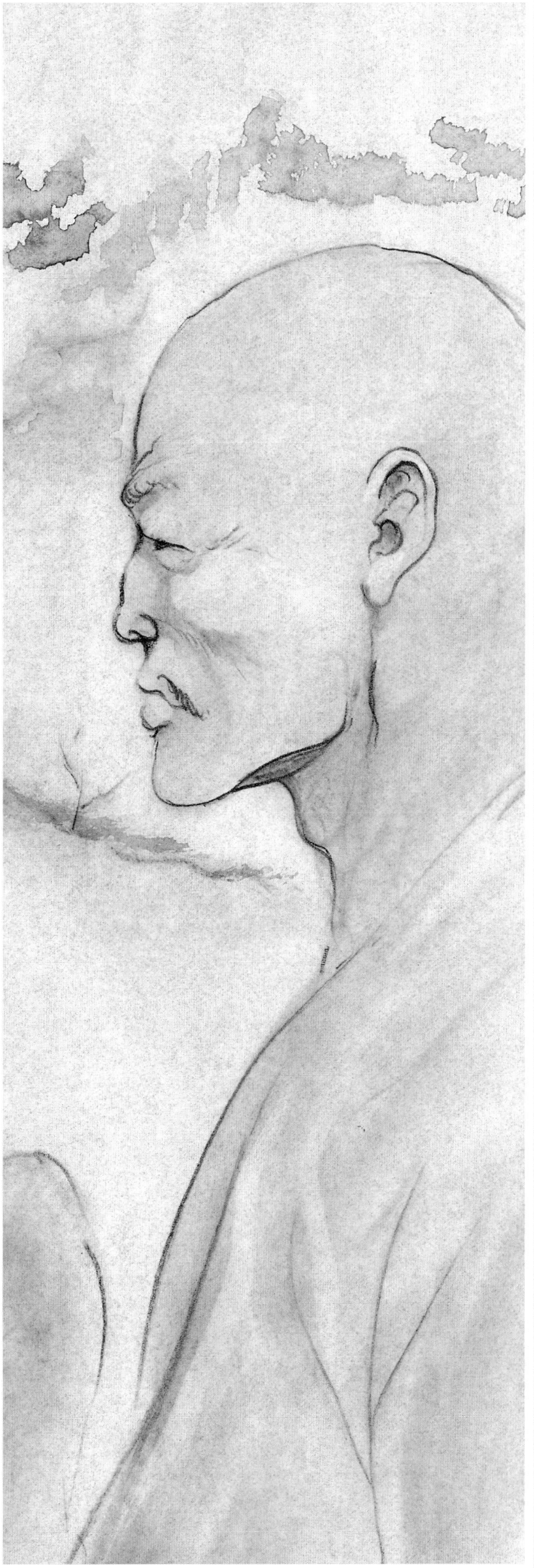

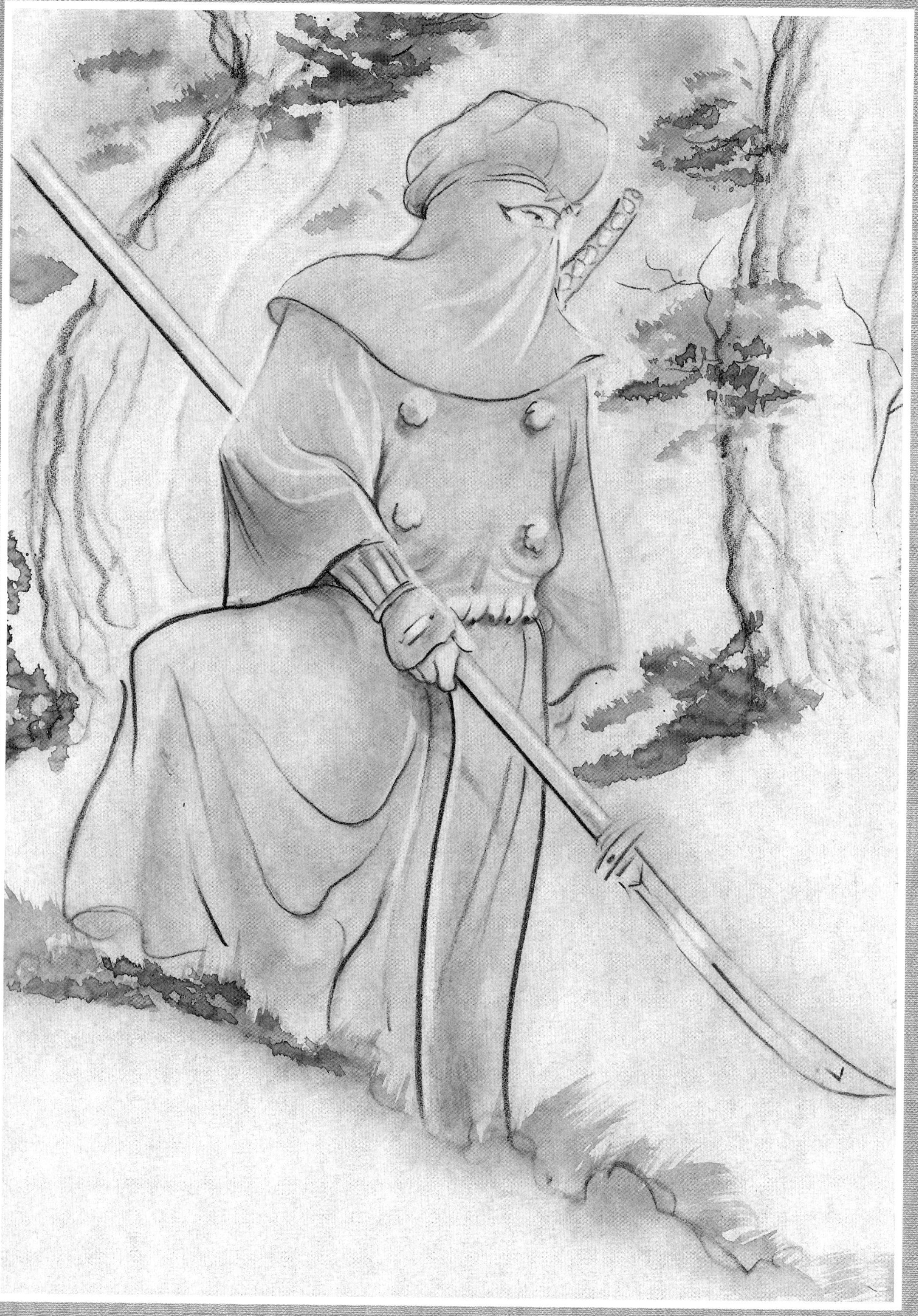

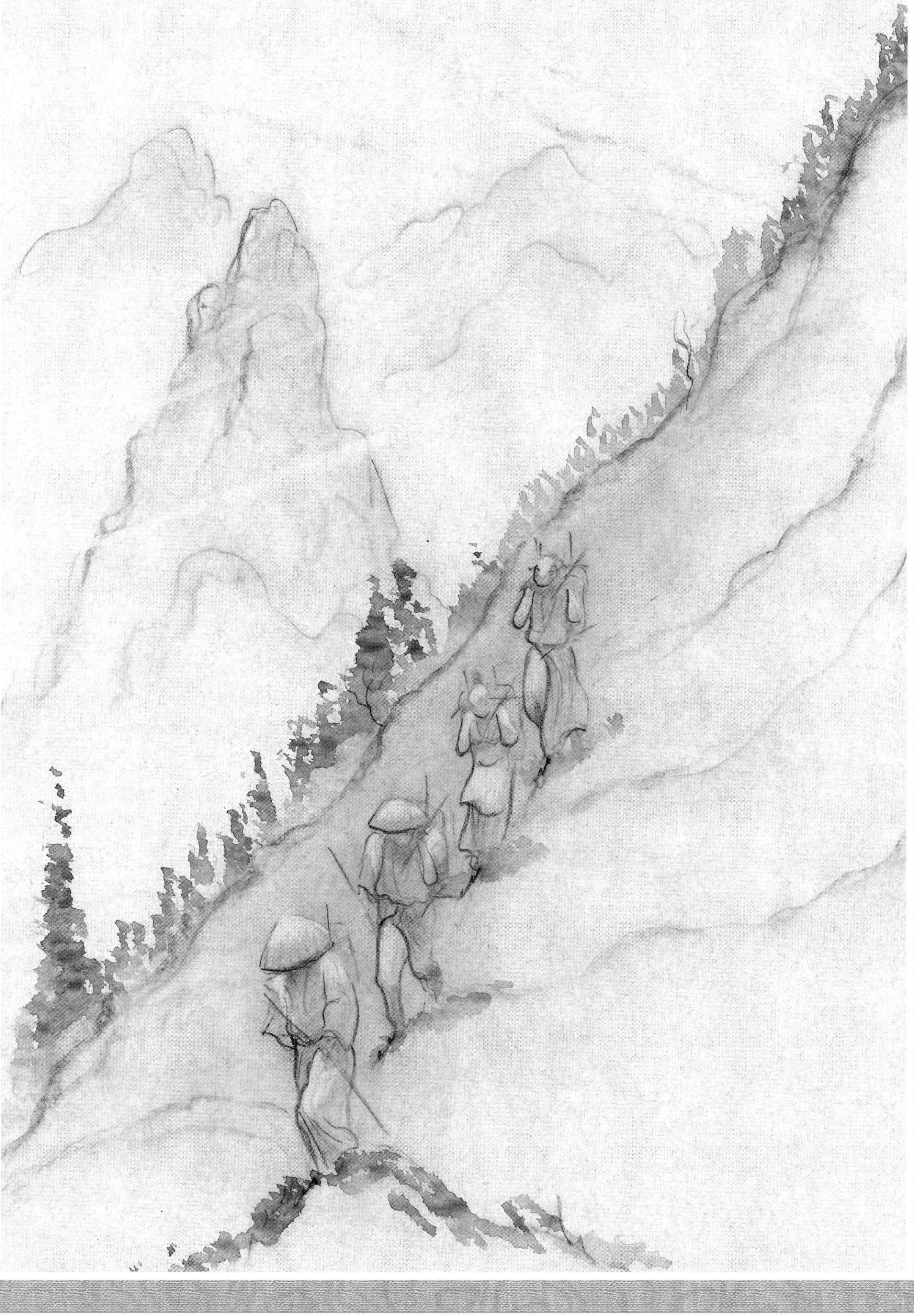

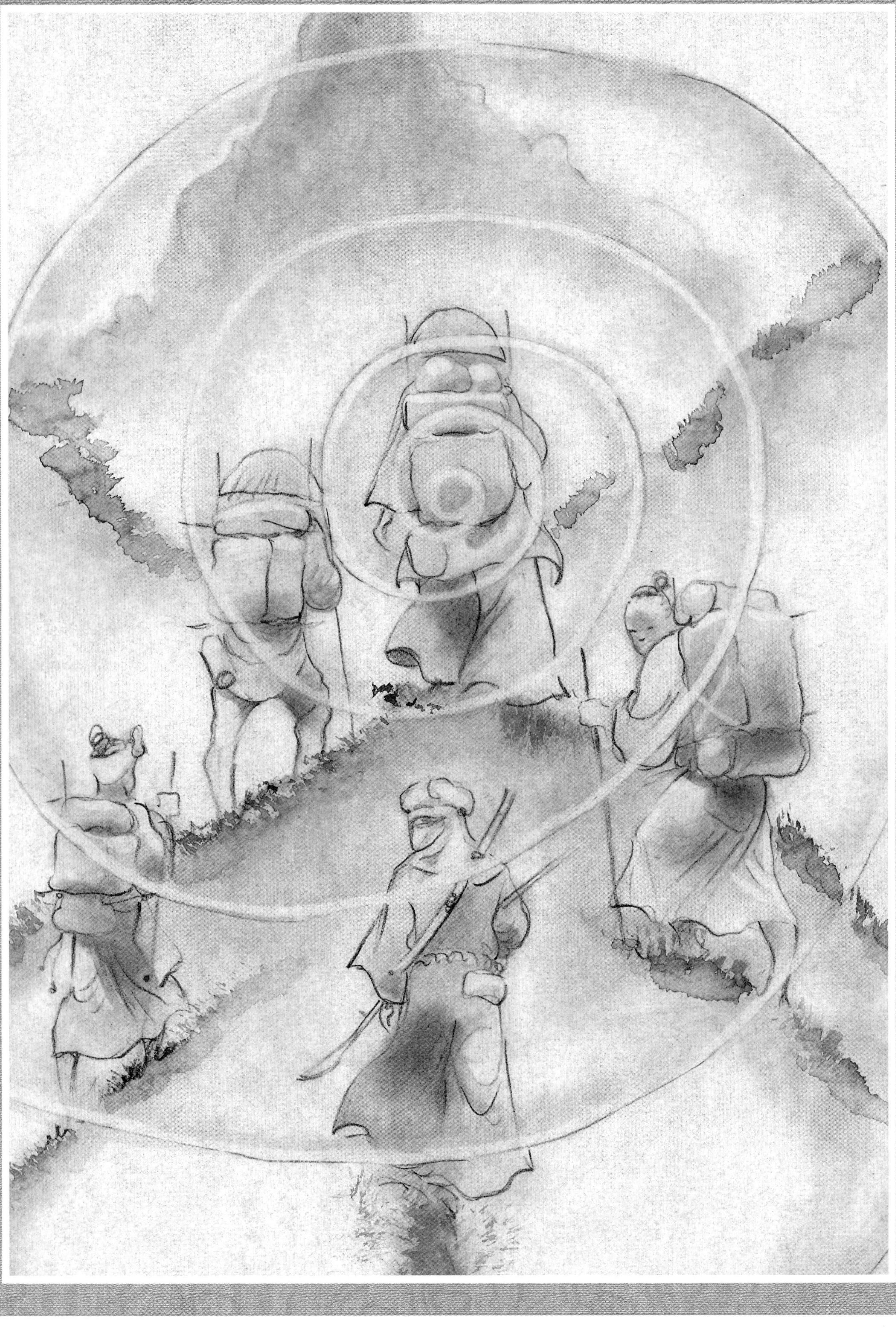

INTERLUDE

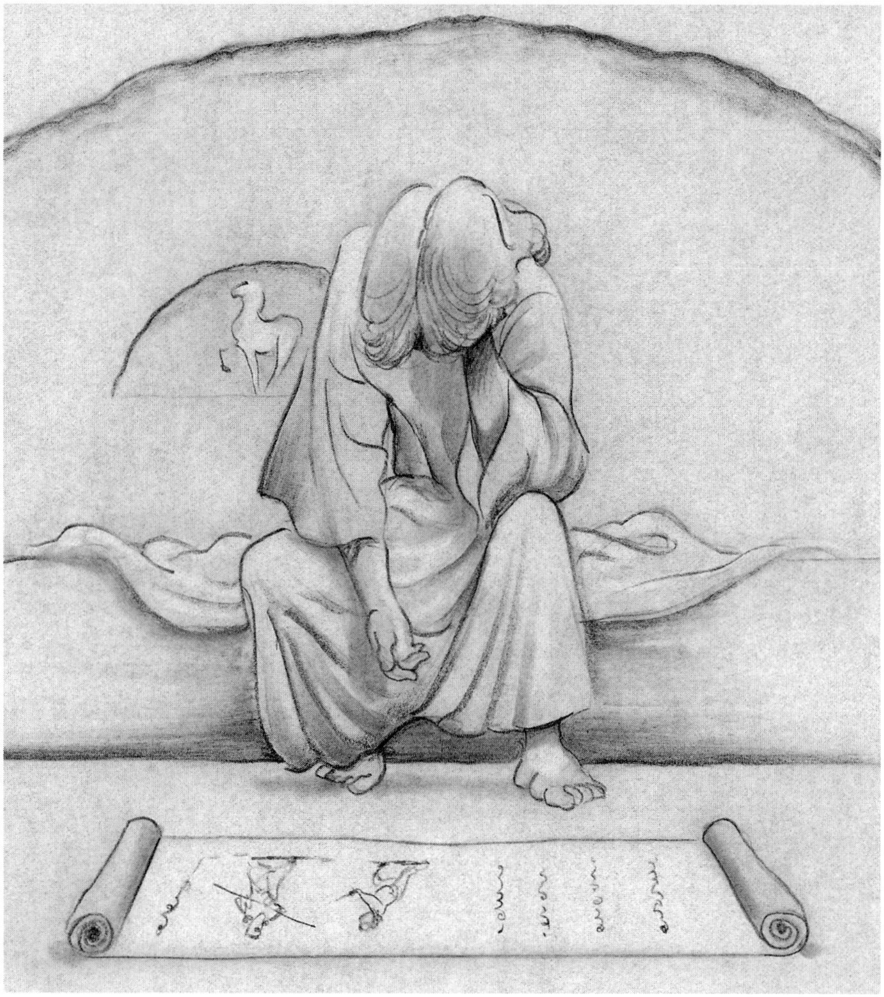

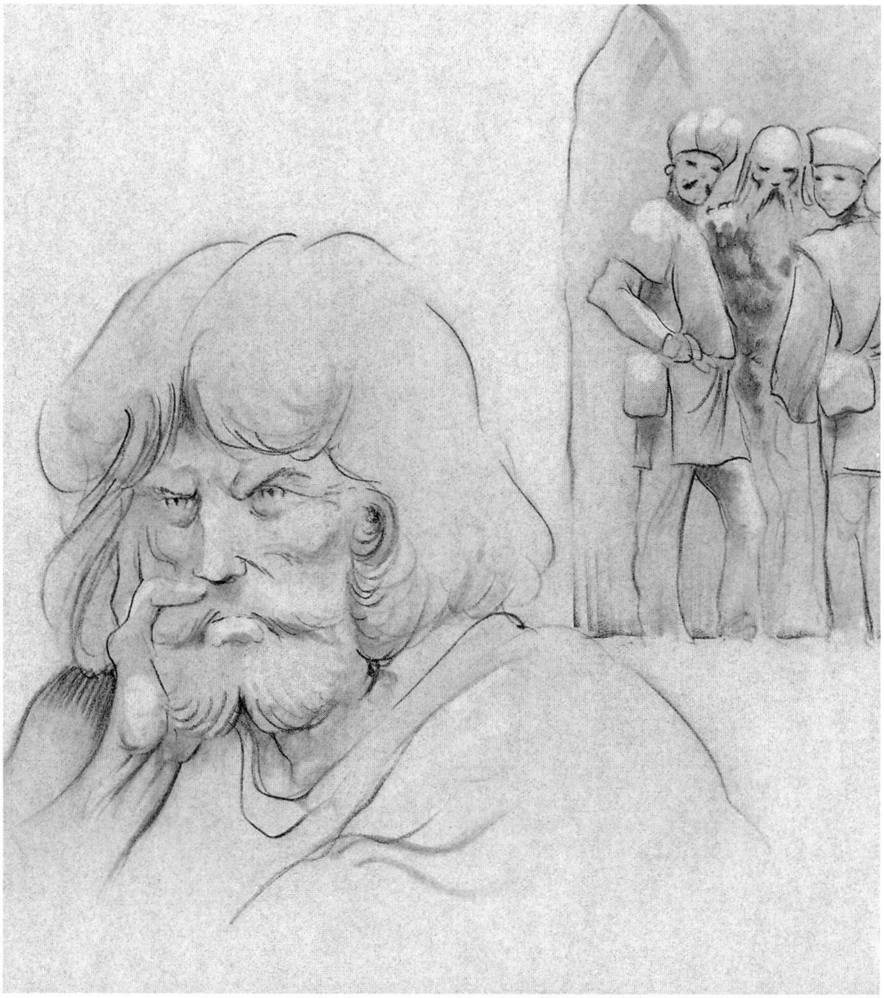

Père Dominic held the *Yamabushi* scroll in his hands for some time after he had finished reading it, staring into space with a bemused expression on his face. Then, with a sudden surge of energy, he rolled up the scroll, placed it carefully to one side, and began pacing back and forth.

Although he was usually eager to discuss his most recent reading with the Residents, he did not seek them out at once this time, but instead remained withdrawn for several days.

His obviously unsettled state of mind did not go unnoticed, however, and several of the Residents expressed their concern to Yu Xia that Père Dominic's recovery might be impeded if he did not find an outlet for his troubled thoughts.

More then one Resident wondered aloud if the tale of the *Yamabushi*, with its descriptions of the harsh realities that had prevailed in the Empire during an earlier age, of the unrestrained violence that had spread throughout the land as monasteries were burned to the ground and villages were pillaged and emptied of their inhabitants, had not proved too much for a man of the cloth who had only recently been subjected himself to similar threats of annihilation.

Perhaps he had found the events that were presented so dramatically in the tale of the *Yamabushi* to be so personally relevant that any discussion of them was too painful to be contemplated?

As a group of the Residents debated the issue near Père Dominic's alcove a few days later, it was Ma Hui who, with her usual bluntness, voiced an exasperated suggestion that reverberated beneath the vaults of the First Level until it reached even Père Dominic's ears. "In the name of the Ultimate Beginning, why don't you just ask him?" Silence settled like a stone as the echo of her words died away under the arches.

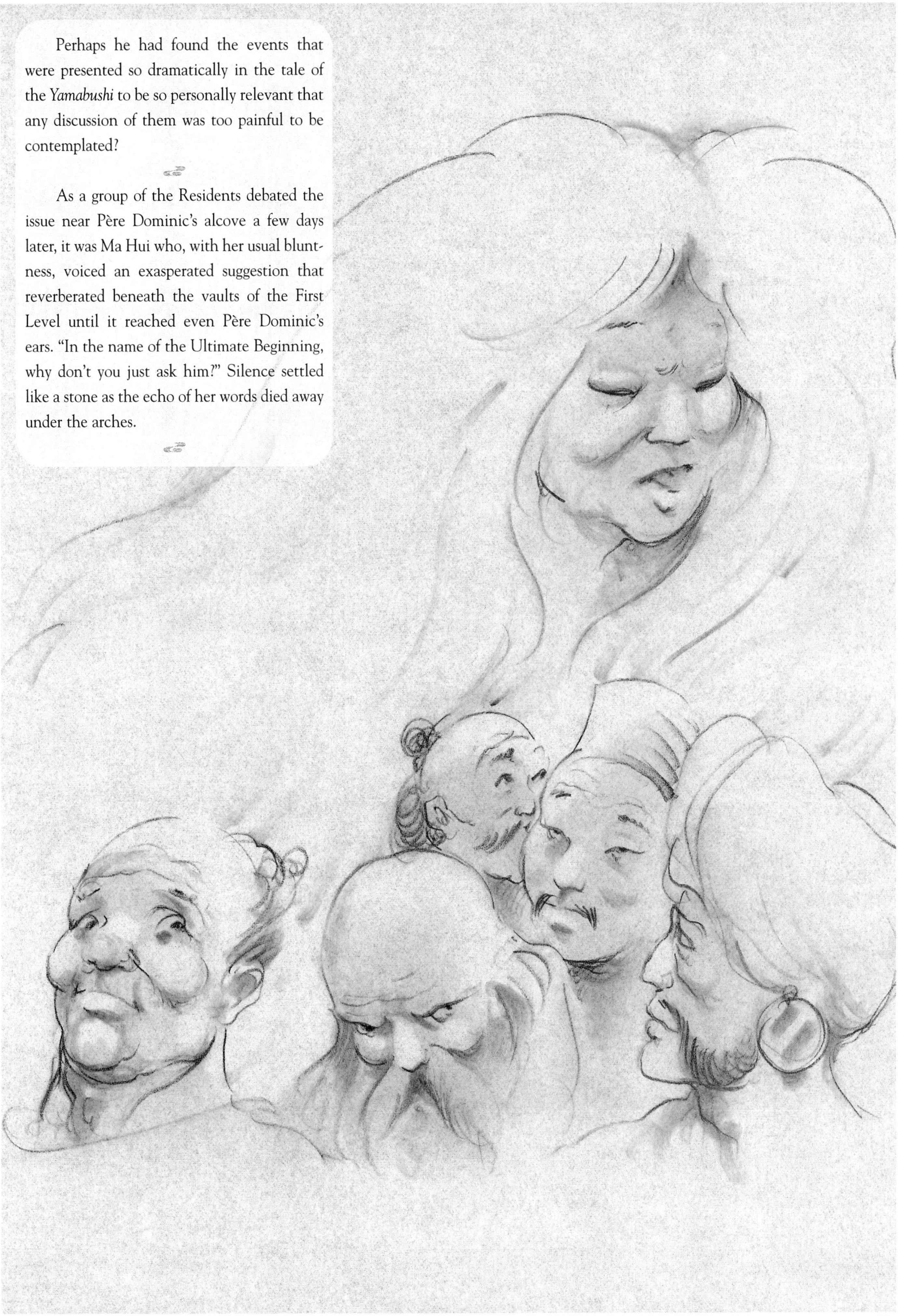

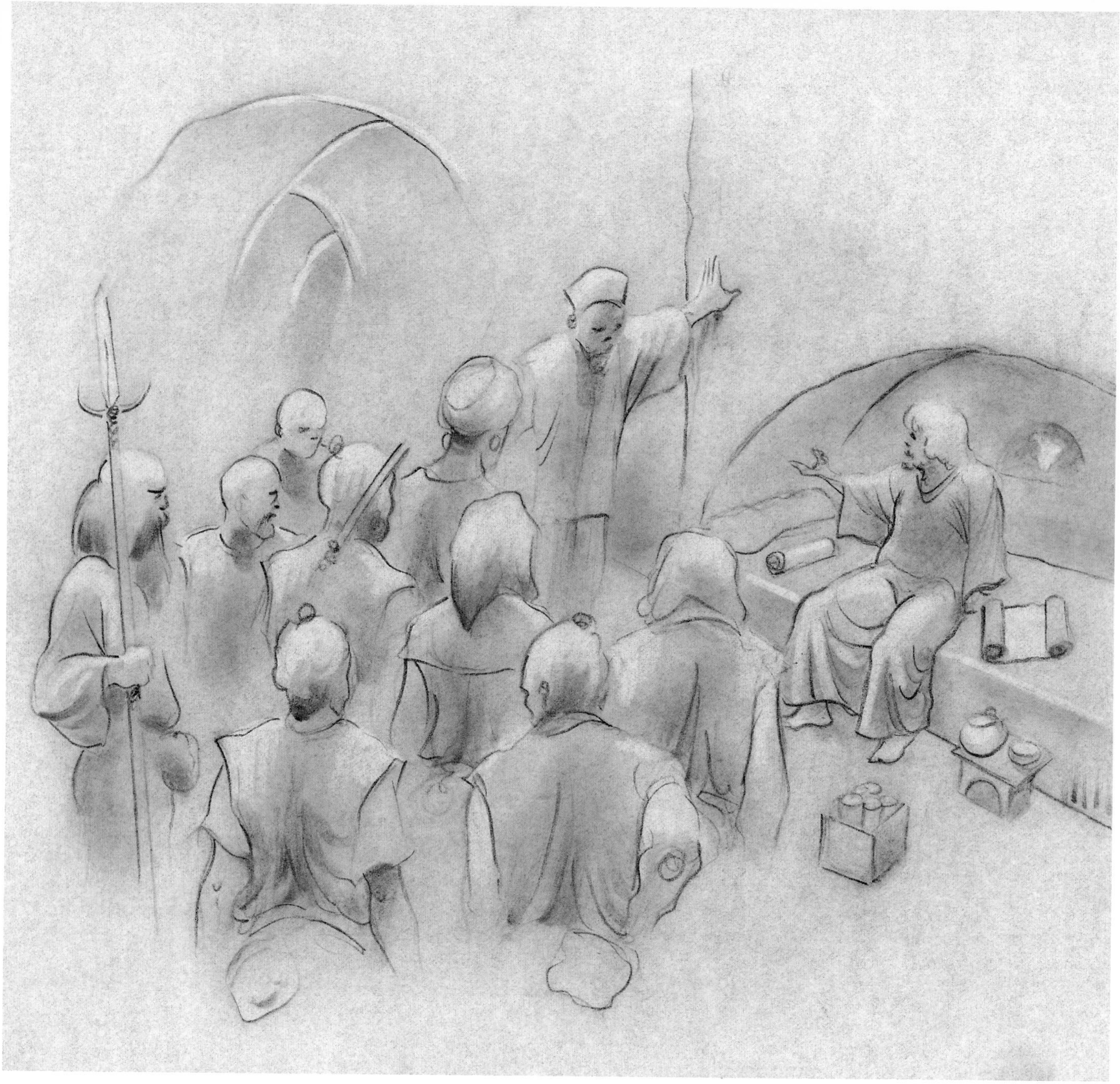

Without further hesitation, the Residents quietly approached Père Dominic's alcove, filling the space in and around it to capacity. Their very presence encouraged him to shake off whatever dark thoughts might have been oppressing him, and he took a deep breath before he spoke.

"When some perplexing issue arises," he explained, "it has always been my inclination to pursue all the aspects of that issue to virtually the total exclusion of everything else. And I must confess to you that my recent visit to the level above this one, and the overall tone of this singular tale, have preoccupied me greatly. I regret any concern I may have caused you, since you have become my friends—as well as my hosts and healers. Permit me to apologize . . ."

Somewhat reassured, the Residents inquired as to the nature of this "issue" which seemed, like a dragon in Chinese mythology, to have transported their guest from the physical world into metaphysical realms, soaring far above the clouds.

With a slight frown, Père Dominic replied: "Well, both the fleeting glimpses I had of the Second Level, and the tale in this manuscript, have reformulated for me a vexing dilemma whose solution has always evaded me . . ."

"Which is, precisely?" Yi Tai inquired.

"In the simplest of terms at this point, I would say that it is the intractable problem of the effective and appropriate response to violence. In the *Yamabushi* scroll, several types of responses are evident, some of which convey the impression—and the hope—that certain methods of combat, as employed by different individuals in this tale, may offer a possible solution . . ."

"Which would be?" The Resident called Dusan, a sturdy figure who had been born in a small Serbian town, asked softly but with a glint in his eyes that told Père Dominic this man and a number of the elder Residents in the group obviously had their own ideas about the issue with which he was now struggling.

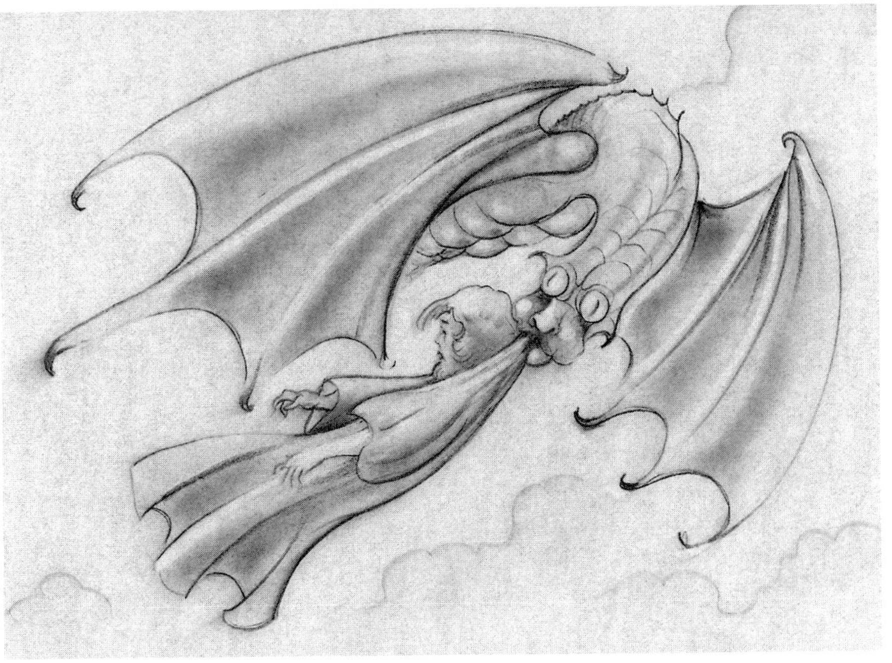

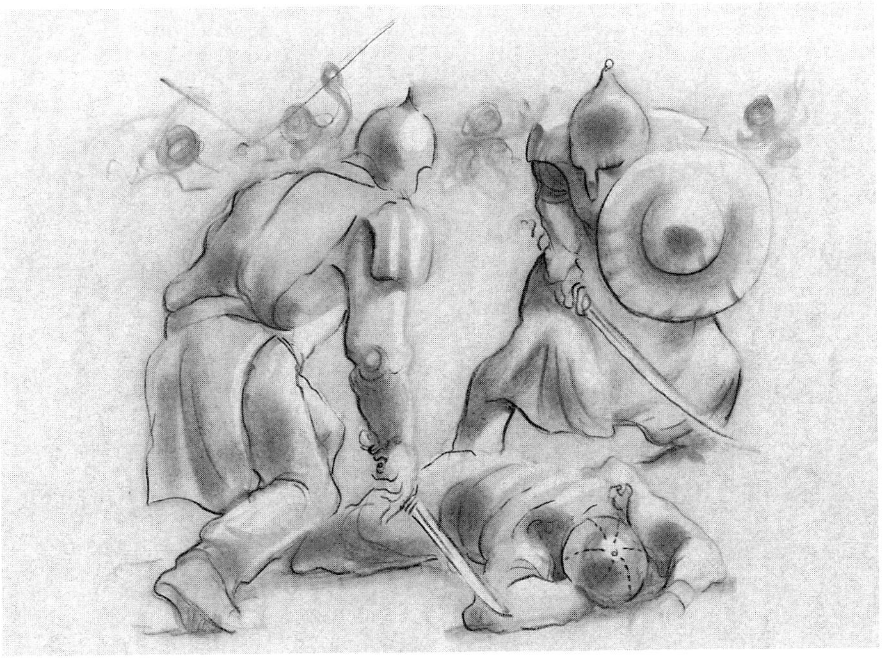

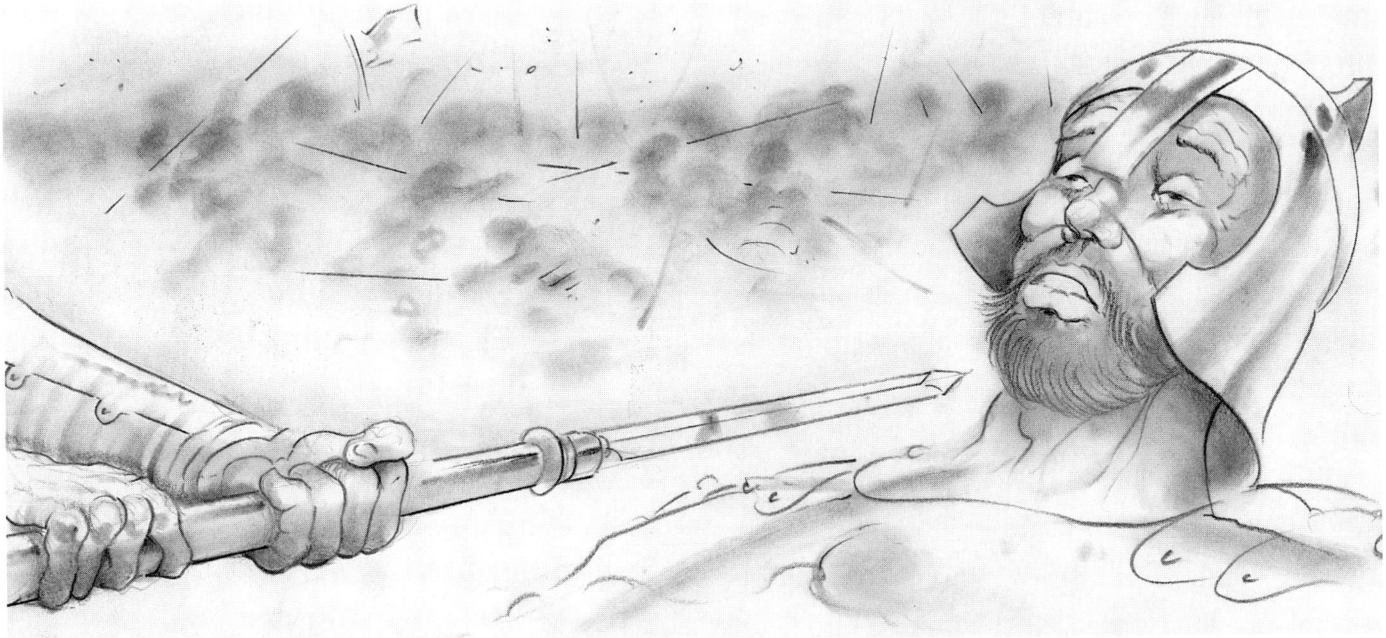

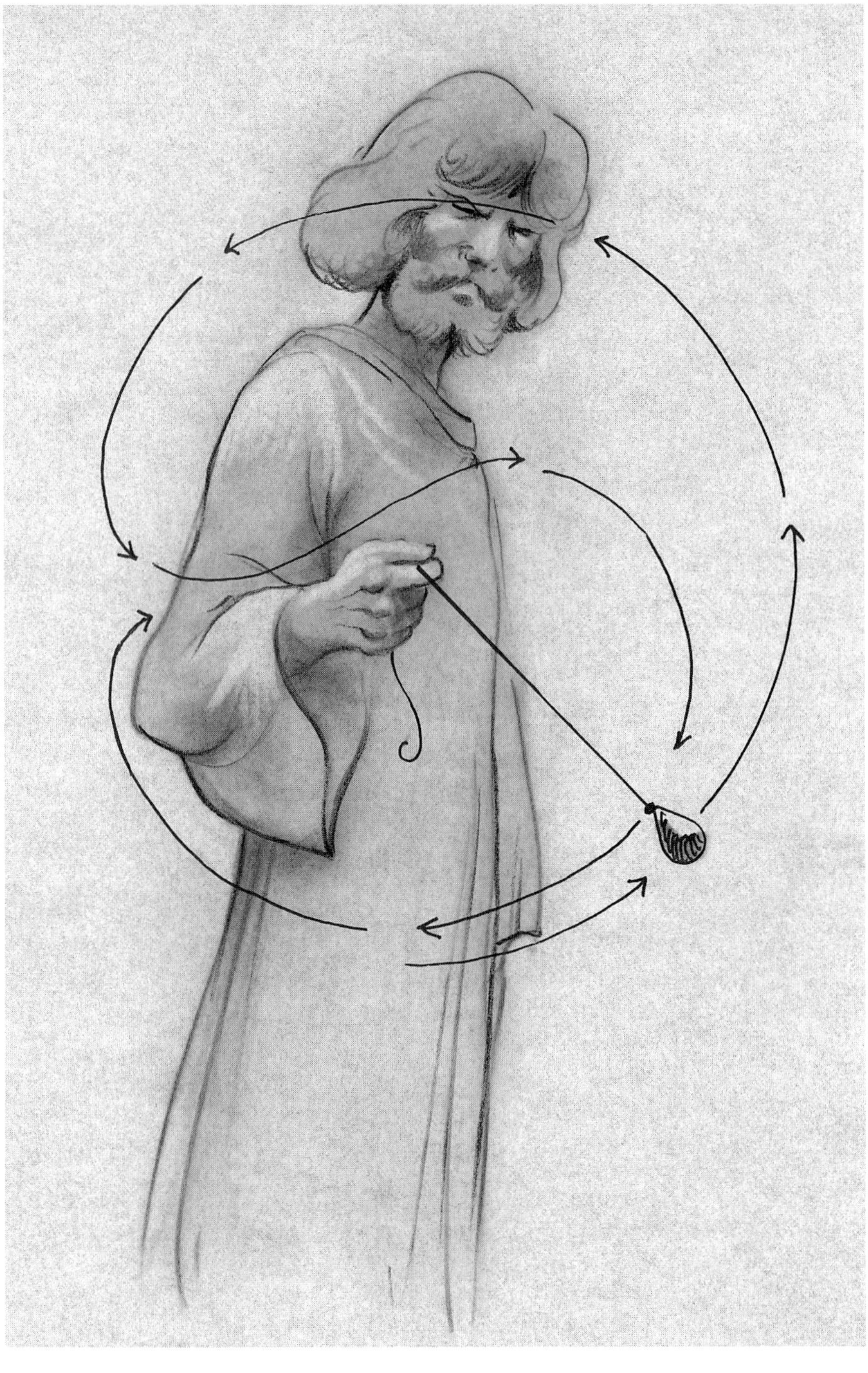

As if aware that he might be stepping onto shifting sands, Père Dominic responded hesitantly: "Well, consider the reaction of Master Naoto, the leader of the small group who return to the village to bury the dead. Twice he is attacked by members of Kisaichi's gang of rogues, and in both instances, he avoids their direct thrusts and, catching them in full motion, as I understand it, spins them into full flight, leaving them shaken and confused, but basically unhurt—at least not irreversibly. It is a type of defense that struck me as quite unusual because it is so inherently different from the response in kind to any attack that I witnessed during my youth in Europe and later, while traveling in the East. And it seemed even more unusual to me because the impression conveyed in the tale is that this form of defense was both effective and appropriate to Master Naoto's vision of life . . ."

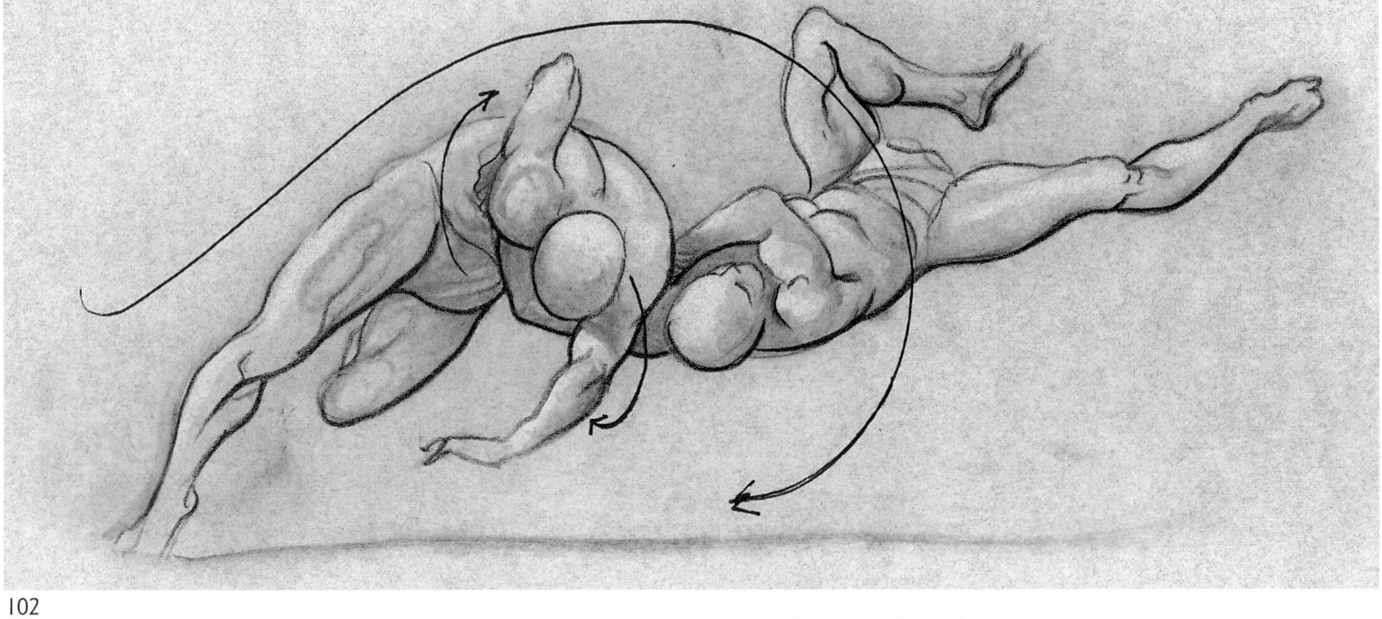

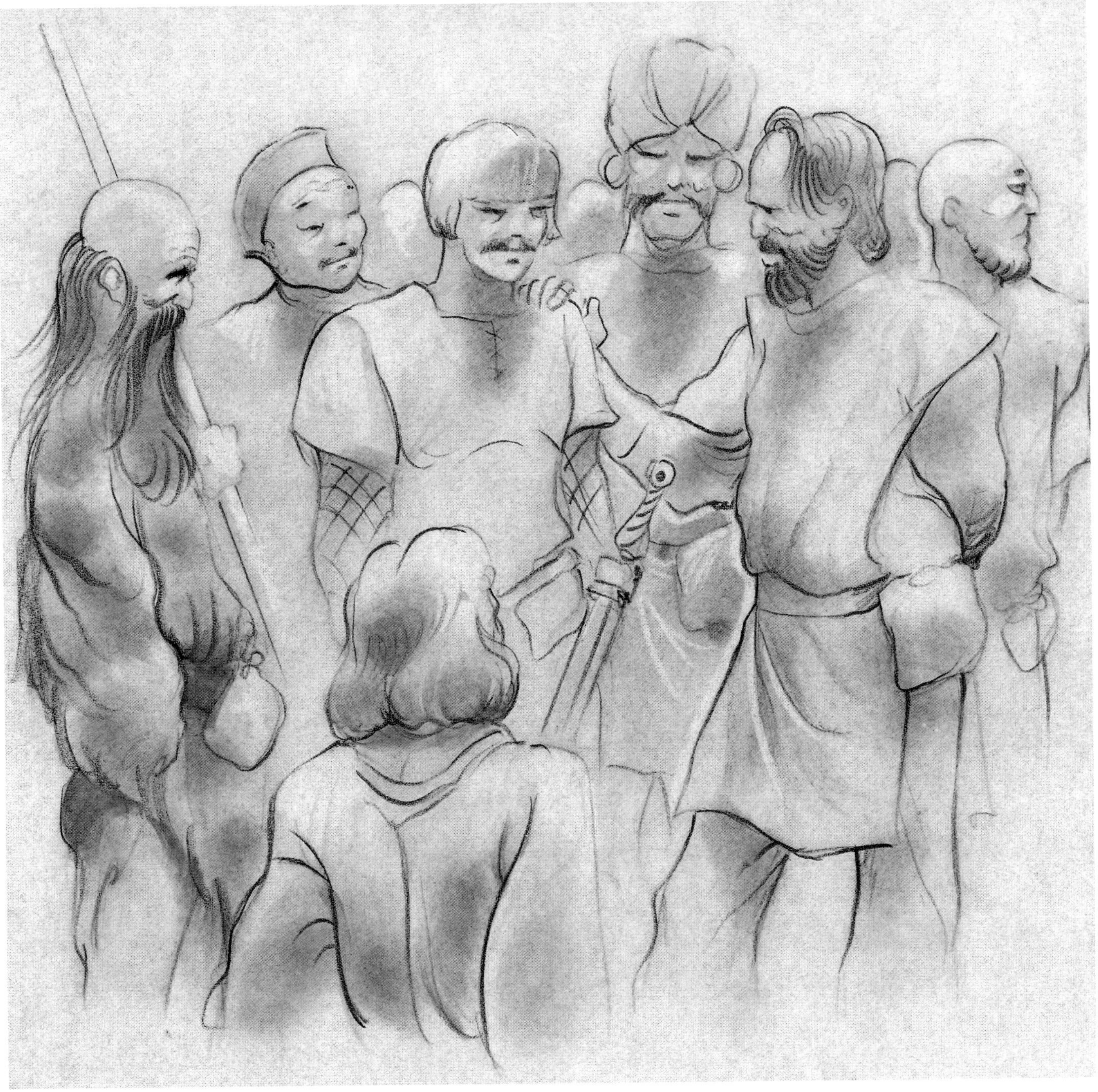

Dusan's exchange of glances with several other seasoned Residents indicated to Père Dominic that they were discussing a subject with which the dwellers on the Summit were well versed. However, they also seemed ready and willing to consider various views on the matter, because the Serbian turned to a younger Resident in the group who, having arrived only recently from Holland after a long and adventurous trek through continental Asia, was still learning the ways of life on the Summit.

Looking him straight in the eye, Dusan said with a smile: "Do you see what can happen when you borrow scrolls from the Library and fail to return them, Piersen? You may unintentionally create problems for others here, who may happen upon them, like this Celt. By the way, Père Dominic, let me introduce you to Piersen von Horen who, as a newcomer like you, is discovering many new aspects of Summit life every day. Like you, he too was impressed with that scroll and its contents. You may find his response interesting. Go ahead, Piersen, tell Père Dominic what you have already related to us about your reactions to the *Yamabushi*.

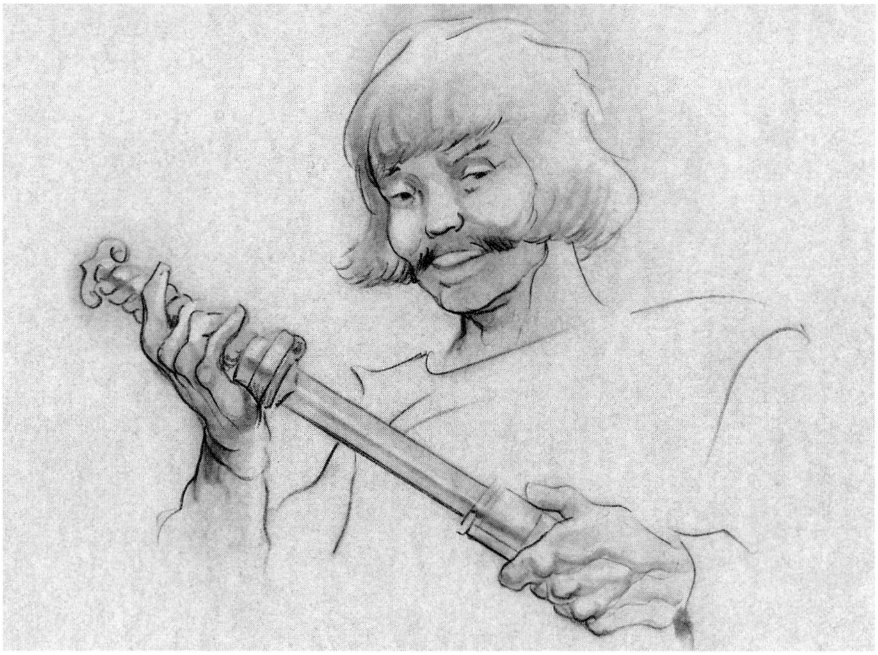

With a slight shrug, the younger man replied: "My reaction to that scroll seems exactly opposite, in terms of effectiveness, at least. I did respond to the bravura shown by Master Naoto in his defensive actions, and to his superior spirit and skills. But were they truly effective, I asked myself? It seems to me that, ultimately, whatever his expertise, nothing that he did was sufficient to save his charges from harm at the hands of another member of Kisaichi's gang of cutthroats."

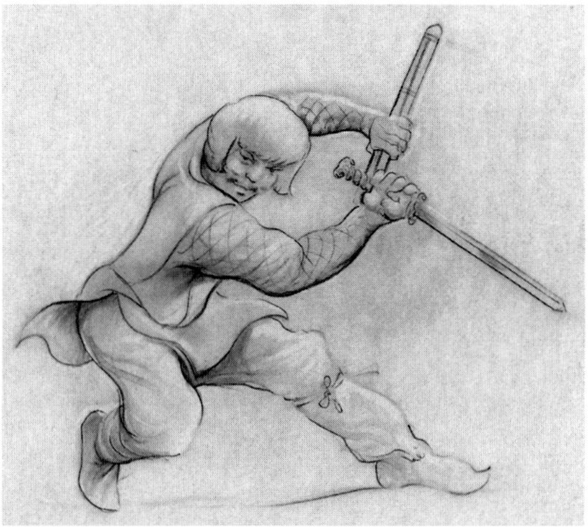

After a slight pause, the Dutchman continued: "This turn of events poses an inevitable question: What was it that actually proved to be effective, in terms of saving lives? And the obvious answer is that the Yamabushi's method, which involved not standing on ceremony, waiting for an aggression to be launched, but rather pre-empting it or meeting it head on through a series of attacks undertaken without hesitation or restraint of any kind, seems to be the approach that truly resolved the situation, dispatching the attackers and saving the innocents. In terms of effectiveness, I don't see that there can be any doubt about who—and what—saved the day. Can you disagree, Père Dominic?"

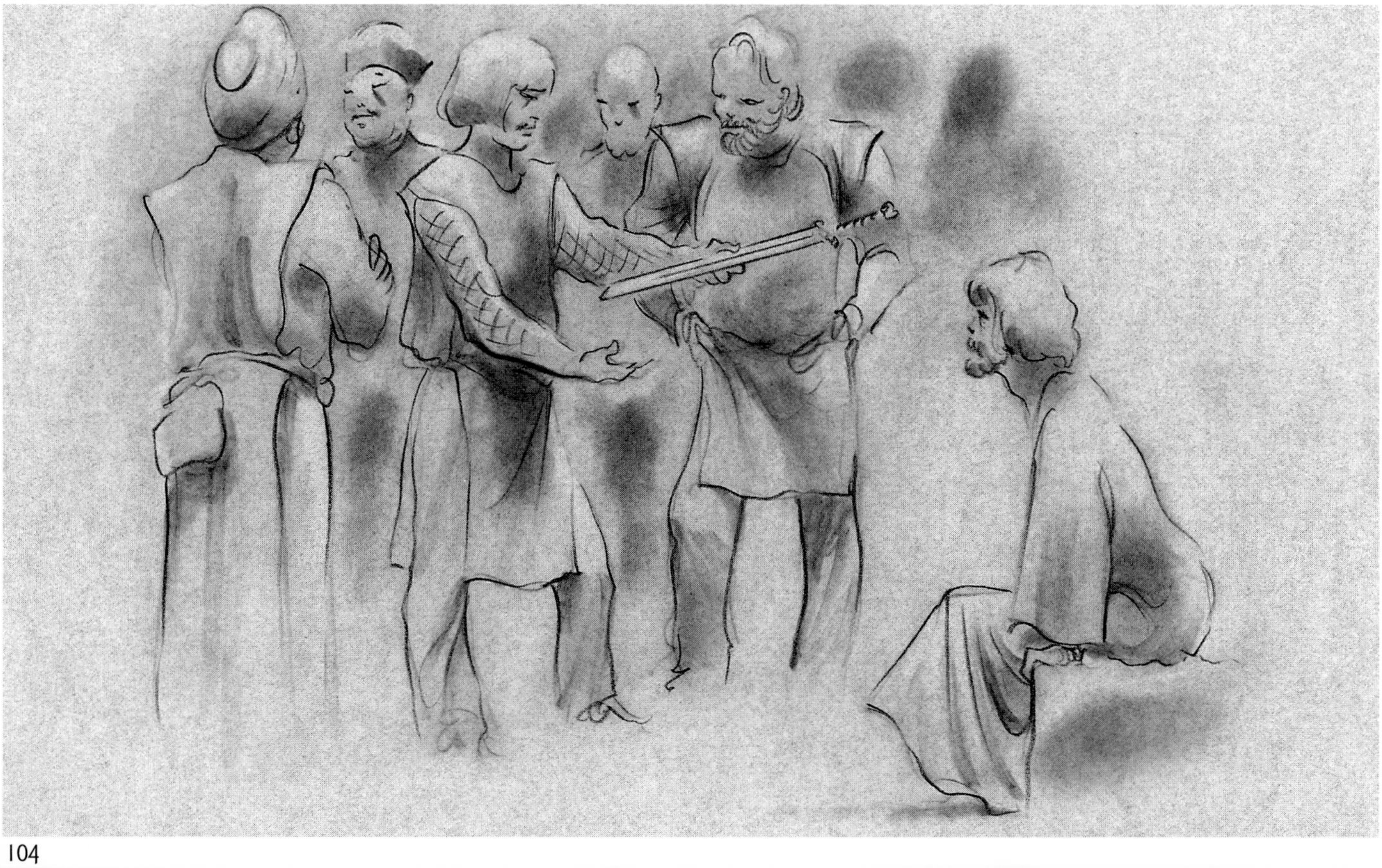

All eyes were on Père Dominic who had listened attentively to Piersen's comments. The Celt shook his head and replied disconsolately, as if this argument were one he had struggled with before: "If it is true that, as our young friend has just stated, violence can be met and overcome only by an equally violent response which, in order to be truly effective, must be quite as terrible, or actually deadly, how does one sustain any hope for the human race if it thus continues to be ruled by that ancient axiom that the Romans expressed so well centuries ago—*mors tua, vita mea . . .*"

"Your death, my life!" Cyrus translated. He was a Resident who had arrived from Persia many years earlier, and took great pride in his knowledge of the classic literature of Greece and Rome. His confreres stood silent for some time, looking at their guest with varied expressions, until Dusan inclined his head toward Père Dominic.

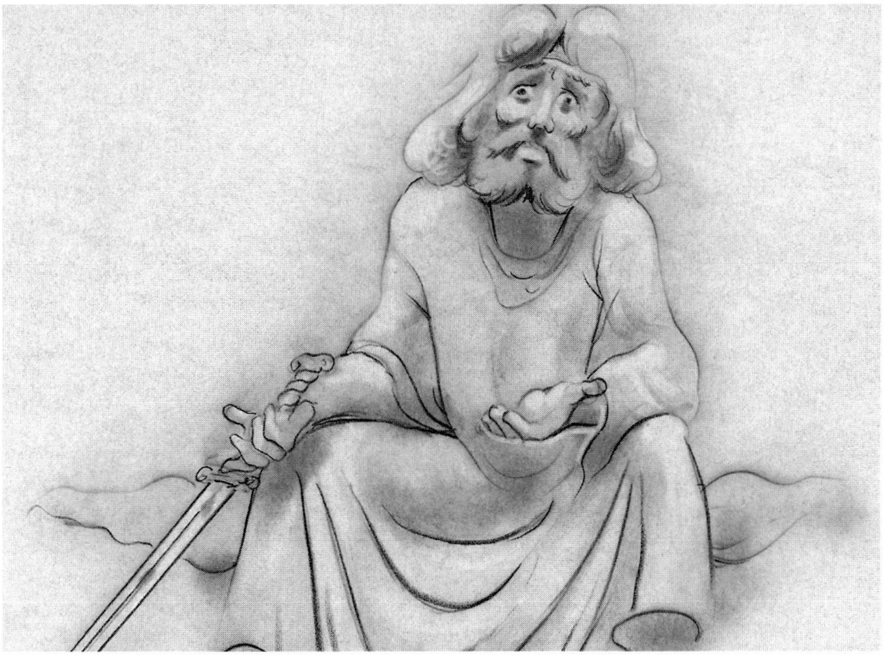

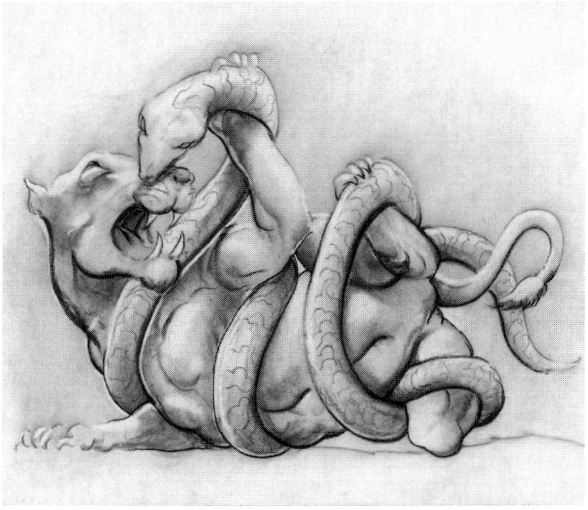

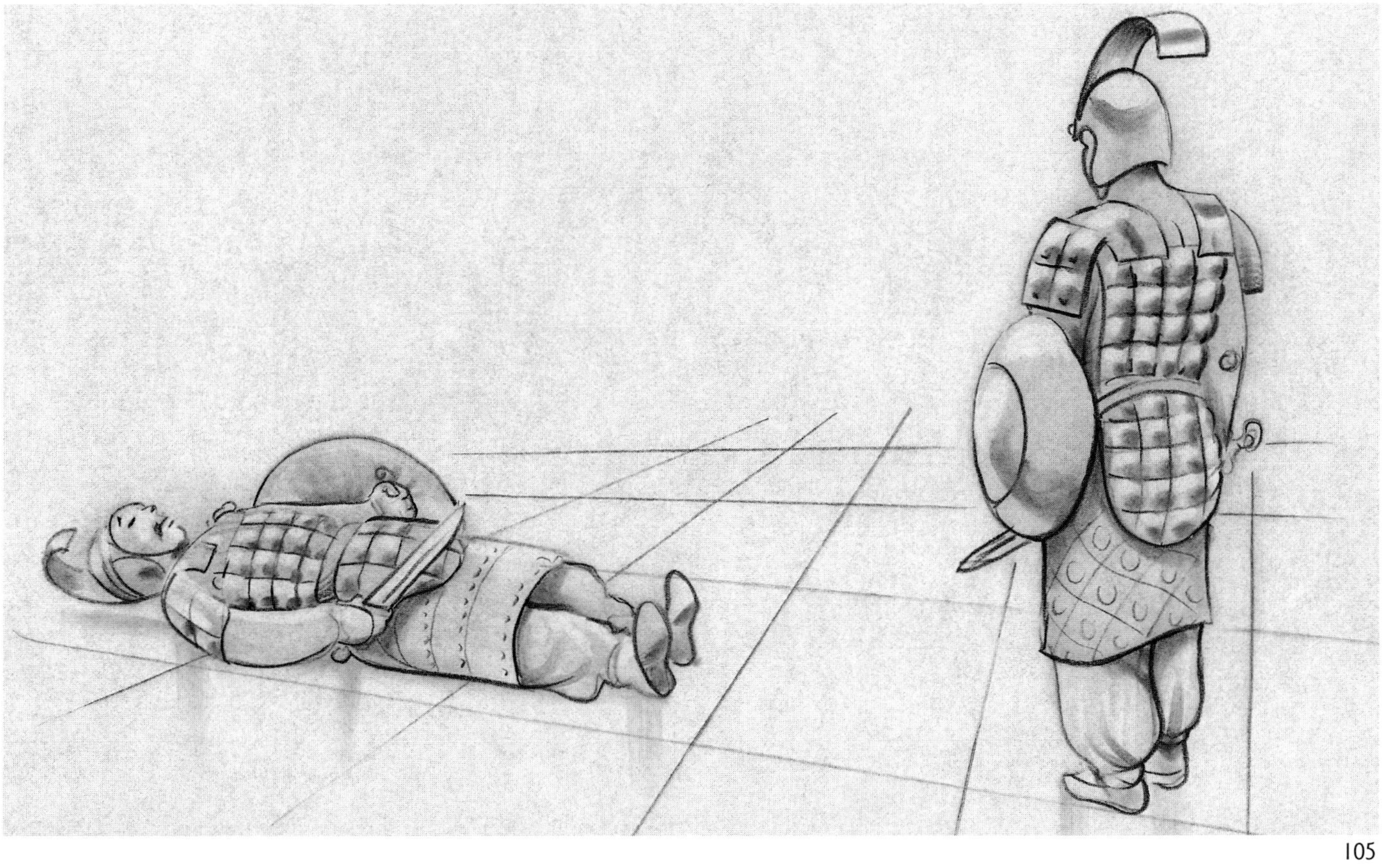

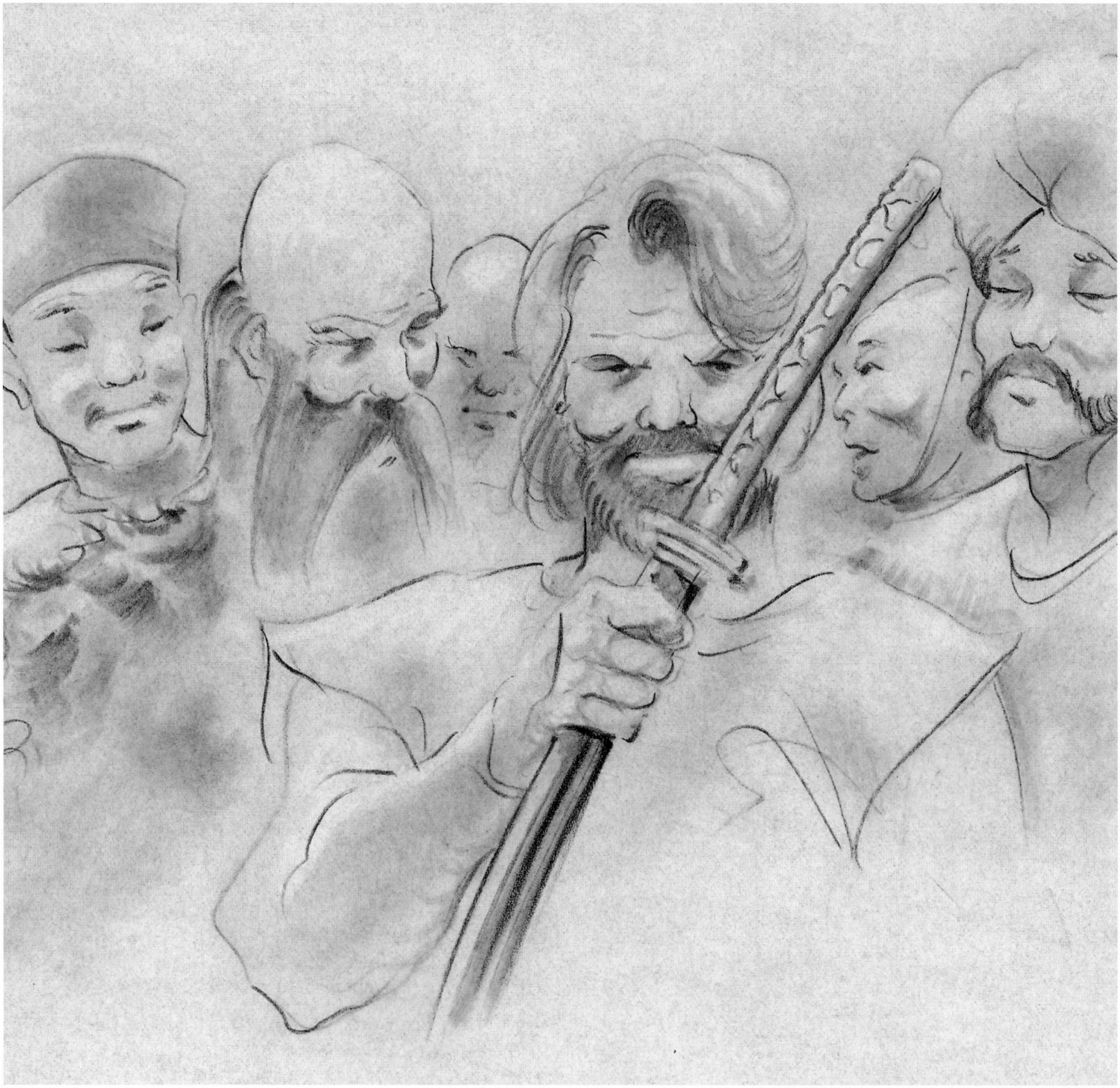

"There is no reason to despair, Celt," he said, breaking the silence decisively. "You are confronting a problem that is very familiar to all of us here. It is an ancient issue, indeed, and one that has vexed many superior intellects since the human race first began to reflect upon itself and the world within which all must live."

"Violence in general, whether man-made or natural—but particularly in the form of personal or individual human violence—never fails to make an impression, even upon the newborn babe. Throughout the ages it has been practiced on the battlefields of every country, or in dim alleyways, by few or by many, endlessly. But it has also been studied in an attempt to discover, if possible, ways and means of reducing or controlling its disastrous effects."

"That study continues, Celt. In fact, it continues intensively in many different places. The Summit is one of them and you happened to stumble upon one such setting on the Second Level, where the theory and practice of the arts of violence, of their weapons, objectives, strategies and techniques, is being examined, re-visited, adapted, and applied in many ways—ways that also include the incorporation of those ethical considerations that you have expressed so vividly . . ."

"Do you mean that, under certain conditions, there may be other effective ways of defending against aggression without necessarily destroying the aggressor?"

As their glances indicated, the Residents sympathized with the eager ring in Père Dominic's voice. Dusan spoke for them all: "That may depend upon how accomplished one can become in the mastery of the ways and means of systematic violence, my Celtic friend. But the training sessions on the Second Level, as anybody here can testify, are very demanding. To begin with, you should clarify the terminology you employ when referring to combat in all its manifestations. For example, you have been using the word 'defense' quite often to define the reactions of both Master Naoto and the Yamabushi to the aggressive behavior of the renegade warrior, Kisaichi, and his band of rogues."

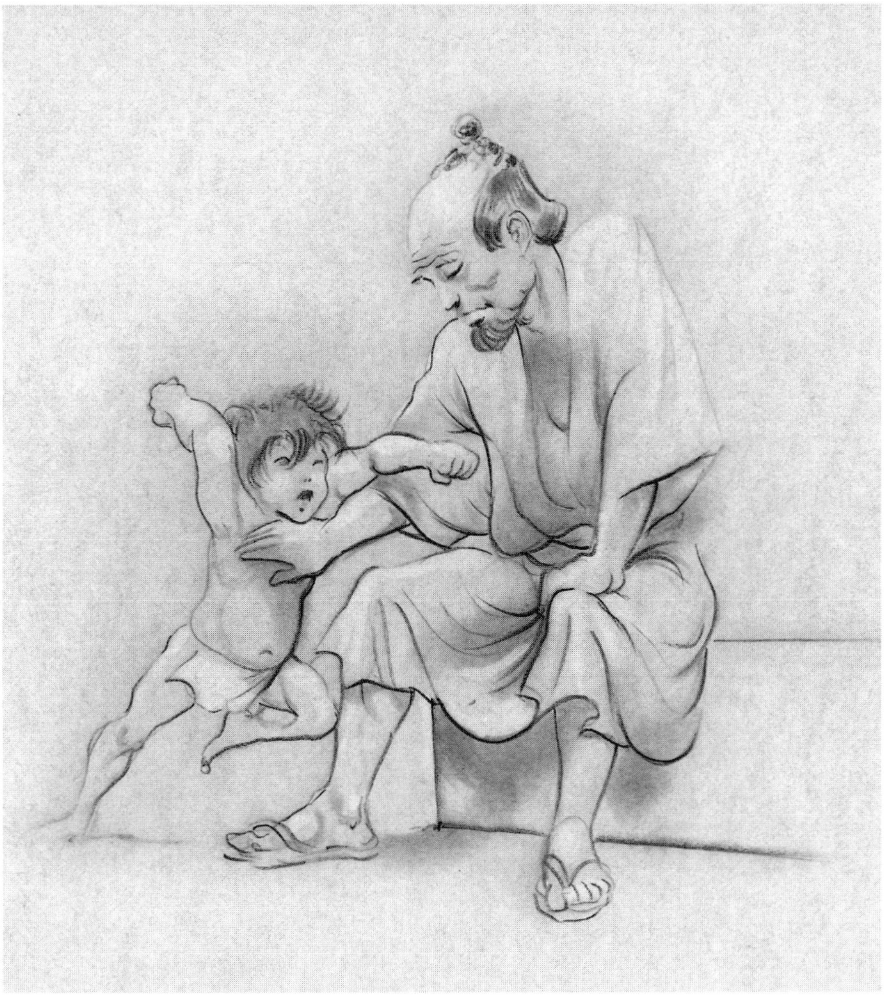

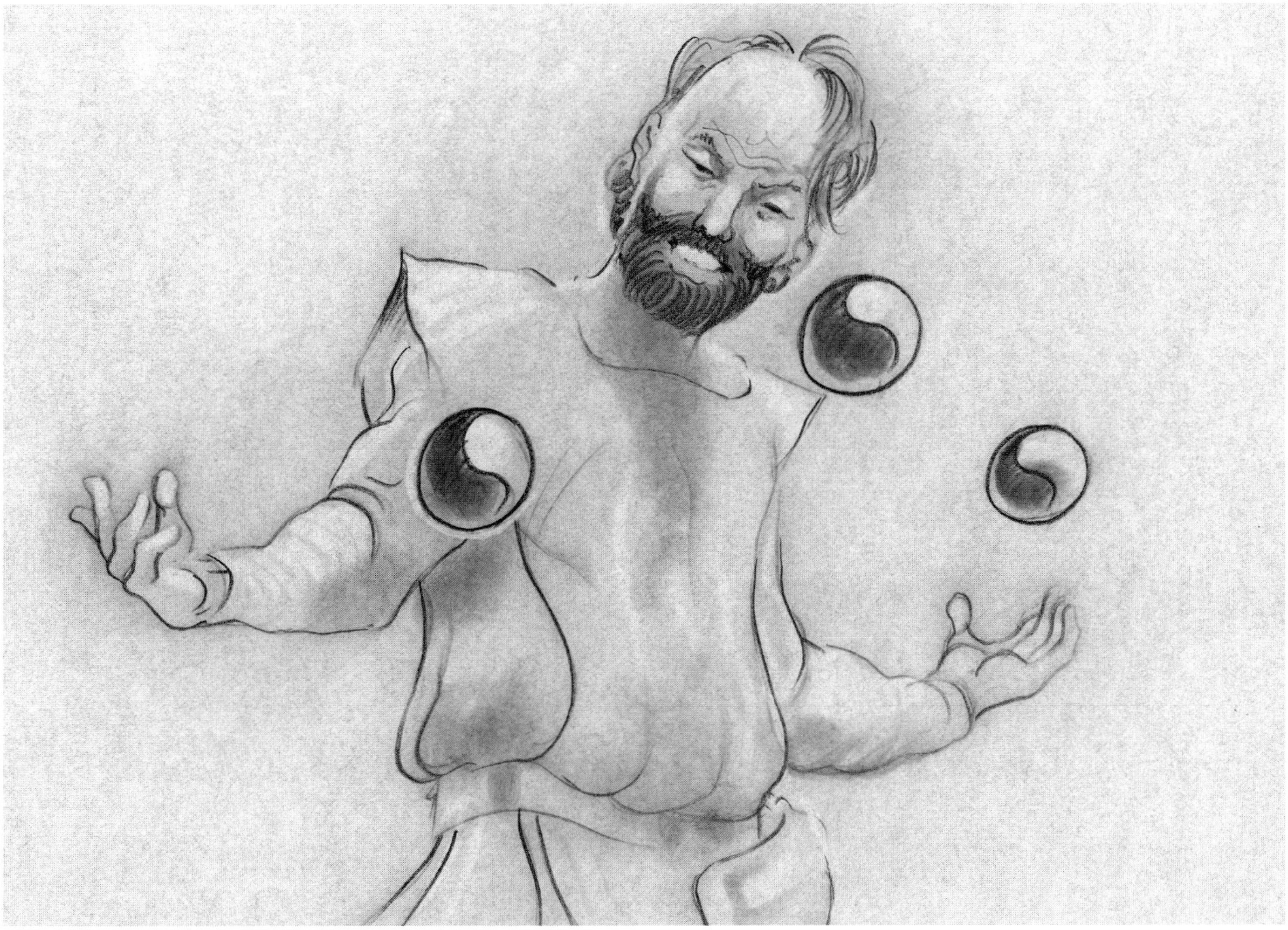

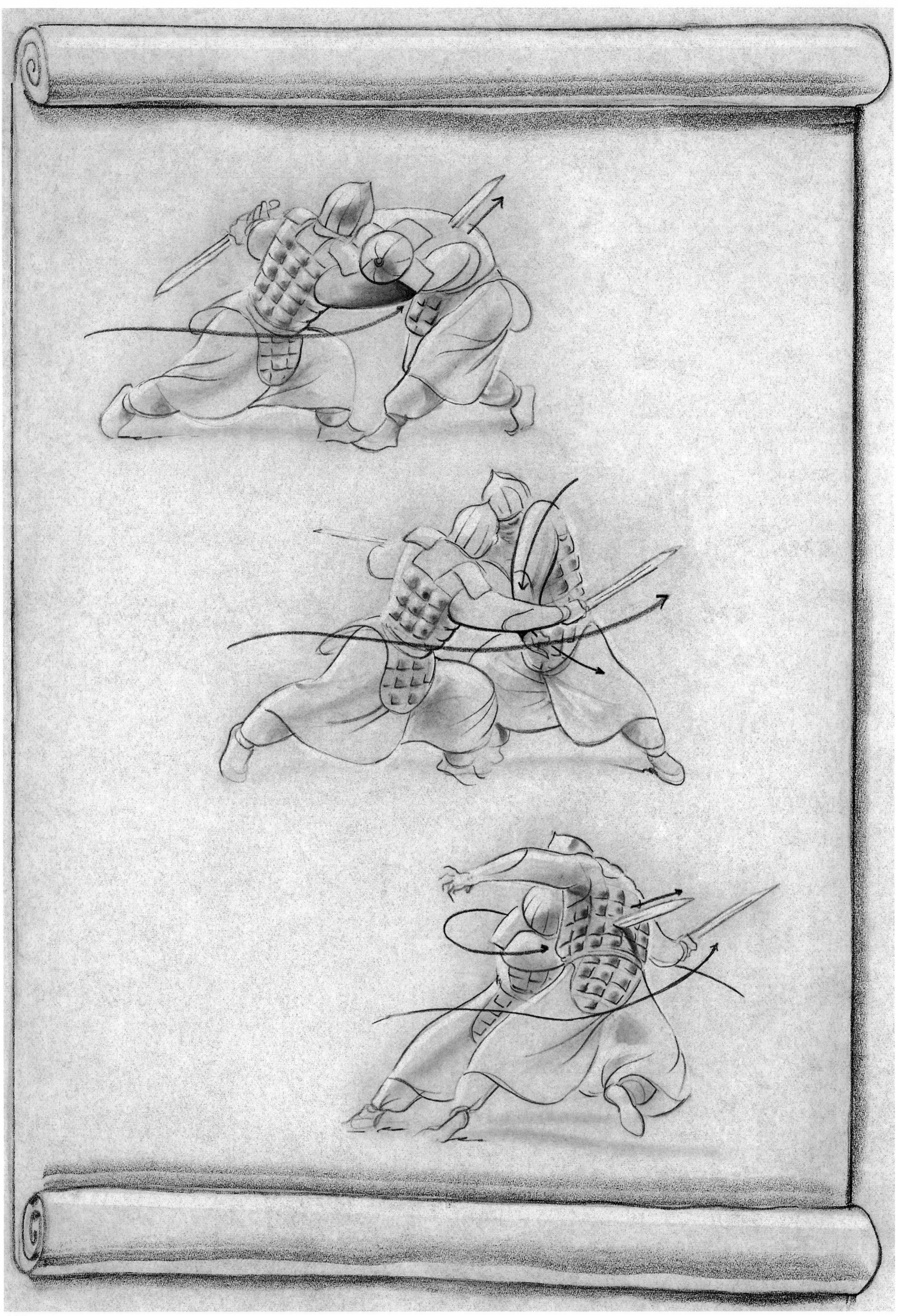

"But your interpretation of their strategies as defense is not quite correct. As you will discover, if you remain here for awhile, and perhaps attend some training sessions (as well as the discussions we often have concerning the issue of systematic violence) you may come to the conclusion that such a term, in describing Master Naoto's response to his attackers, applies only to the moment during which he avoided the direct stream of violent actions directed toward his body as the target, which he did not allow them to contact. That moment represents the clearest and most accurate definition of 'defense' as we have come to conceive of it in our theory of combat: preventing an attack against you from reaching its target."

Dusan held up his hand at the expression of dissent on Père Dominic's face. "I know," he continued. "Master Naoto did more than that. Having avoided the direct force of the attack with his strategy of defense, he took advantage of the opening thus created and proceeded to whirl his attackers into an irresistible flight that projected them through the air. But this is a different strategy with its own appellation, Celt. Here, we call it 'counterattack' to indicate a strategy that may follow a successful defensive action but should not be confused with it."

Père Dominic had been following Dusan's explanation carefully and now asked: "How would you qualify the Yamabushi's actions, then?"

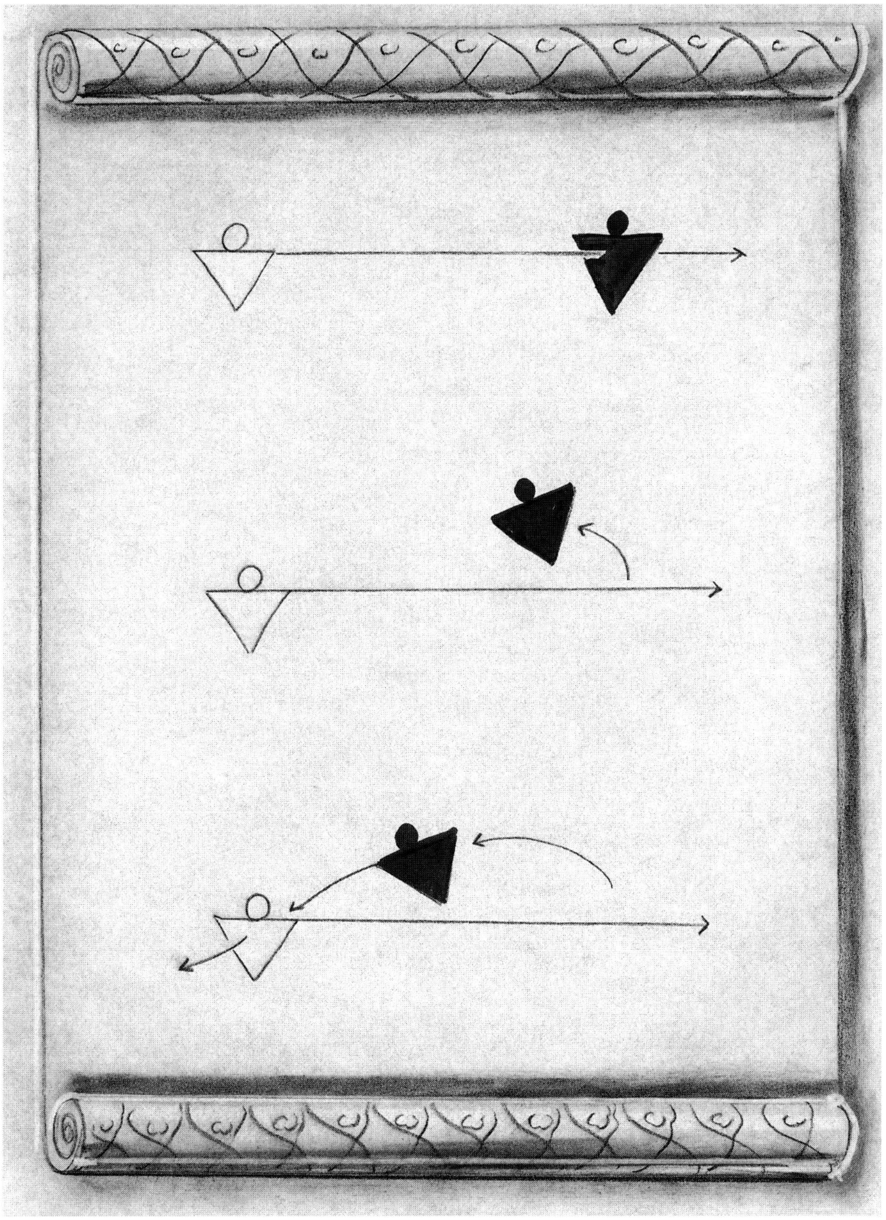

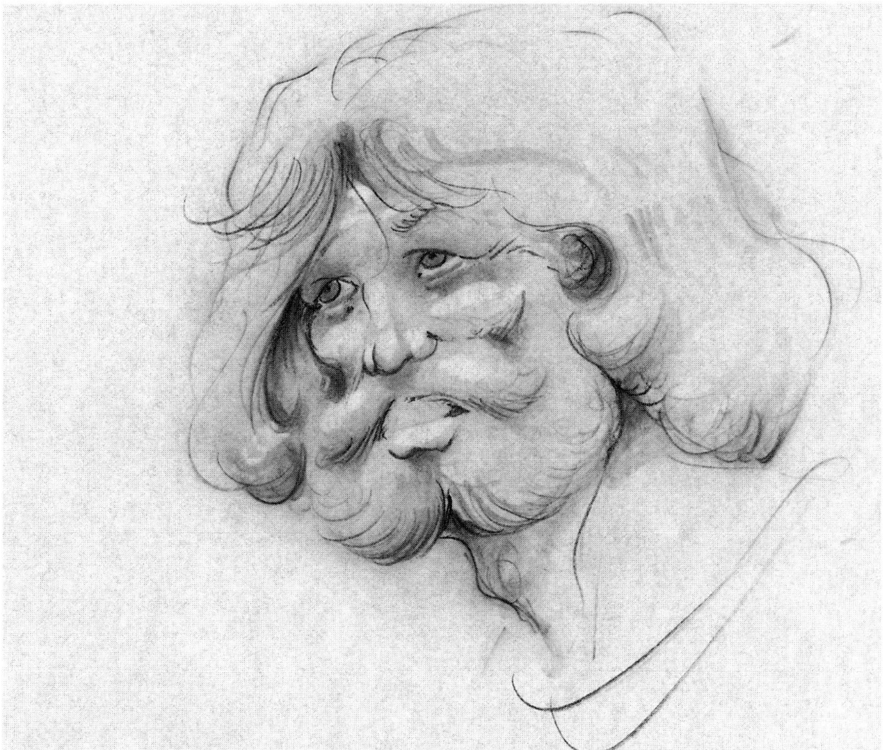

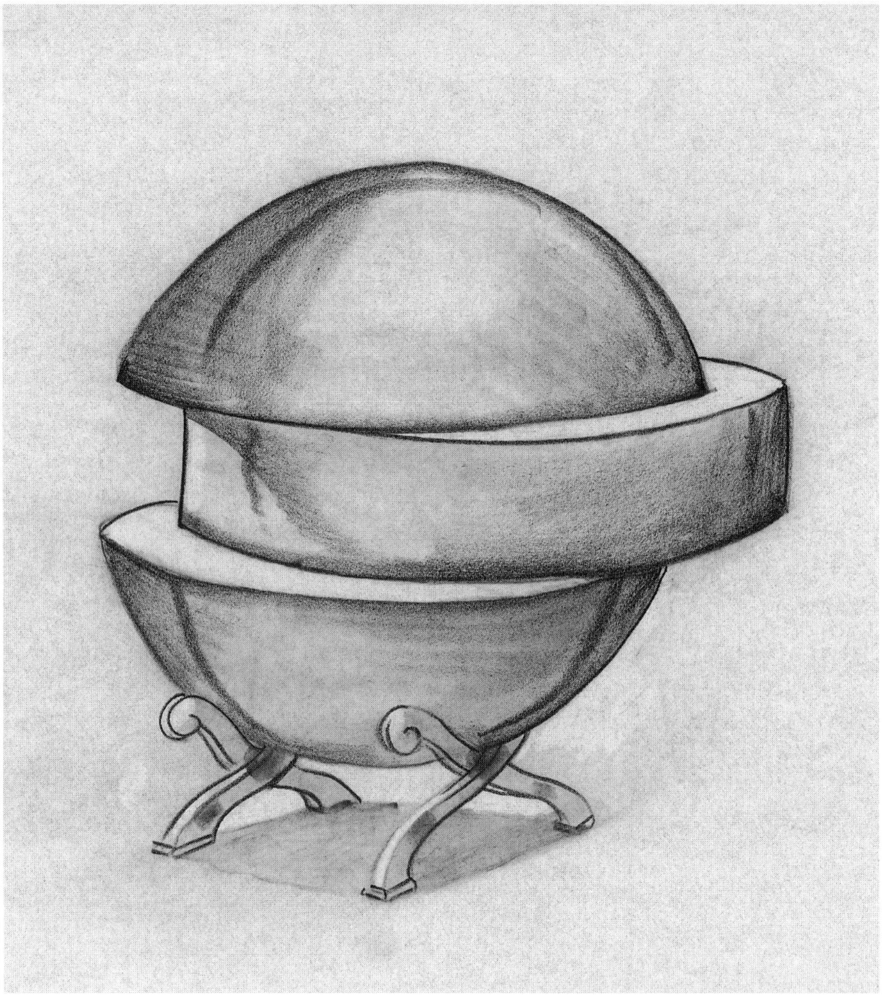

"The Yamabushi's actions, as he dispatches his opponents one by one or in pairs, also cannot be termed "a defense" in the sense that I have tried to convey to you. As related in the scroll, the Yamabushi clearly attacked in each and every case, either in a pre-emptive fashion, or deliberately, and followed all of his actions through to the bitter end."

"Have I managed to confuse you entirely by emphasizing the differences in these strategies, Celt? If it is of any consolation to you, it has not been a simple matter for us to reconcile our notions of combat before we arrived on the Summit with those concepts and terms we had to consider when we began our study of the Art of Combat on this Range. But isn't that part of the process of discovery that any human being undertakes every day of his or her life, until that final breath is drawn?"

Père Dominic did not respond at once. His mind was in turmoil as he tried to absorb all of the issues and perspectives that Dusan's analysis had presented.

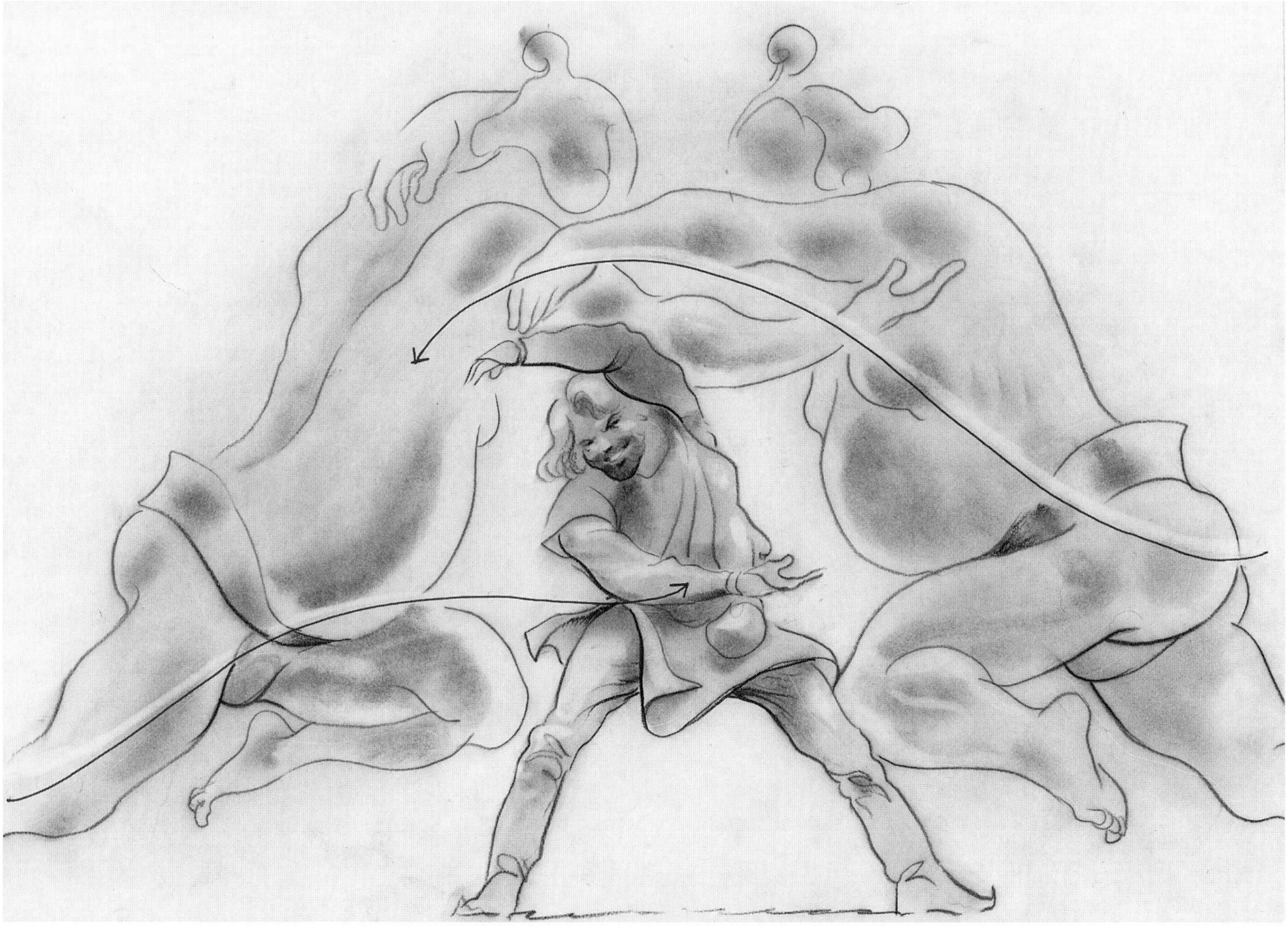

"He obviously needs more time to reflect," Cyrus suggested. "Initially, our guest had interpreted everything for himself in terms of 'defense.' Now, he must reconsider the actions in the tale he has just read in terms of 'attack' and 'counterattack'—all of which is enough to drive any student of the martial arts to distraction, wouldn't you say? Come, let us leave Père Dominic in peace—at least for the moment."

Exchanging asides and some good-natured jostlings, the Residents began to disperse, leaving Père Dominic's mind awhirl with new clarifications concerning a subject that had concerned him so intensely for years and about which he had come to certain conclusions that it now seemed he must revisit.

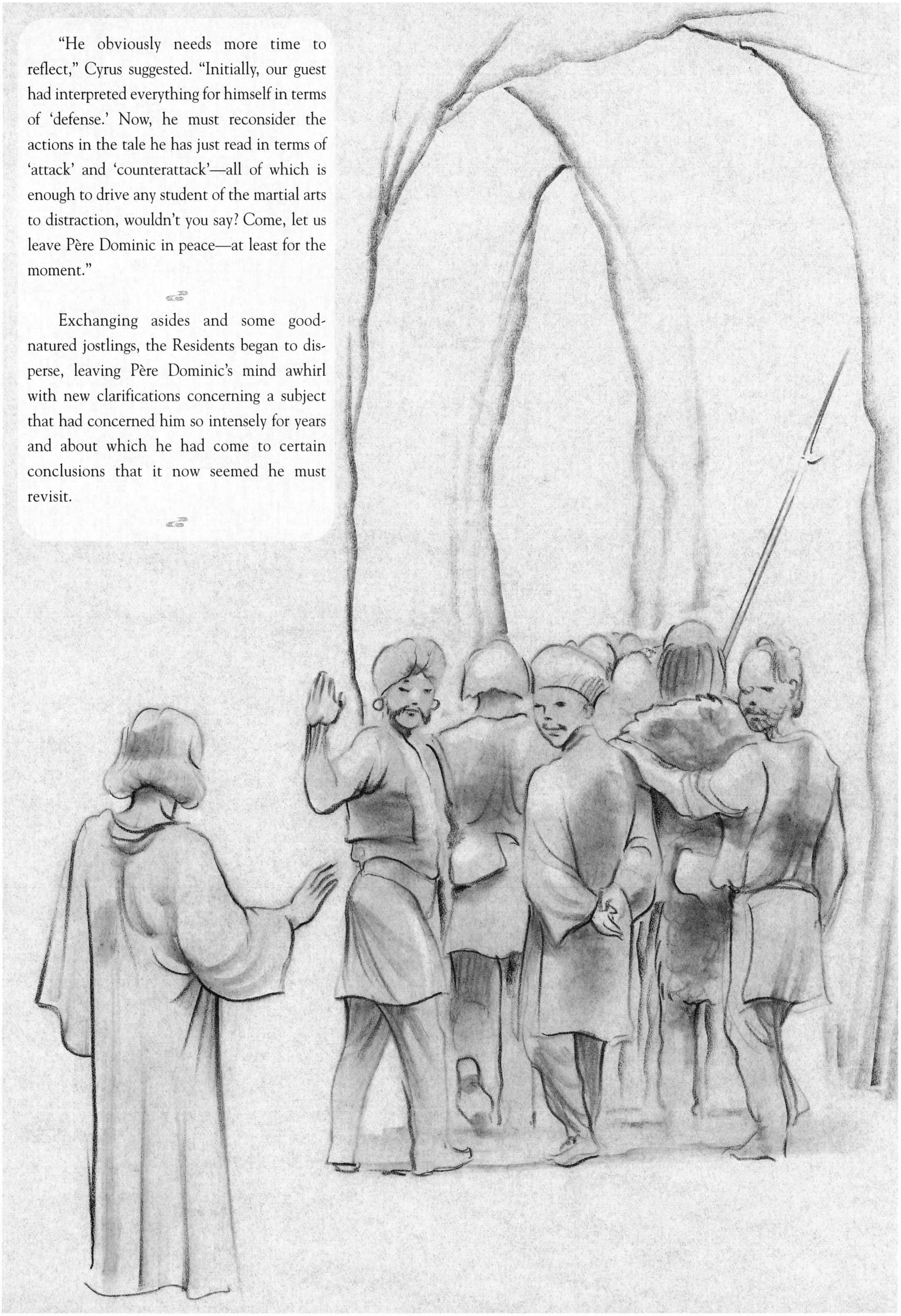

But beyond the technical aspects of violence, such as strategies of attack, counter-attack, and defense, it was the moral and ethical questions that most troubled Père Dominic.

How far was it permissible for an ethical person to go in defense of the innocent? And how skillful did one have to become to engage effectively in such defensive actions? Even more to the point, if one believed that there was never any excuse for the taking of human life, didn't that lead to the logical conclusion that men of ill will would always triumph against all those unable or unwilling to defend themselves, and others, to the death?

In the scroll he had just read, if the Yamabushi had not intervened, there would still have been dead bodies littering the ground, but they would have been those of Master Naoto and his followers, not their attackers.

There would obviously be no easy answers.

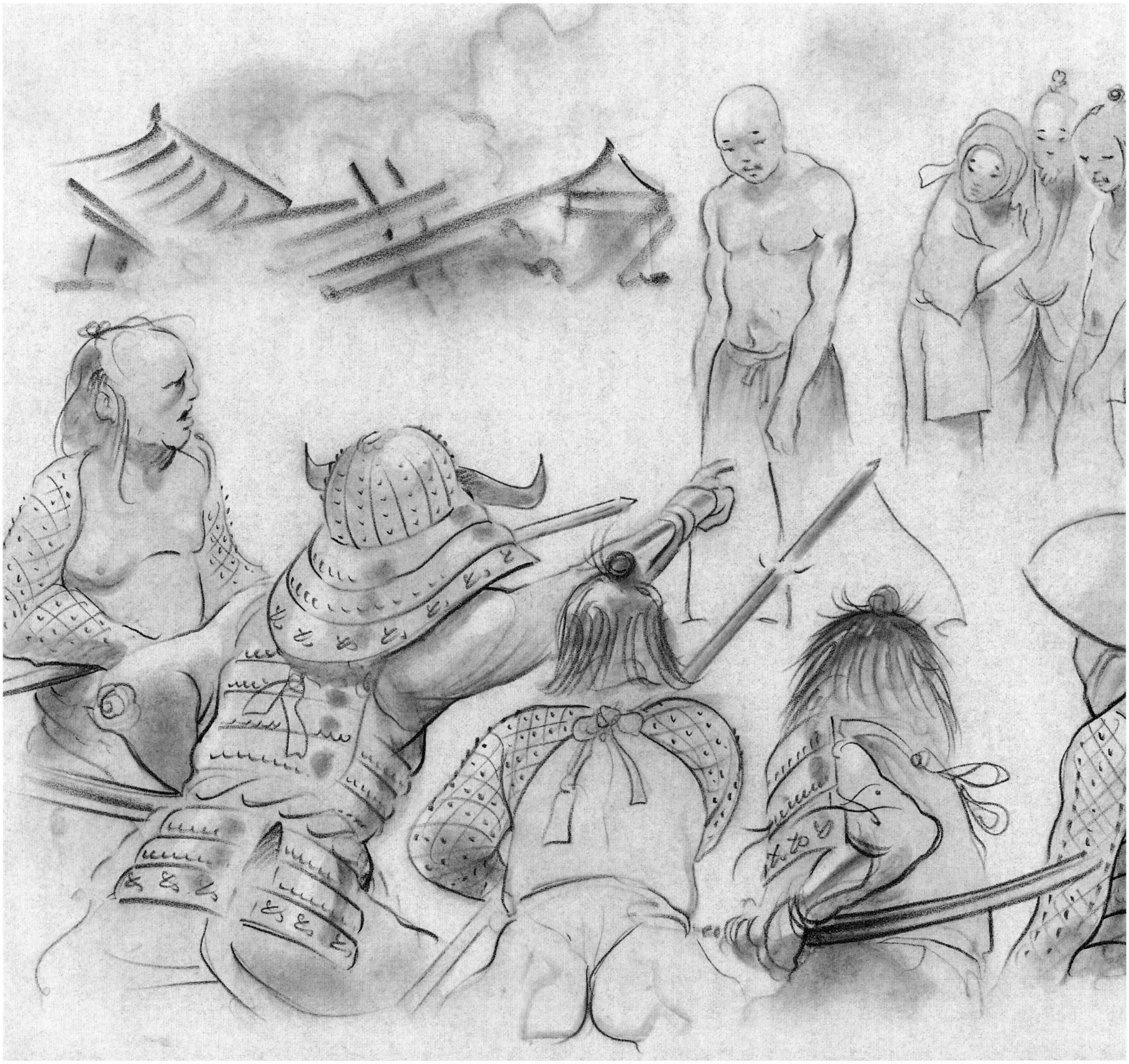

Involuntarily, Père Dominic shivered as he struggled with his doubts. Should he return to the caves, chambers, and vaults arching over those forbidding collections of weapons and armors whose images still haunted him? How far would he have to go in this new quest, and who would guide him?

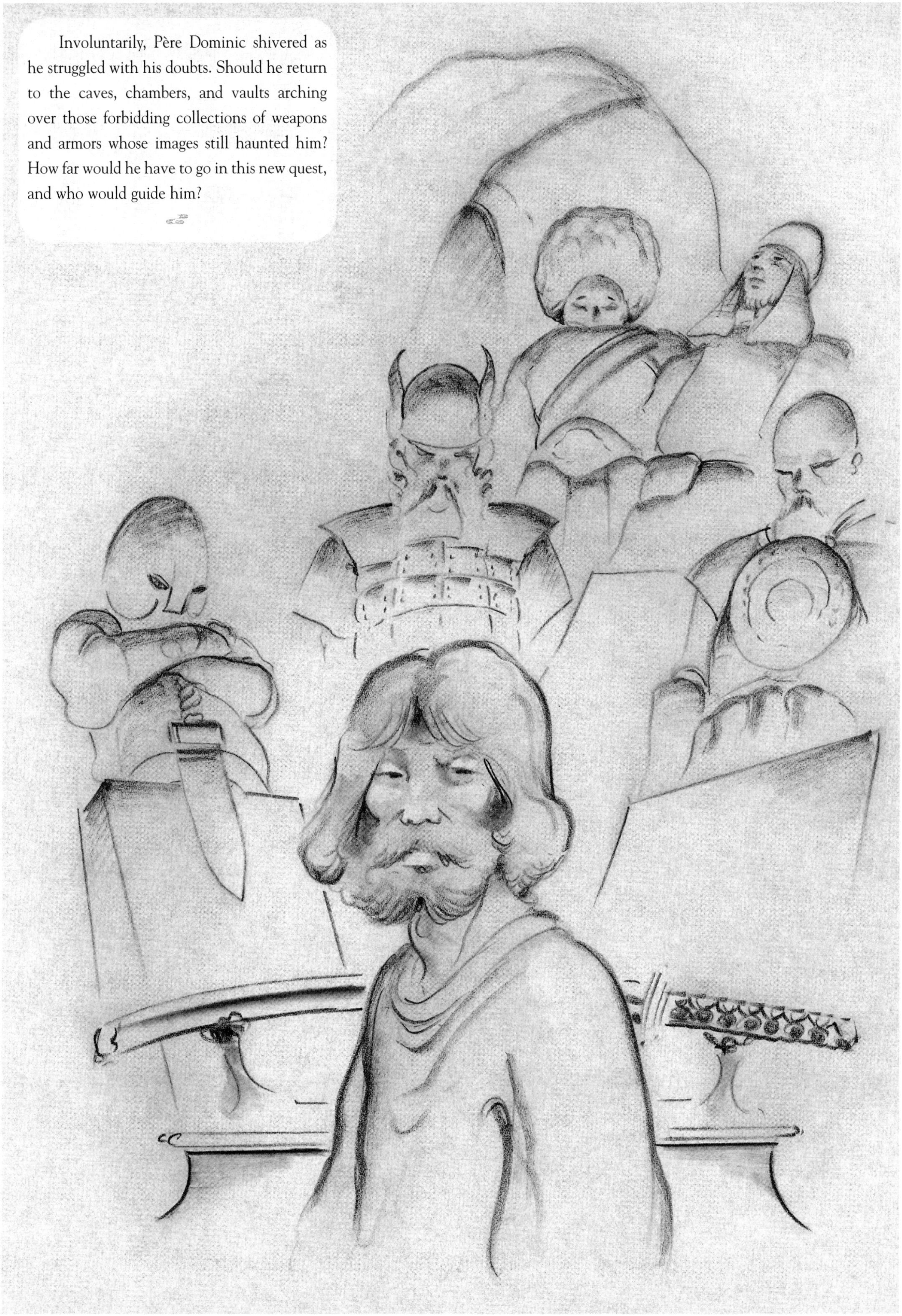

To distract himself from thoughts of what might await him in the shadows, Père Dominic reached for the other scroll he had discovered on the Second Level, which—as Yu Xia had informed him—also belonged to the martial tradition of the Empire. He found himself wondering about the title, as he unrolled the second scroll that also bore only a single word on its cover: *Homecoming*.

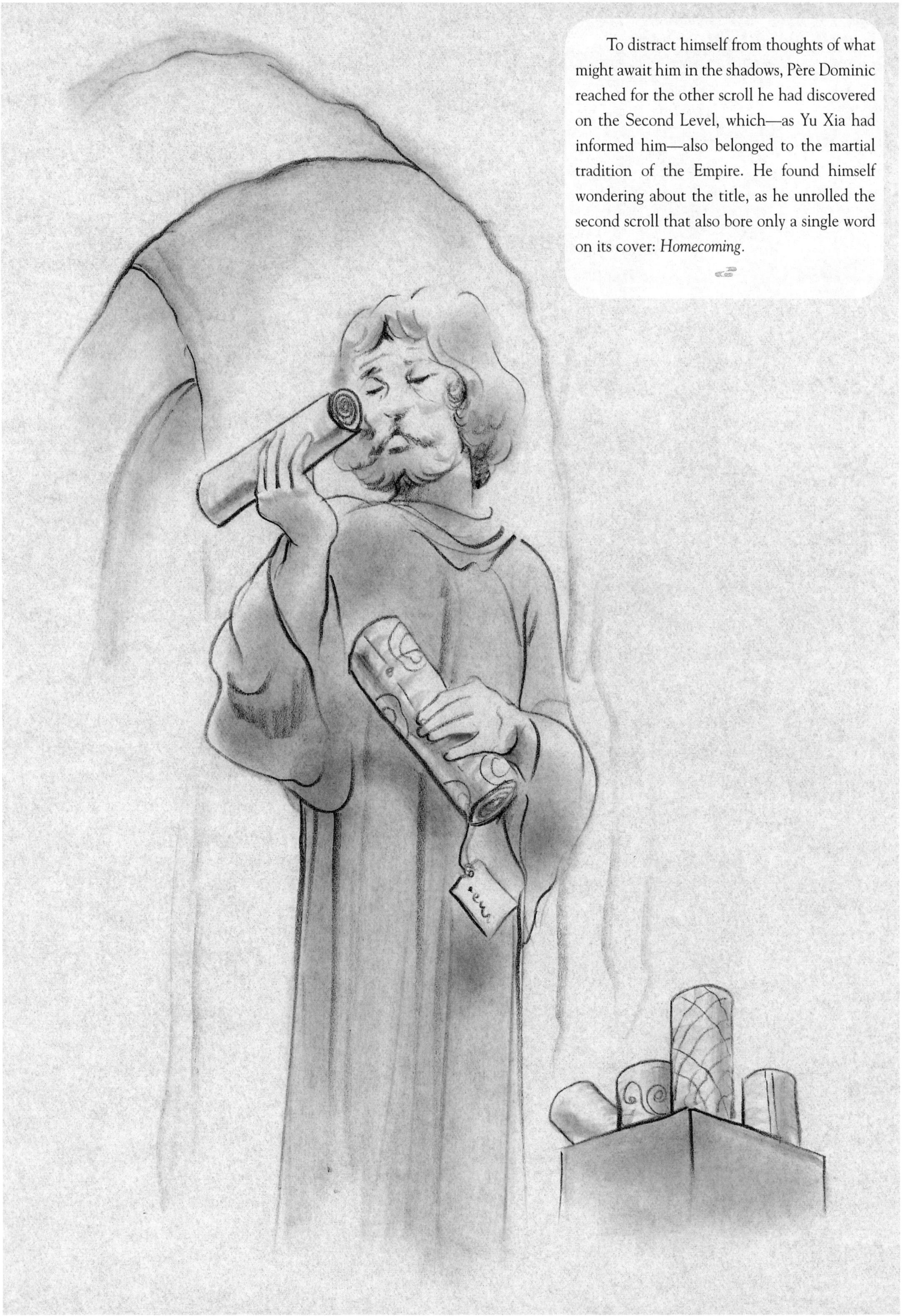

HOMECOMING

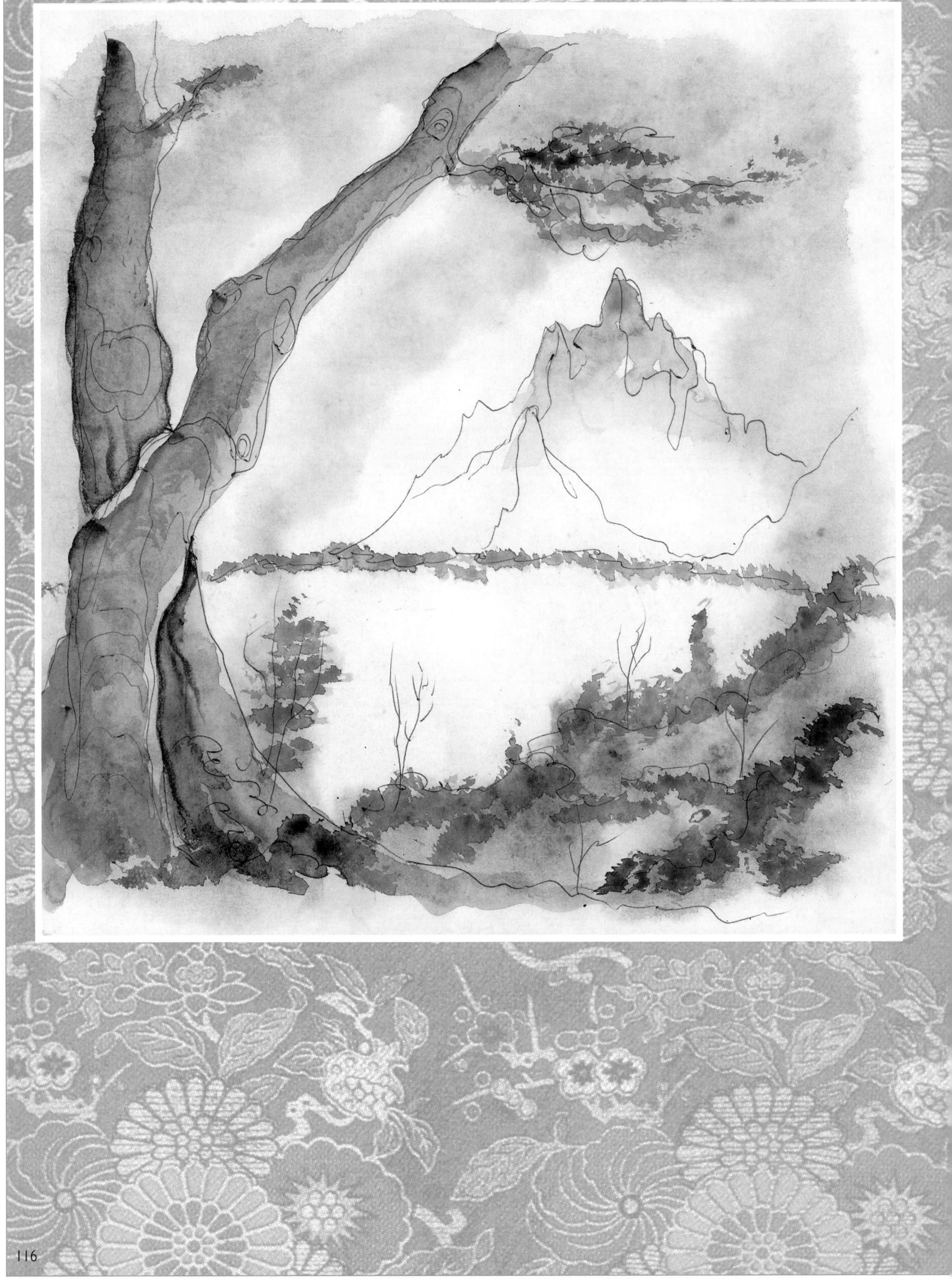

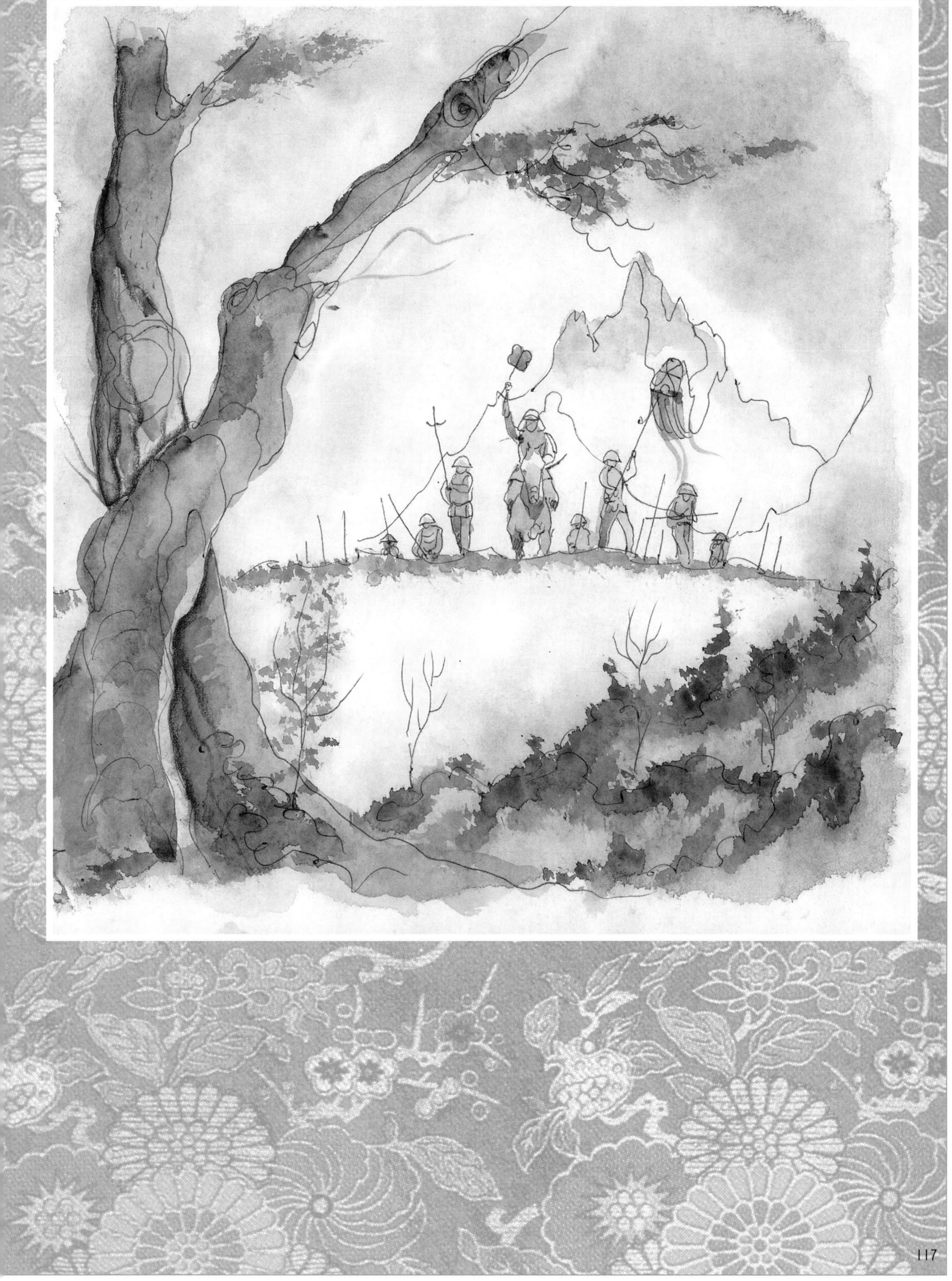

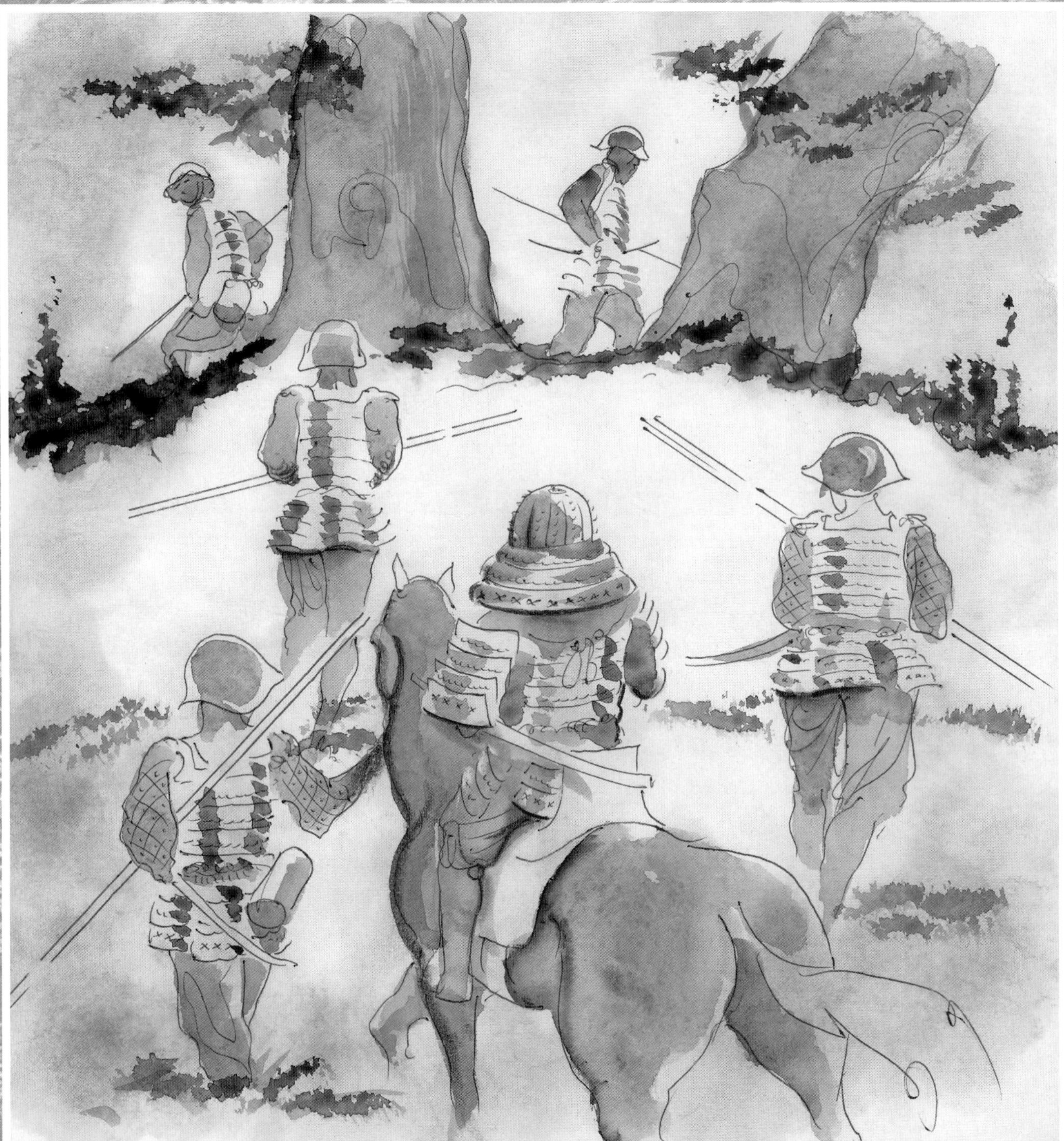

"Hello, there."

"Anything?"

"Not over here. And you, Yokoru?"

"Not anything alive."

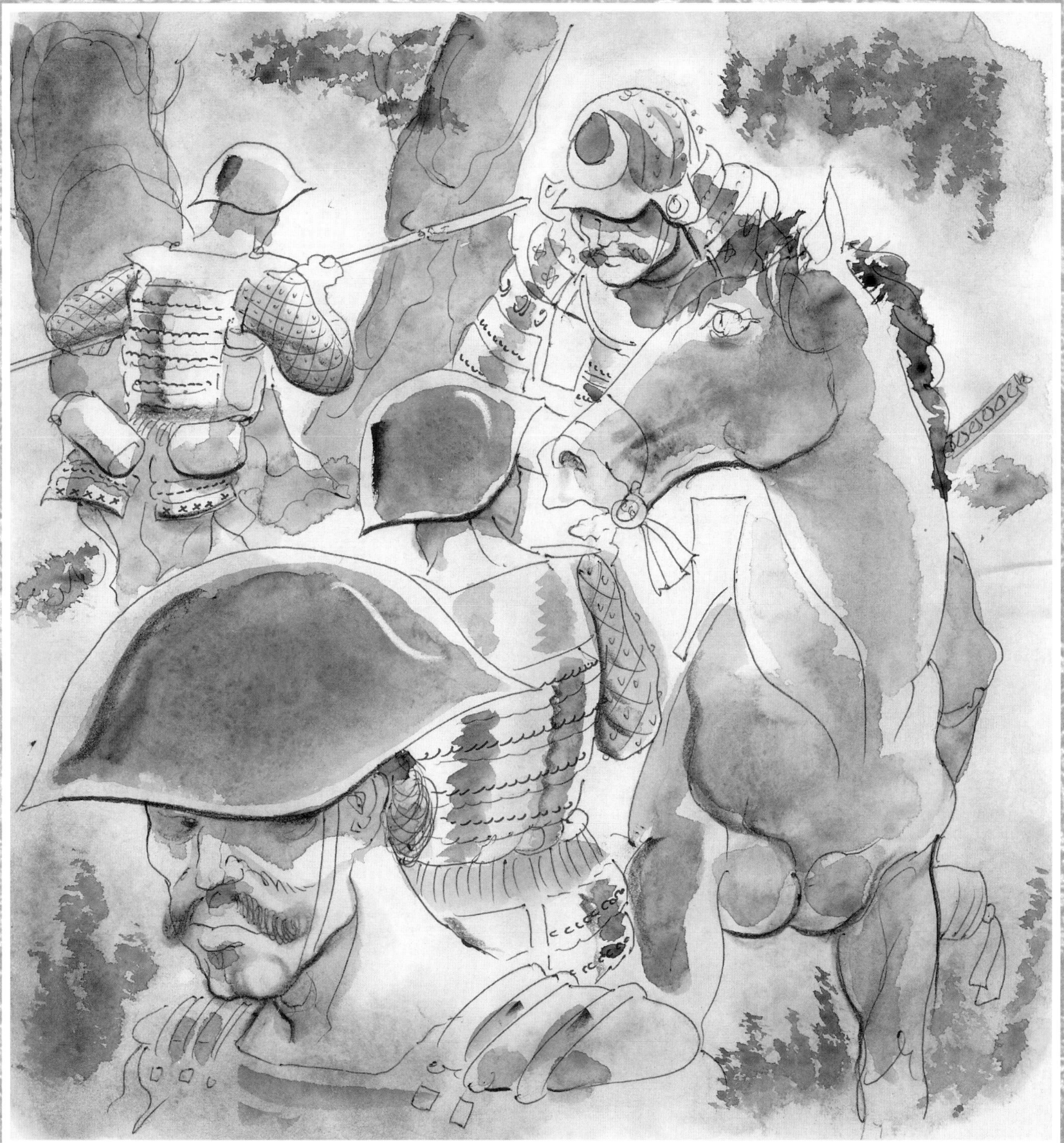

"Nothing yet?"

"Nothing, Sir. Not on this side."

"But that's impossible! They saw him ride straight into the thicket. And he couldn't have climbed the cliff on the other side of these woods, not with all those wounds. Separate into pairs and spread out, signaling at intervals to keep in contact. Quickly! The fog is beginning to thicken!"

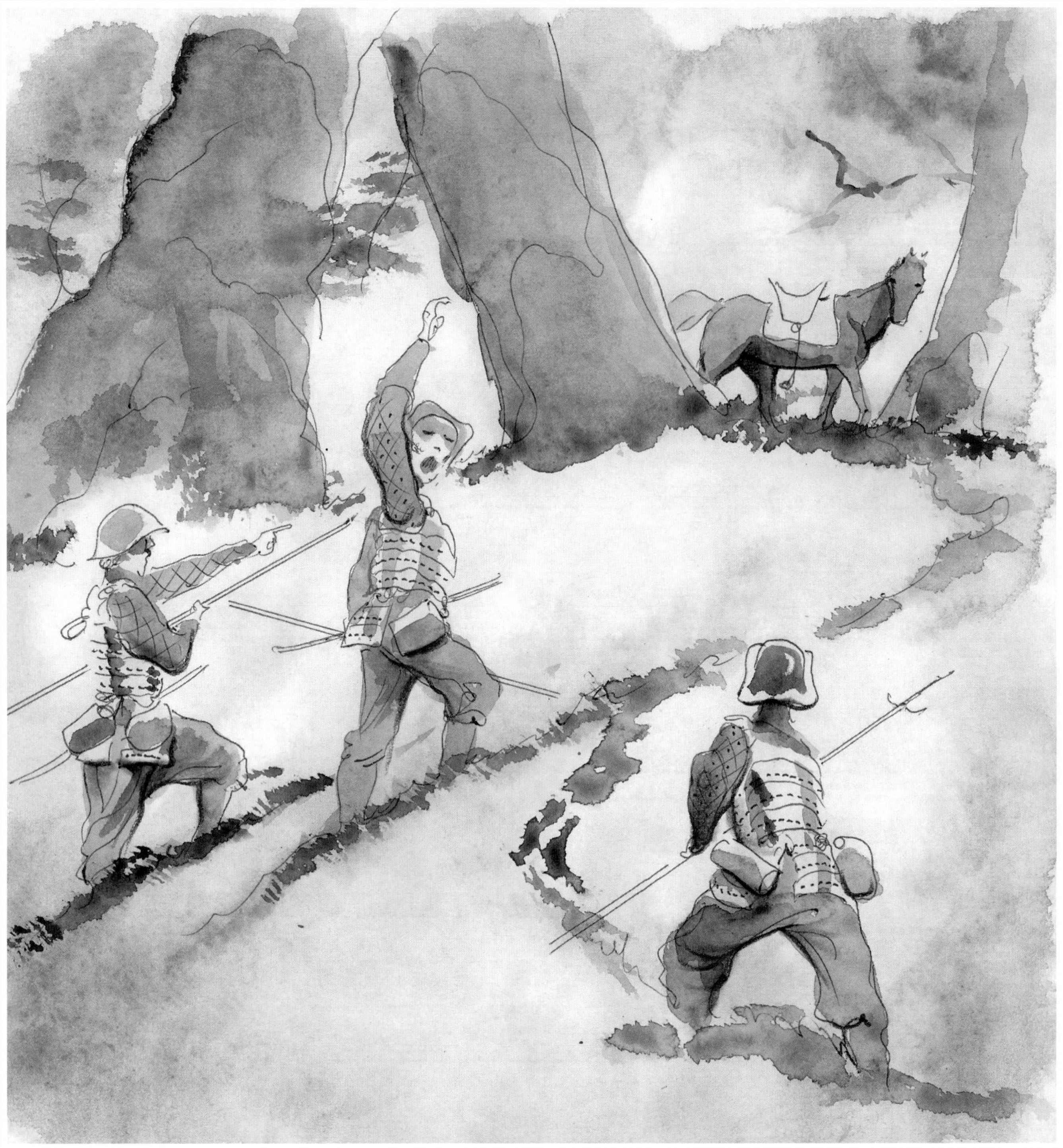

"Be quiet!
Something is moving on the right, I can see it!"

"I can't see anything at all."

"Well, there's something there—I'm sure of it!
Circle toward it, slowly.
Now! Move in now!"

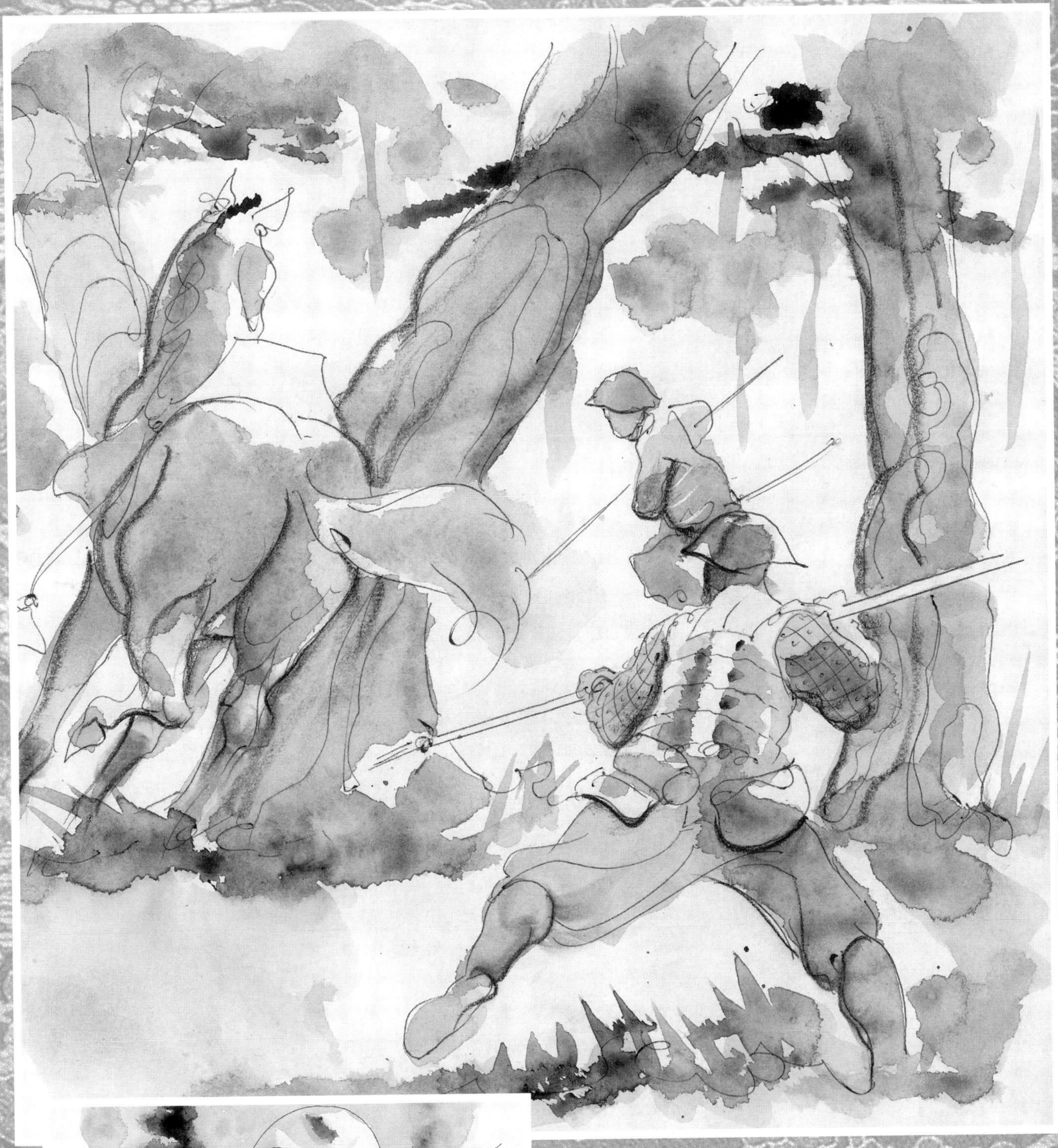

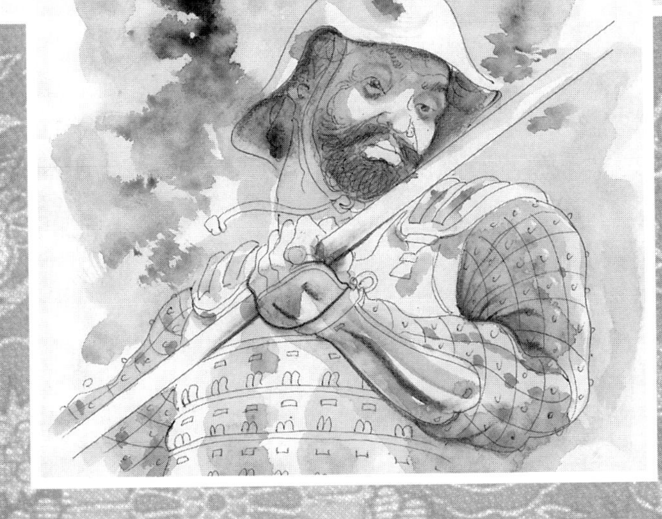

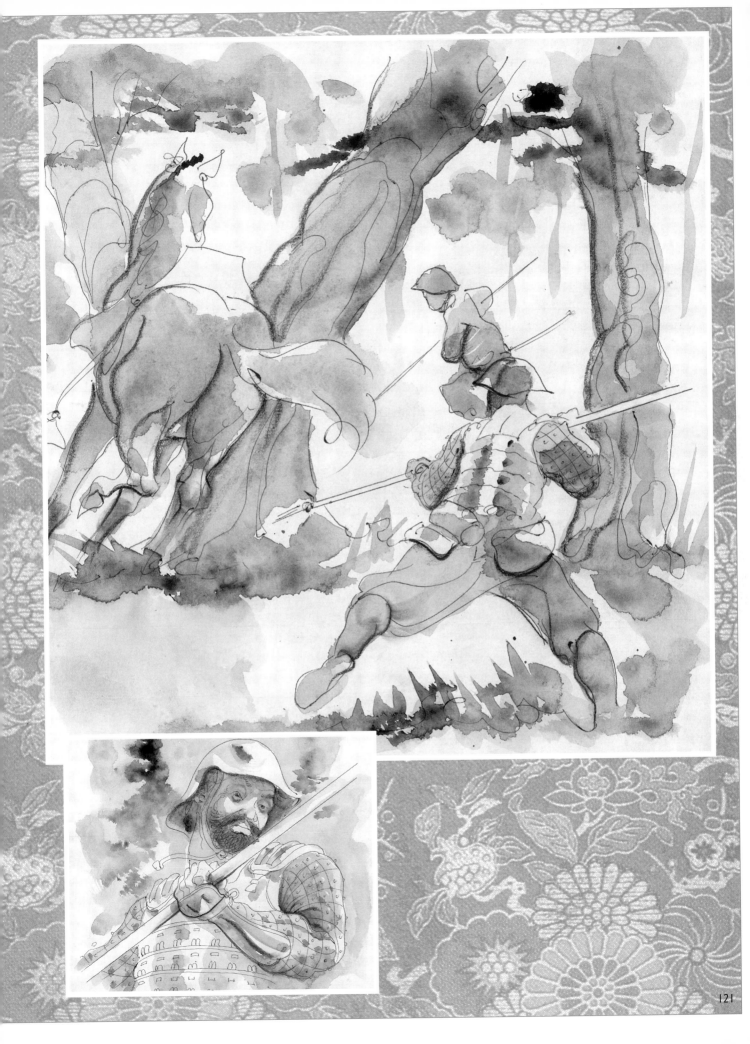

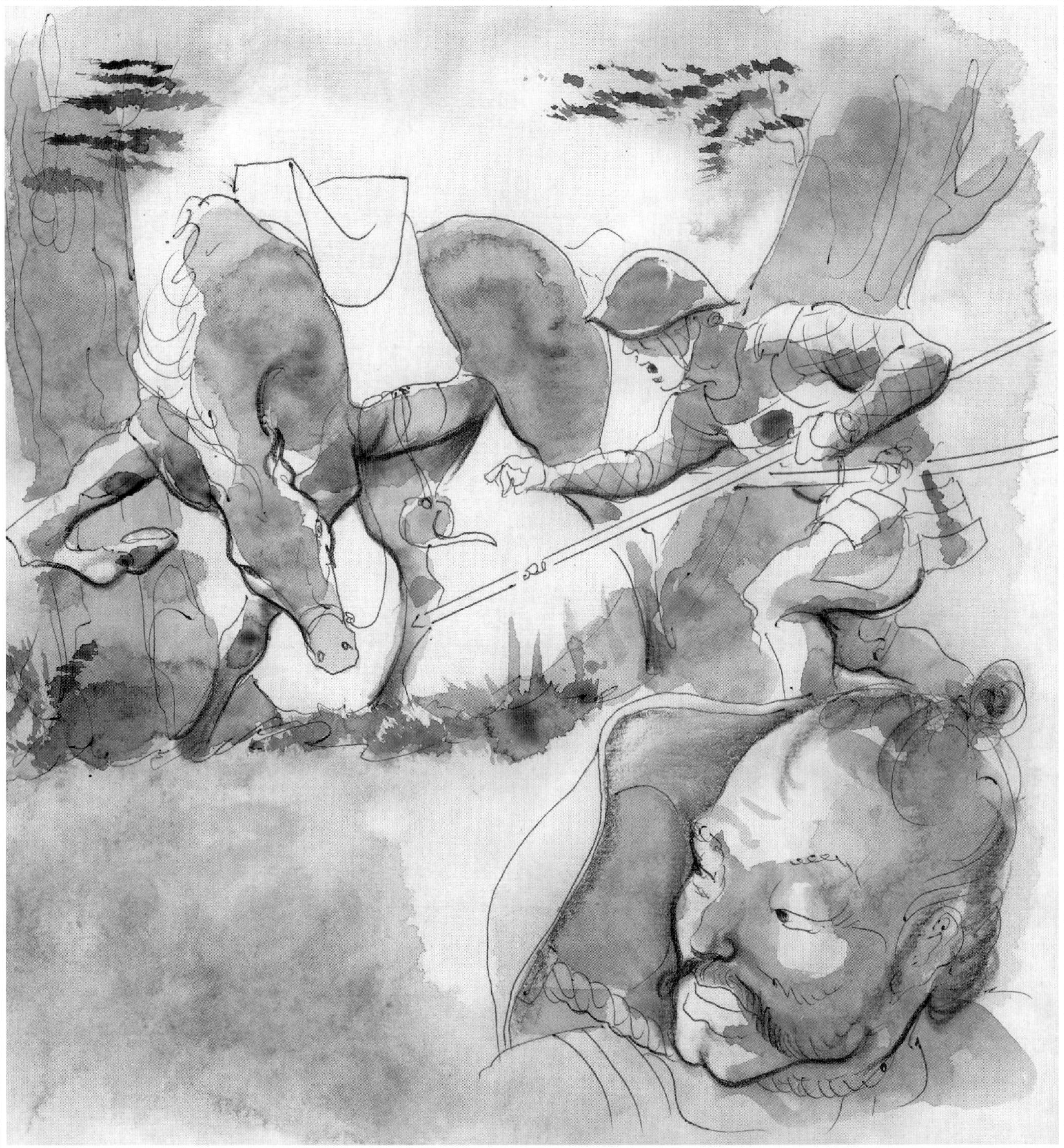

"Is this horse one of those he rode this morning?"

"Can't you see his crest, you fools?"

"Let's call the lieutenant."

"Why? So that we can help to advance his career?"

"You mean, if he finds the fugitive?"

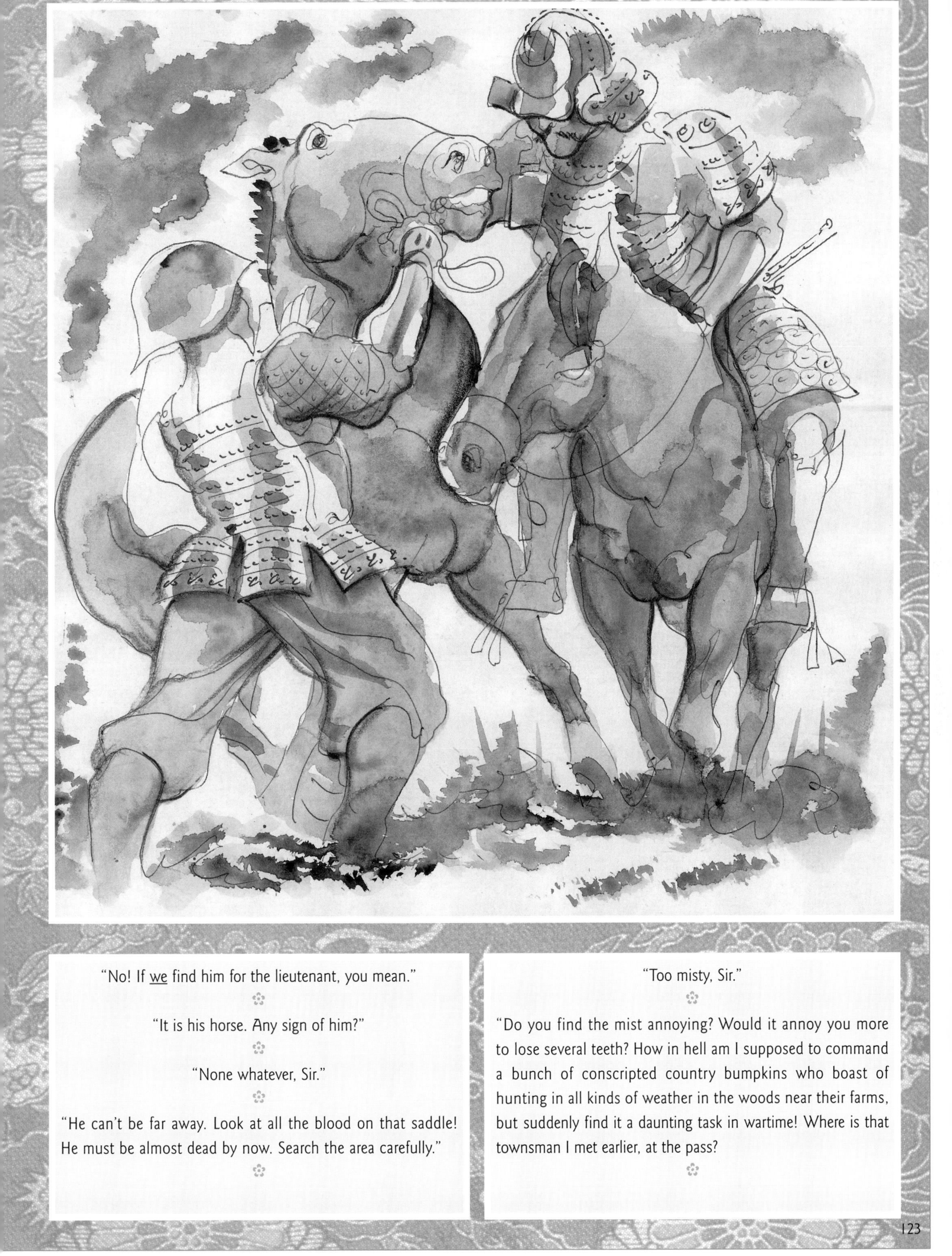

"No! If we find him for the lieutenant, you mean."

❀

"It is his horse. Any sign of him?"

❀

"None whatever, Sir."

❀

"He can't be far away. Look at all the blood on that saddle! He must be almost dead by now. Search the area carefully."

❀

"Too misty, Sir."

❀

"Do you find the mist annoying? Would it annoy you more to lose several teeth? How in hell am I supposed to command a bunch of conscripted country bumpkins who boast of hunting in all kinds of weather in the woods near their farms, but suddenly find it a daunting task in wartime! Where is that townsman I met earlier, at the pass?

❀

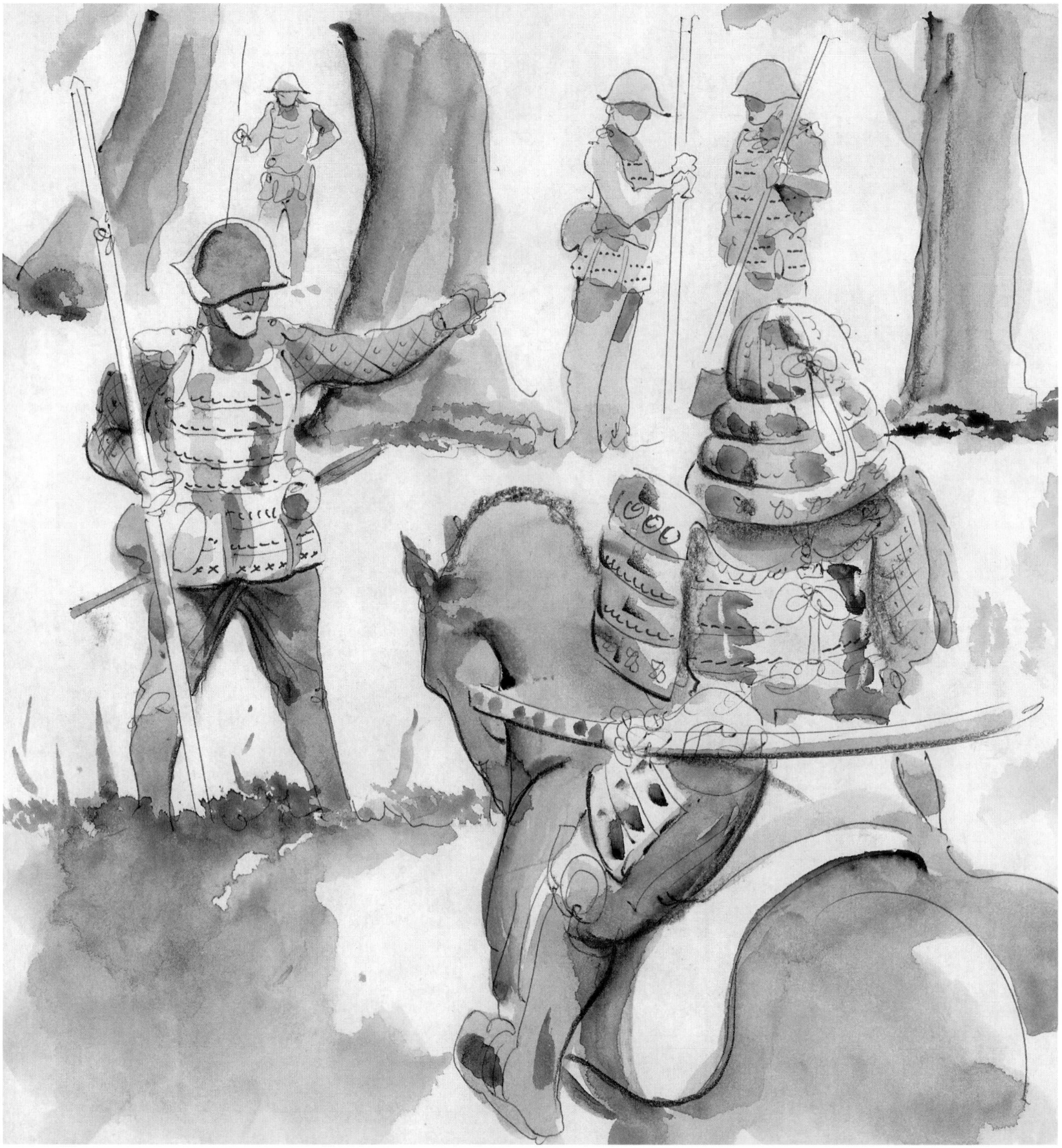

"Here I am, Sir."

"Good. Would you have any idea as to how we might find our man?"

"Your earlier suggestion seems an excellent one to me. If we split up into several two-man patrols and comb the woods straight to the river on the other side, keeping in touch by sound signals, we should be able to locate his hiding place—if he is still around here, Sir."

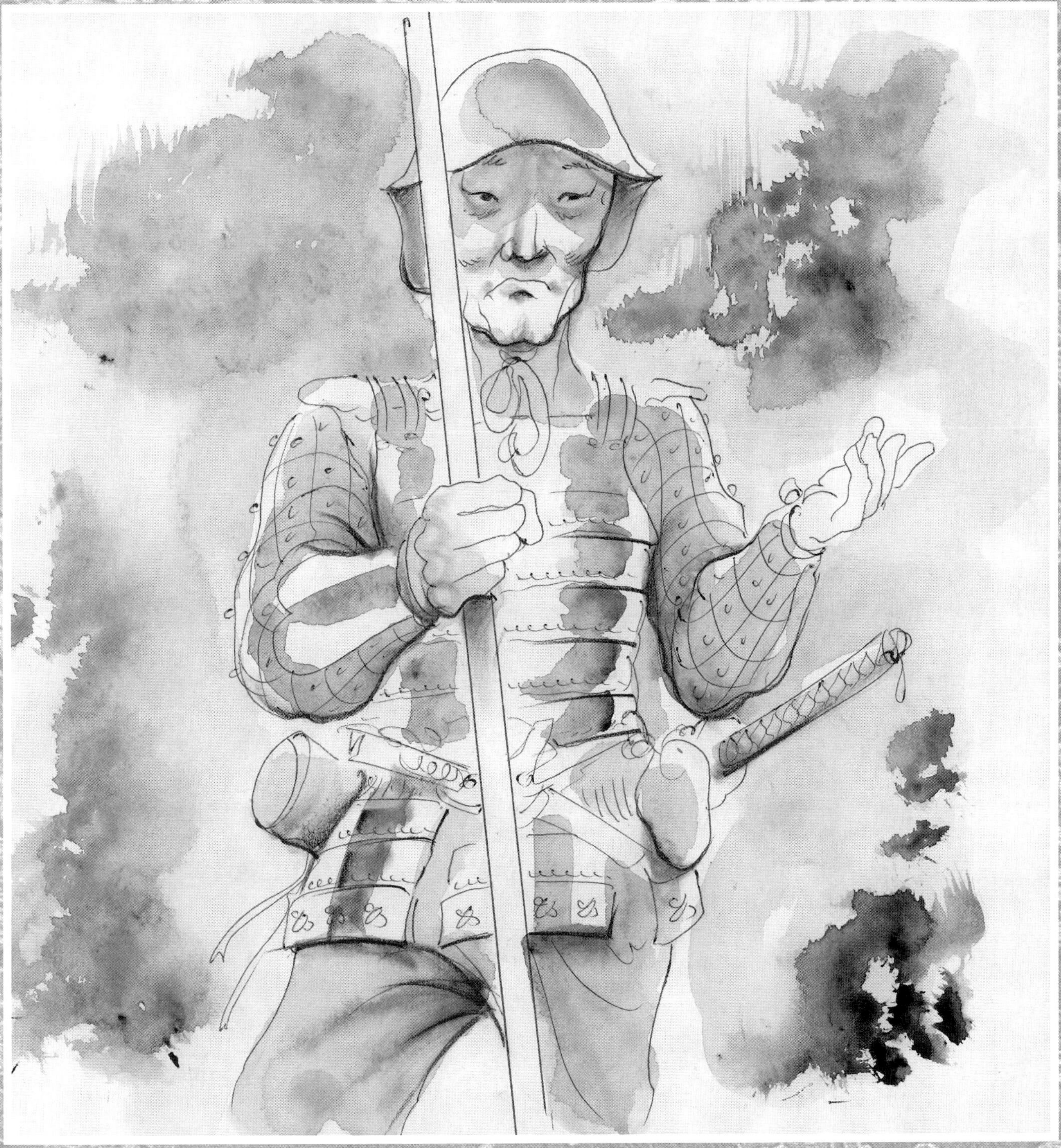

"You can count on that. Pass the plan along to the platoon leader and choose a partner for yourself. I have been noticing your enterprising spirit. Find the man we are after, and there may be more of a reward than the stipend promised when the current clan warfare began. Our overlord needs talented men for service at the castle when we have won this war. Do you understand what I mean?"

"Perfectly, Sir. And I am very grateful."

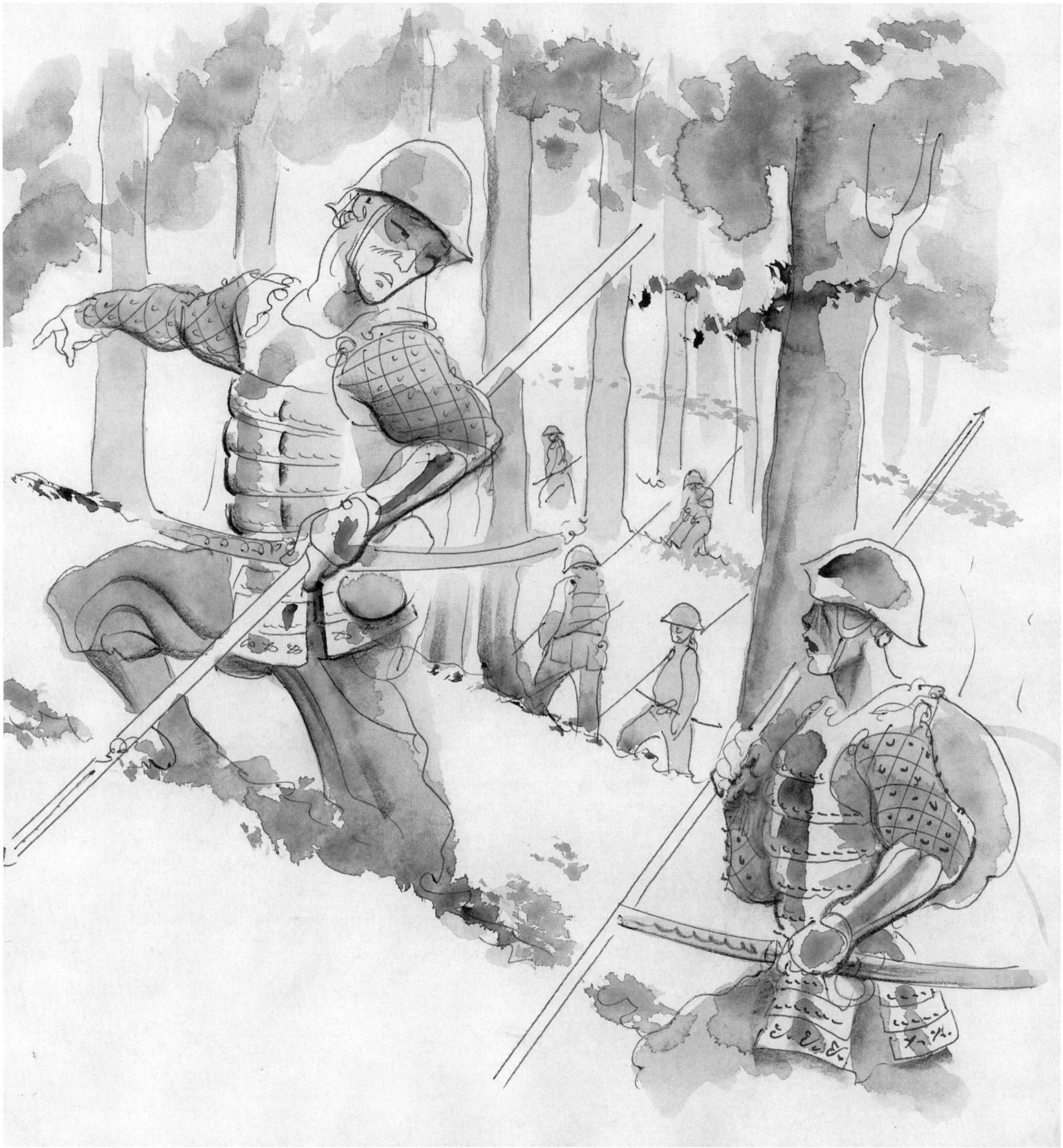

"You, over there—the farmhand trying to pass himself off as a spearman. Follow me! You heard the lieutenant. We will take this corridor in the woods that seems to divide it into fairly equal areas. Search each side and investigate any cluster of bushes or trees where a fugitive might try to hide himself. Our quarry is bound to be around here somewhere. Come on—put some life into those steps!"

"Do you think he is still alive?"

"I hope so. But not lively enough to be able to put up much of a fight any more. Wasn't he already badly wounded when they saw him disappearing into the woods?"

"Yes. There were even some arrows still stuck in his armor. Those, I mean, that he hadn't been able to tear out. And they kept bobbing up and down as he galloped away, the poor devil!"

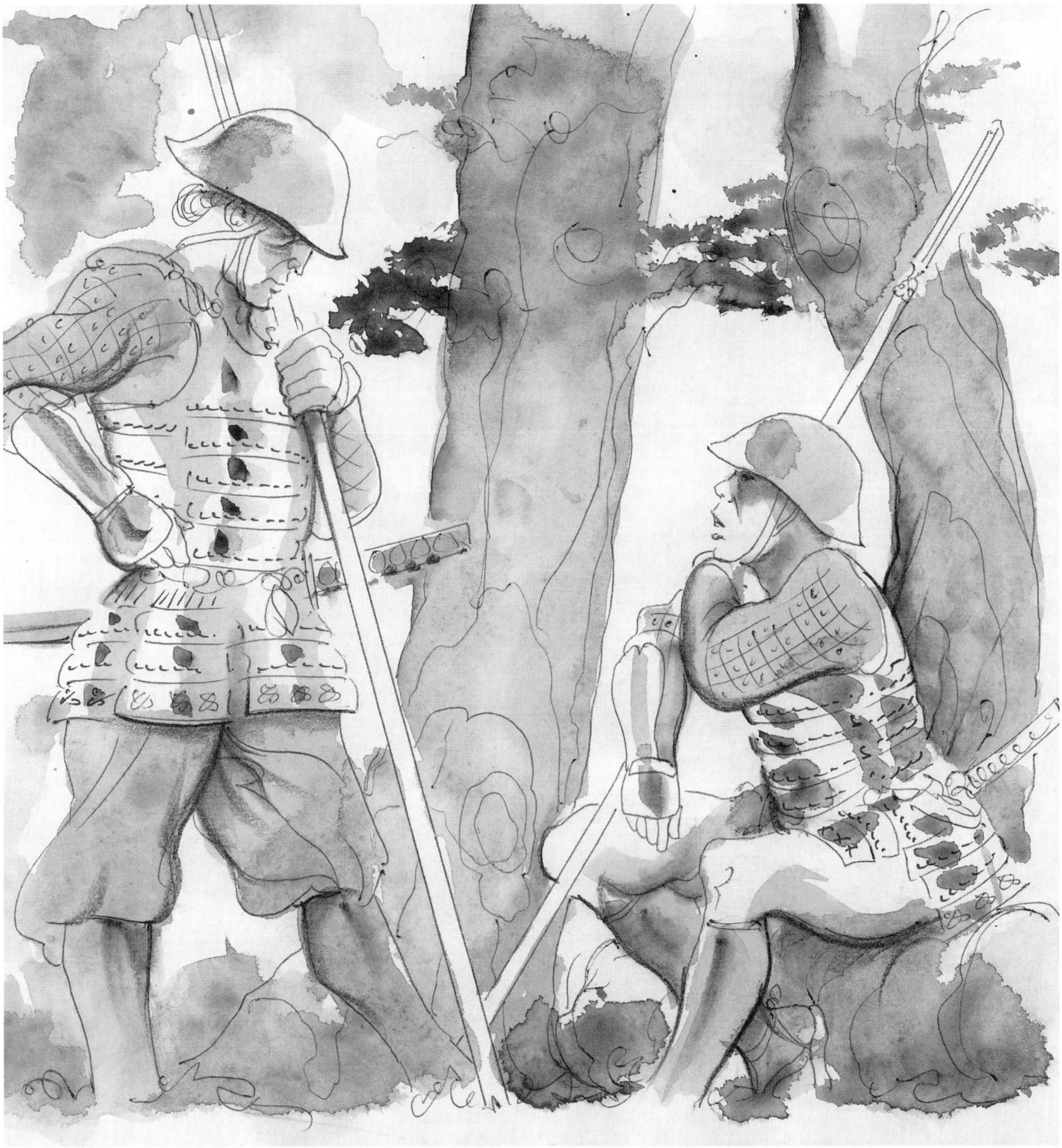

"Poor devil? He's a viper on a horse, like the one in charge of our platoon. Keep your eyes open and if you catch sight of him, let me take care of the rest. I'm better armed, anyway. You farmers are hardly even decently covered, much less properly outfitted with weapons. I can't figure out how you can stand the chill in these damned woods."

"The cold doesn't bother me at all. Or the forest. It's men who bother me. And these spears. . . ."

"What are you doing now?"

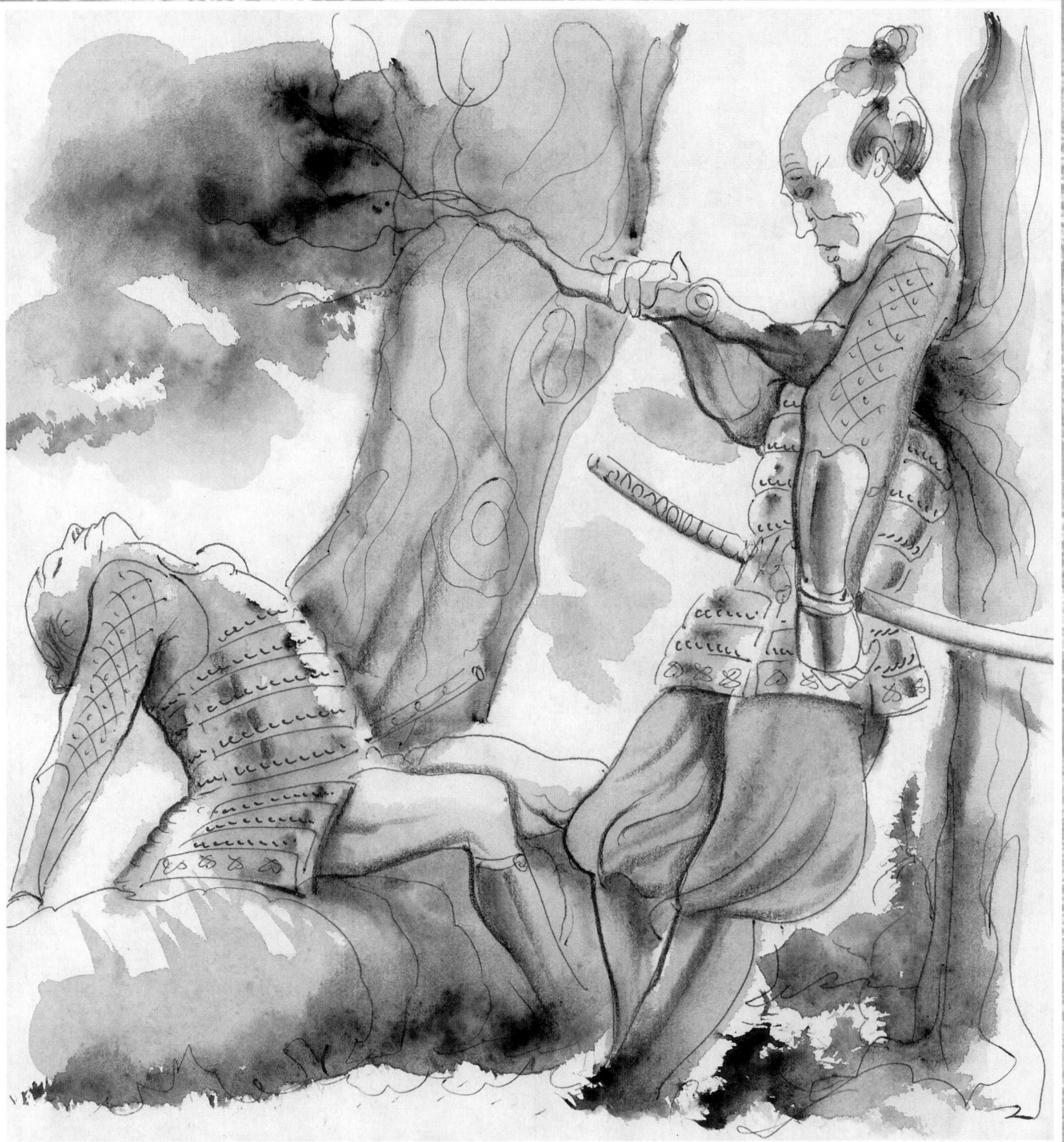

"Sitting. And resting awhile. Actually, I'm not at all eager to come face-to-face with him. Or with that long sword of his. Not at all."

"Frightened?"

"Why wouldn't I be? Aren't you?"

"Of a man half dead?

"What are you talking about? Do you know who it is we are looking for? None other than Kunio Takahashi, First Rank Cavalry Officer of the Kishikami Clan. No wonder they assigned an entire platoon of spearmen to try to track him down in these woods, however badly wounded he may be. And you want to tackle him all by yourself? You must be crazy!"

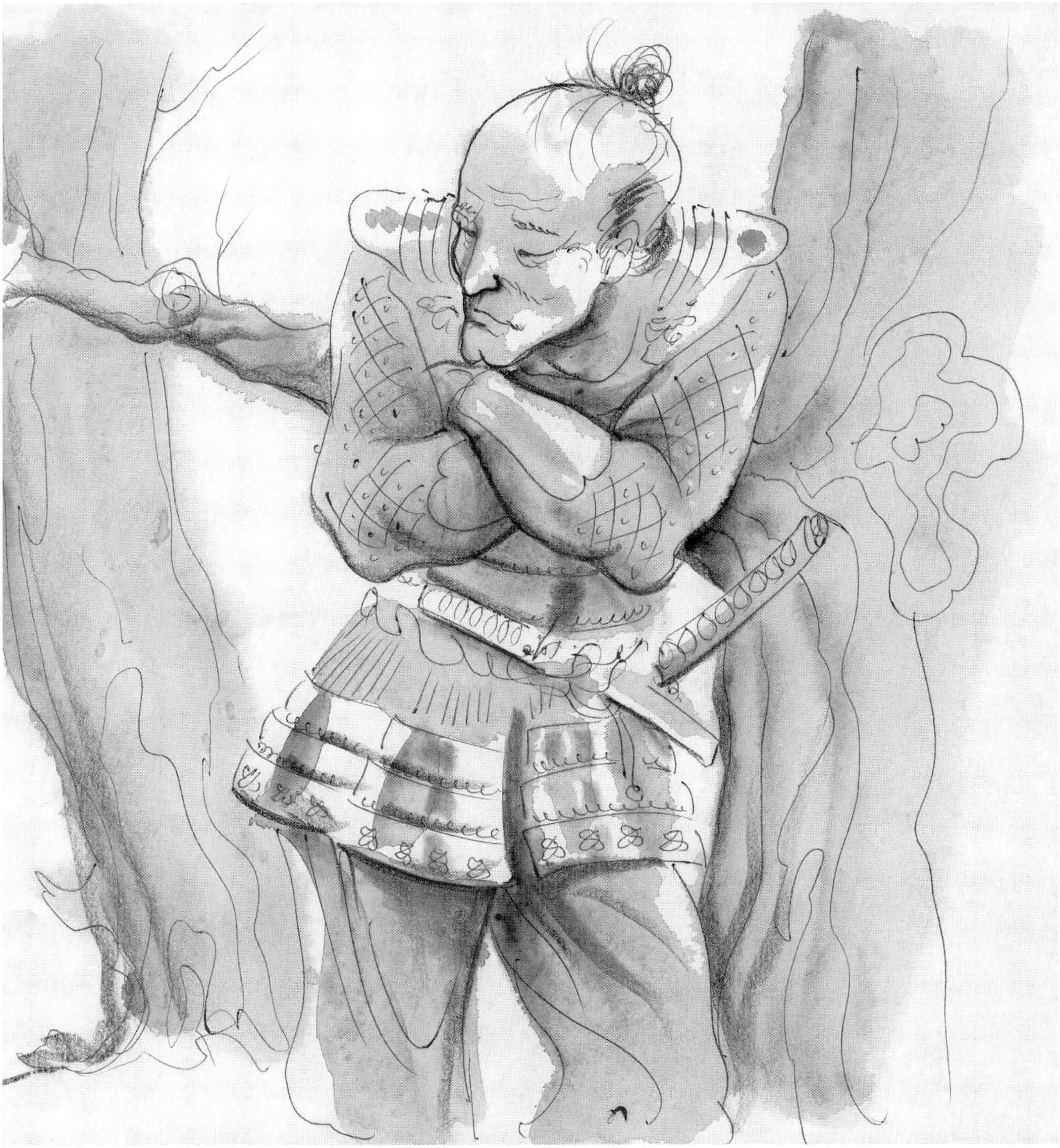

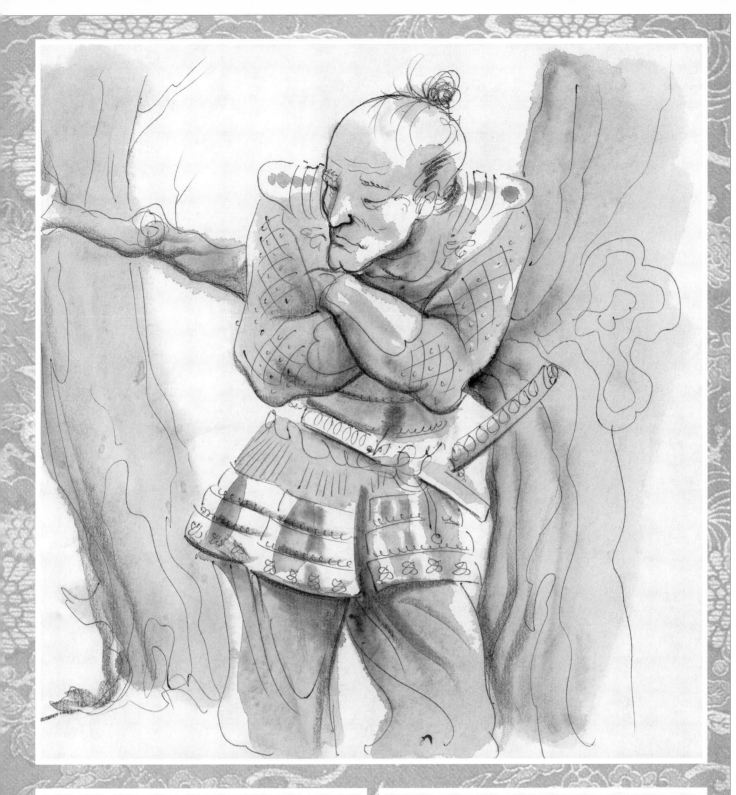

"Not a bit. I know exactly what I'm doing. You saw him this morning, didn't you? And you said yourself that he's seriously wounded, isn't that right?"

"So?"

"So, let's find him and finish him off. Those damned warriors on horseback always carry some gold with them. I have no intention of leaving that for the scavengers. No, I intend to have his money and whatever other valuables he may be carrying, not to mention his weapons, which will be of the finest quality. Such gentlemen don't go into battle as poorly equipped as you and I, believe me."

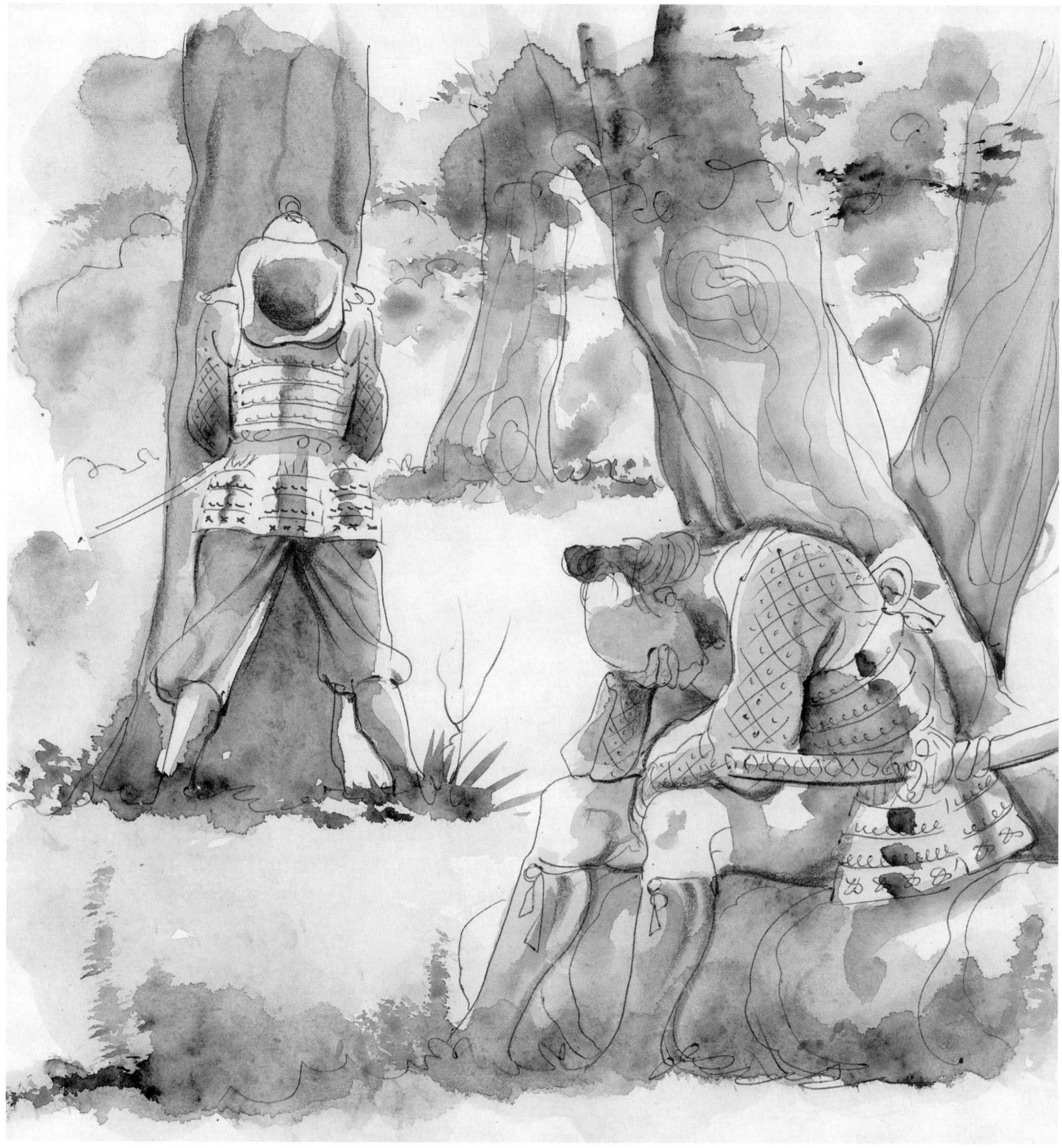

"Well, they are different."

"In what way?"

"What do you mean? They are gentlemen."

"Is that so! And what is that supposed to mean? They eat and drink as we do, don't they? And they bleed just like us when they are cut, and then they die, as we all do. I don't see any real differences, farmer! Something tells me that this gentleman is hiding somewhere around here, in this very section of the woods."

"I sincerely hope not. What do you have against him, anyway?"

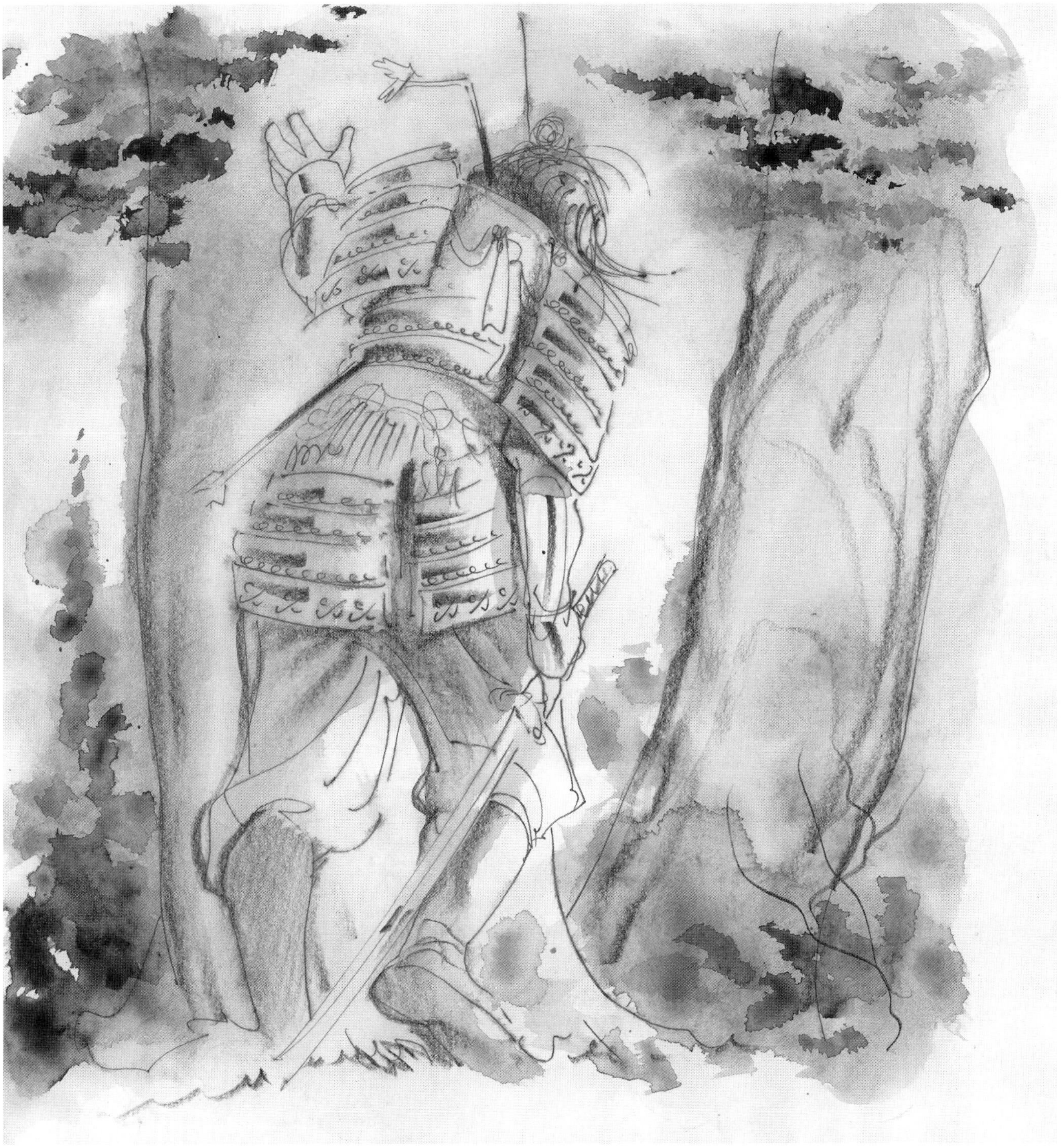

"What a question! He's an enemy commander, isn't he?"

"Well, then, let our commanders catch him. Why you should be so eager to find him yourself is beyond me. You didn't actually volunteer for this search party, did you?"

"I most certainly did."

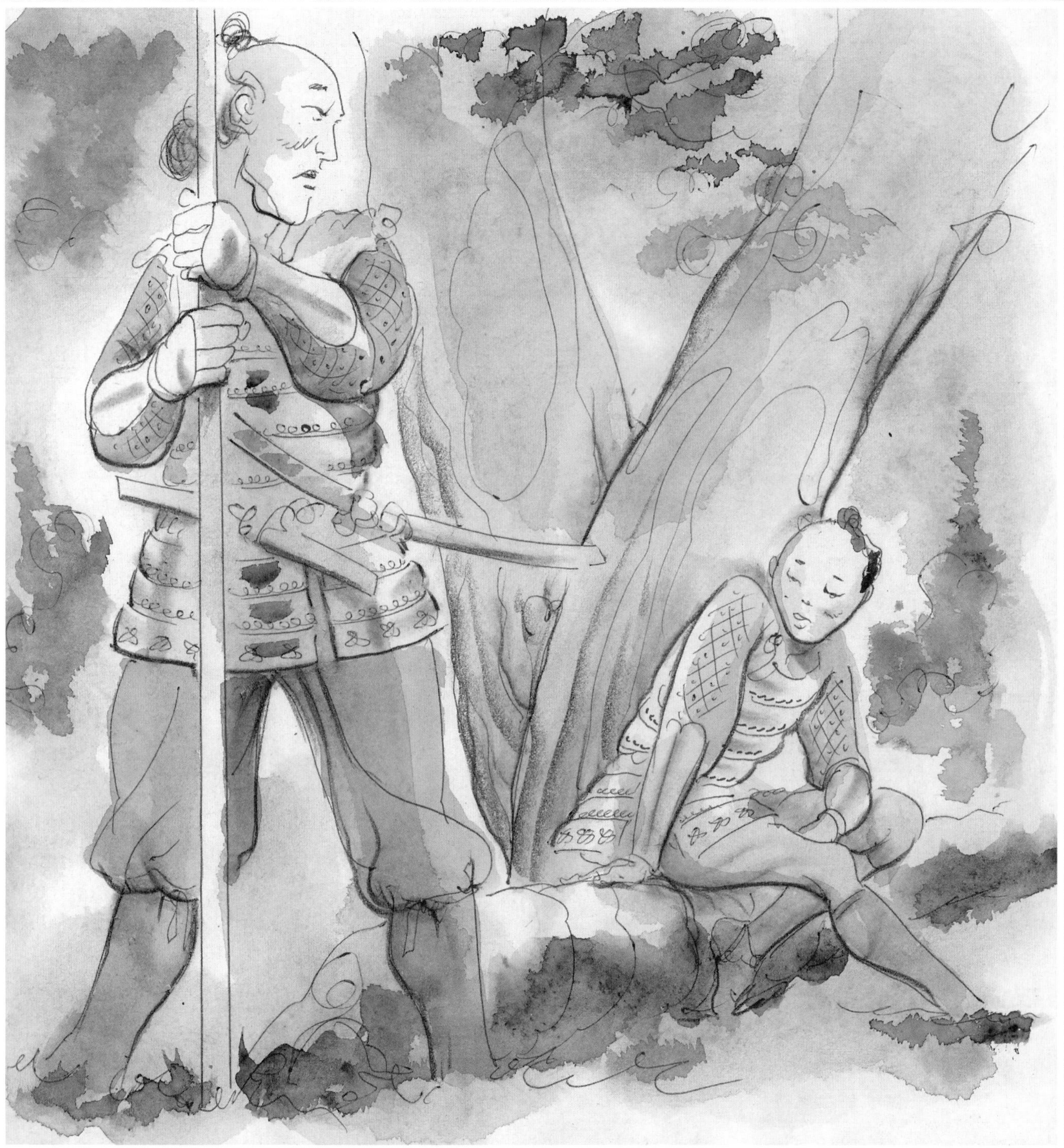

"And did you volunteer to participate in this cursed war?"

"Naturally. You, I gather, are a conscript—aren't you? You speak like a peasant whose only desire is to return safely to his tiny plot of mud and stones. . . ."

"Of course I want to go home! And the sooner the better. You obviously have other ambitions and hope to advance yourself through a career in the armies of Lord Kawasaki, Governor of our province. My best wishes to you, soldier!"

"What the hell are you doing among spearmen, then? Why aren't you home with your wife and children?"

"Because the authorities came and dragged me away, that's why. Any refusal would have resulted in public decapitation—as a means of inspiring other farmers with the necessary martial fervor. Otherwise, that's exactly where I would be now, my warlike comrade, sitting at my own hearth with my family around me."

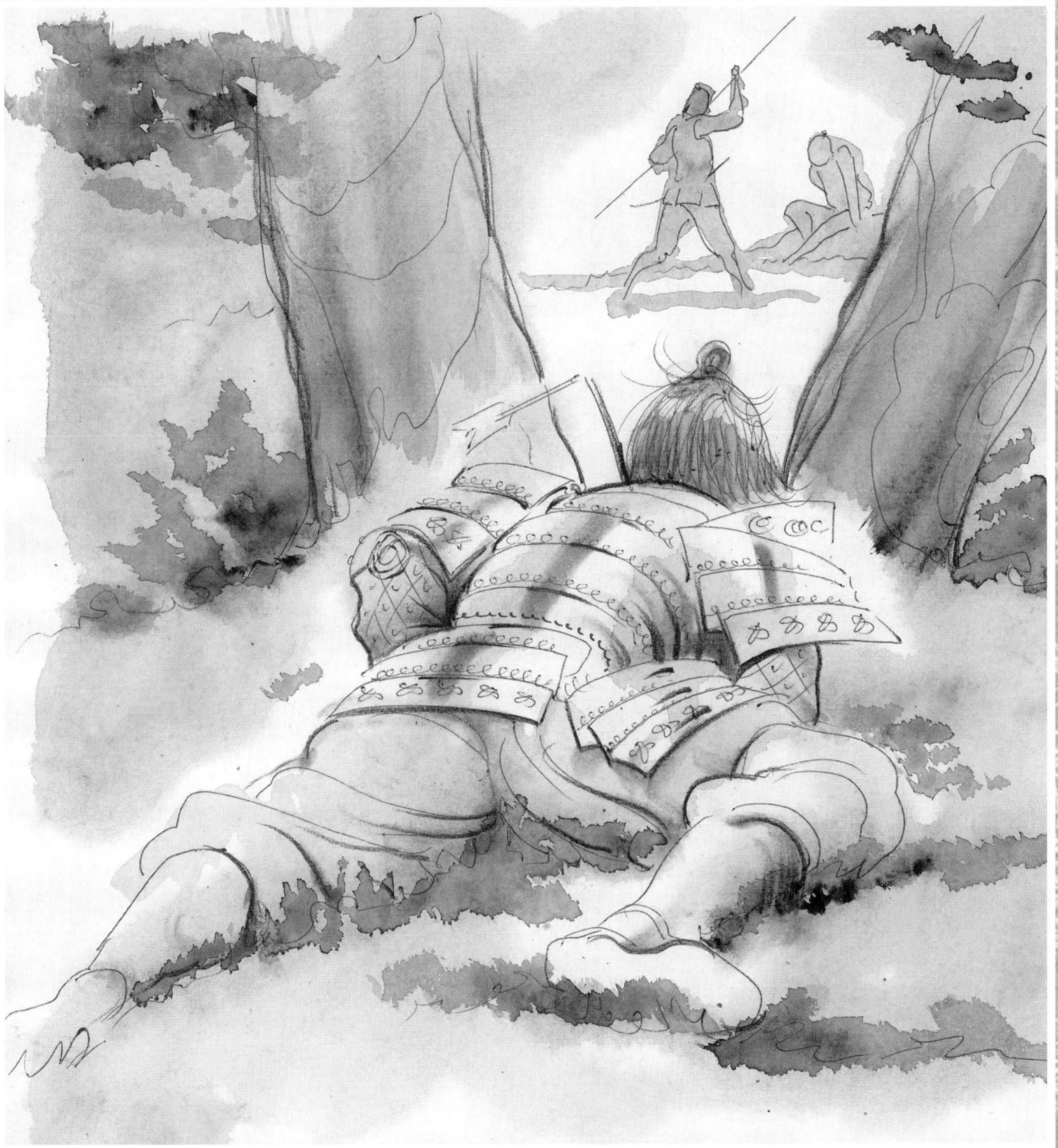

"Quiet!"

"What is it?"

"I thought I heard labored breathing and the sound of someone moving. He must be close by, I'm sure of it. I can feel it!"

"If you're right—and I hope you're not, for my own sake—why don't we call the others? We were instructed to keep in close contact with them, or have you forgotten?"

"We're not going to call anyone!"

"Why not? If that madman should rush us, we would be finished—both of us. Finished."

"By all the evil gods of the forest! Why must I always be paired with a coward?"

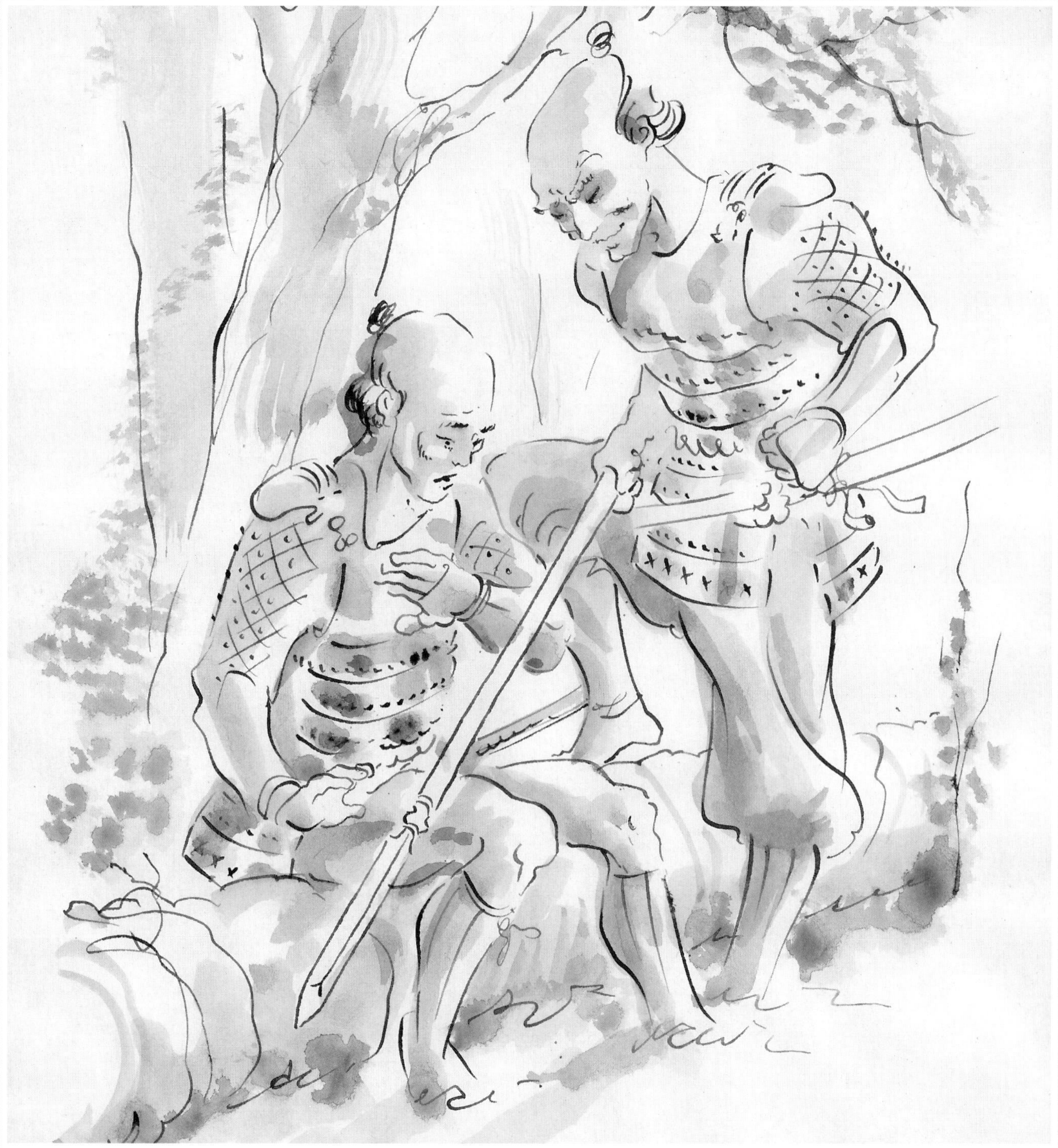

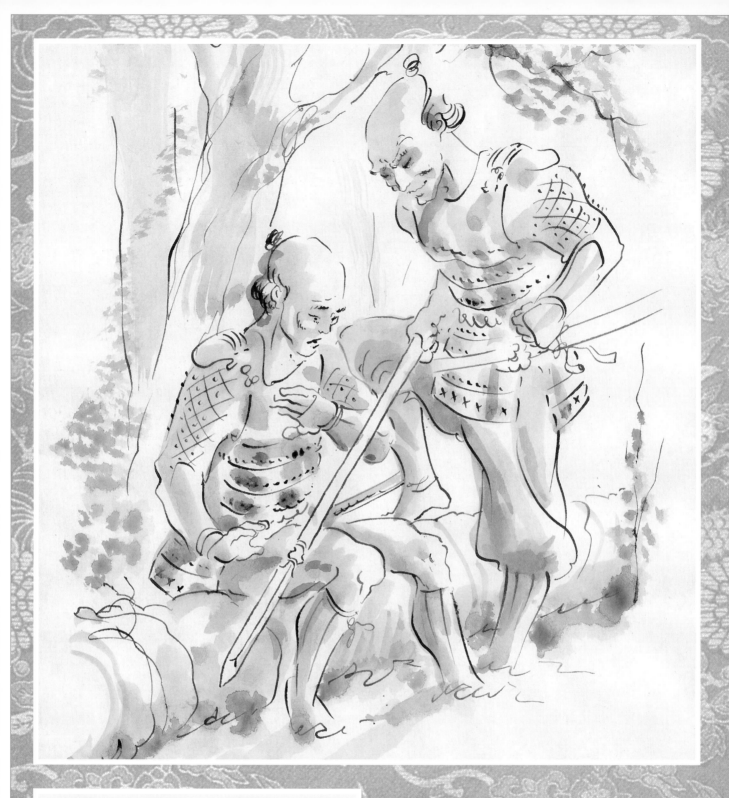

"Why are you so afraid of a man who is probably half-conscious and already bleeding to death beneath those bushes with all those arrows still protruding from him? If we call the others, how much do you think we'll get of the spoils? The lieutenant will appropriate his weapons, his money, and his head as a trophy. The others will snatch whatever is still worth taking of his armor. You and I will be left with what even the vultures don't want. No thank you. Just keep your mouth shut. We'll find him, finish him off if he should still be breathing, strip him of his valuables and then—only then—will we call the others."

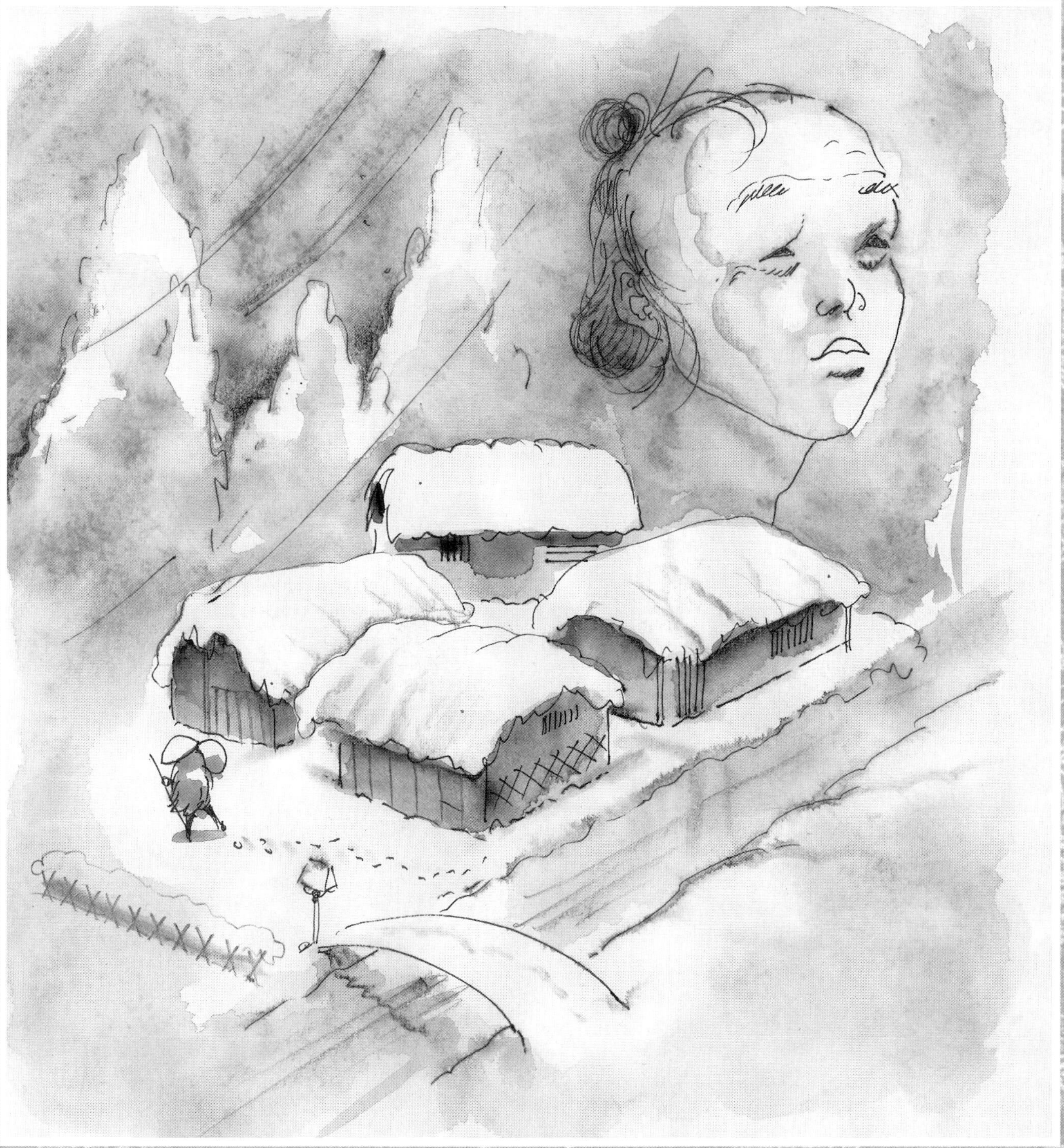

"And if I start to call them now?"

"Then you will find the blade of this spear lodged in your throat right now, or in your back the first chance I get when we're sent into battle again, you toad!"

"What a life! If a foe doesn't kill me, my comrade will."

"Listen to me. Would you like to return home in one piece?"

"I have no other ambition at the present moment, believe me!"

"Good. Then follow me and keep your mouth shut. That's all you have to do."

"Soon it will begin to snow in my village. We stay indoors during the winter, indulge our children, repair our tools, or play games of chance with one another. It's very warm near the hearth, in the kitchen. Tell me something: you've never been on a farm, have you?"

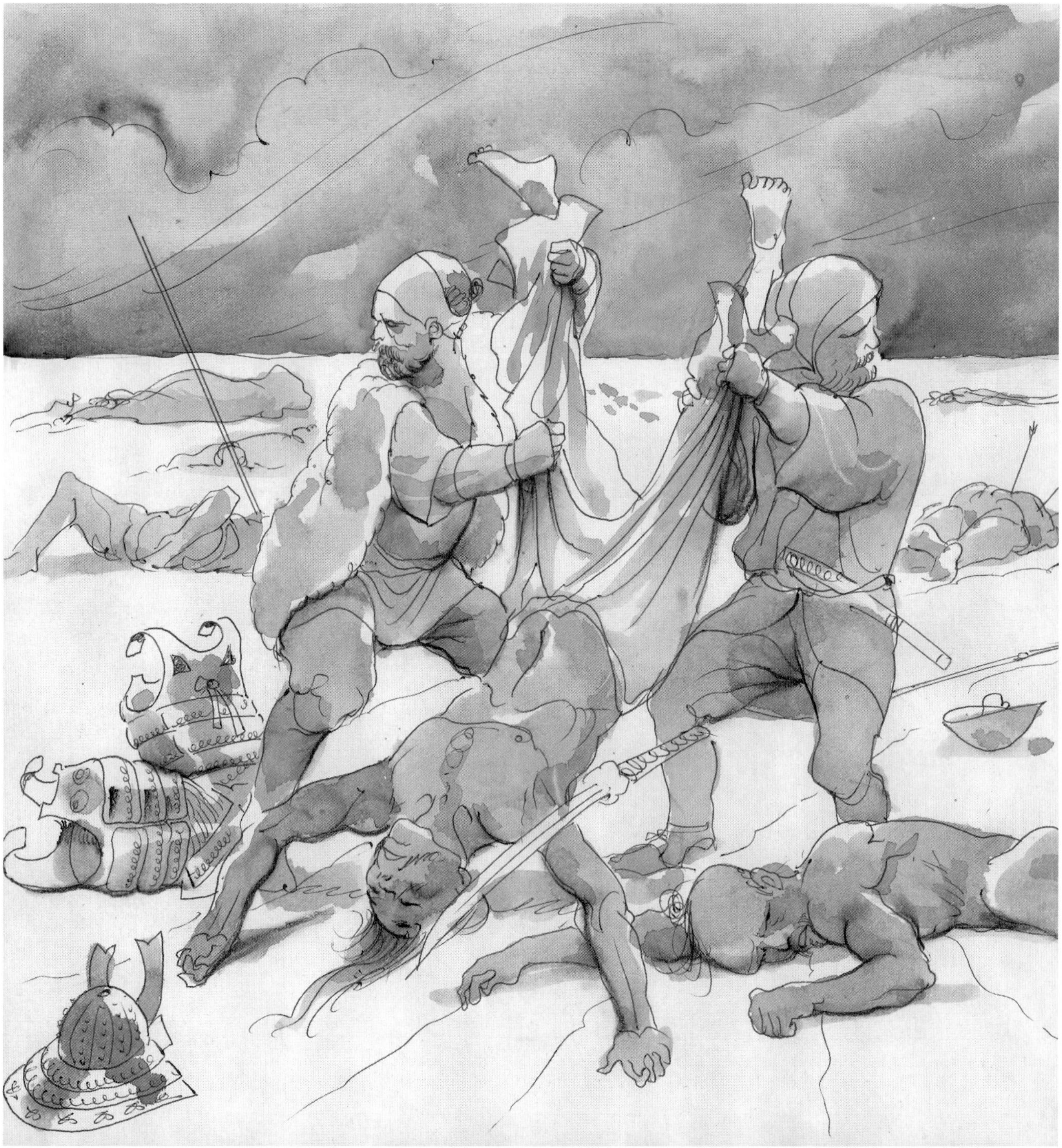

"No. I'm from the city. I was a wood-worker, duly registered with my neighborhood association. Until, one day, I realized that it took me a year to earn the same amount I could make in a month as a soldier—with any luck, sometimes in a week!"

"By looting, you mean?"

"Don't be so damn smug, farmer. You peasants don't waste any time when it comes to looting, either. Nor do you and your friends hesitate to finish off wounded warriors who can't lift a finger to protect themselves. I have seen their carcasses after your fellow farmers have picked them clean. I'm just more honest about it, that's all. These are times for grabbing whatever you can get your hands on, and I grab. What else is there? Prestige? Glory? Those are luxuries that only warriors on horseback, with great names and huge estates behind them, can afford. But, in the end, even they grab whatever they can. And their reach is much longer than yours or mine, believe me. Woe to anyone who finds himself in their way when they want something!"

"Being a soldier is a dangerous profession, though. I'd much rather till the land. At least it doesn't rush at you with a raised sword and a crazed shout. . . ."

✿

"No. It just allows you to starve quietly, your precious land, because of a mere accident of flood or drought, or whatever! No, even if it is rather precarious, the life of a mercenary soldier is much simpler. All you have to do is choose the ascending clan, join its ranks, and make sure to carry several different clan badges in your bag when you go into battle—just in case things go badly for your side."

✿

"You mean, then you would just change badges? Strange sense of honor you city folks seem to have."

✿

"The ultimate goal is survival, farmer. Not understanding that is why so many peasants end up fertilizing their own plots of earth."

"You seem to know all the tricks. Perhaps you can tell me how to rid myself of this armor, hand my spear back to the armory officer, get my long overdue pay, and an official release from the camp's bursar."

✿

"All of that can be arranged."

✿

"How? Are you serious?"

✿

"Of course, you idiot!"

✿

"Could you do it?"

✿

"Not me, stupid. It's money that can do it."

✿

"You mean . . ."

✿

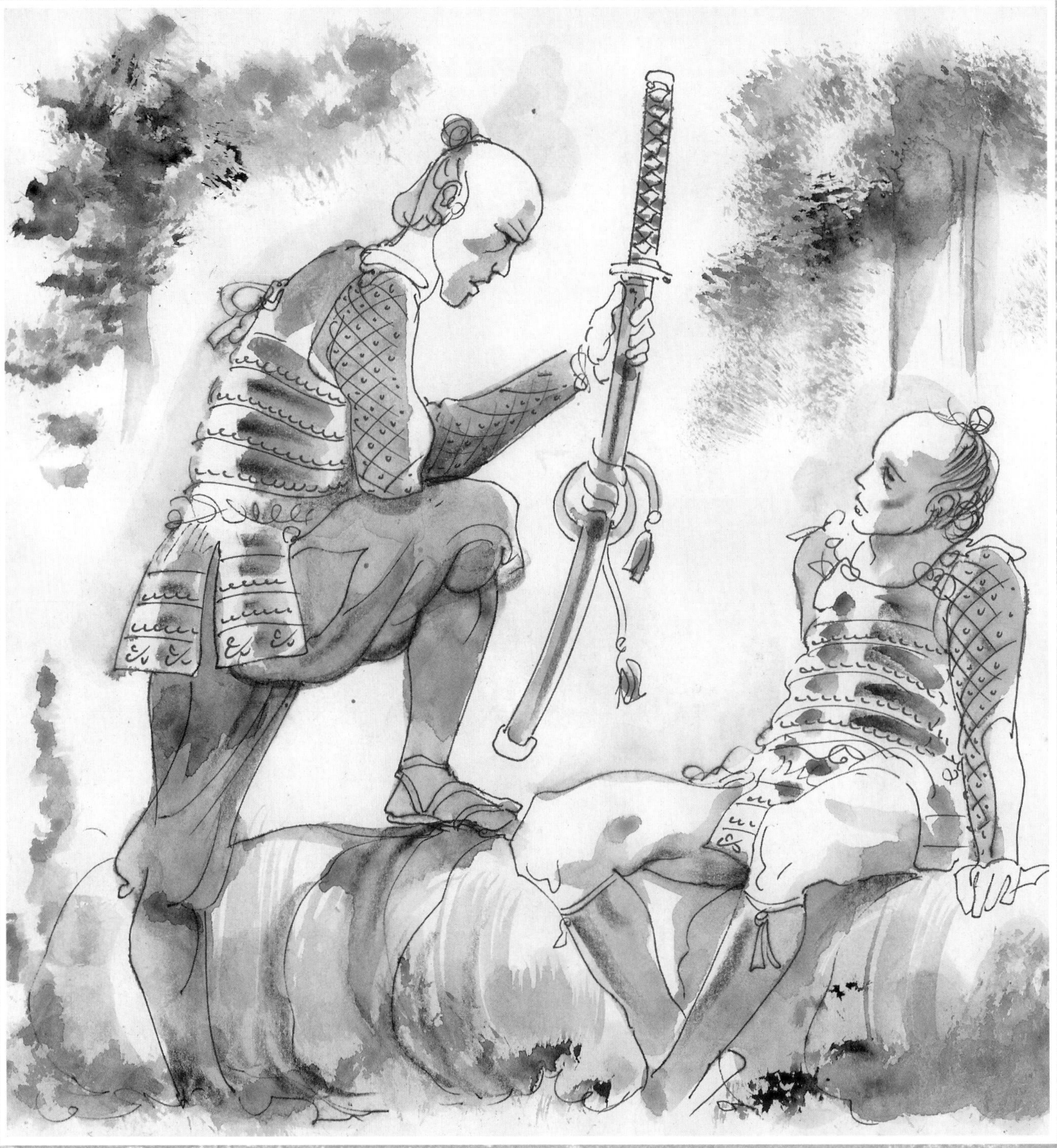

"A bribe. That's right. An appropriate amount of gold and both those officers will be more than happy to send you home with an official seal of discharge attached to your pass."

"You really do know all the tricks!"

"I certainly hope so. In times like these, it could be worth your life to wander around wearing blinders about such things."

"Even so, it's still very dangerous, this martial profession that you have chosen, my city friend."

"Of course it is. That's why it is so profitable. So far, I have done fairly well with the spear, which has been long enough to keep me well beyond the reach of trouble. As soon as I can afford it, though, it's the sword that I want to learn how to use well. Look at this—I took it from a dead samurai. I want to find a real teacher who can show me all the best techniques. Not some fool of a corporal who knows less about the sword than I do."

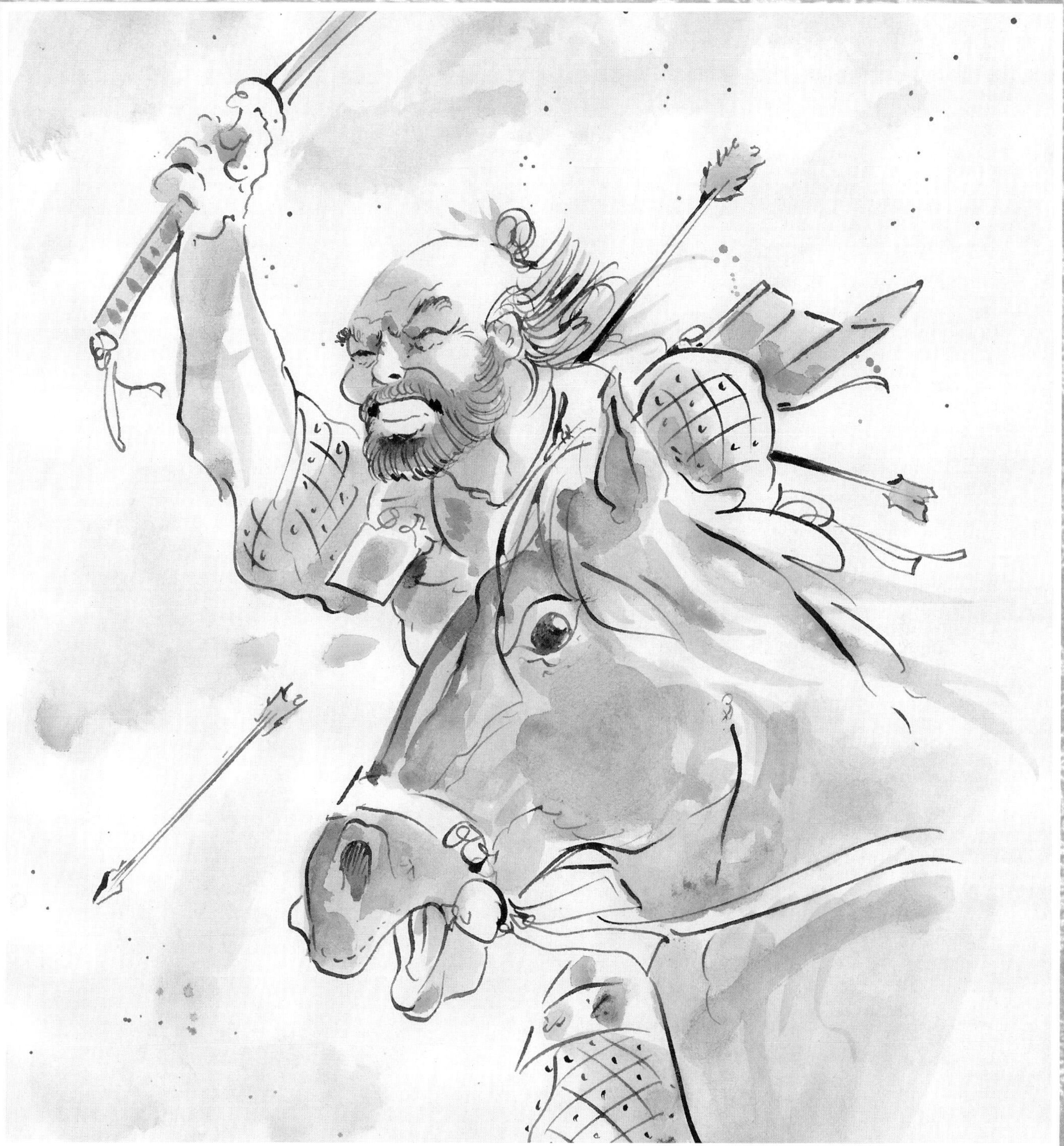

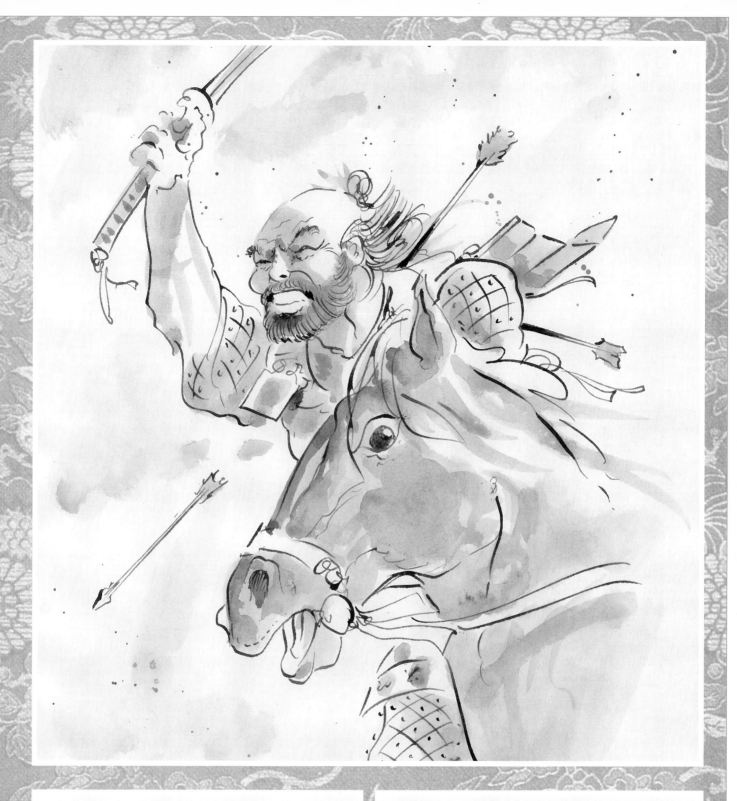

"Why the sword?"

"'Why the sword,' he asks. How could you expect to become a gentleman and rise through the ranks if you don't know how to handle this weapon as a gentleman should?"

"Like the man we're looking for?"

"Yes."

"I think he must have made good his escape by now."

"I'm sure you hope he has, farmer, but I know better. He's still somewhere around here."

"If you had seen him in battle this morning, you'd also be hoping he has left these woods far behind, believe me."

"Why, did you actually see him fight?"

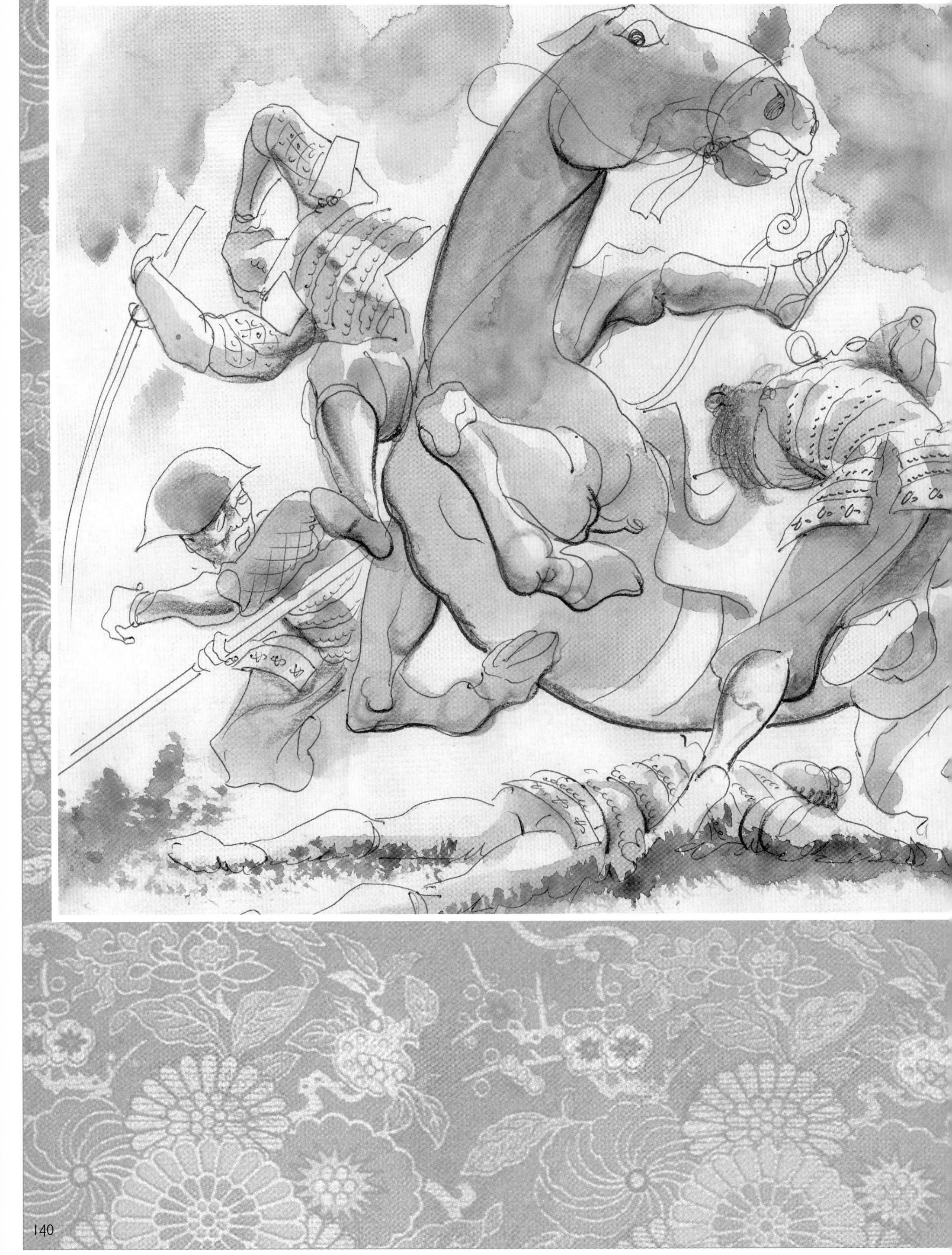

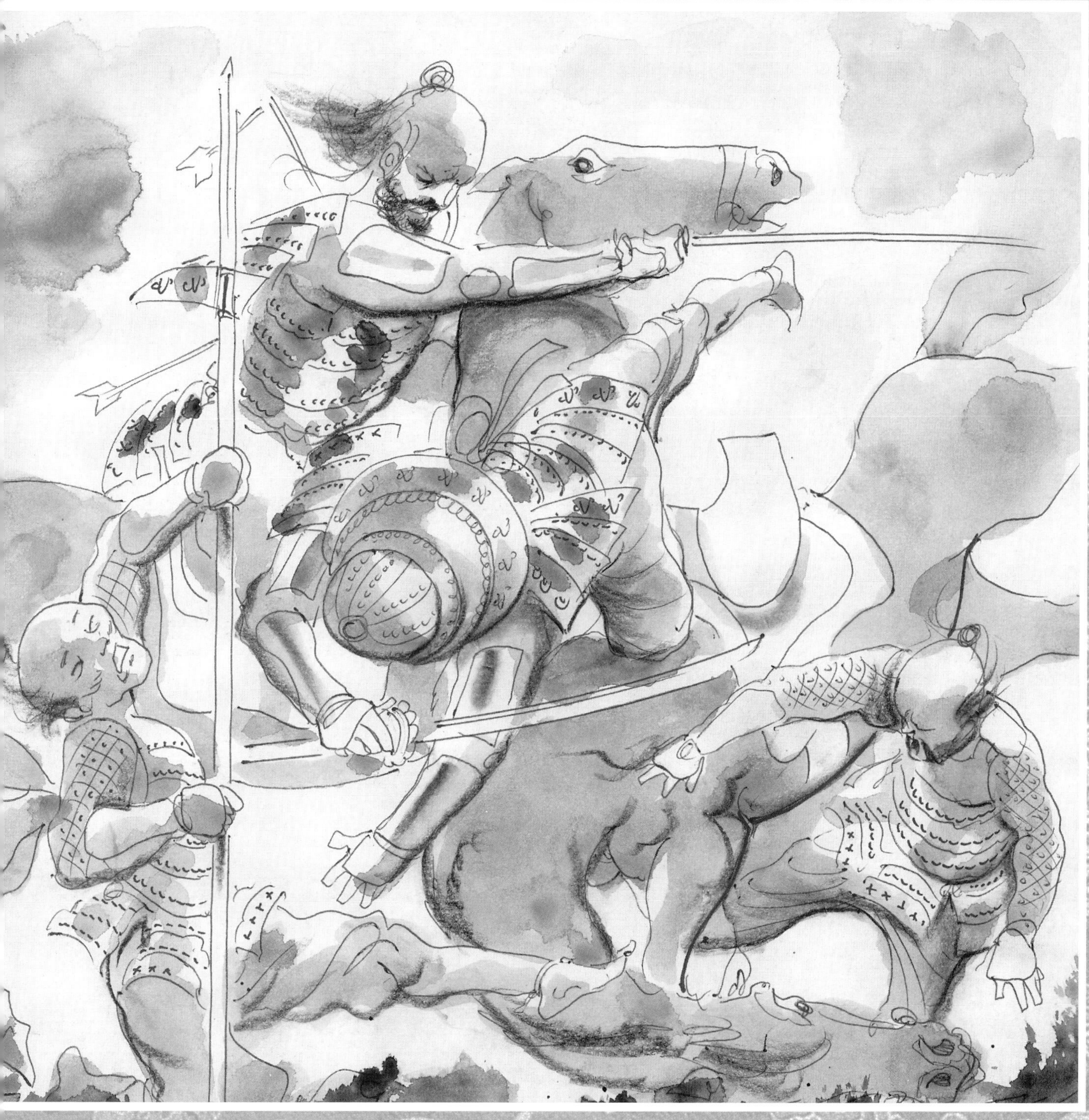

"I certainly did! That's why I'm not eager to meet him again. He maneuvered that long sword of his as if it were as light as a paper fan. I saw an acrobat at a festival once, who did astonishing things with a fan. This warrior was much faster and his movements even more unpredictable. He cut down two mounted warriors before my very eyes, and I don't know how many of the spearmen who surrounded him. . . . Do you remember 'Spear Head,' the corporal?"

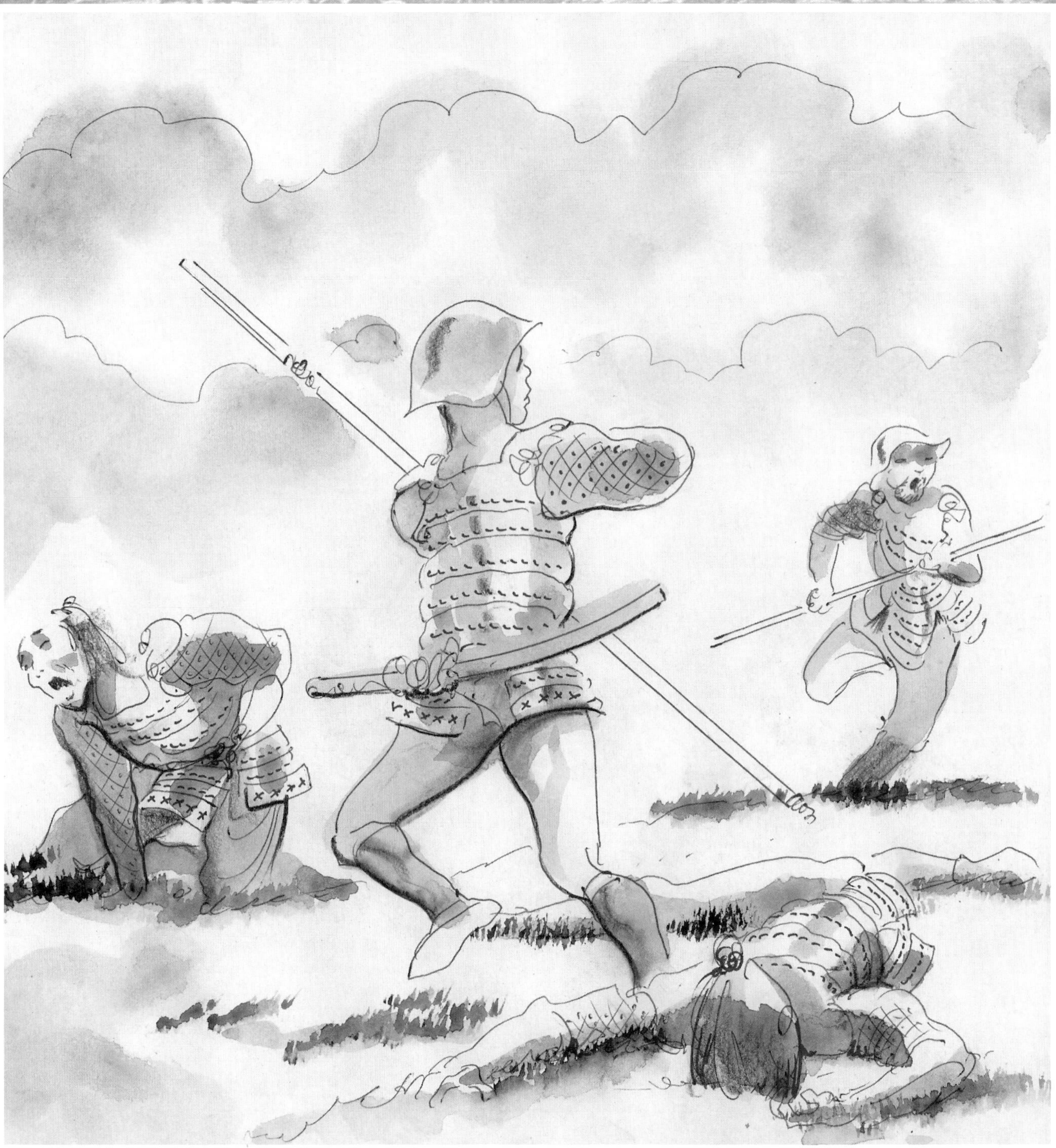

"The 'veteran' squad leader? I remember him only too well. Did he bite the dust, as well?"

"Yes—with only one cut. But he managed to sink his spear into the man's thigh before he fell—only an instant before a shower of arrows brought Sir Takahashi crashing down as well, almost on top of him."

"Good riddance! I'm glad that Spear Head isn't around anymore. First, because—once he recognized that I had potential and

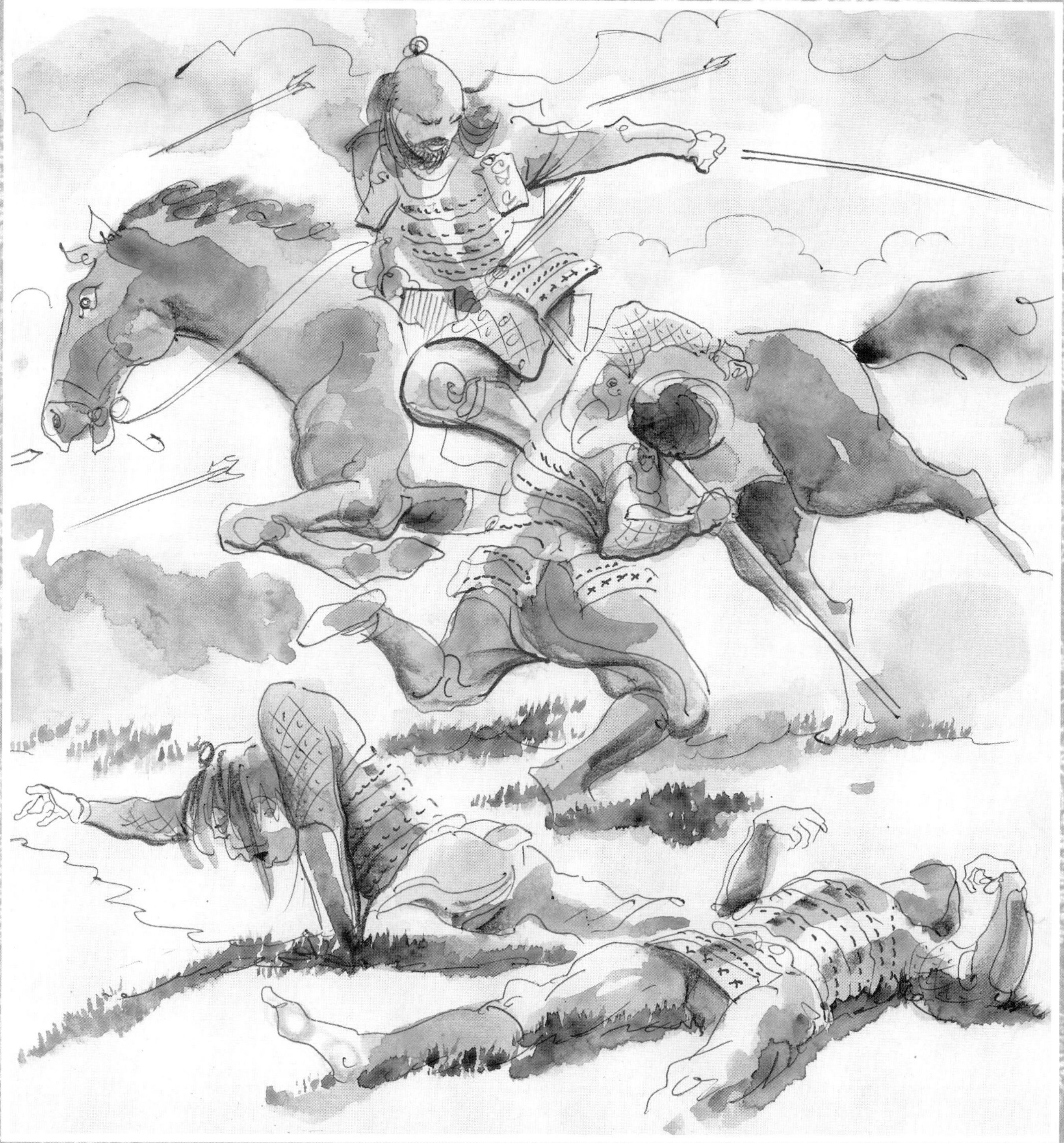

might represent a threat to him in the future—he tried to break my spirit during our training at the castle. He would hit me at every opportunity with the butt of his spear. That, supposedly, was his way of teaching me 'the noble art of spearmanship'—or so he liked to claim. All he actually did was land me in the medical ward more than once. Now he is no longer barring my way, is he? But never mind about him—it's what happened to the rest of his squad of spearman that interests me. . . ."

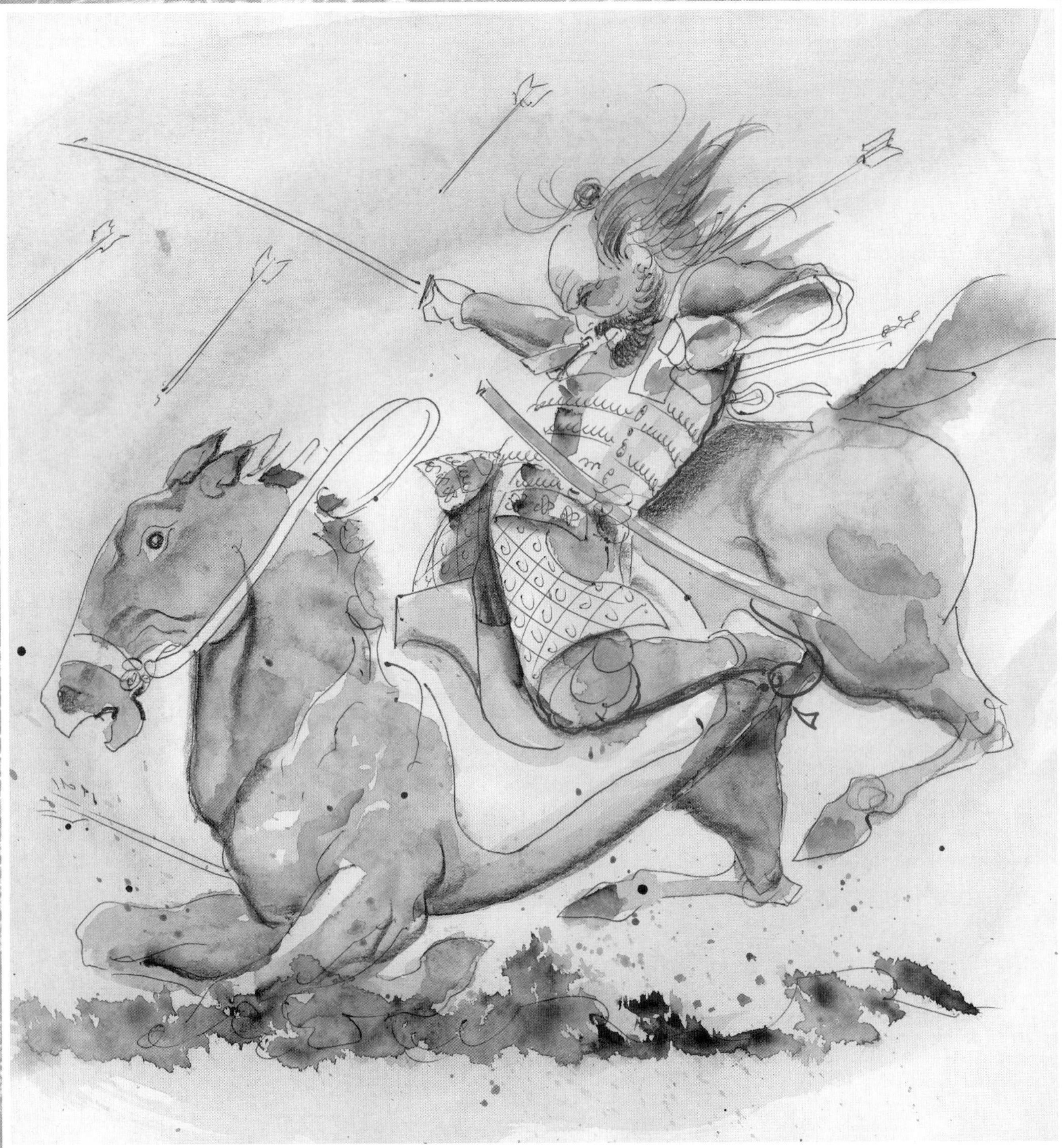

"Yes, undoubtedly the most extraordinary thing, my friend. Sir Takahashi, upon whose fallen body the few surviving members of Spear Head's squad were eagerly converging, roaring in expectation that the arrows and the heavy fall had killed or incapacitated him, disentagled himself from his convulsing horse and rose like an angry specter to meet them halfway.

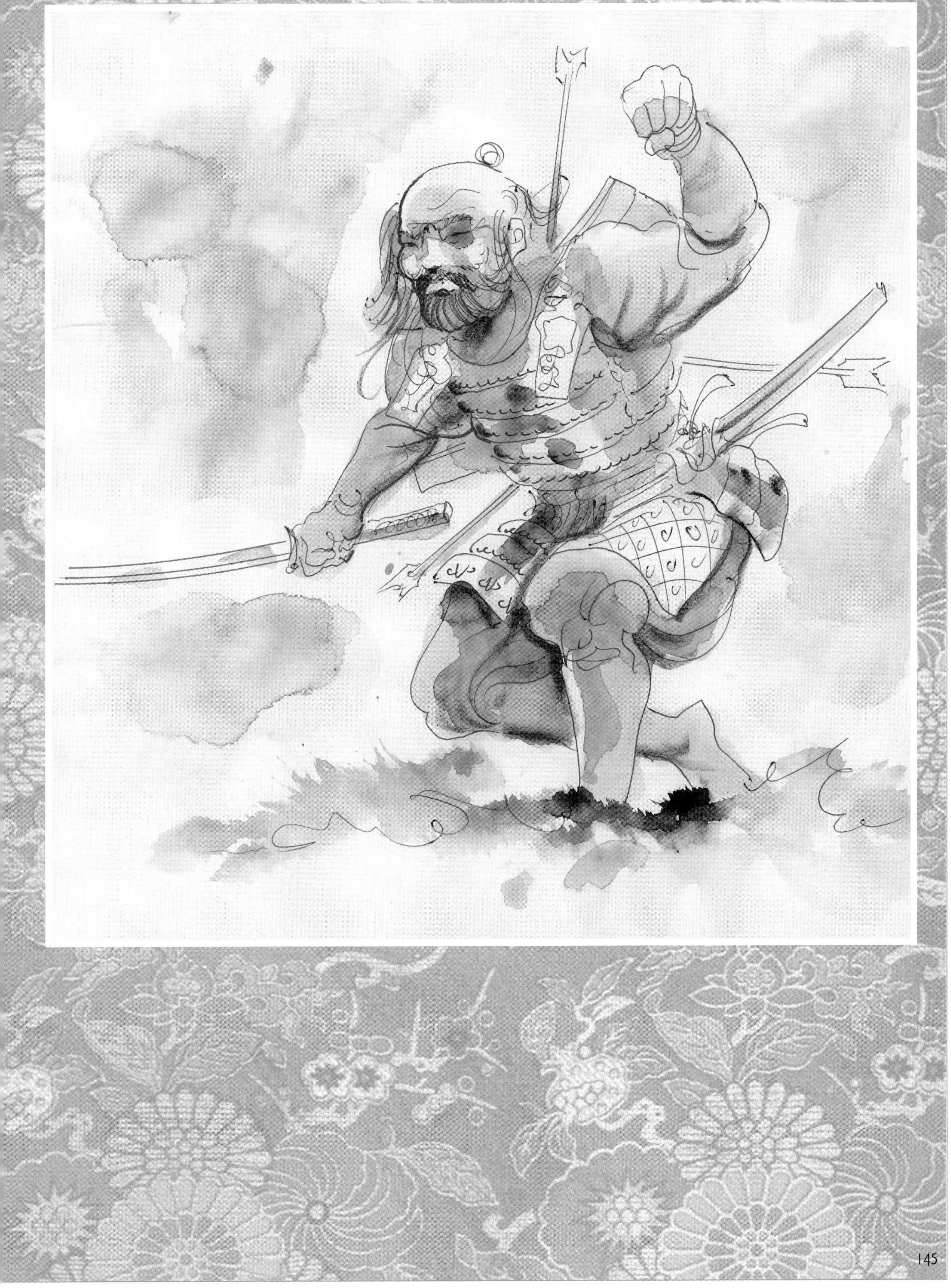

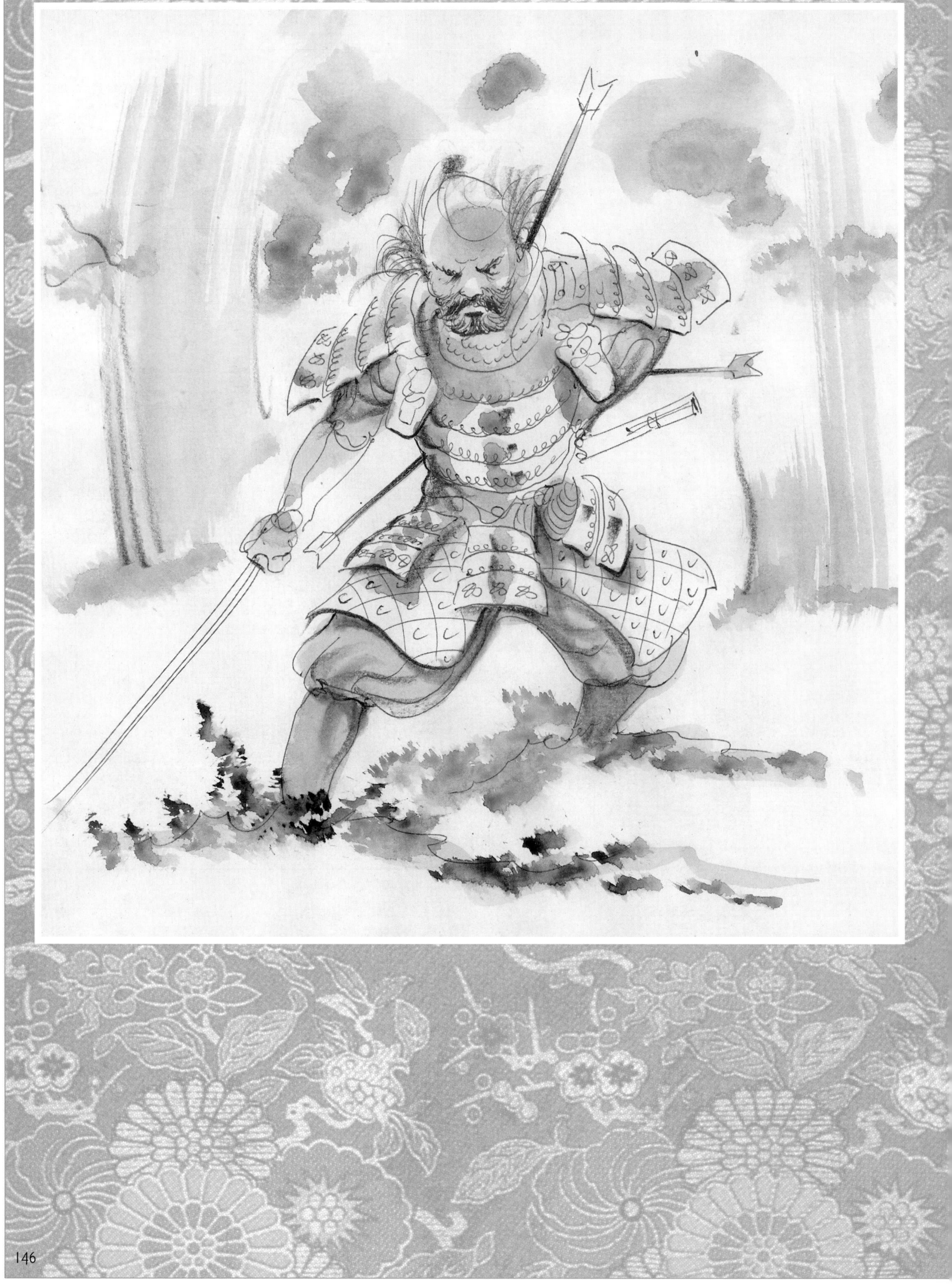

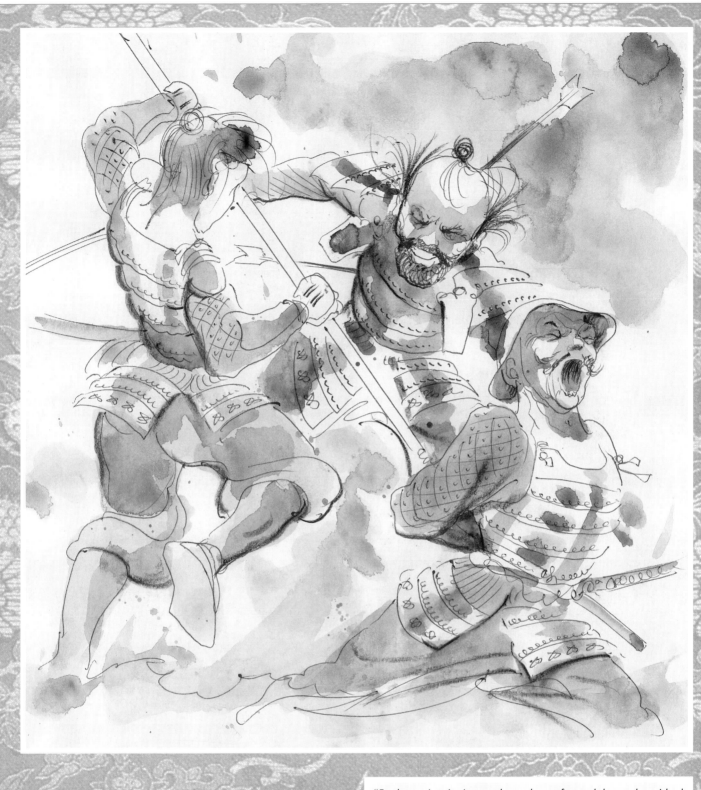

"At that point, I witnessed a cyclone of swordplay such as I had never seen before. Outnumbered, riddled with arrows that were still drawing blood through the scales of his armor, it was he who attacked them, as if incensed that they had the impudence to even imagine they could drive their spears into him."

❀

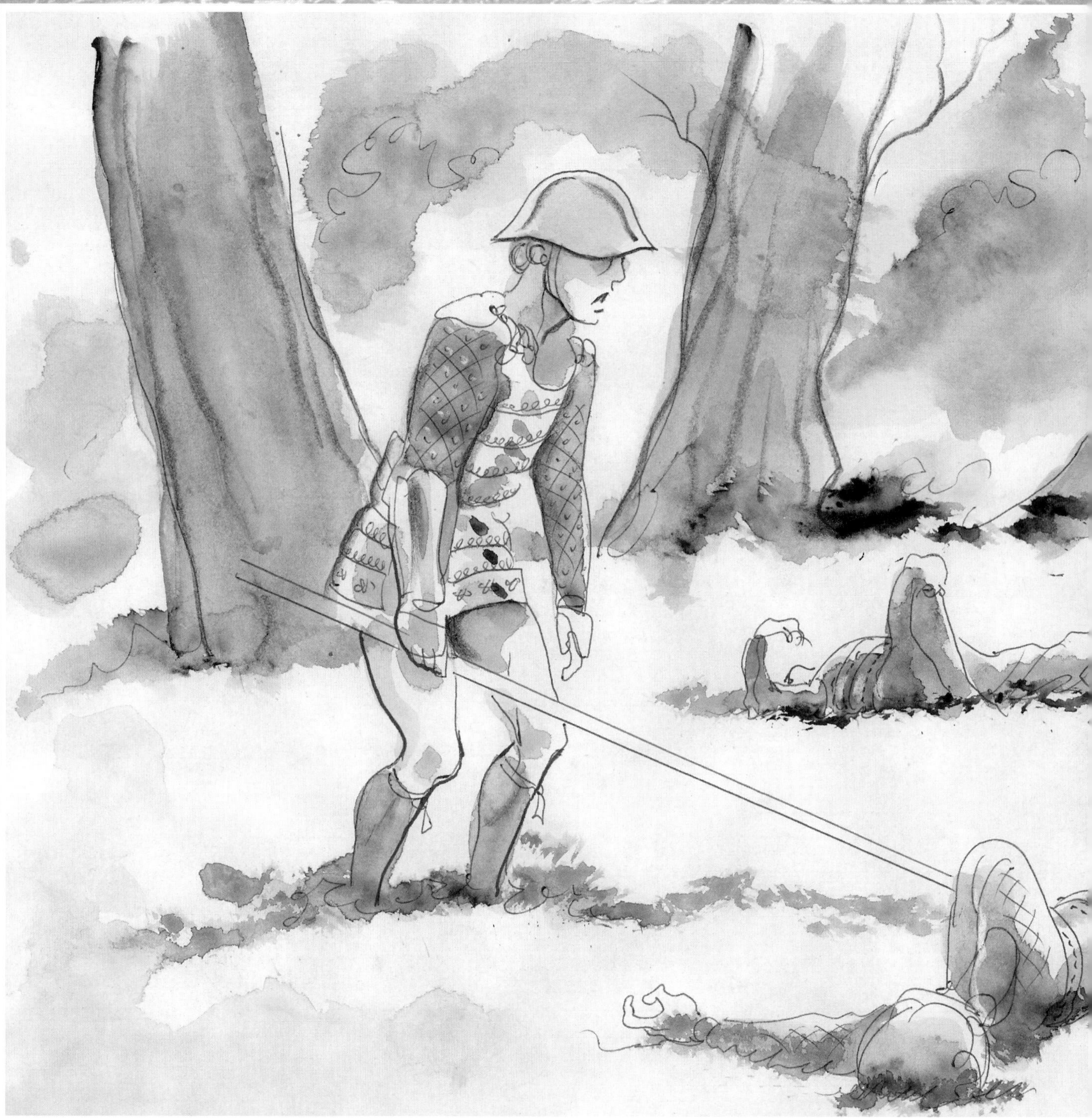

"By the time they realized what was happening and how outclassed they were in any confrontation with a swordsman of that caliber, it was too late—he gave them no chance to withdraw . . ."

"What happened next?"

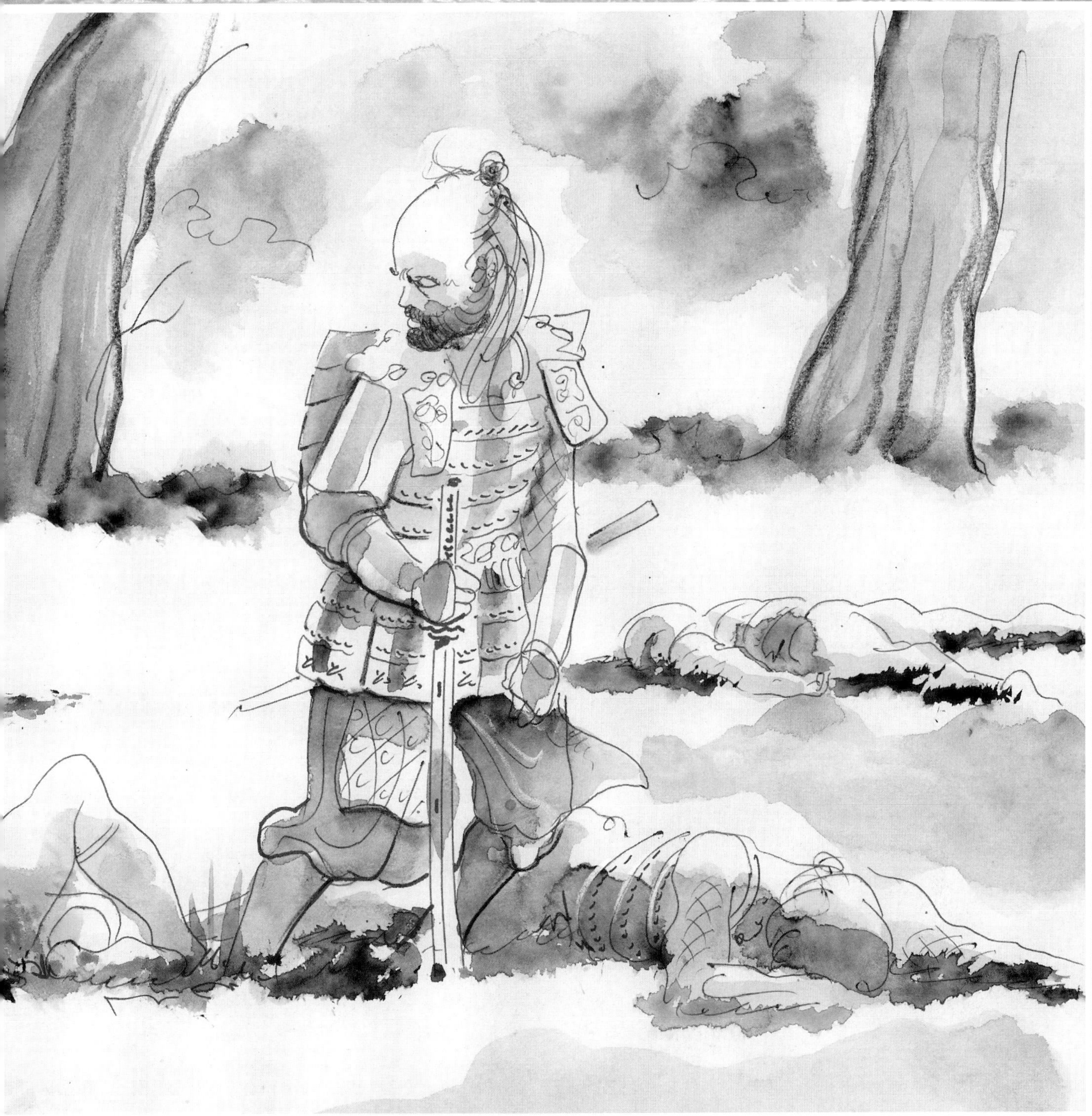

"It was all over in a matter of seconds. With bodies strewn all around him, he turned around and saw me, at the edge of the melee, frozen in amazement and terror at the sight of him and of what he had done with that incredible weapon of his. He took a long look at me and then—as if I had not seen enough marvels that morning—he turned toward the woods, grinning. . . ."

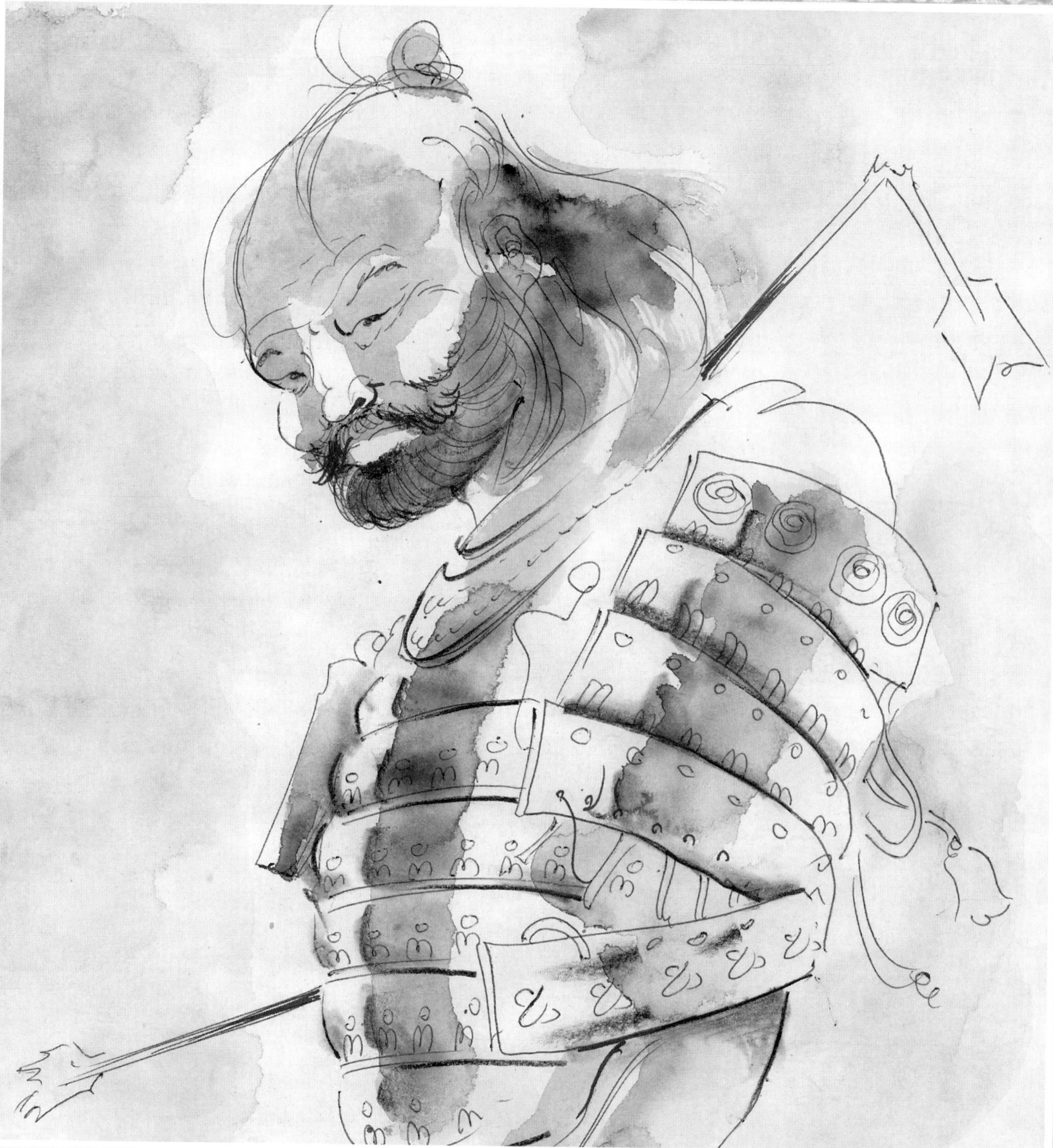

"Grinning?"

"I think so. He wasn't wearing a face protector and I'm sure I saw his teeth flash white against the blackness of his beard. But why would he have done that?"

"That's simple. With your moronic face, eyes shut, and your whole body shaking like a leaf, you must have been quite a sight! He was probably having a good laugh at your expense. Or perhaps he was grimacing at the thought that, with opponents such as you, his clan had still lost the battle."

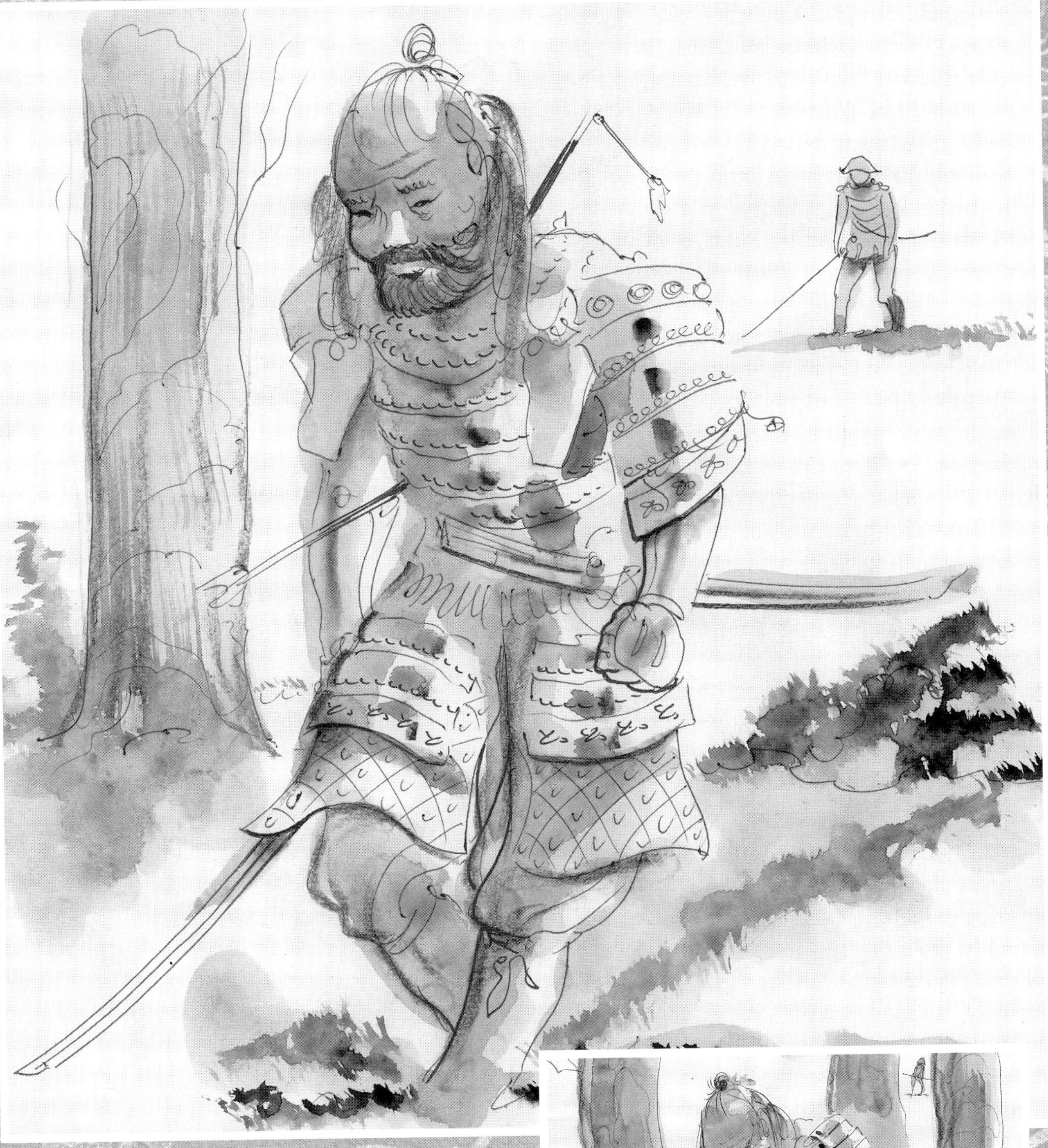

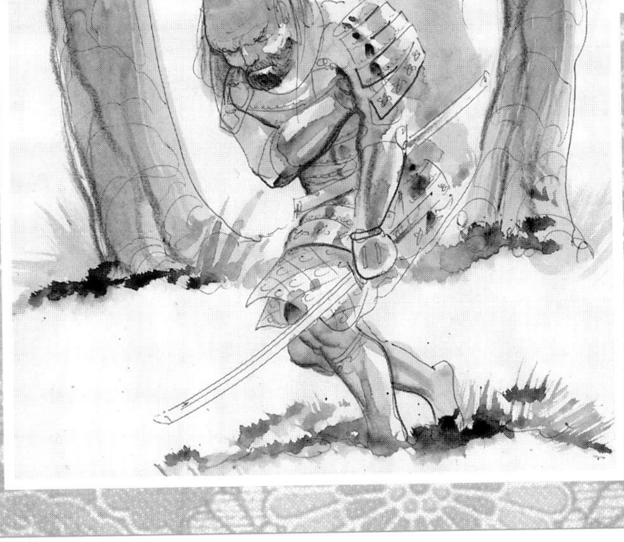

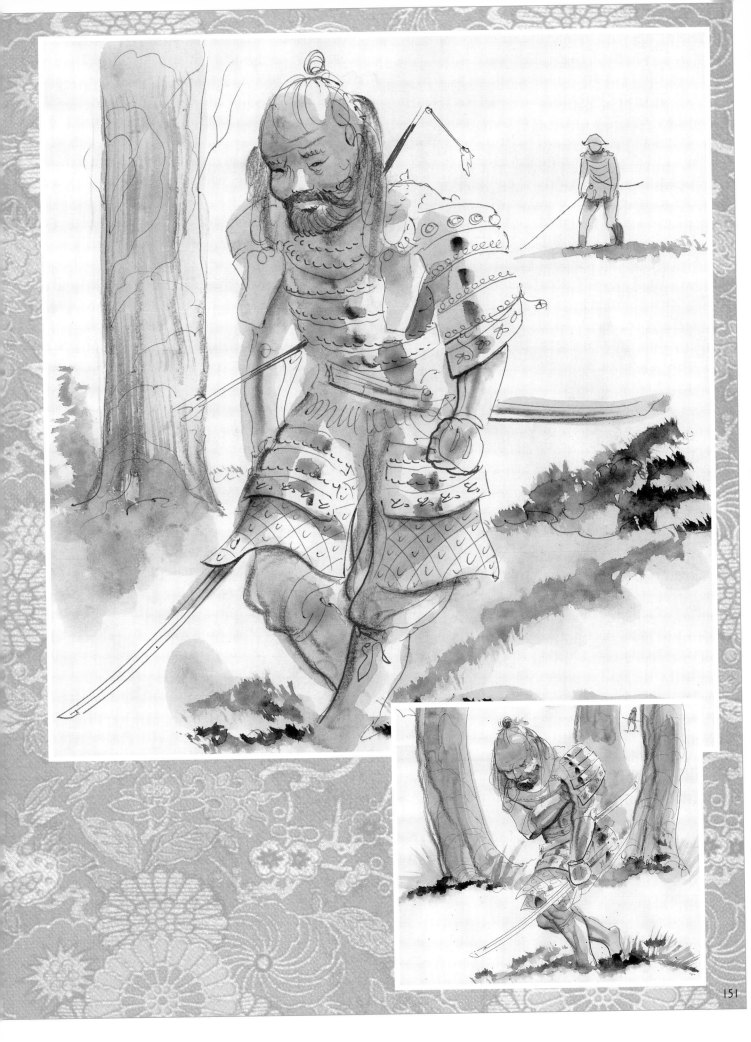

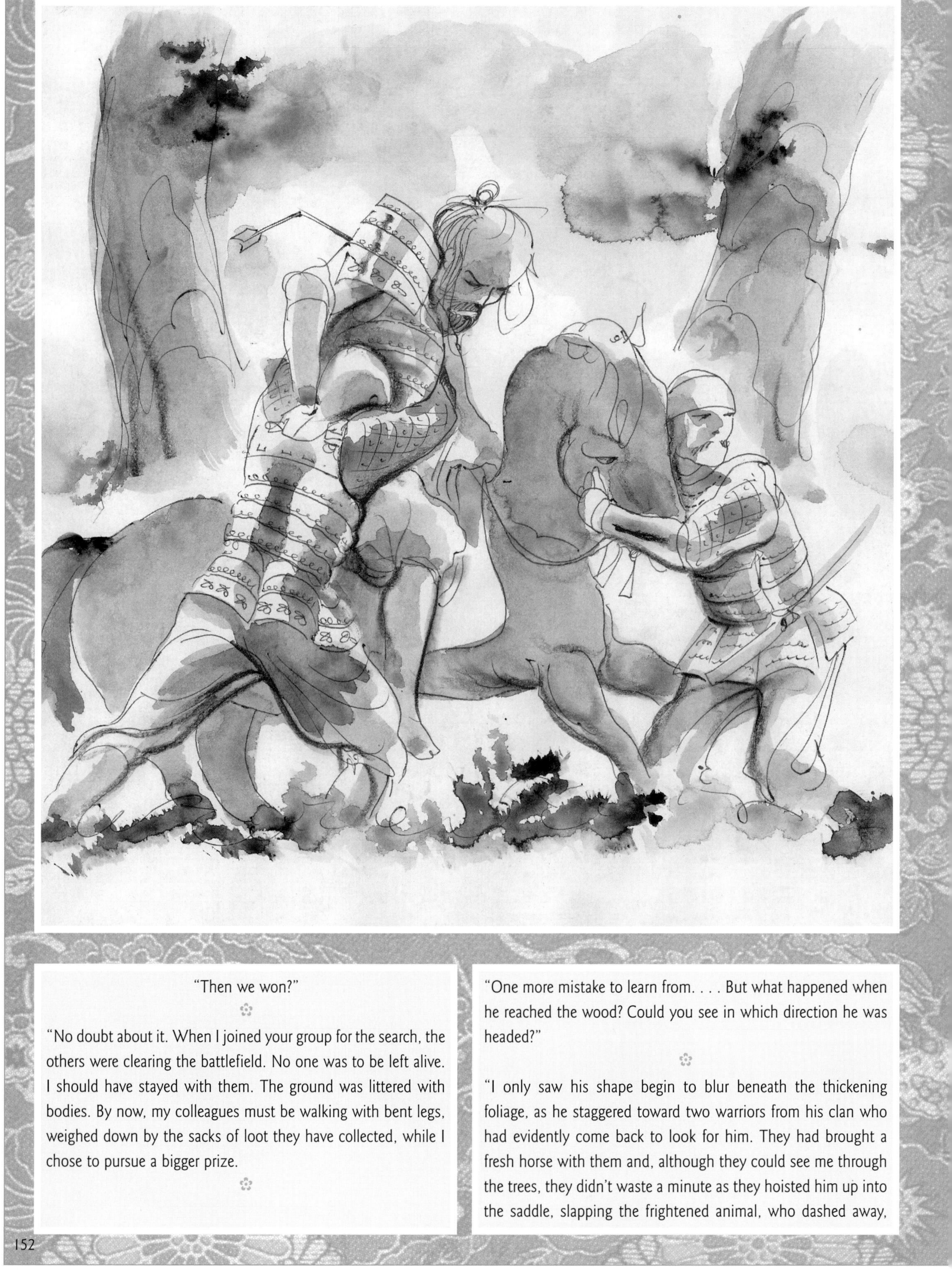

"Then we won?"

"No doubt about it. When I joined your group for the search, the others were clearing the battlefield. No one was to be left alive. I should have stayed with them. The ground was littered with bodies. By now, my colleagues must be walking with bent legs, weighed down by the sacks of loot they have collected, while I chose to pursue a bigger prize.

"One more mistake to learn from. . . . But what happened when he reached the wood? Could you see in which direction he was headed?"

"I only saw his shape begin to blur beneath the thickening foliage, as he staggered toward two warriors from his clan who had evidently come back to look for him. They had brought a fresh horse with them and, although they could see me through the trees, they didn't waste a minute as they hoisted him up into the saddle, slapping the frightened animal, who dashed away,

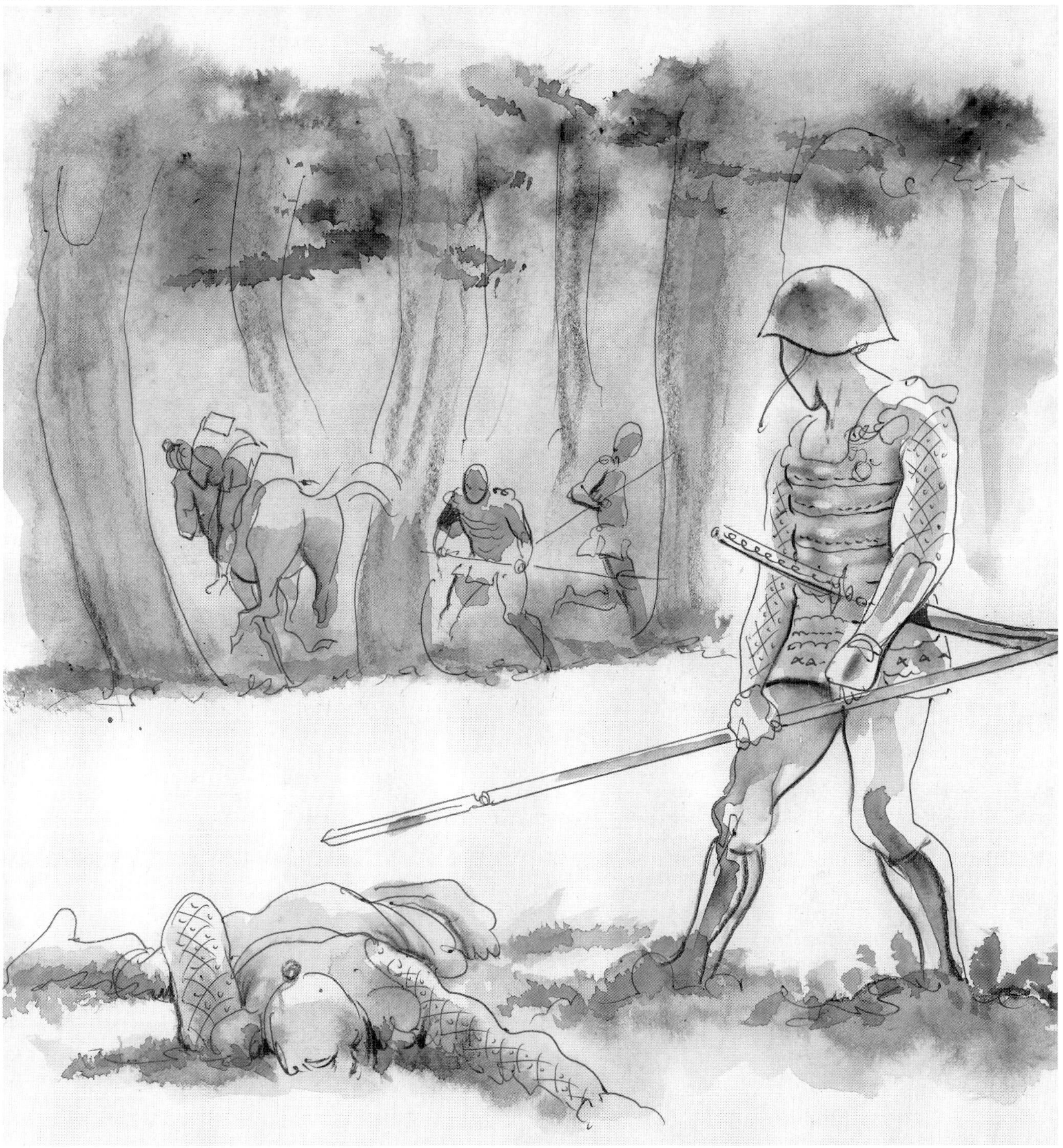

toward the densest area of the woods, before they disappeared themselves.

"And as far as the direction his horse took as it moved deeper into the woods, it seemed to me that neither he nor his master were sure where they were going. They stumbled right and then left, as if totally disoriented, which should not have surprised anyone, considering what the rider had been through earlier, and the loss of blood he had sustained—thanks to all those arrows that had managed to penetrate the metal tassels of his body armor. Now, do you still wonder why the last thing I want in this life is to meet such a swordsman again?"

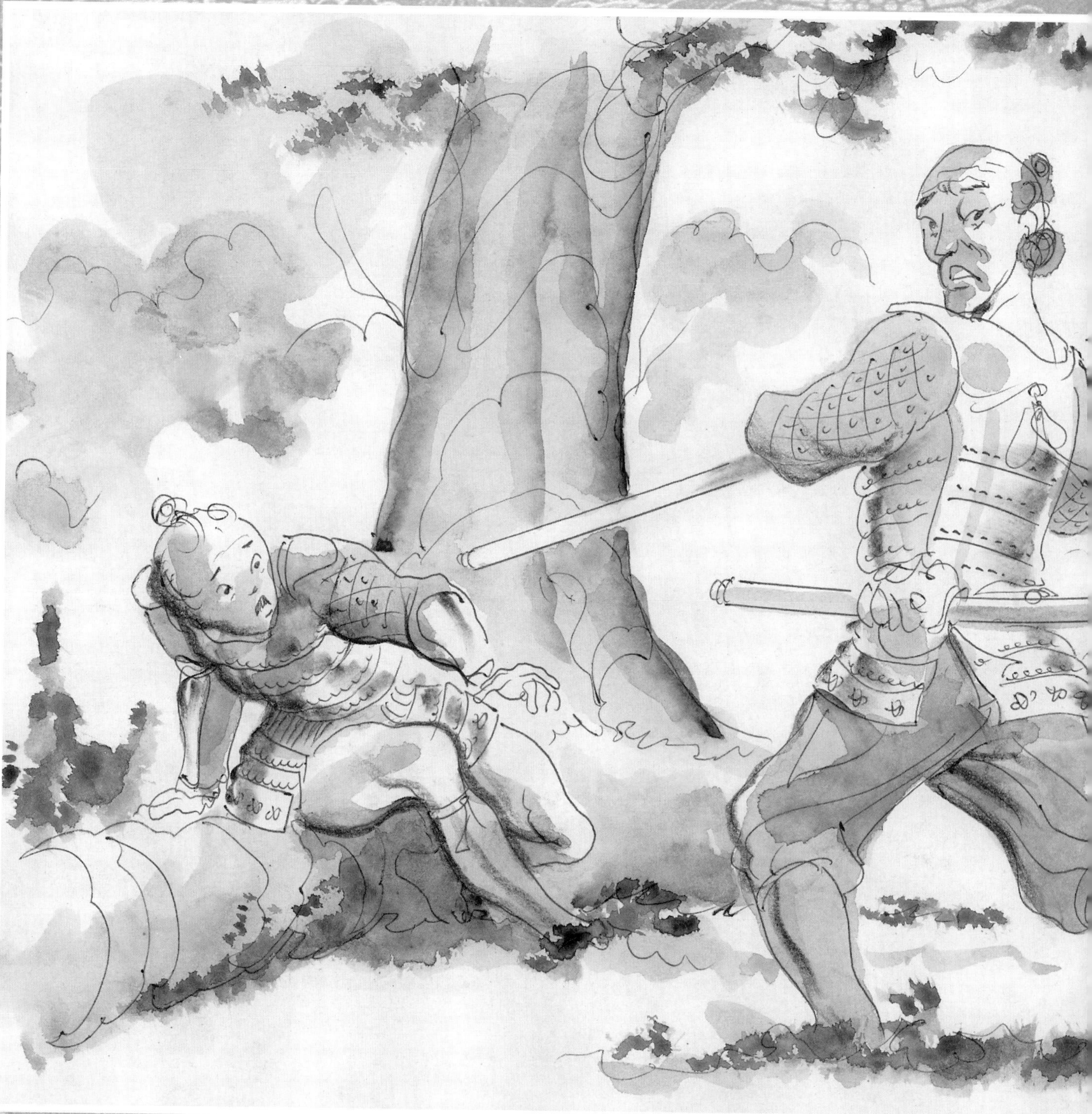

"A dying man, you mean, farmhand? I have no fear of him. What I fear is that we are wasting time talking about him instead of searching for him. What is the matter now? Have you seen a ghost?"

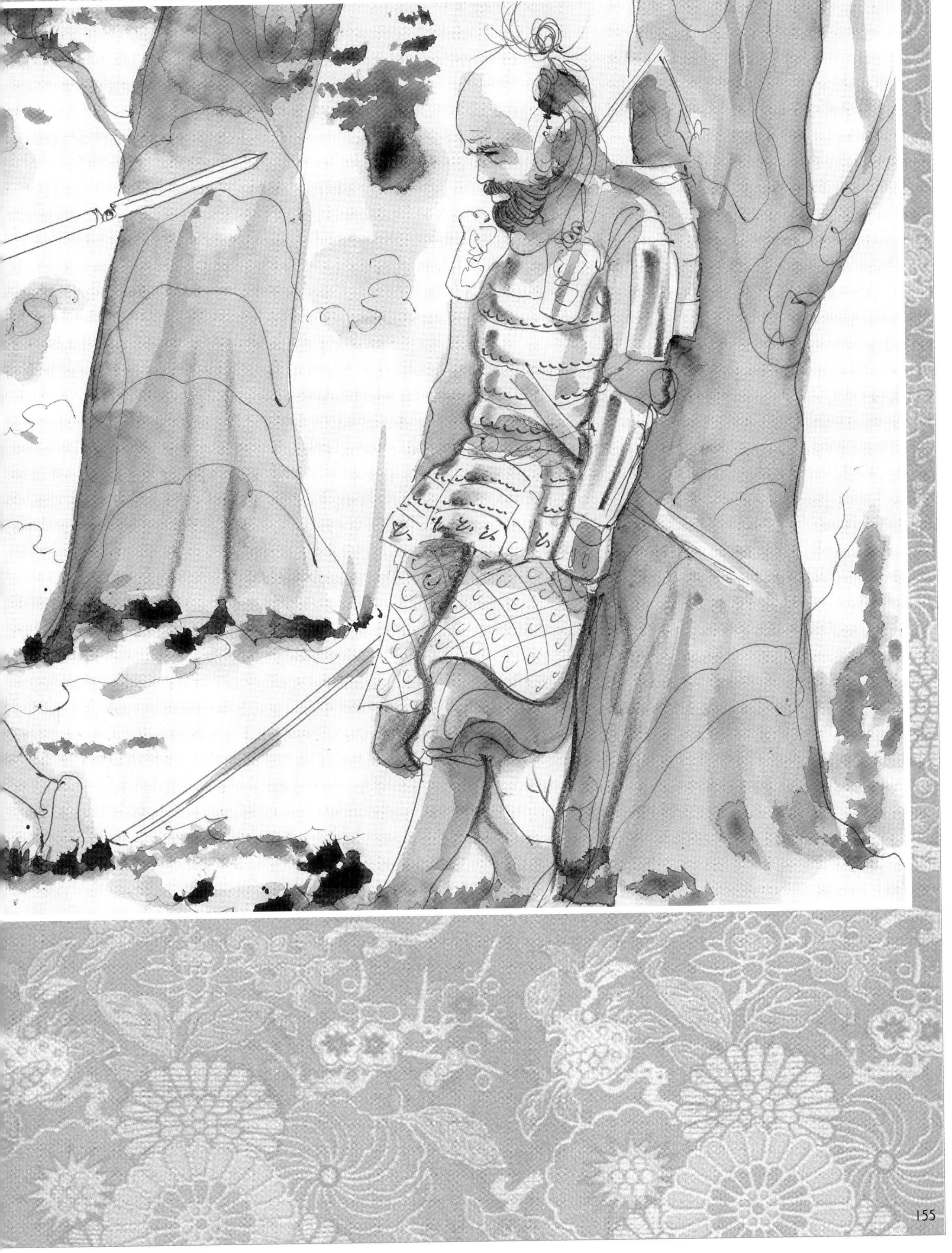

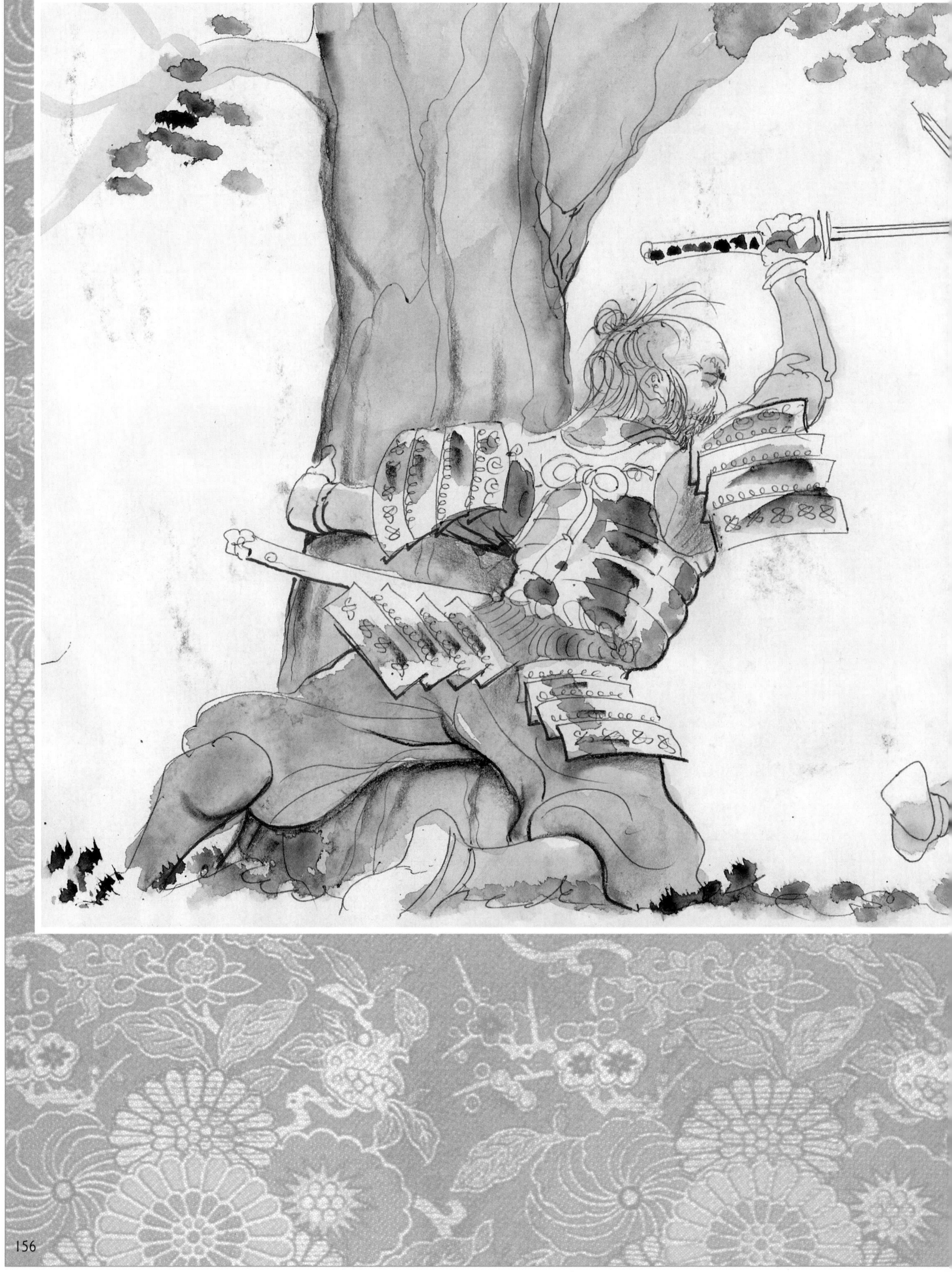

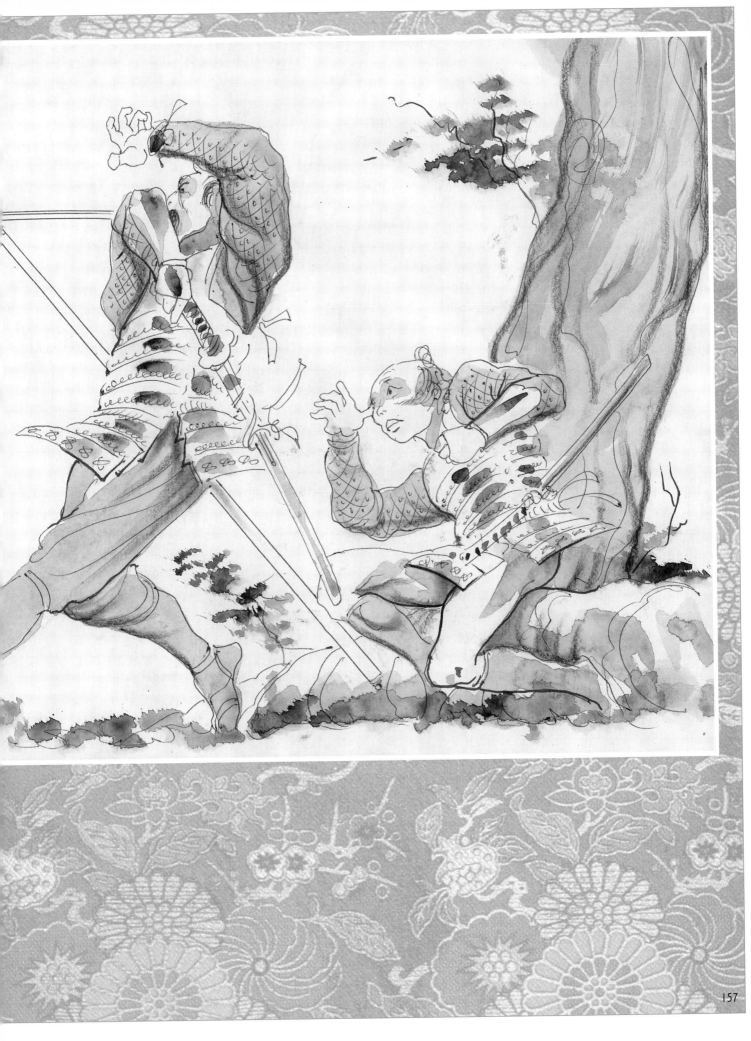

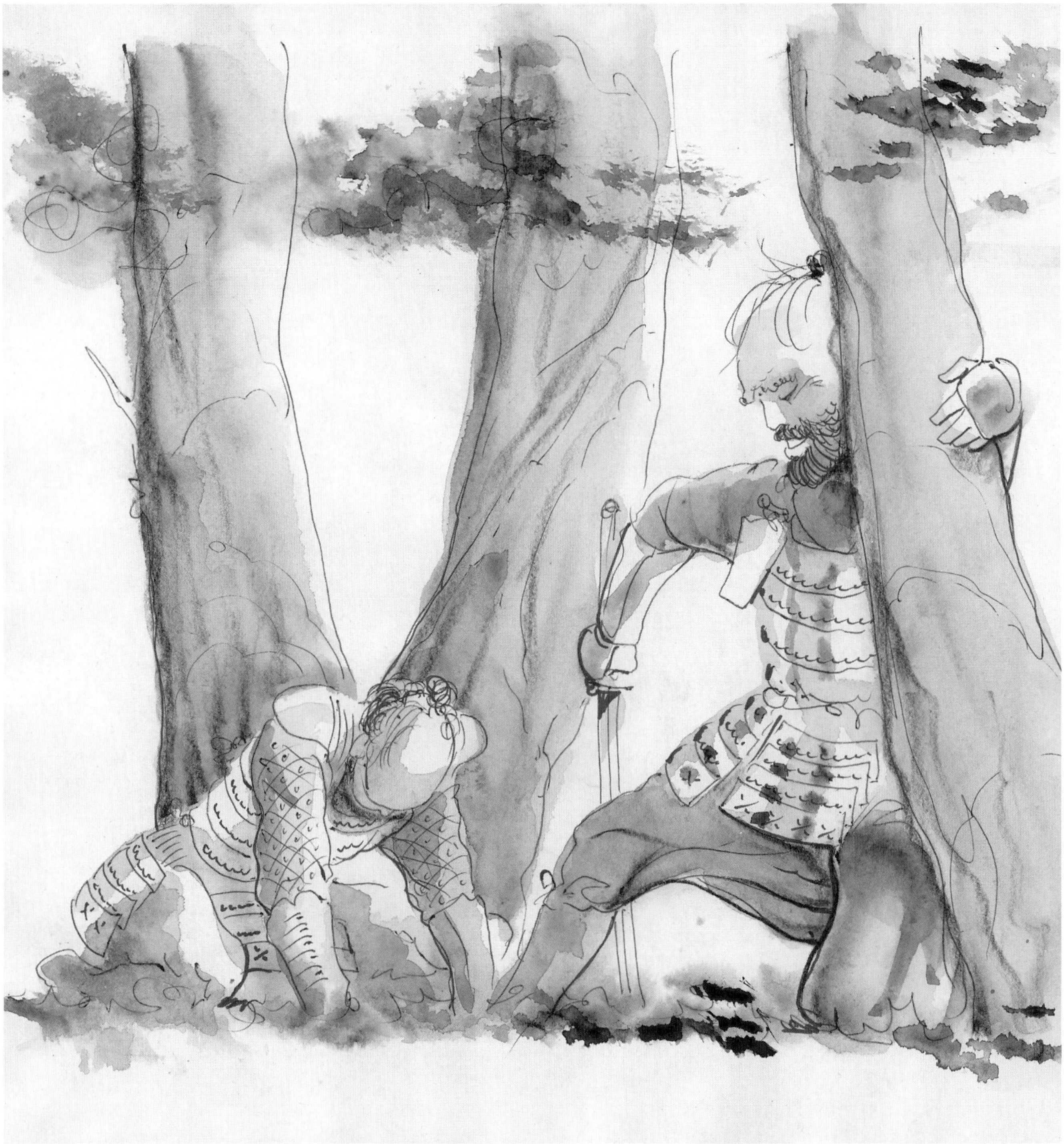

"You had to go for your sword, footsoldier, didn't you? And you, farmer, I hope you are not as foolish as your partner from the town, are you? My suggestion to you is that you do not call out to anyone. What do you say to that?"

"No, Sir. I mean, yes, Sir. That is, whatever you think best, Sir."

"So we meet again. . . . Tell me something."

"Yes?"

"Do you know anything about medicine?"

"Medicine? No, Sir. Only animal husbandry, that is . . ."

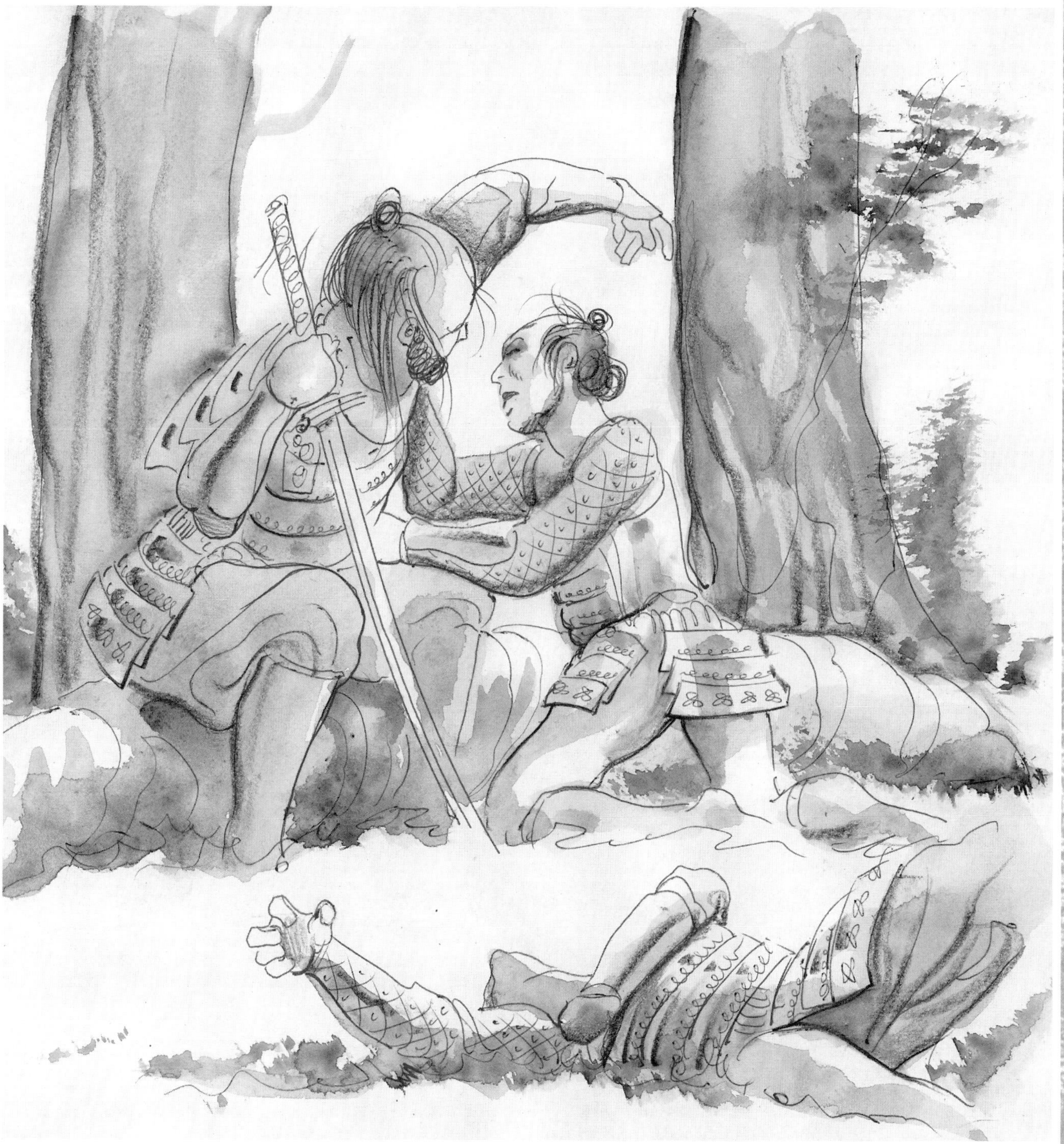

"Right. Well, see what you can do about this particularly annoying piece of metal in my side. I can't seem to breathe properly with it stuck in there. Don't be afraid. Come closer. Can you see it?

"Which one? There are so many cuts . . ."

"This one—the one under my arm."

"I see it, Sir. It seems to have penetrated very deeply."

"Not much of a novelty. Can you see the shaft of the arrow?"

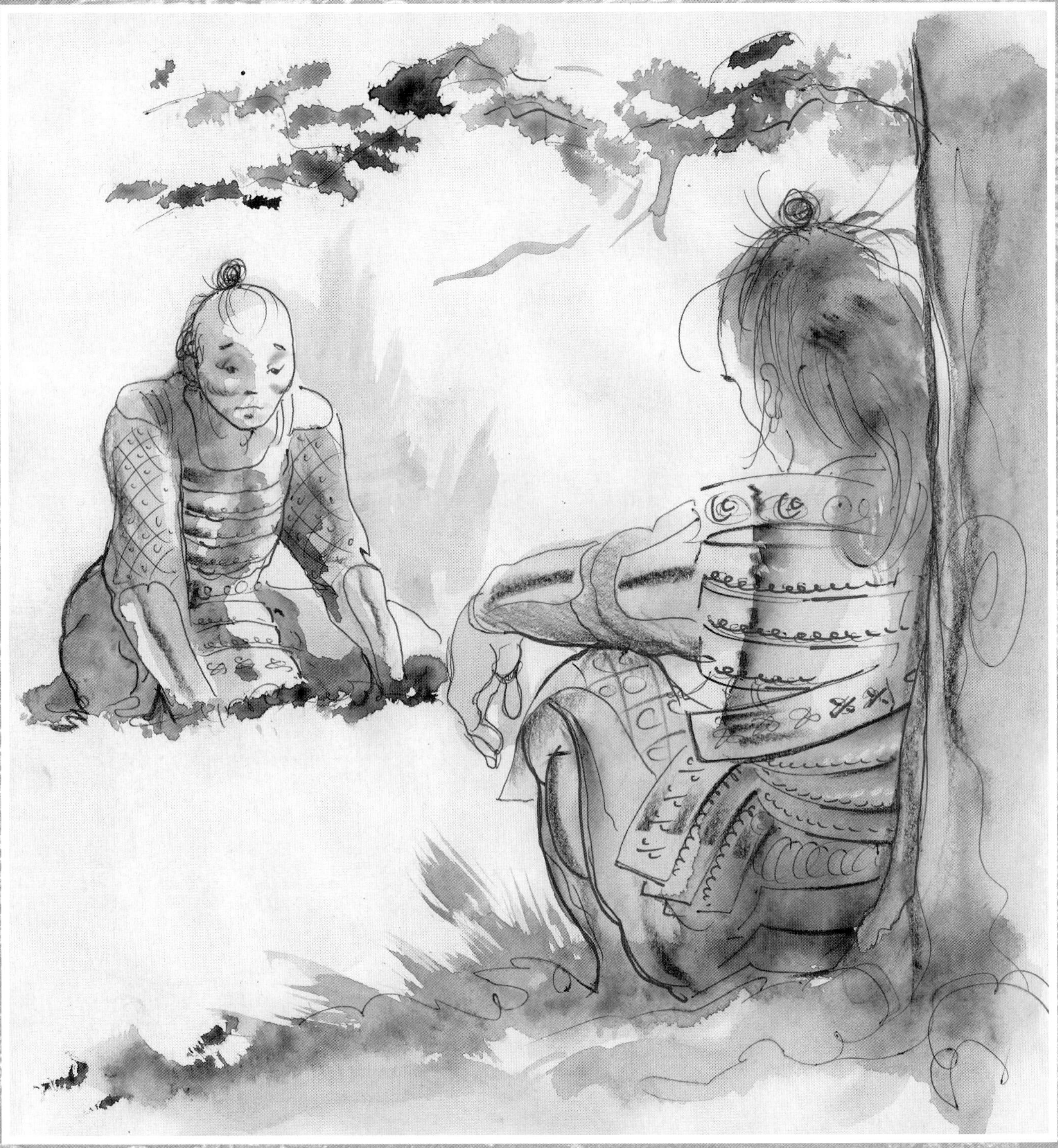

"No. There's too much blood, and the flesh around the wound is all inflamed and swollen shut—so much so that even the bleeding seems to have stopped there. Not from the other wounds on your back, though."

"I see. That is the one that will kill me, then. I see that I must resign myself to the inevitable. What do you say, farmer?

"I suggest that we call my superior, Sir."

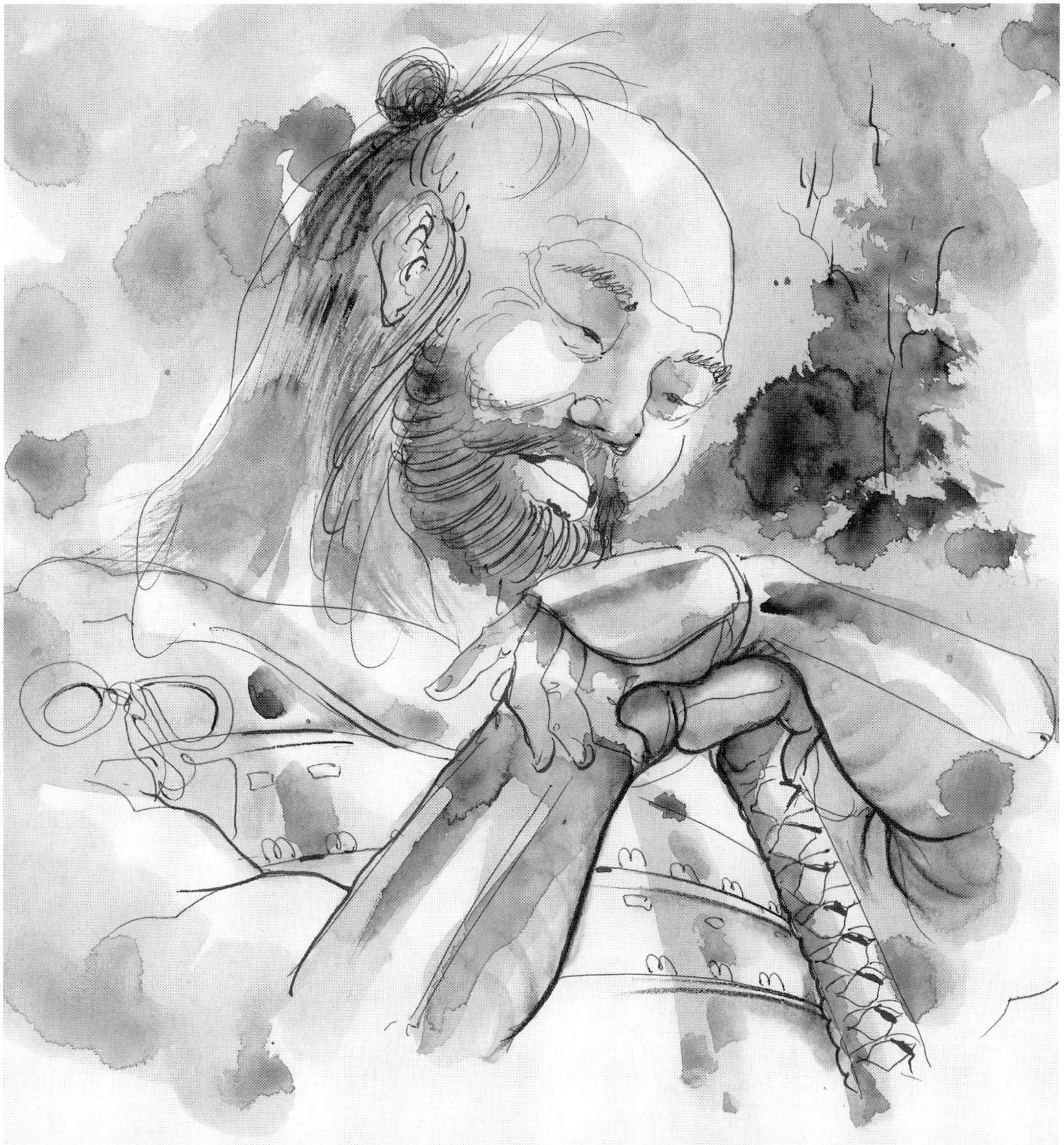

"Are you jesting?"

"No, Sir. He has an army physician with him. If the other spearmen find you first, they will close in on you with their spears and then strip you of any valuables you may be carrying."

"And just what do you think your superior would do? You heard the order that was given on the battlefield. Your friend there was well informed. No, be quiet. It won't take long now."

"Yes, Sir."

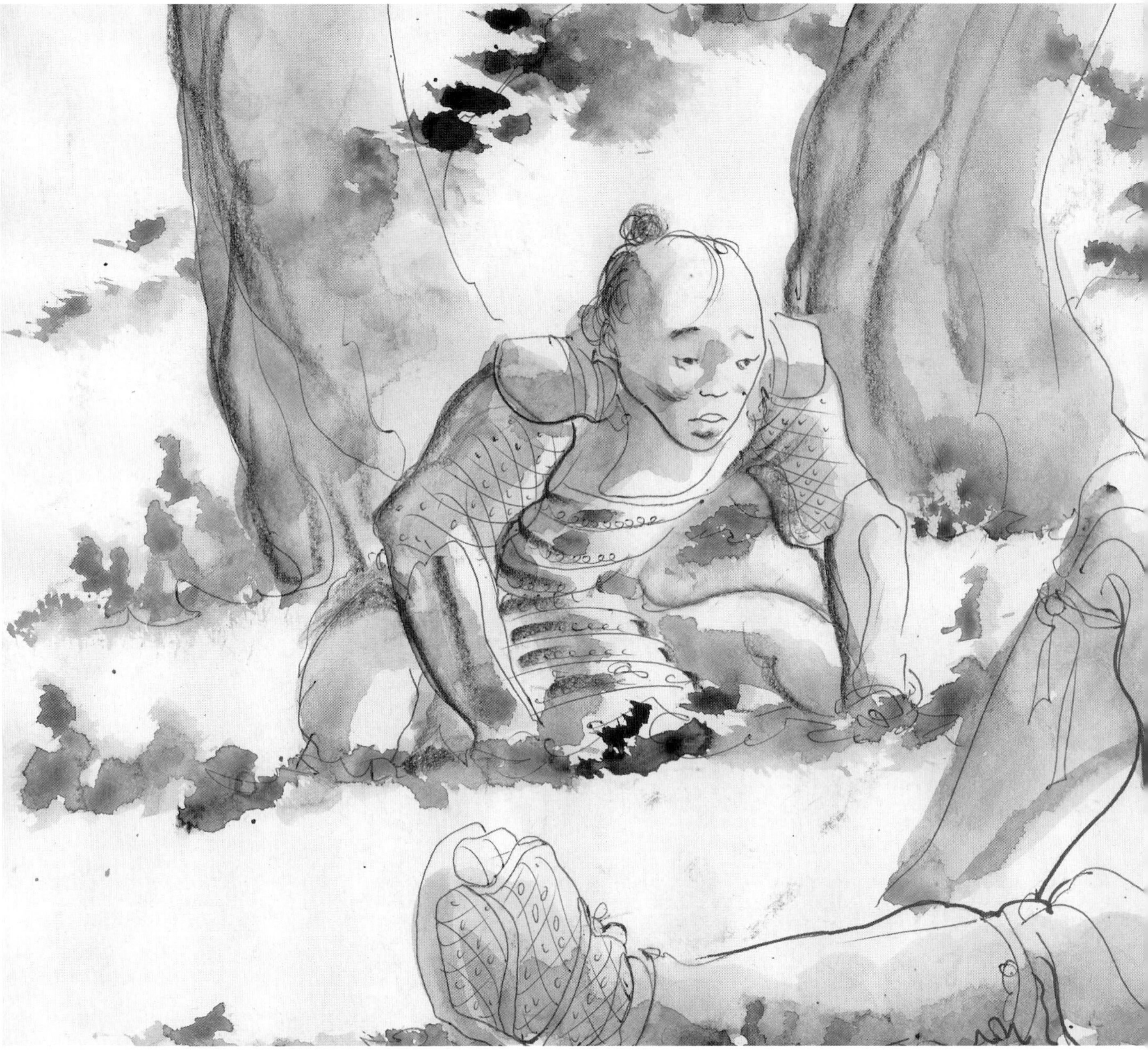

"Of course, we could hasten matters a bit. Tell me something."

"What is it, Sir?"

"Have you ever used a sword?"

"Never, Sir. How could I have learned swordsmanship? No, swordplay is far beyond me."

"You mean you never found a sword, like your comrade over there? There are so many blades lying around these days. . . ."

"I'm not a looter, Sir. Believe me."

"I do. You like a warm kitchen and your family around you. I heard you before. Nothing wrong with that. . . ."

"Well, as you have heard, Sir, I never wanted to be a warrior, and yet, wherever I turn, I find somebody who insists upon forcing a spear into my hand and pushing me into the thick of some battle or other. But you, Sir, you are a real warrior. I saw you this morning. Those were amazing things you did with that sword. Does it take long to learn such skills?"

"A lifetime. And even then, as you can plainly see, it's still not enough. . . ."

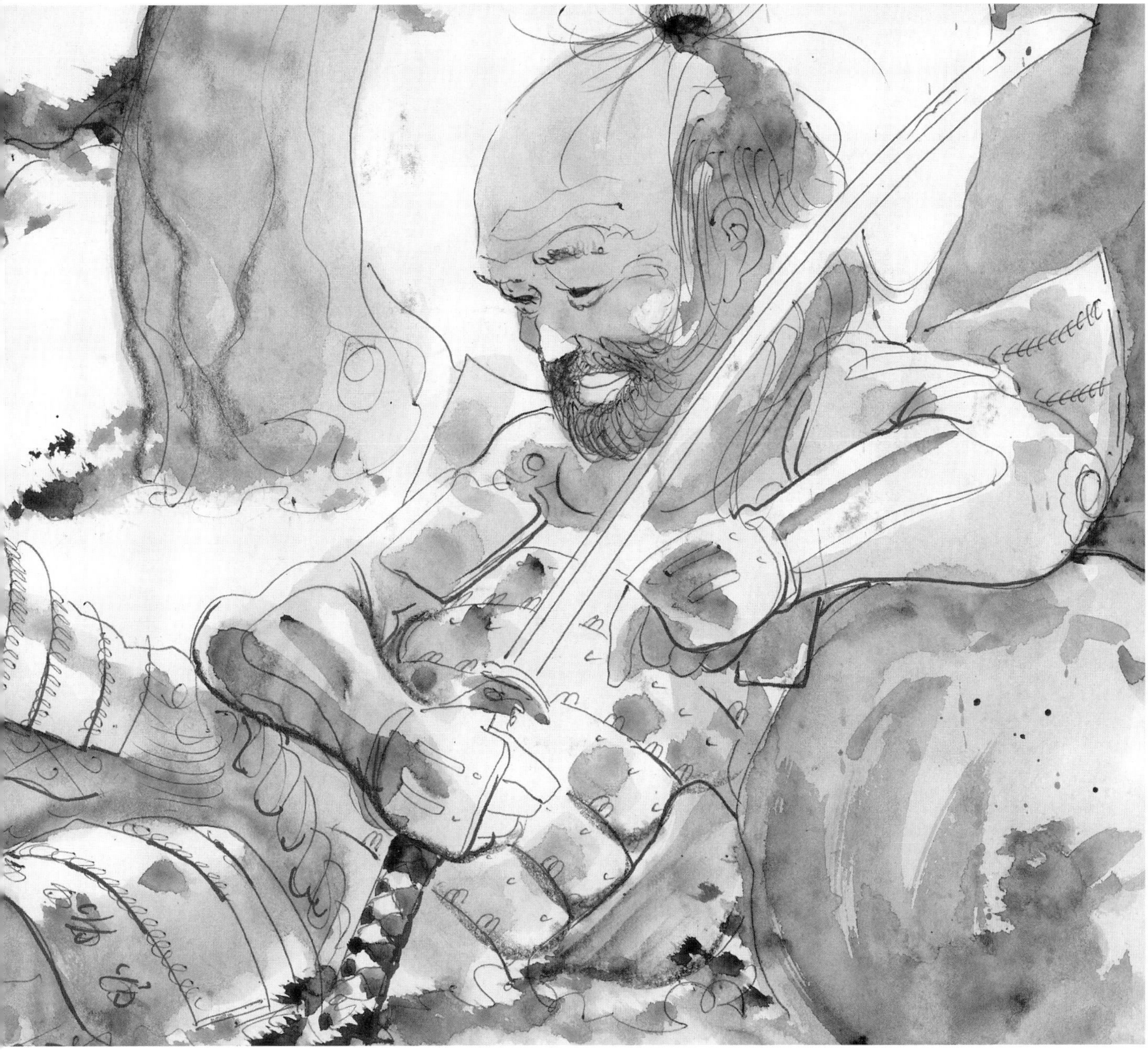

"You're still losing blood, Sir. It's seeping through the scales of your armor."

"I hope it continues and even more quickly. I haven't a great deal left, anyway, nor much energy, either. Listen to me: can you at least wield an ax?"

"You mean for cutting wood? Of course I can. How else would I be able to chop wood for the winter?"

"Show me. With this."

"But that's a sword, not an ax."

"How perceptive of you. Of course it's a sword. I don't happen to carry an ax. But don't worry, you can use this blade just as you would an ax to chop wood, can't you?"

"I don't know, Sir. I never tried to chop wood with a sword."

"It's never too late to learn a new skill. See that low branch over there?"

"Yes, Sir."

"Try to chop it off with a single stroke. Grasp the handle with both hands and imagine you are holding the handle of an ax. Cut right through that branch. Go on . . . try it!"

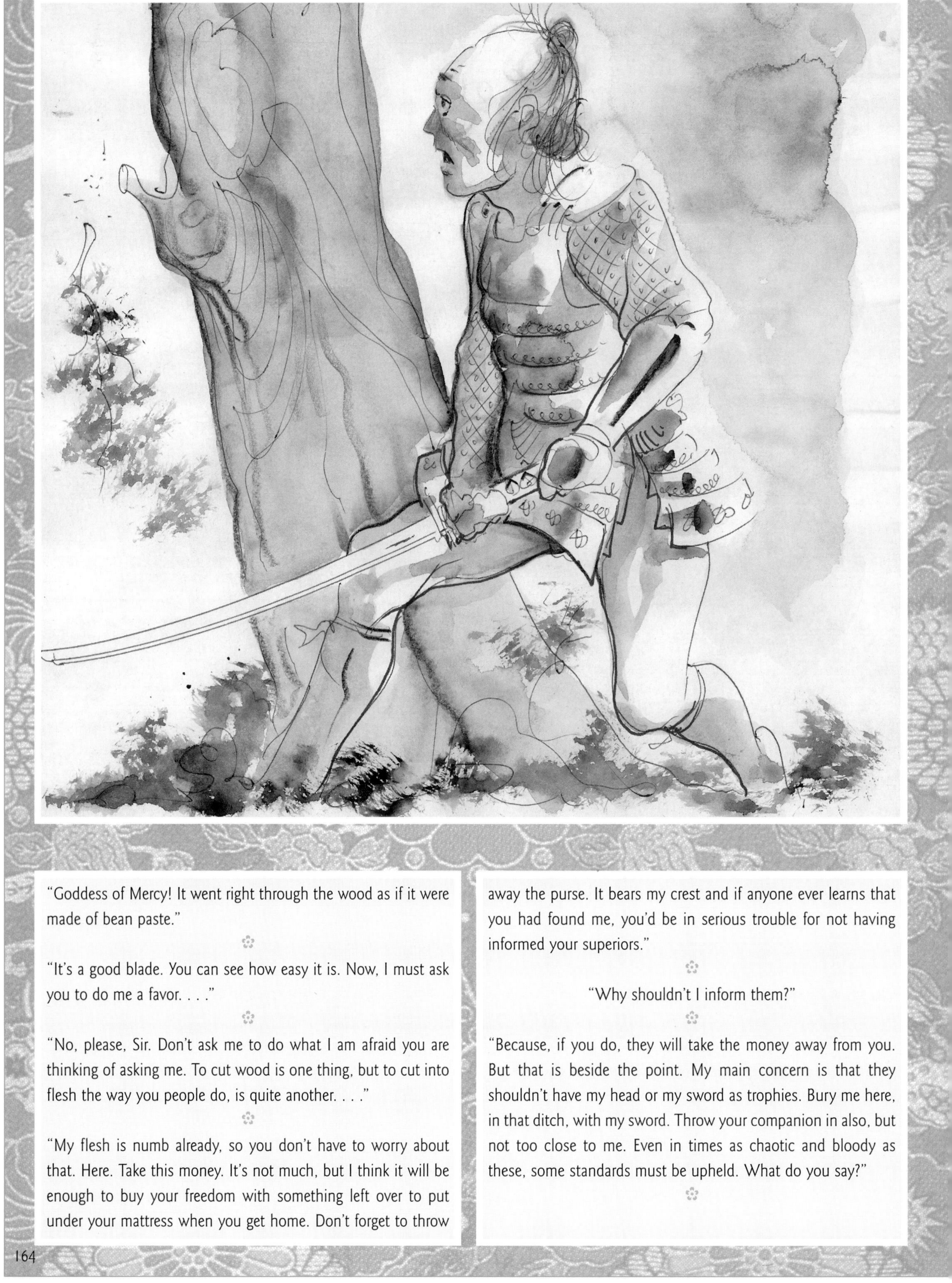

"Goddess of Mercy! It went right through the wood as if it were made of bean paste."

"It's a good blade. You can see how easy it is. Now, I must ask you to do me a favor. . . ."

"No, please, Sir. Don't ask me to do what I am afraid you are thinking of asking me. To cut wood is one thing, but to cut into flesh the way you people do, is quite another. . . ."

"My flesh is numb already, so you don't have to worry about that. Here. Take this money. It's not much, but I think it will be enough to buy your freedom with something left over to put under your mattress when you get home. Don't forget to throw away the purse. It bears my crest and if anyone ever learns that you had found me, you'd be in serious trouble for not having informed your superiors."

"Why shouldn't I inform them?"

"Because, if you do, they will take the money away from you. But that is beside the point. My main concern is that they shouldn't have my head or my sword as trophies. Bury me here, in that ditch, with my sword. Throw your companion in also, but not too close to me. Even in times as chaotic and bloody as these, some standards must be upheld. What do you say?"

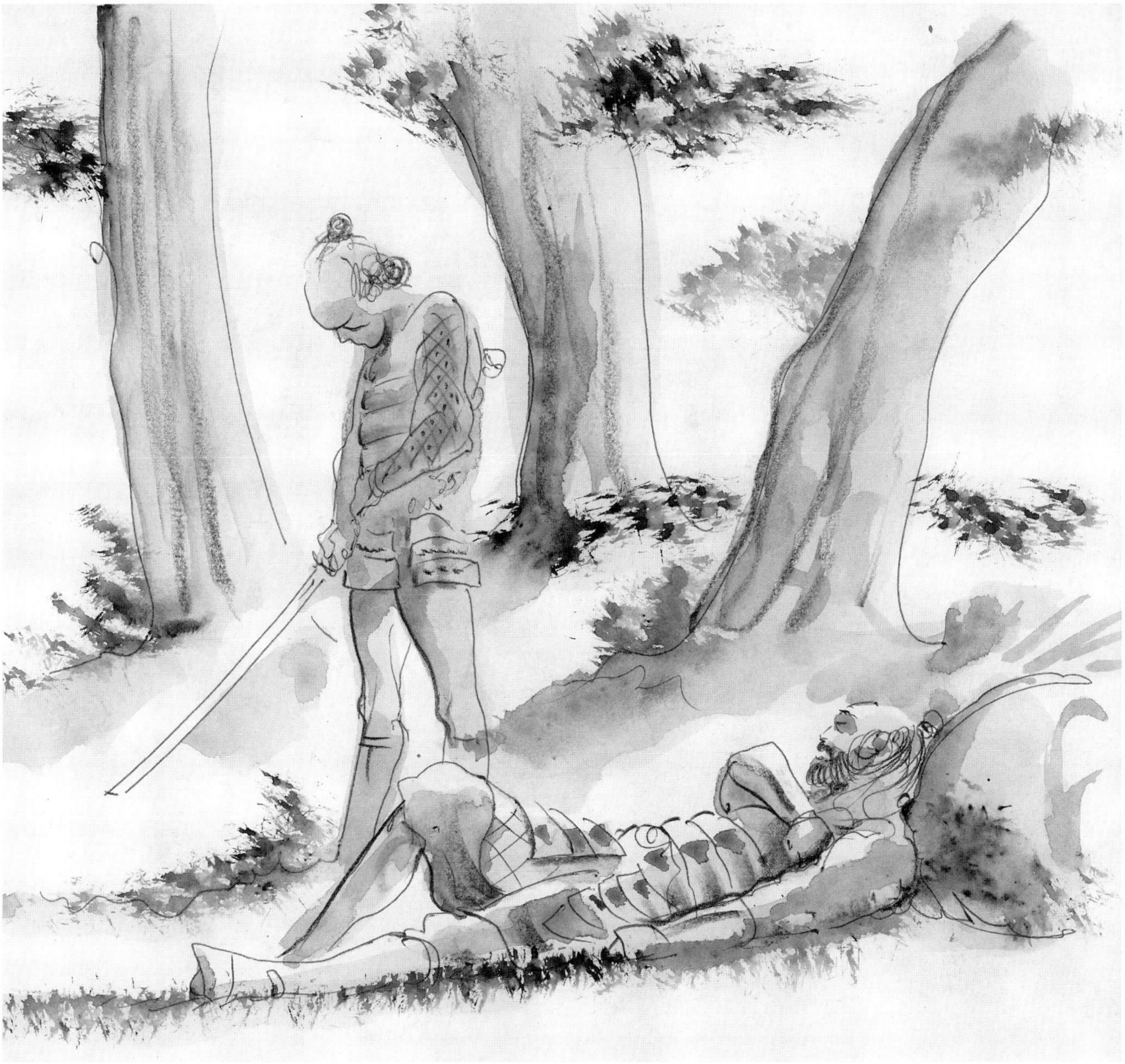

"I can't, Sir. I really can't. I know that it is considered a great honor among gentlemen such as yourself to be selected to perform such duties, but I am not a member of your class. . . ."

"You are an honest man, farmer. I wish that more 'gentlemen' had your sense of honor. To have encountered you is the first bit of luck I have had during all these months of one disaster after another. My clan has been destroyed and my family along with it. My only wish now is for a decent burial, without further disgrace and mutilation."

"I'm sorry, Sir. I cannot do it."

"Listen to me, farmer. I would do it myself, if I had sufficient strength left in my arms. But if I attempted it in my present condition, I would only make a mess of everything and probably attract the attention of your other friends, as well. My heart is still too damned strong—it doesn't realize that we are finished. Must I remind you that I have spared your life twice today?"

"It is not a gentlemanly thing to remind me of my obligation."

"I'm not much of a gentleman now, farmer. First and foremost, I'm a dying man. Pay me this last courtesy, at least."

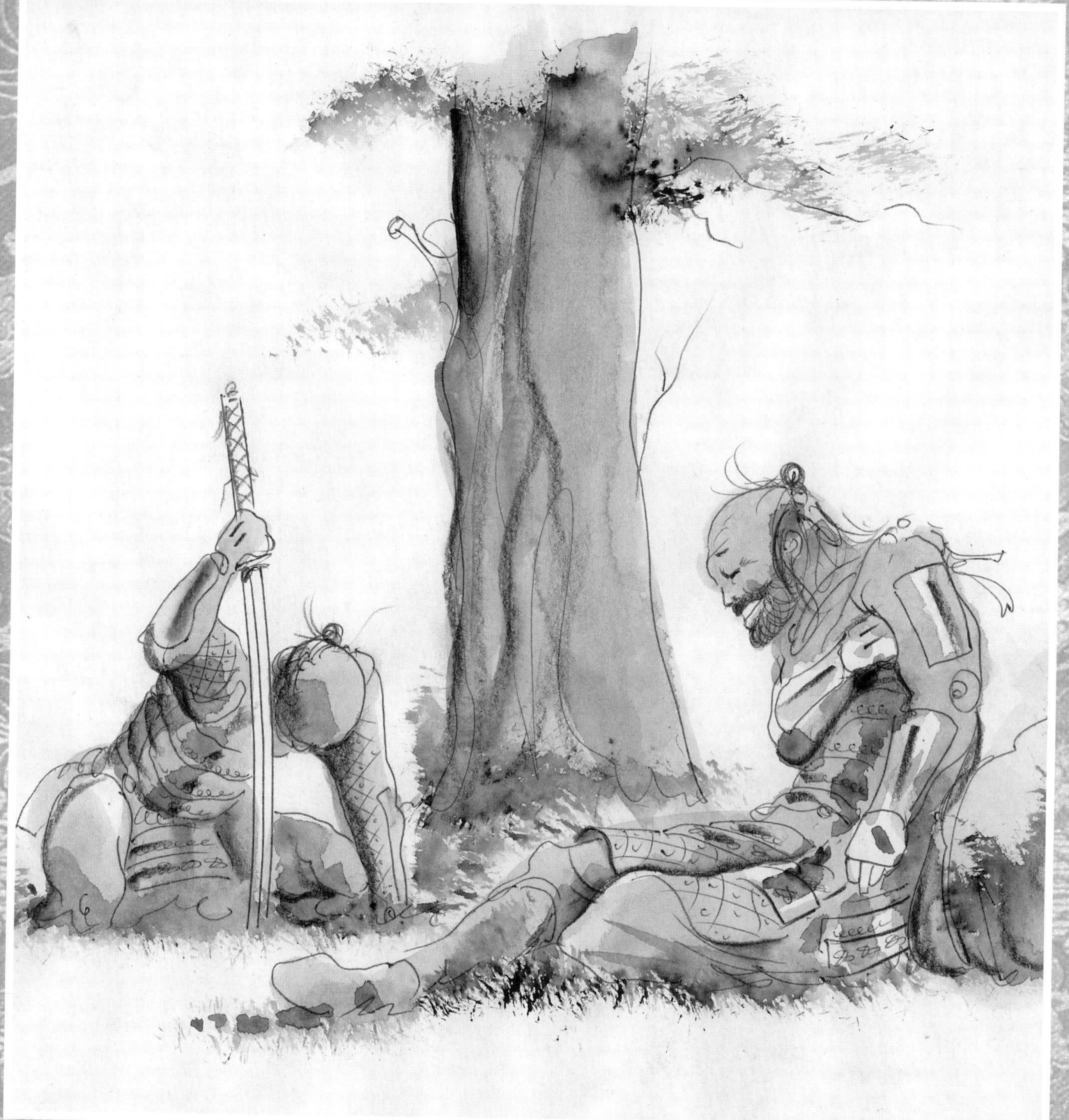

"But why me?"

"Because all my old comrades-in-arms are gone. And because I trust you. Think of it as a single stroke. It is an excellent blade and it has served me well in the past. It will surely not fail me—or you—now. It also deserves to rest at my side. Cut cleanly, bury me and my sword, and then rejoin your group so that you can buy your freedom and return home. But use some discretion. Don't flash your money around like some country bumpkin at an Edo festival, and don't draw attention by making it obvious that you have something to hide, like an incompetent apprentice spy. That's all."

"But I never . . ."

"I know. Look: do you see this stem?"

"Yes."

"I will hold it for you. Cut right through it. Think only of cutting

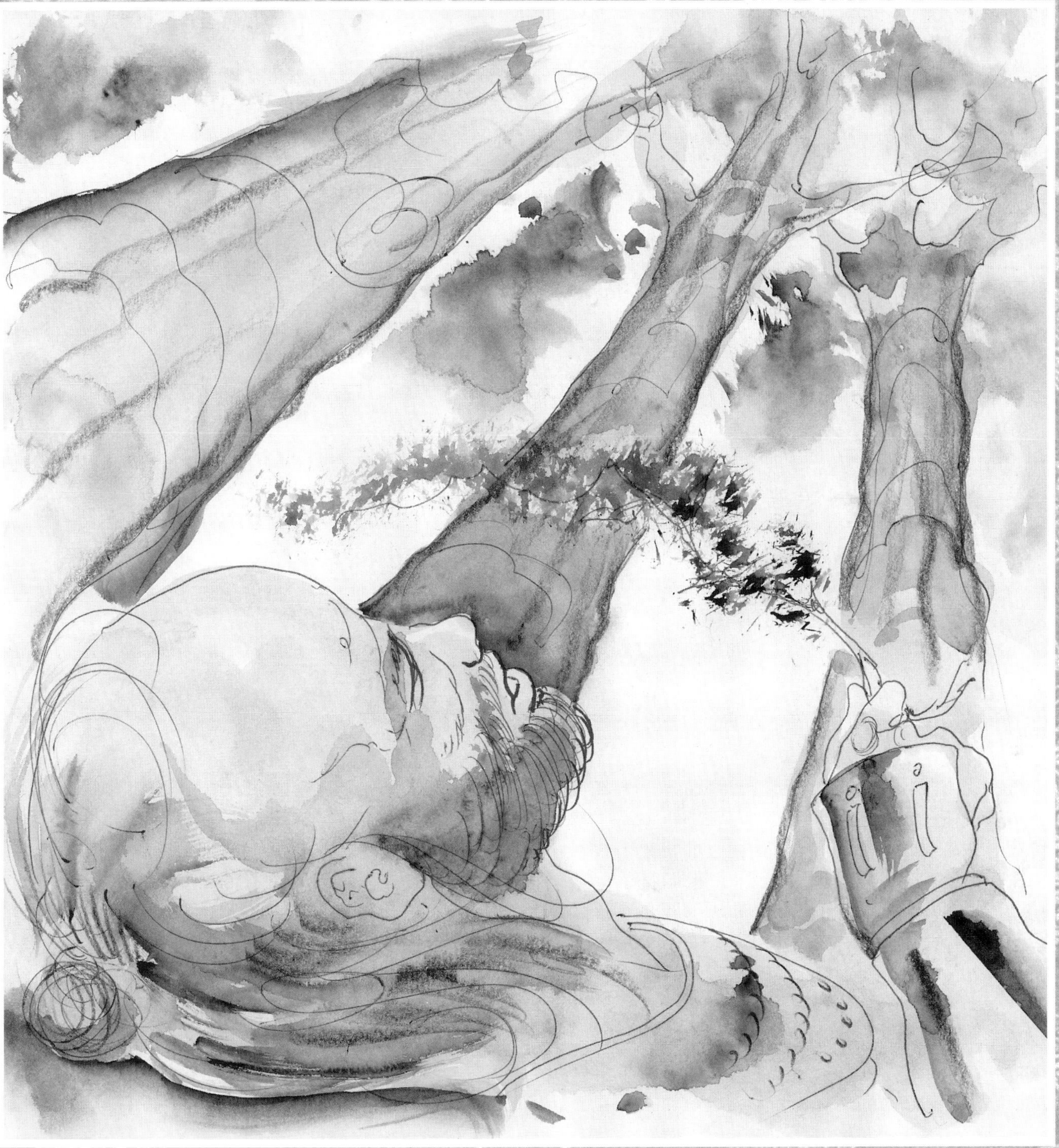

through this stem. Remember that it is easier to cut through a large, strong branch than through a thinner, elastic one. The first provides some body and resistance to a blow. The other gives and then snaps back. . . ."

"I know. When I was young, my father told me the same thing. You can hurt yourself chopping carelessly. I remember once . . ."

"Not now, farmer. Some other time—when we meet again. Just concentrate now and cut right through—all the way through."

"I wish I were home, Sir. I truly wish I were home. It seems as if this madness will never end. . . ."

"It will be over soon. I had never seen how beautiful the trees are when observed like this, from below. It will soon be winter, and your homecoming should be a welcome event. . . ."

"Sir . . ."

"Cut! Cut the stem! One single blow! Now!"

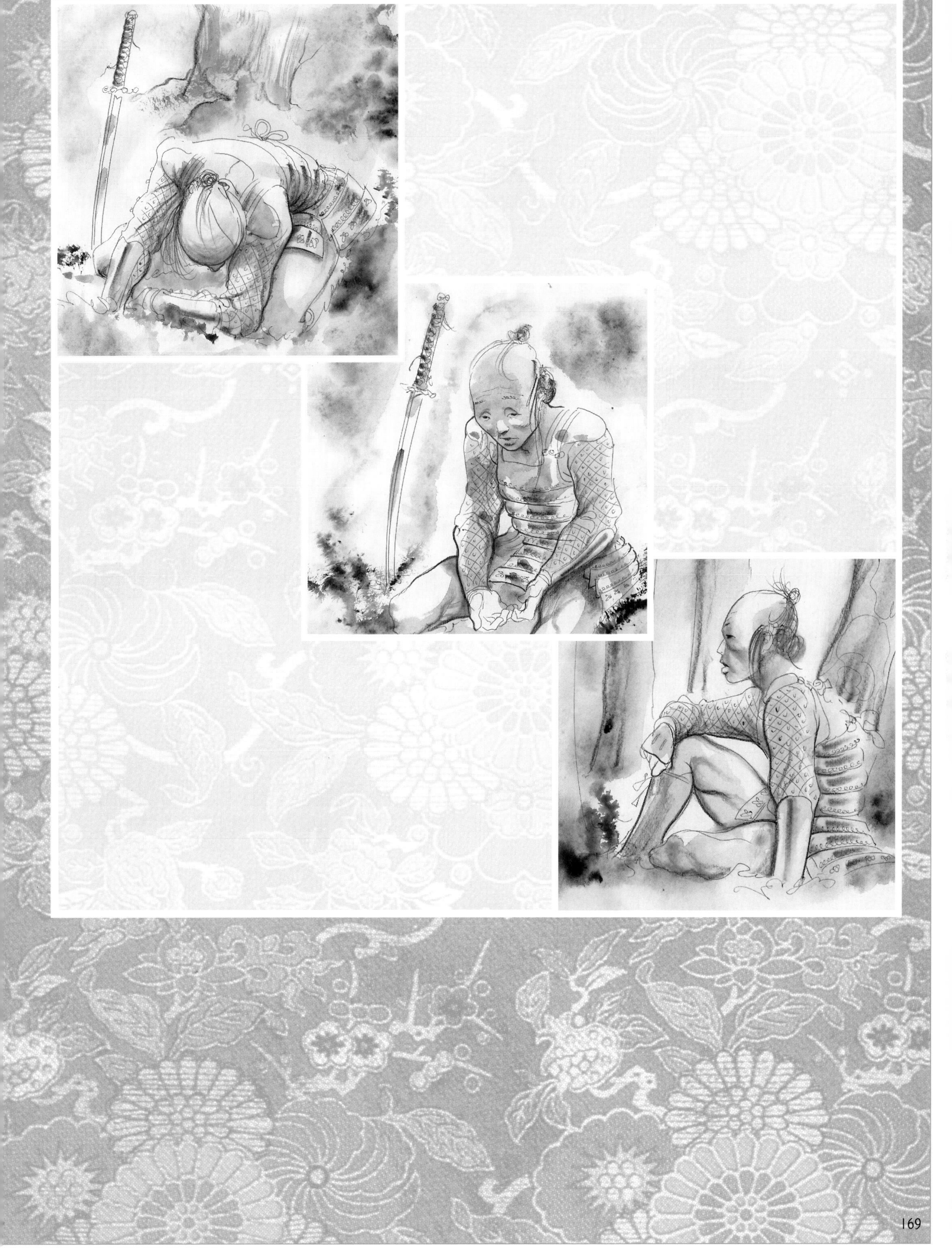

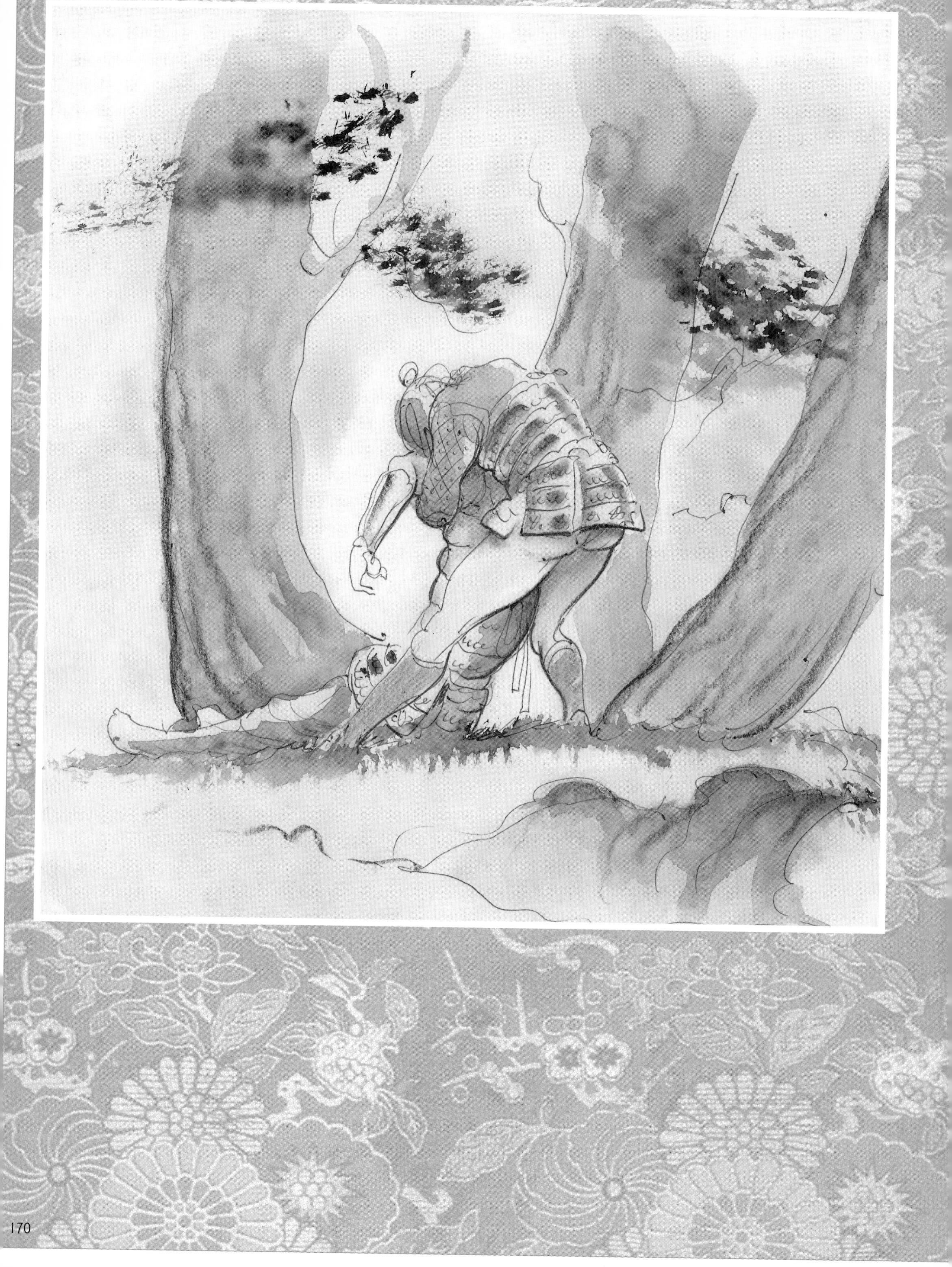

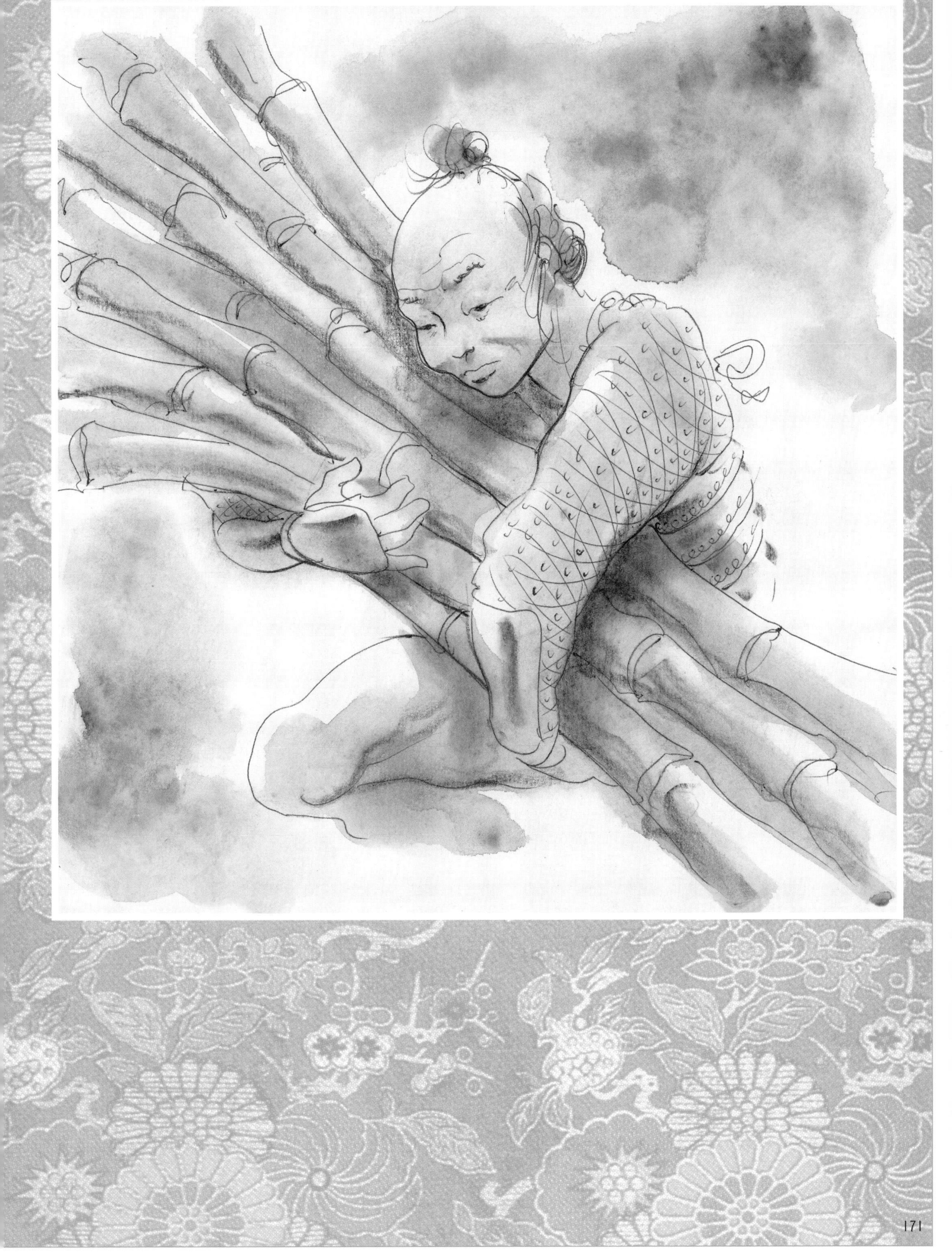

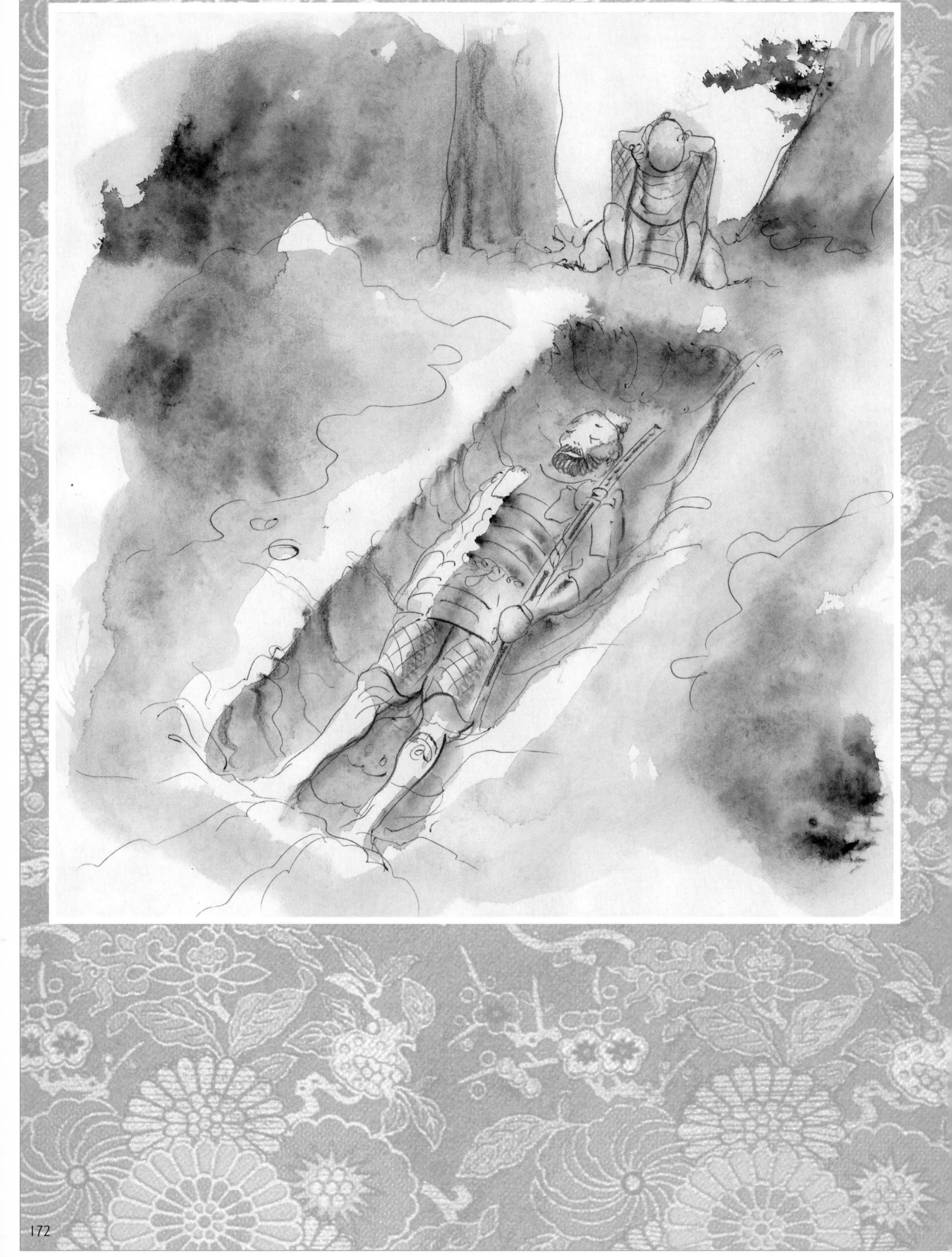

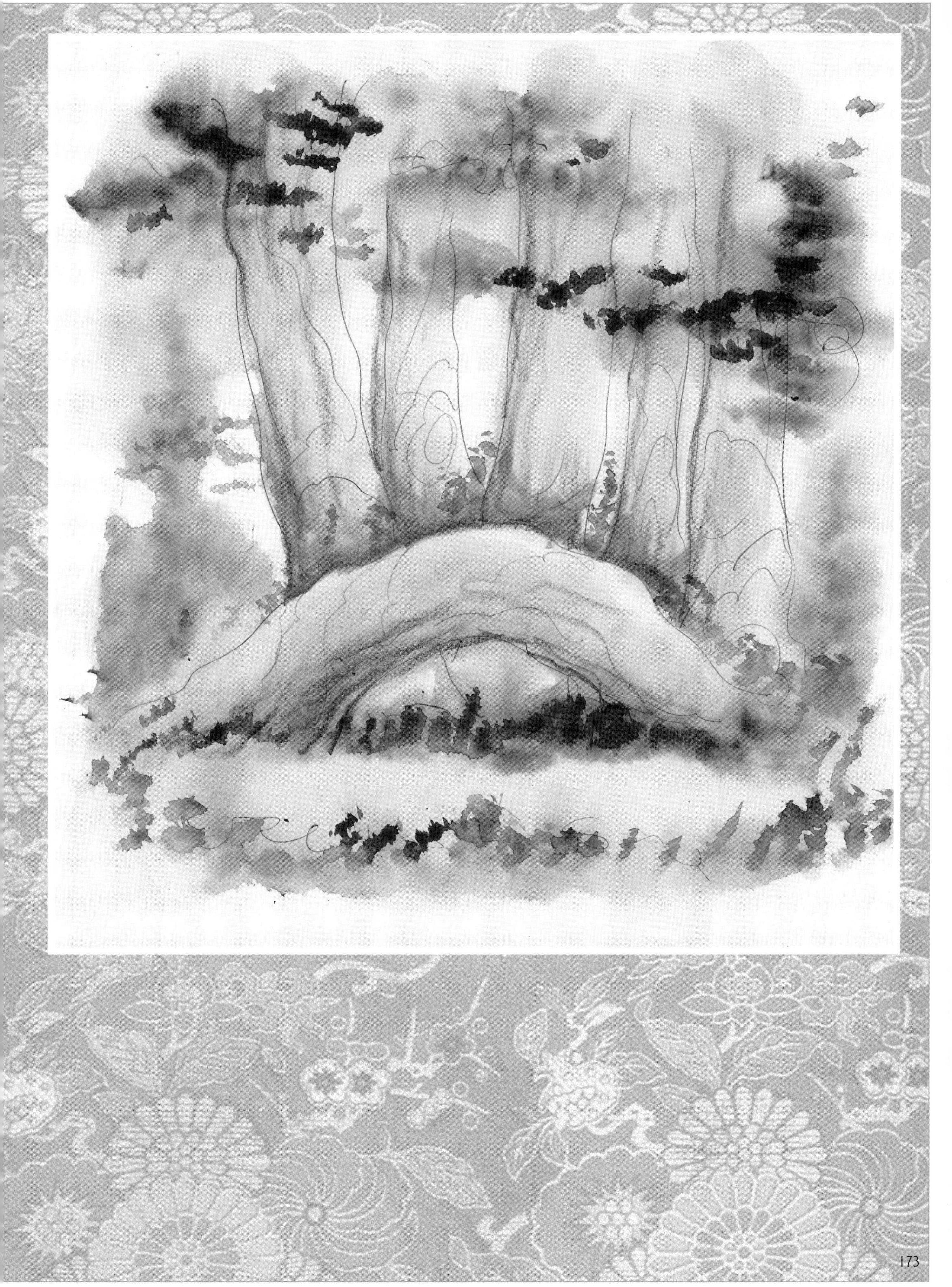

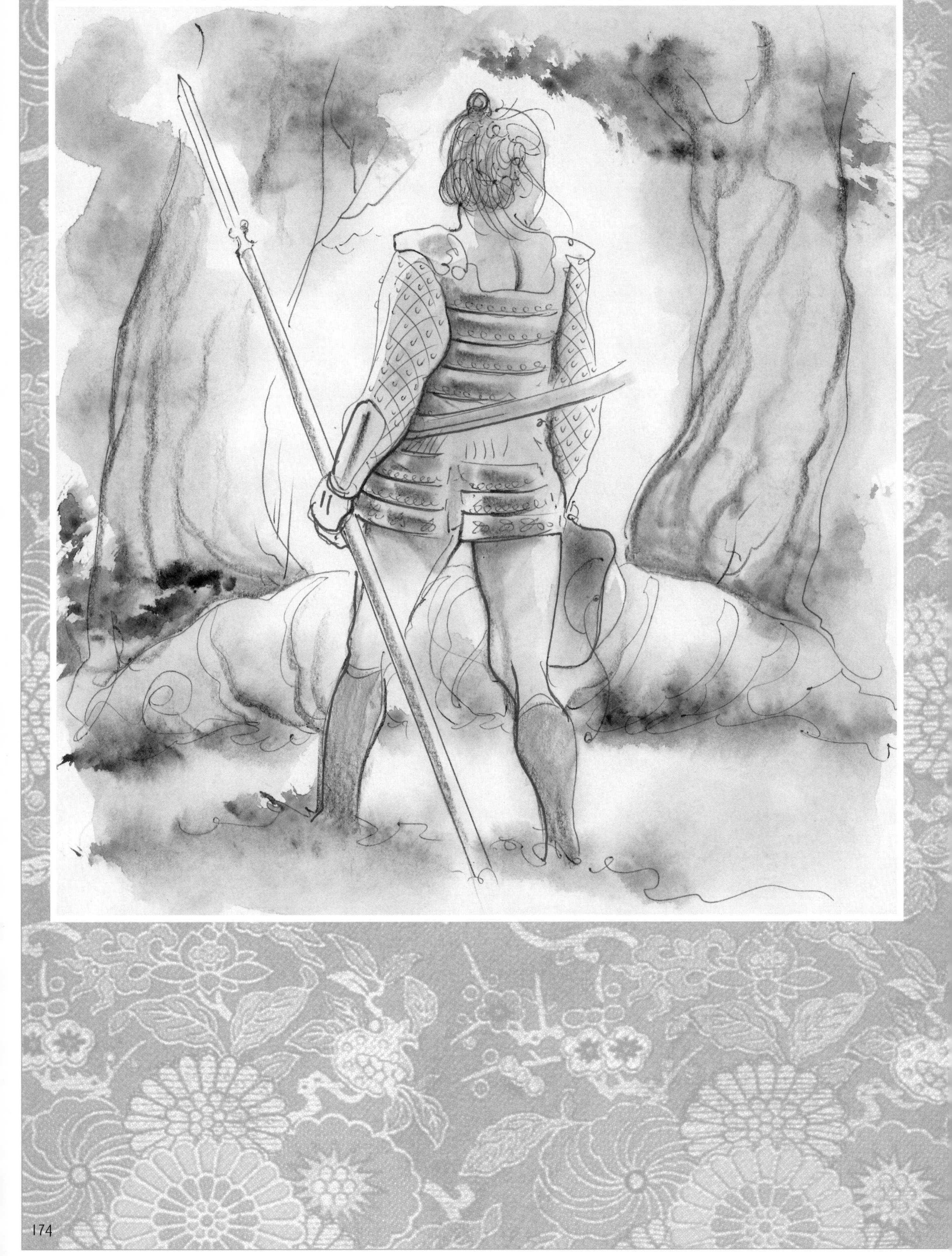

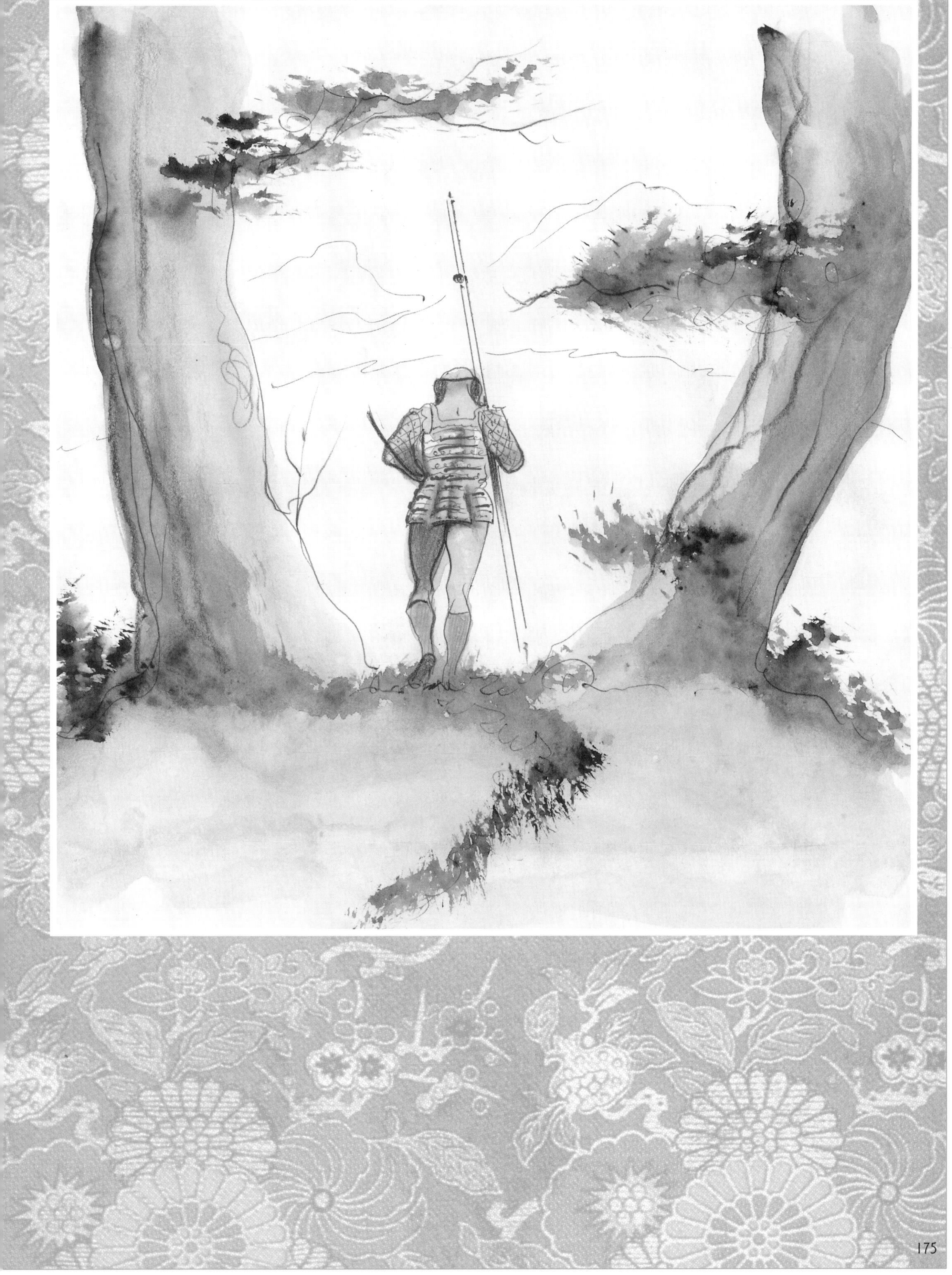

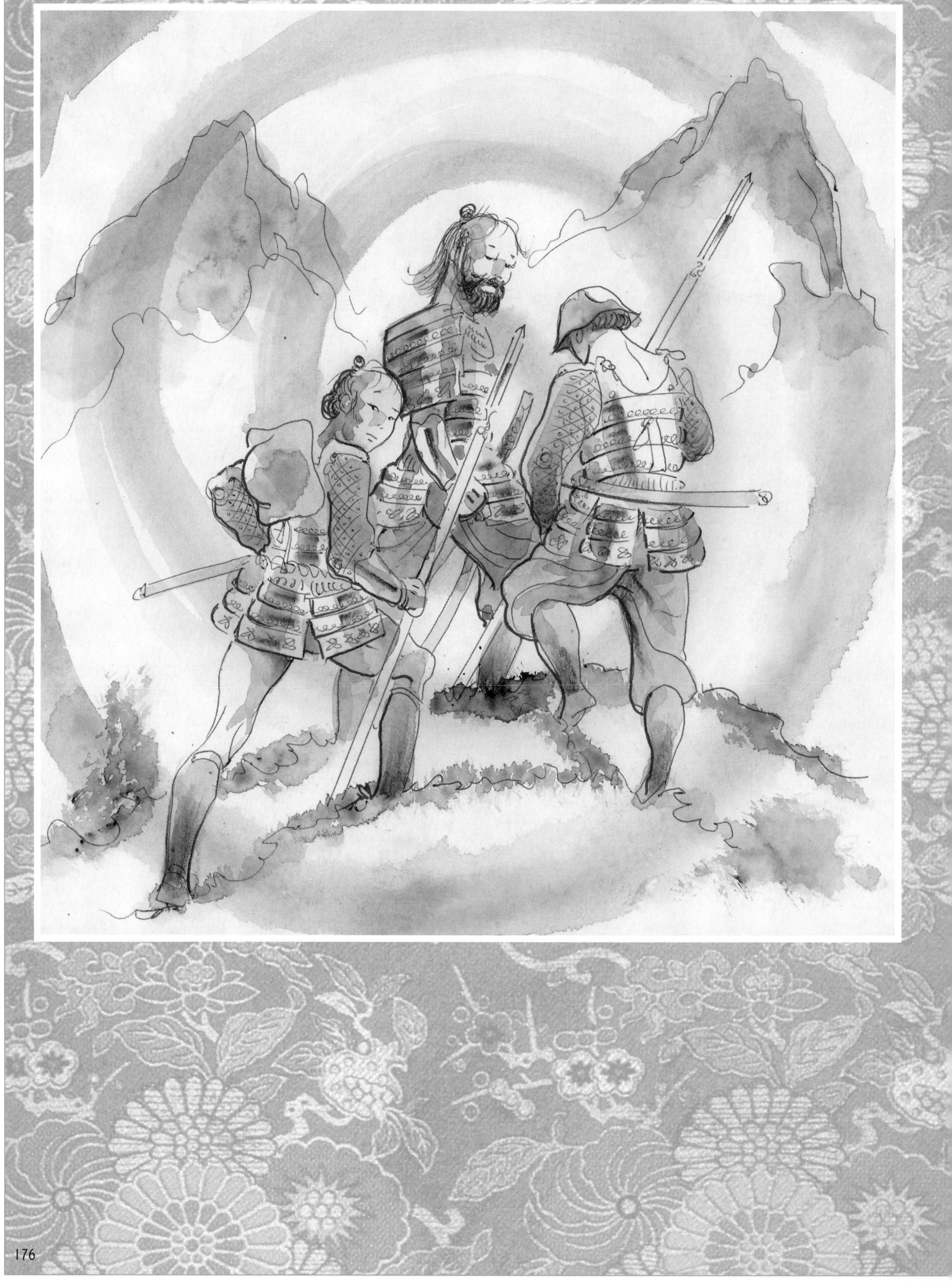

EPILOGUE

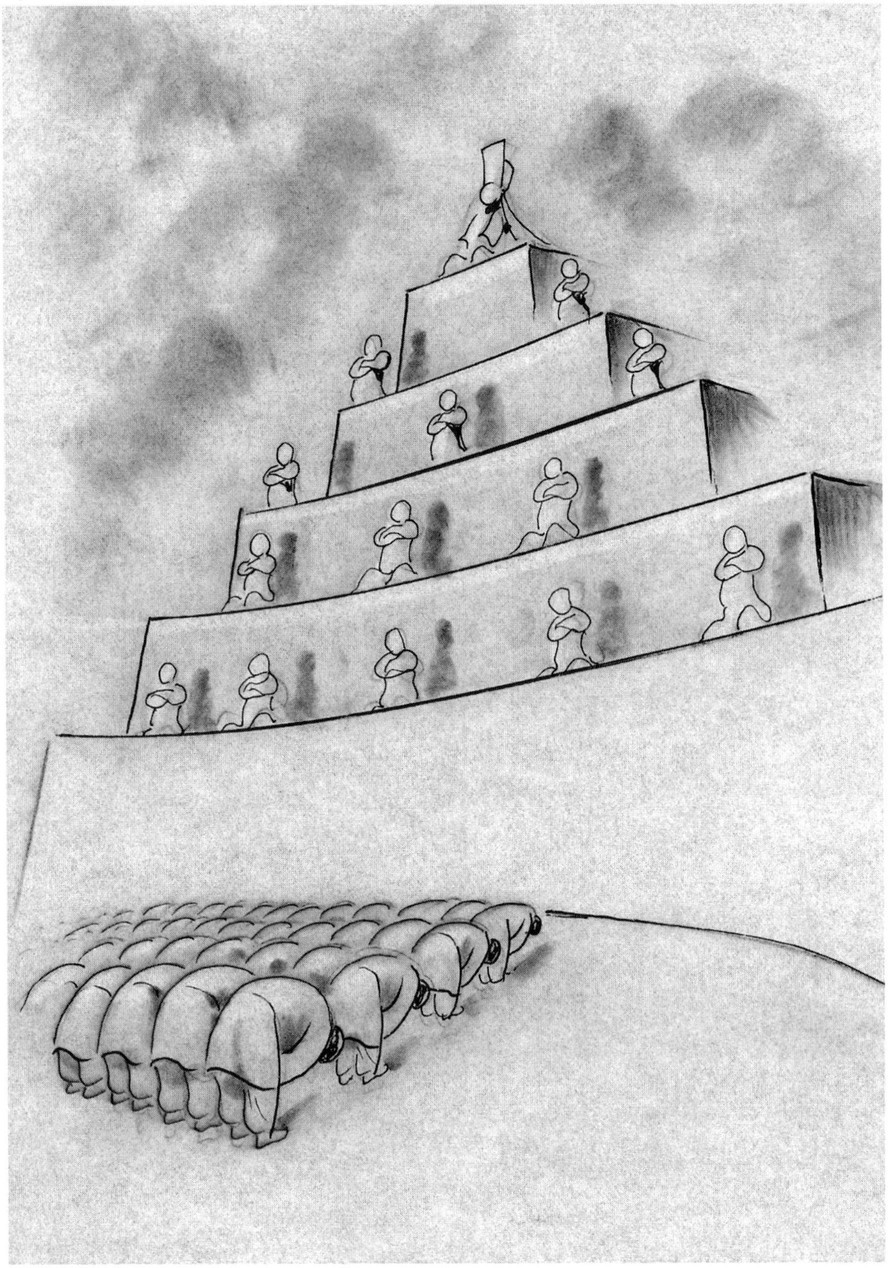

As he finished reading *Homecoming*, Père Dominic found himself wondering about the breach of boundaries this tale embodied. For, since his arrival in the Islands Empire, all his experiences had reinforced everything he had learned in Europe and observed during his travels in the East, concerning the strict (and strictly enforced) codes of behavior and class hierarchies in these Eastern societies.

Even in his native land of Eire, everyone knew that precedence must be given to the warrior who proudly displayed the markings of his association with systematic violence and death, or to the druid mystics, whether male or female, who gazed fixedly at their countrymen, as if they saw through and beyond them into worlds that the others could not discern.

It became clear to Père Dominic that, even without any mystical confirmation from other dimensions, as in India (or in Eire), social distinctions such as those he had noted in other tales he had read or in encounters he had witnessed personally, were vigorously maintained, often through the inexorable authority of a sharp blade.

He was to recollect one such unforgettable incident later, during discussions with some of the Residents and their Students in the House of Initiation. But when he broached the subject at some length, these experienced veterans of past battles who had been exposed to more than their share of systematic violence and social dissonances, did not seem overly interested in delving too deeply into those complexities which, as they expressed it, "delight scholars who have made a point of pursuing cultural loops for professional aggrandizement, while carefully avoiding any exposure to real danger!"

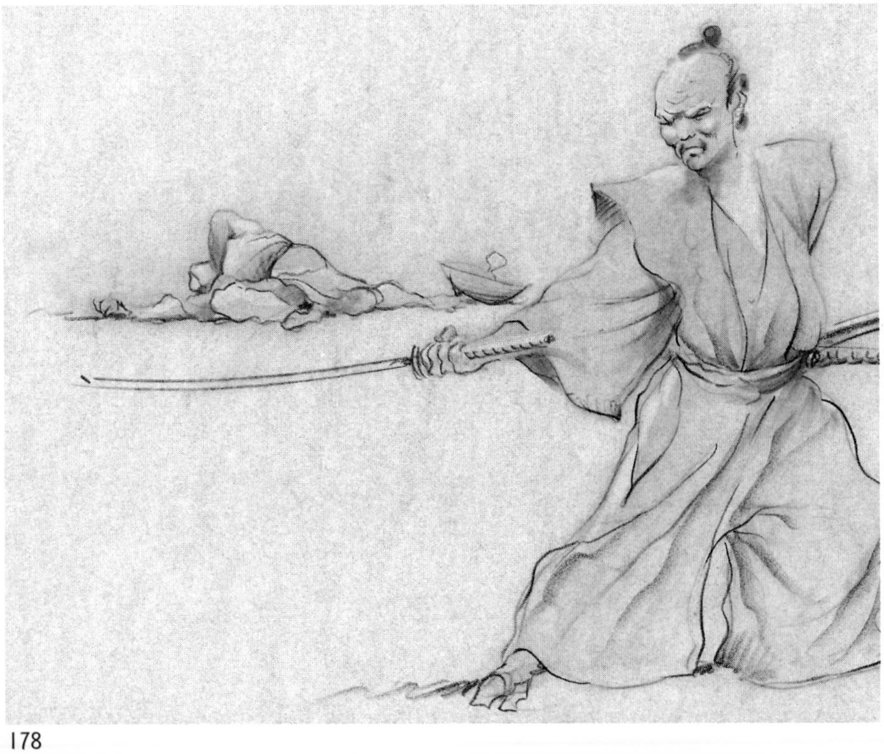

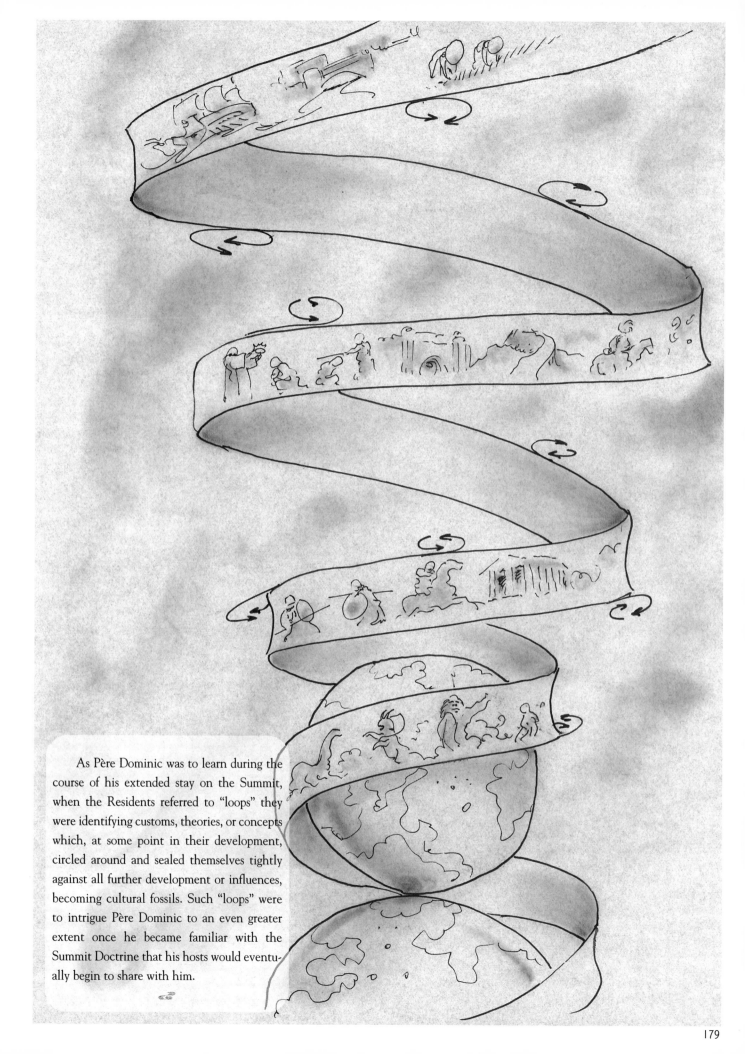

As Père Dominic was to learn during the course of his extended stay on the Summit, when the Residents referred to "loops" they were identifying customs, theories, or concepts which, at some point in their development, circled around and sealed themselves tightly against all further development or influences, becoming cultural fossils. Such "loops" were to intrigue Père Dominic to an even greater extent once he became familiar with the Summit Doctrine that his hosts would eventually begin to share with him.

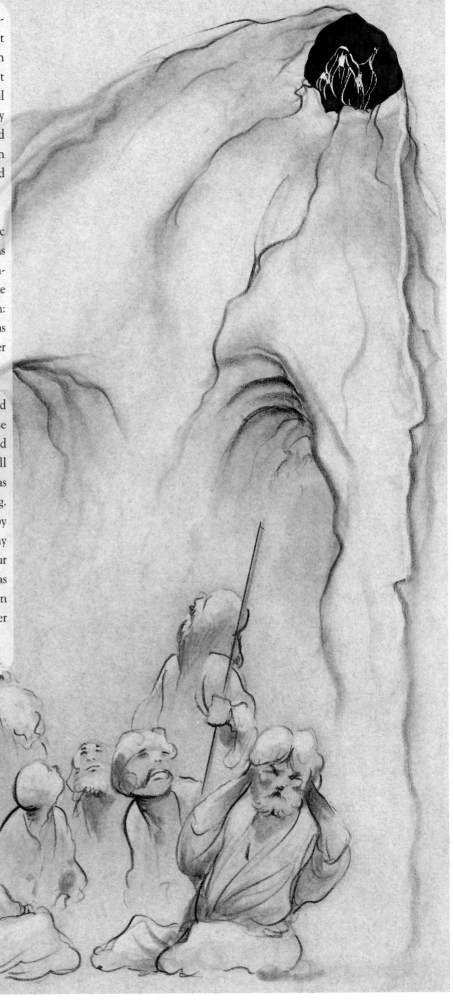

At this point, however, Père Dominic stubbornly insisted upon returning to the subject of such an unusual breach of social separation that would induce a lowly farmer to assist an aristocrat of the warrior class at the final juncture of his life, and to dispatch him as only an aristocratic peer was customarily permitted to do (thus honoring him in the only fashion the warrior class recognized, whether toward friends or foe on the battlefield).

Despite some discussion, Père Dominic was not convinced by any of the opinions advanced by his hosts as to how such an eventuality might have become possible. At one point, he threw up his hands in exasperation: "It seems to me that the author of this scroll has expressed only wishes, hopes, or dreams! After all, the tale itself is purely fictional, isn't it?"

At this point, Ma Hui's unique voice had intruded into his mind, as well as into those of the circle of Residents who surrounded him, reverberating under the arcades all around them, while filtering from within, as this ancient shaman was so skilled in doing. "Perhaps it might be worthwhile to begin by examining your definition of 'nobility,' my dear mountain colleagues, as well as that of our Celtic guest. If I recall correctly, the term was originally associated with a unique position associated with wealth and prestige, however acquired."

There was a reflective pause before her voice enveloped them once again: "But hasn't it also acquired another, broader meaning, and become associated with the idea of a greatness of spirit, an elegance of manners, a modest but accurate sense of one's own worth that stands as a barrier against boorish or overbearing behavior, while facilitating the recognition of, and respect for, similar qualities in others?"

The Residents remained silent, while listening intently to their inner interlocutor, whose voice was so familiar to them. As her discourse continued, they exchanged amused glances among themselves as they observed Père Dominic's reaction to Ma Hui's intervention—a reaction that was to reflect a pronounced element of apprehension for some time, before he, too, through determined practice, learned how to adapt to this form of mountain exchange and could begin to make extensive use of it himself.

Ma Hui's tone became softer as it echoed in their minds and under the arcades: "If 'nobility' denotes a state of worthiness not merely because of a biological association, or as the result of violently imposed power, but identifies a quality of mind or spirit that is inherent or acquired independently by an individual, then it is not impossible that your wounded warrior recognized a kindred spirit in the lowly farmer who had manifested his own integrity and sense of decency within the system that encapsulated him. If this was indeed the case, then the warrior spoke to the farmer as to a peer and received an appropriate response. At least, this provides an explanation that may be worth your consideration, wouldn't you agree, friends?"

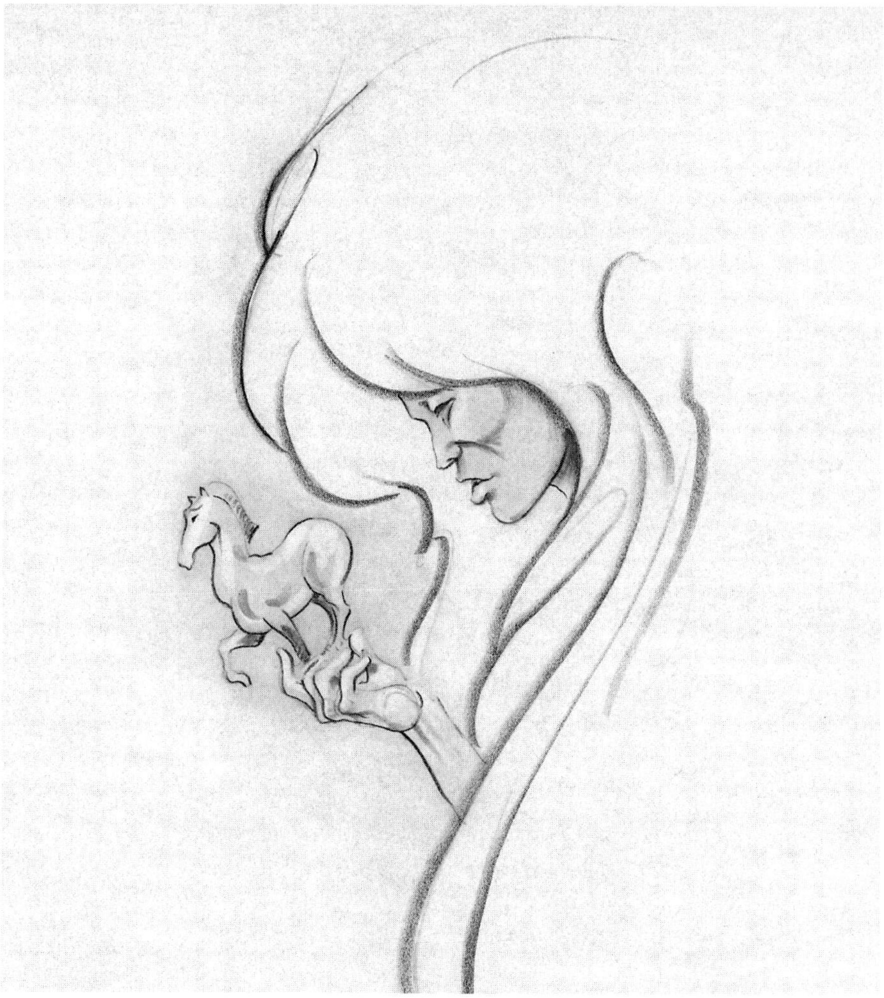

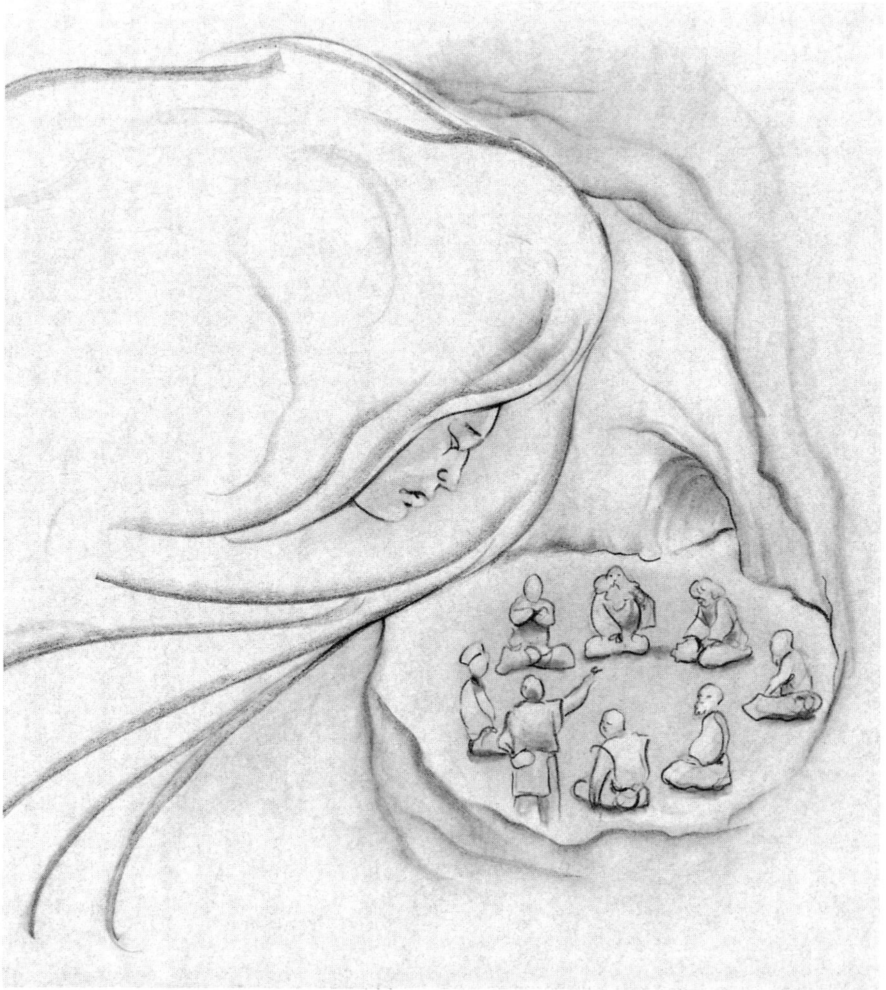

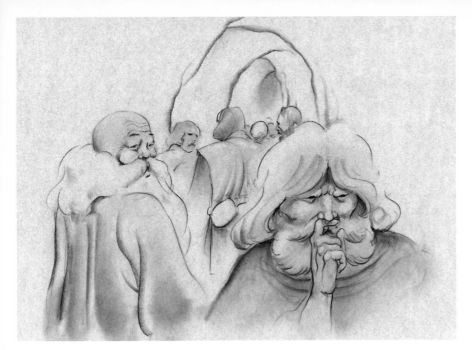

As Ma Hui's voice began to fade away, the group of Residents sat silently for awhile and then gradually began to disband, each preoccupied with his or her own thoughts on the subject of a nobility of spirit as proposed by this shaman of the Summit's Ninth Level and beyond.

Yu Xia, who had been listening to the exchange of views without offering any comments of his own, now moved closer to Père Dominic and said with a smile, "I think I should tell you that there are other scrolls in the Library that reflect the sometimes eccentric or amusing ways in which certain individuals are inclined to view Reality and respond to its challenges. The flow of life also embodies a great deal of humor, expressing Creation's store of good will and bonhomie—another way for the Yin to balance the Yang that might appear oppressively present in some of the tales that you have examined thus far."

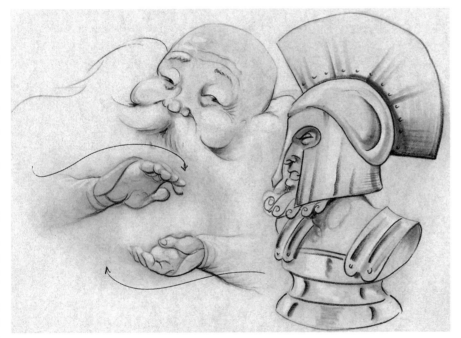

"If I have understood it correctly, the god of war depicted in the classics that inspired the early stages of your culture never smiled, because his nature could not be ameliorated. Mars could only sneer, growl, or shout, whether in triumph or in pain. Perhaps, if the violence so evident in combat could be expressed in a different manner . . ."

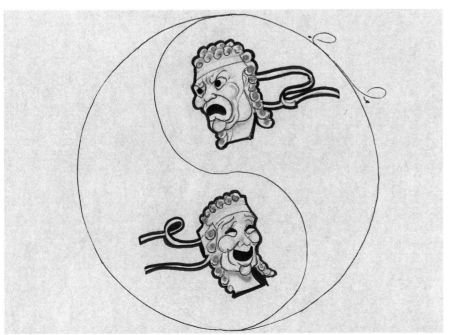

"Can it, Yu Xia?"

❧

"To determine whether it can or cannot is one reason why so many of us have been drawn to this Summit, my friend. We are all explorers and travelers in this vast wilderness of possibilities and, although many of our findings may have seemed distressing at first, very few of us have lost hope. In fact, many of the training disciplines developed here are actually encouraging . . ."

❧

With an air of hesitation, Père Dominic said: "I realize that I am an outsider, Yu Xia, but could you tell me more about these disciplines?"

❧

Yu Xia responded judiciously: "Well, to allow you to plunge immediately, and without adequate preparation, into the technical and experimental aspects of our research might do more harm than good, since you are still so strongly influenced by those harsh realities that forced you to flee for your life."

❧

"But the subject of physical violence and its manifestations is so pivotal . . ."

❧

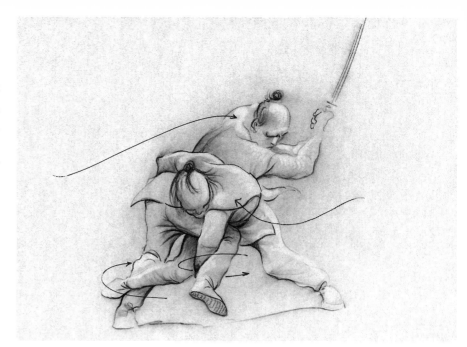

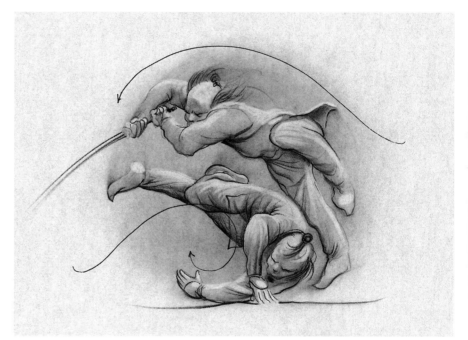

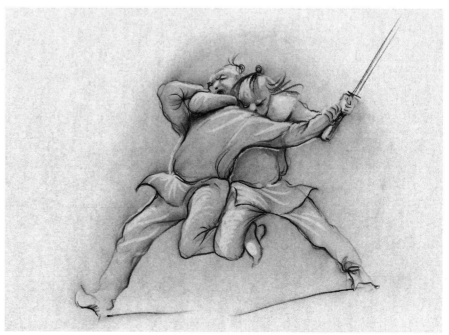

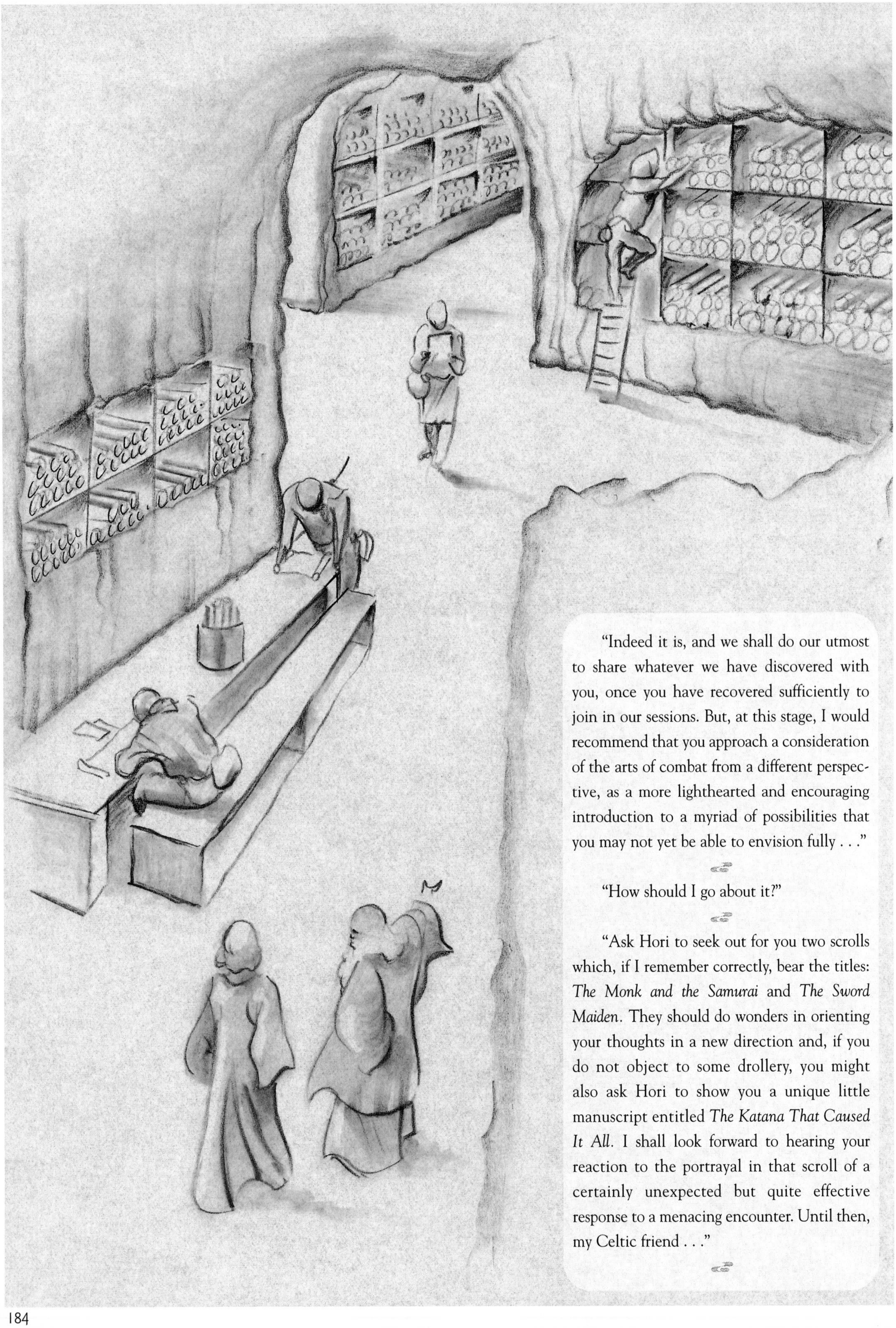

"Indeed it is, and we shall do our utmost to share whatever we have discovered with you, once you have recovered sufficiently to join in our sessions. But, at this stage, I would recommend that you approach a consideration of the arts of combat from a different perspective, as a more lighthearted and encouraging introduction to a myriad of possibilities that you may not yet be able to envision fully . . ."

"How should I go about it?"

"Ask Hori to seek out for you two scrolls which, if I remember correctly, bear the titles: *The Monk and the Samurai* and *The Sword Maiden*. They should do wonders in orienting your thoughts in a new direction and, if you do not object to some drollery, you might also ask Hori to show you a unique little manuscript entitled *The Katana That Caused It All*. I shall look forward to hearing your reaction to the portrayal in that scroll of a certainly unexpected but quite effective response to a menacing encounter. Until then, my Celtic friend . . ."

Tales of the Hermit

Volume III:

The Monk and the Samurai

The Sword Maiden

&

The Katana That Caused It All

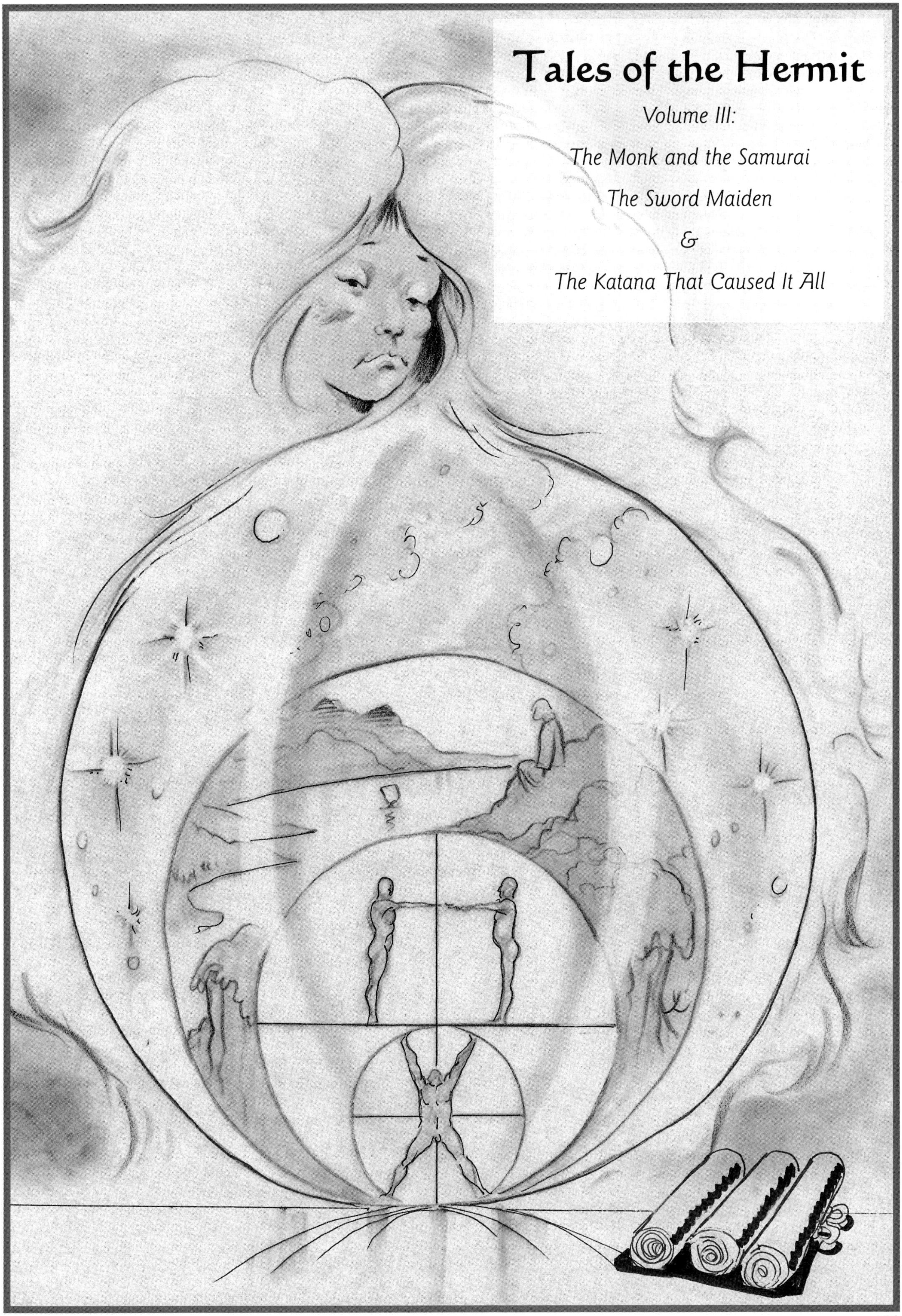

Scenes from Tales of the Hermit Volume III

The Monk
and the Samuari

❖

The Sword Maiden

❖

The Katana
That Caused It All

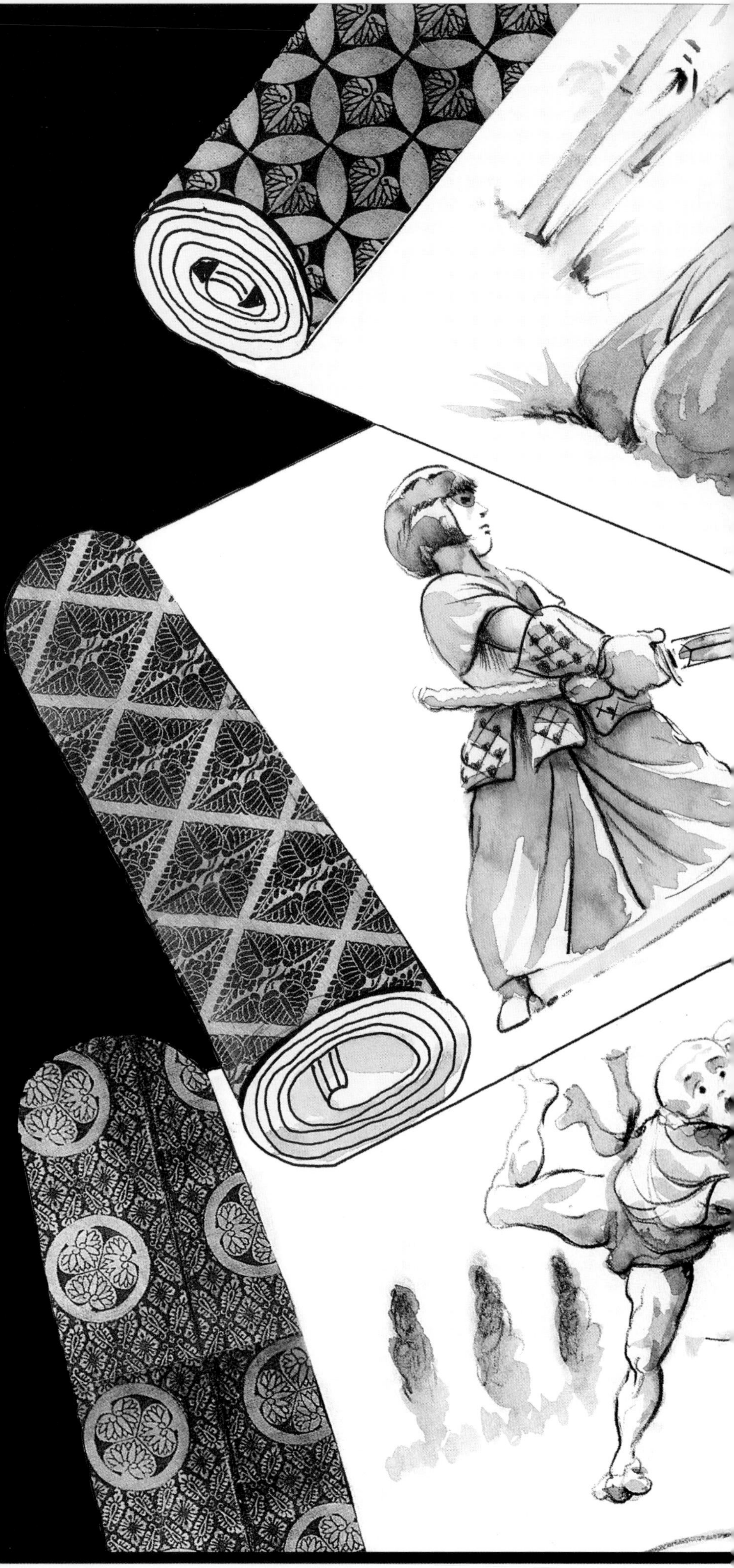

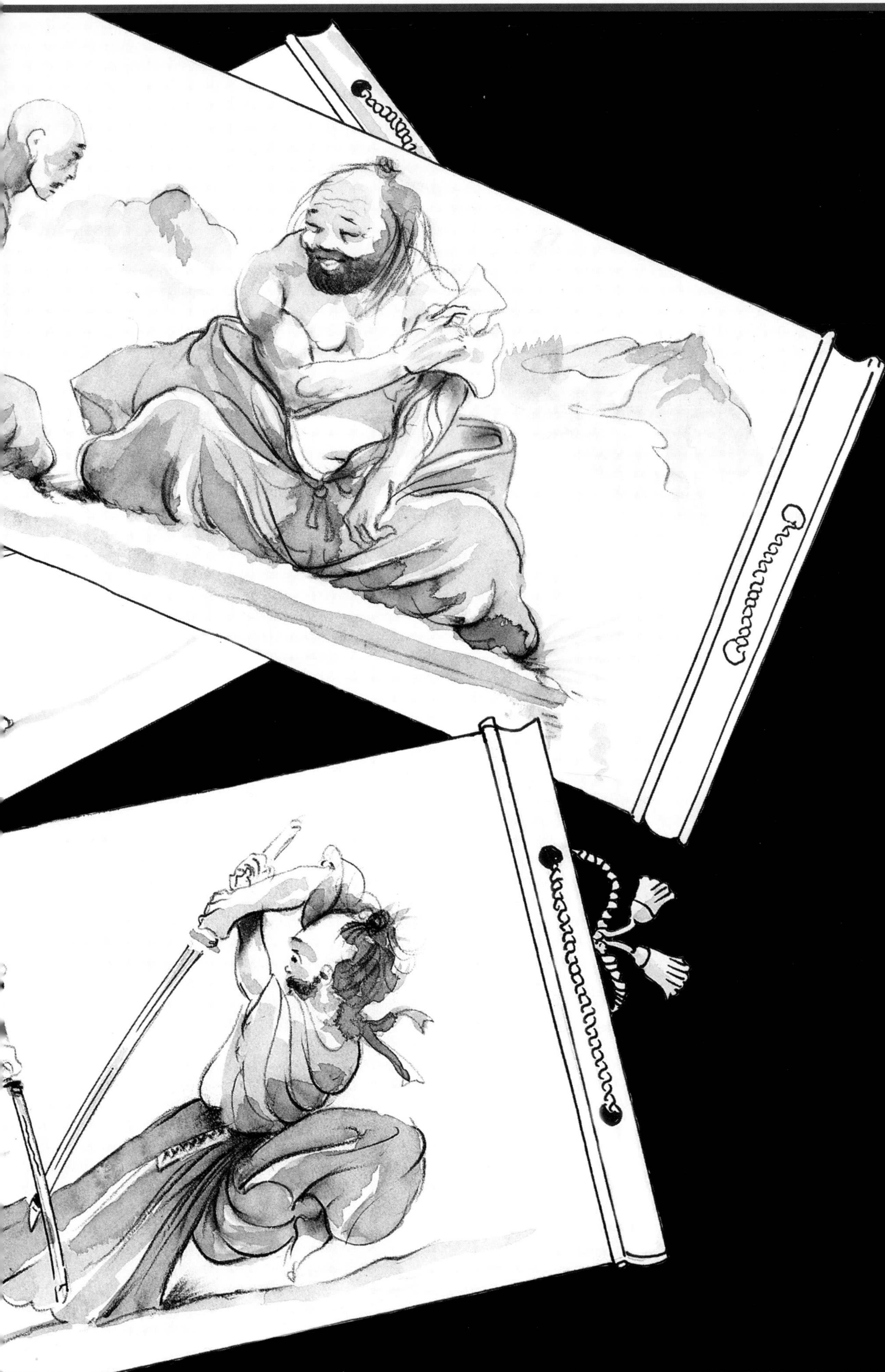

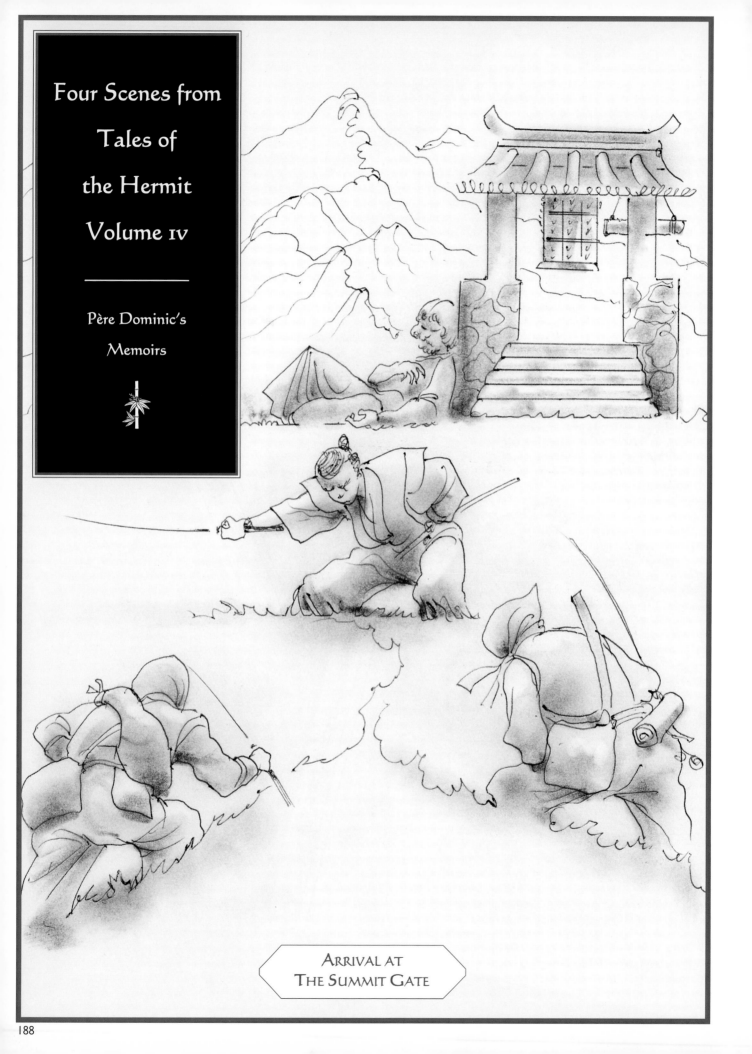

Four Scenes from
Tales of
the Hermit
Volume IV

Père Dominic's
Memoirs

ARRIVAL AT
THE SUMMIT GATE

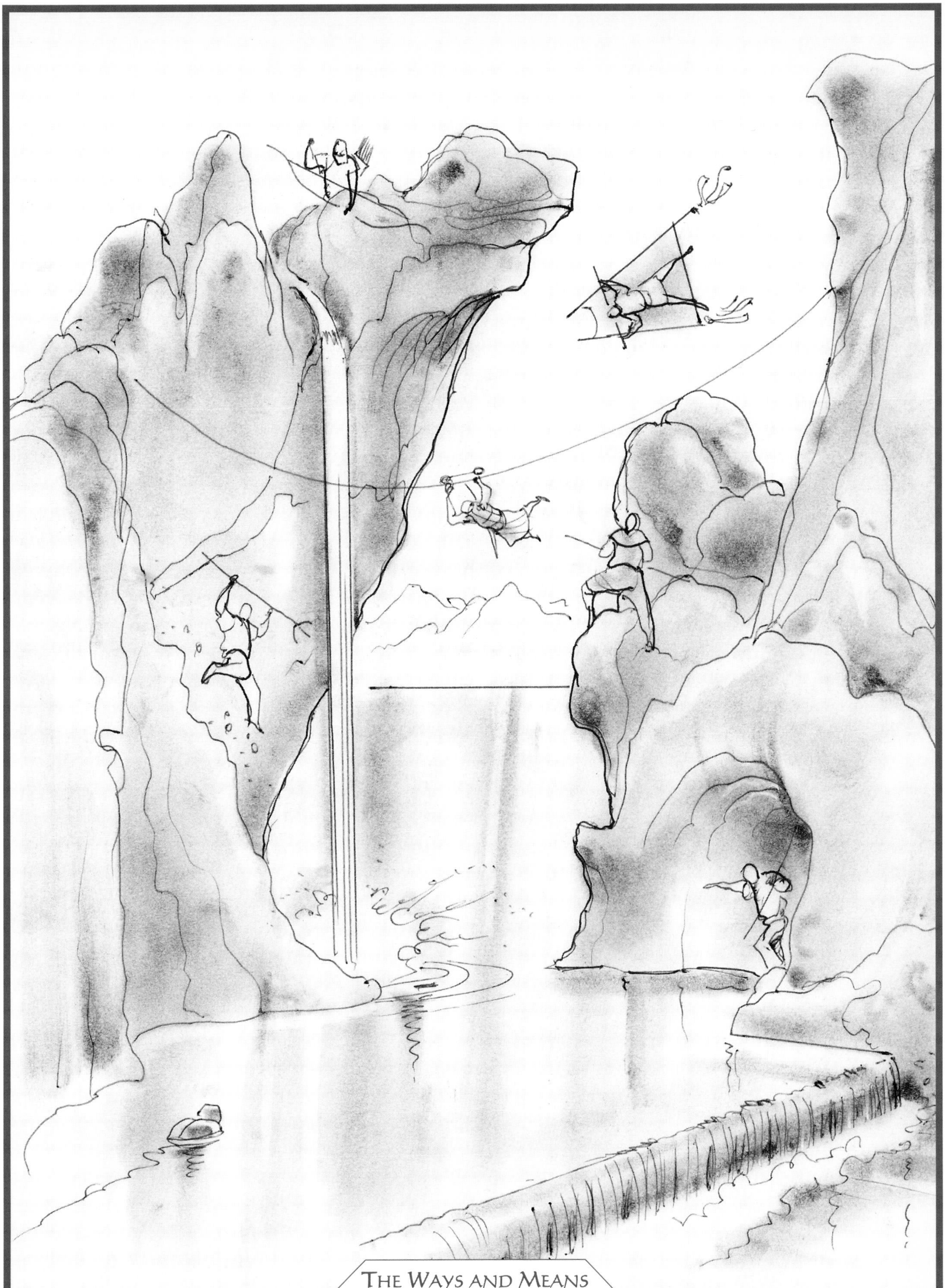

The Ways and Means of the Mountains

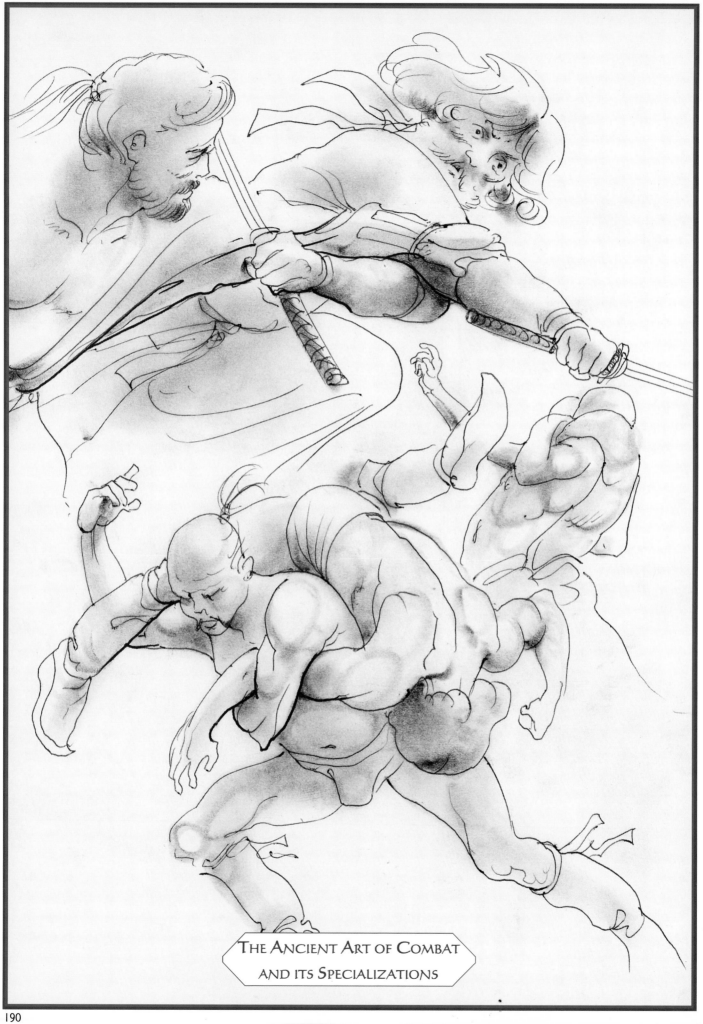

THE ANCIENT ART OF COMBAT
AND ITS SPECIALIZATIONS

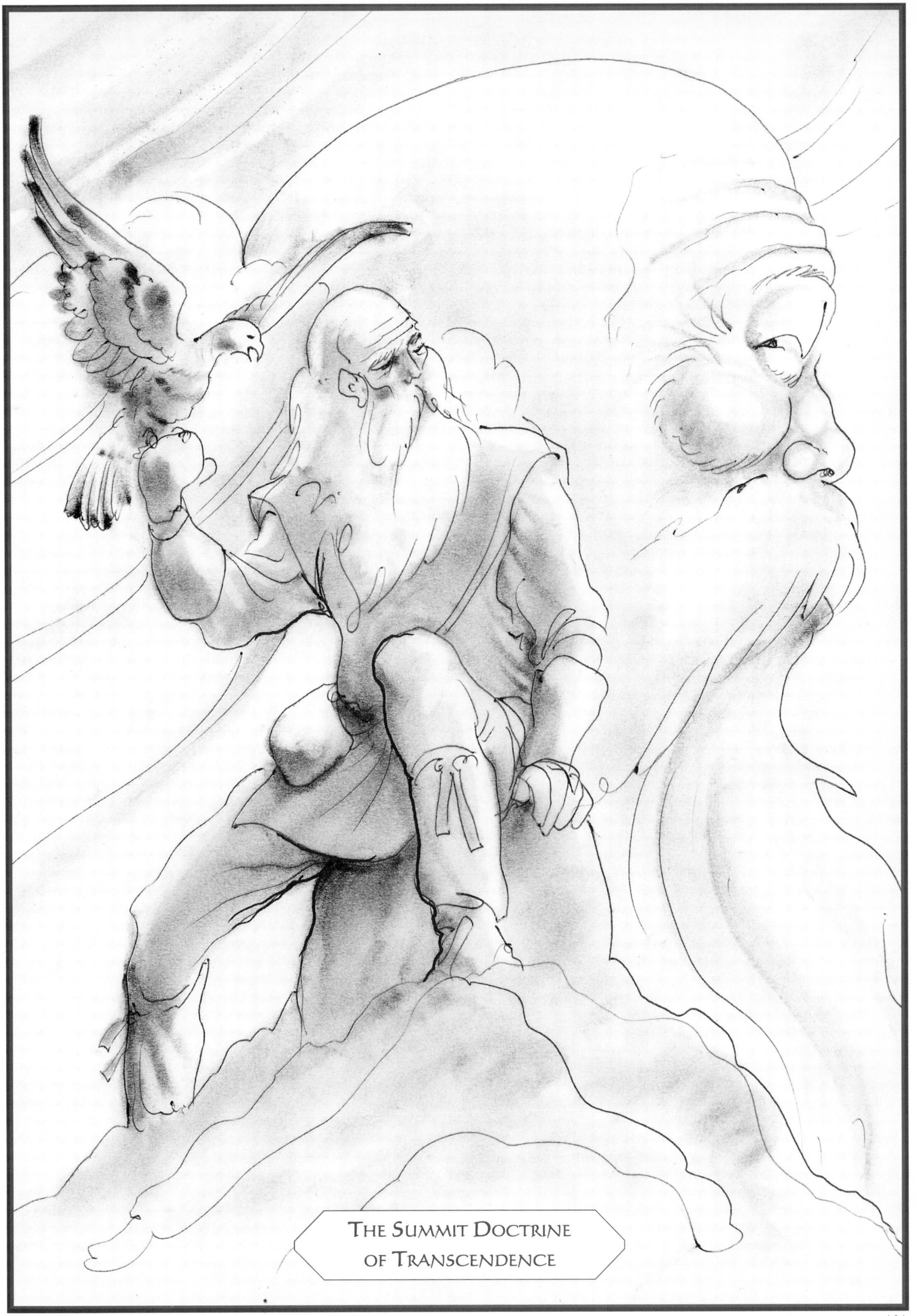

The Summit Doctrine of Transcendence